CORPORATE AFTERSHOCK

CORPORATE AFTERSHOCK

The Public Policy Lessons from the Collapse
of Enron and Other Major Corporations

Edited by Christopher L. Culp and William A. Niskanen

WILEY

JOHN WILEY & SONS, INC.

Published by John Wiley & Sons, Inc., Hoboken, New Jersey.
Published simultaneously in Canada.

For general information on our other products and services, or technical support, please
contact our Customer Care Department within the United States at 800-762-2974,
outside the United States at 317-572-3993 or fax 317-572-4002.

Wiley also publishes its books in a variety of electronic formats. Some content that
appears in print may not be available in electronic books. For more information about
Wiley products, visit our Web site at www.wiley.com.

Library of Congress Cataloging-in-Publication Data:

Corporate aftershock: the public policy lessons from the collapse of
Enron and other major corporations / edited by Christopher L. Culp and
William A. Niskanen.
        p. cm.
Includes bibliographical references.
   ISBN 0-471-43002-1 (cloth)
   1. Disclosure in accounting.   2. Corporations—Accounting.
3. Industrial policy. I. Culp, Christopher L.   II. Niskanen, William A.,
1933–
   HF5658.C667   2003
   332—dc21

                                                          2002156132

Printed in the United States of America.

10 9 8 7 6 5 4 3 2 1

CONTENTS

ABOUT THE EDITORS

Christopher L. Culp is an adjunct professor of finance at the Graduate School of Business of the University of Chicago, where he teaches graduate-level courses on derivatives, alternative risk transfer, risk management, and investments. He also offers a graduate seminar on insurance during winter quarters as a guest professor of risk and insurance in the Institut für Finanzmanagement at Universität Bern in Switzerland. A principal at CP Risk Management LLC, Culp provides consulting services on corporate financial strategy, risk management, and capital allocation to nonfinancial and financial institutions. He also provides litigation consulting and expert testimony as a principal for Chicago Partners LLC. In addition, Culp is a senior fellow in financial regulation at the Competitive Enterprise Institute, and is a nonexecutive independent director of IDACORP, Inc., and Idaho Power Company, Inc., where he sits on the Audit and Corporate Governance Committees of both boards of directors. Culp's latest book, *Risk Transfer: Derivatives in Theory and Practice* is forthcoming in the summer of 2003 from John Wiley & Sons. He is the author of two prior books, also published by Wiley—*The ART of Risk Management: Alternative Risk Transfer, Capital Structure, and the Convergence of Insurance and Capital Markets* (2002), and *The Risk Management Process: Business Strategy and Tactics* (2001)—and he co-edited *Corporate Hedging in Theory and Practice: Lessons from Metallgesellschaft* (Risk Books, 1999) with Merton H. Miller. He writes frequently on corporate finance, risk management, and valuation, and is co-editor for derivatives and risk management of the Financial Management Association's online journal *FMA Online*. He is a member of the editorial advisory boards of the *Journal of Applied Corporate Finance*, the *Journal of Risk Finance*, and *Futures Industry* magazine. Culp holds a PhD in finance from the University of Chicago's Graduate School of Business and a BA in economics (Phi Beta Kappa) from the Johns Hopkins University.

William A. Niskanen, an economist, has served as chairman of the Cato Institute since 1985, following experience in academy, government, industry, and other policy institutes. He joined Cato after serving as a member and acting chairman of the Council of Economic Advisers under President Reagan. His prior experience in the government included serving as an assistant director of the Office of Management and Budget under George Schultz and as director of special studies in the office of Secretary of Defense Robert McNamera. As a professor of economics, Niskanen taught at the University of California at Berkeley and Los Angeles. He also organized and directed a program to teach economics and systems analysis techniques to military officers. His first position out of graduate school was as a defense analyst at the Rand Corporation, and he later served as a division director at the Institute for Defense Analyses. In the late 1970s, he was the director of economics at the Ford Motor Company. Niskanen has a BA from Harvard and an MA and PhD in economics from the University of Chicago. His professional specialties have been public finance and public choice. He is the author of the following books: *Bureaucracy and Representative Government; Reaganomics; Going Digital!; Policy Analysis and Public Choice,* a fifth book that will be published later this year, and many articles. His primary reward as a co-editor of this book, he relates, is continuing a lifelong learning experience with new issues and techniques.

ABOUT THE CONTRIBUTORS

Richard Bassett is the cofounder and managing director of Risktoolz, an international corporate finance consulting and software firm (www.risktoolz.com). Bassett's career in finance has included working in the merchant banking division of Security Pacific Bank in London and New York, where he was a registered securities dealer in the institutional bond and equity markets. He was managing director of Alcar Europe as well as managing director of Corporate Performance Systems worldwide. Bassett has led assignments that include: more than 35 M&A transactions with a cumulative value in excess of $60 billion; development of a corporate credit system for a major U.S. bank involving credit evaluation in 85 countries and the attendant problems in reconciling, or not, competing accounting practices; developing a series of strategic planning systems for global corporations, often involving hundreds of participants in scores of countries; worked extensively in developing optimal capital structure programs for large, diverse, multinational firms; and has been a pioneer in the introduction and establishment of shareholder value programs working with more than 100 companies since 1987. Prior to his finance career, Bassett worked as a ministerial assistant for the Minister of Fisheries and Oceans, Minister of Health, and the Cabinet Secretariat, in the governments of Canada and British Columbia. Bassett completed his undergraduate degree at the University of Victoria, Canada, and earned an MBA through a combined program at Boston College in the United States and Insead in France.

Keith A. Bockus is a principal at Chicago Partners LLC and at CP Risk Management LLC. Chicago Partners provides a multidisciplinary approach to consulting services on matters of economics, finance, accounting, and technology. Through its subsidiary, CP Risk Management, the firm offers specific consulting services for measuring and managing financial risks. Bockus specializes in microeconomics and financial analysis. He has consulted on various risk management matters, with a particular concentration of clients in the banking and energy sectors. He also consults in various commercial litigation matters and testifies on damages issues. Bockus is also active in Chicago Partners' forensic accounting practice. He holds MBA and PhD degrees from the University of Chicago Graduate School of Business, and a BA in economics (Phi Beta Kappa) from the Johns Hopkins University. Previously he worked as an information technology consultant to various U.S. government agencies.

Doron F. Ezickson is a partner in the Trial Department in McDermott, Will & Emery's Boston office. He is partner-in-charge of the Boston office, co-chair of the firm's Energy Practice Group and serves on the firm's Management and Executive Committees. His energy practice involves a wide array of federal and state regulatory issues and litigation relating to the development and operation of the wholesale and retail electric markets. From 1991 to 1993, Ezickson worked for Massachusetts Governor William F. Weld, as deputy chief of staff/chief of operations and as assistant chief of staff. His responsibilities included management of the governor's office operations, coordination of Cabinet activities, and policy development and implementation. Ezickson is also the former executive director of the Massachusetts Office of International Trade and Investment. Ezickson received his bachelor's degree in Asian studies from Dartmouth College in 1981. He graduated magna cum laude in 1985 from Boston University School of Law, where he was an articles editor for the *Boston University Law Review*. Ezickson then served as a law clerk for the DC Circuit of the U.S. Court of Appeals. Ezickson is admitted to practice in Massachusetts; Washington, DC; and Pennsylvania.

Steve H. Hanke is a professor of applied economics and co-director of the Institute for Applied Economics and the Study of Business Enterprise at the Johns Hopkins University in Baltimore. He is also a senior fellow at the Cato Institute in Washington, DC, and a principal at Chicago Partners LLC in Chicago. In addition to writing a regular column in *Forbes* magazine, he is a contributing editor at *Forbes Global* magazine, *Central Banking*, and the *International Economy*. A distinguished associate of the International Atlantic Economic Society, Hanke was named by *World Trade* magazine as one of the 25 most influential people in the world in 1998.

Alton B. Harris is a founding partner of Ungaretti & Harris and heads the firm's Financial Practices Group. He concentrates his practice in the areas of corporate finance and financial regulation, focusing particularly on the federal regulation of financial institutions and financial products and services. He was named by the *National Law Journal* as one of the 50 outstanding securities lawyers in the United States. Harris graduated from Harvard College and Harvard Law School. He is an adjunct professor of law at Northwestern University Law School where he teaches courses on the regulation of derivative products and the financial markets. He served as a consultant to the Reporter for the American Law Institute's Federal Securities Code. He was a member of the Legal Advisory Board of the National Association of Securities Dealers. He is a member of the American Law Institute and the Committee on Securities Regulation of the American Bar Association. He is a life trustee of the American Bar Foundation.

John Herron is internationally recognized as a global expert and a leading entrepreneur in the financial markets. He was previously the CEO, founder, and developer of the Australian Derivatives Exchange (ADX), which was a pioneer among electronic exchanges. Herron's vision of a competitive and efficient financial industry within a global market led him to Chicago, where he assisted in the establishment of Fair Market Associates (FMA), an industry consulting group. He is also a contributor to numerous financial market publications, and has recently been appointed as a nonexecutive director to 4DTrading, a U.K. financial software company. Prior to establishing ADX, Herron held senior banking positions within the Australian financial markets for over 15 years. He has lectured extensively at the Securities Institute of Australia and several universities. Herron holds a bachelor of economics, a bachelor of arts, and a master of commerce from the University of Sydney in Australia.

Barbara T. Kavanagh is a principal at CP Risk Management LLC, Chicago, Illinois. She has many years of experience as a risk management consultant working with major corporations and financial institutions all over the world. Her work has focused on trading markets, cash and derivative financial instruments, and structured finance and securitization for nearly 15 years. Prior to her current position, she was the senior credit officer in ABN AMRO's investment bank in North America, a risk management consultant with KPMG and Ernst & Young, and worked for many years within the Federal Reserve. During her career inside the Federal Reserve, she was involved in a number of public policy making matters, including those relating to trading markets, structured finance and securitization, and trade clearing, payments, and settlements systems.

Andrea S. Kramer is a partner in the law firm of McDermott, Will & Emery, in its Chicago office. She is the head of the firm's Financial Products, Trading, and Derivatives Group. Kramer focuses her practice on tax and regulatory counseling and defense, legislative consulting, regulatory advice, documentation of customized and OTC financial products, risk management policies and procedures, and bankruptcy and creditors' rights issues. She advises clients on the design, trading, and risk management applications of highly complex and rapidly evolving OTC products, such as securitized assets, electricity derivatives, emission allowances, weather derivatives, equity swaps, credit derivatives, contingent debt instruments, and hybrid products. Kramer devotes a substantial amount of time to representing taxpayers in contested tax matters. She is a frequent contributor to trade and professional journals, having written over 100 articles and publications on derivative financial products. She is the author of *Financial Products: Taxation, Regulation, and Design* (Panel Publishers, 3rd ed., 2000) a three-volume, 3,600-page treatise that is kept current with annual supplements. As the leading treatise on financial products law, it has been cited by the courts and commentators on several occasions. She is also co-editor-in-chief of the quarterly CCH *Journal of Taxation of Financial Products*. A frequent speaker at conferences and workshops, Kramer has presented close to 200 speeches and full-day workshops on trading activities and financial products. She has developed and conducts full-day training courses on the documentation and negotiation of swap transactions, financial product tax issues, and foreign currency tax issues.

David Mengle is head of research for the International Swaps and Derivatives Association, with responsibility for education and survey activities. He also teaches courses in economics and risk management at the Fordham University Graduate School of Business. Prior to joining ISDA in November 2001, Mengle worked in the Derivatives Strategies Group at J.P. Morgan in New York. During that time, he was active in ISDA educational and policy initiatives. Before that, he was a research economist with the Federal Reserve Bank of Richmond, specializing in bank regulation, payment system risk, and market value accounting. Mengle holds a BA from the Citadel and a PhD in economics from the University of California, Los Angeles.

Andrea M. P. Neves is a principal at Chicago Partners LLC and CP Risk Management LLC, where she provides economic consulting services in the areas of financial risk, derivatives valuation, and market mechanisms. She focuses on asset pricing issues arising from volatile market activity. She also provides expert witness testimony in these areas for litigation and arbitration resolution. Her typical clients include multinational corporations, investment banks, broker/dealers, asset managers, and derivatives exchanges. Neves has worked extensively with electric utilities and power marketers on the crises that have affected the wholesale electricity trading markets in the United States over the recent years. Some of her most rewarding projects have been helping such clients incorporate risk management for a trading operation into an overall financial risk management strategy and framework. Neves also teaches a course in financial risk management in the executive education program at the University of Chicago's Graduate School of Business, and she has authored numerous publications in financial journals. Neves received her BS in Physics from Mary Washington College, a MS in Physics from Texas A&M University, and a MA in Economics with an emphasis in finance from Virginia Polytechnic Institute in Northern Virginia.

W. Dana Northcut is a principal of Chicago Partners LLC, a consulting firm that specializes in the application of economic theory to a variety of legal and regulatory issues. He consults in the areas of accounting, finance, and valuation and has testified on damages issues. He is also adjunct associate professor of accounting at the University of Chicago Graduate School of Business where he regularly teaches accounting and financial analysis. Northcut has held other academic teaching and research positions and has professional experience as a Certified Public Accountant.

Paul Palmer is the CEO of Capital Credit, a merchant bank and asset management boutique that focuses on complex credit risk. He is former president of Enhance Structured Products at Asset Guaranty/Enhance Financial Services Group where he was responsible for creating credit risk transfer products for financial institutions and industrial companies globally. Palmer has created several innovative asset-backed structures for domestic and international clients, including the first-ever supply bond for an emerging market future flow securitization, the first-ever insured check remittance securitization, and the first synthetic capital product for stock and commodities exchanges. Palmer spent eight years with Asset Guaranty and was a member of the Board of Directors of Asset Guaranty Insurance and Enhance Reinsurance Companies. Prior to that, he was at American International Group where he worked in the financial product development and lending areas. Palmer has underwritten and managed over $30 billion in credit risk transfer exposures from global financial institutions. He has a BA in economics from the City College of the City University of New York, and has completed executive management courses at Stanford and Tuck business schools. Palmer's work in the credit risk management arena was recognized by *Risk* magazine in January 1999.

Paul J. Pantano Jr. is a partner resident in McDermott, Will & Emery's Washington, DC, office and is a member of the firm's Executive and Management Committees. He heads the firm's Energy and Derivatives Markets Practice Group. He practices primarily in the areas of commodities, energy, and insurance law. Pantano represents energy companies, brokerage firms, electronic exchanges, trade associations, insurance companies, and financial industry professionals in a wide variety of transaction, regulatory, and litigation matters. He has considerable experience negotiating and drafting structured commodity and derivative transactions and structuring electronic trading systems. Pantano regularly represents clients in investigations and proceedings before the Commodity Futures Trading Commission, the Federal Energy Regulatory Commission, state insurance commissions, and other government agencies. He also counsels financial services, energy, and association clients on regulatory matters affecting their businesses.

Fred L. Smith Jr. is the founder and president of the Competitive Enterprise Institute (CEI), a public interest group dedicated to the principles of free enterprise and limited government active in a wide range of economic and environmental public policy issues. Based in Washington, DC, CEI works to educate and inform policymakers, journalists, and other opinion leaders on market-based alternatives to regulatory initiatives, ranging from antitrust and insurance to energy and environmental protection, and engages in public interest litigation to protect property rights and economic liberty. Smith is a frequent guest on national television and radio programs to discuss and debate regulatory initiatives. He has appeared on ABC's *This Week,* CNN's *Crossfire,* the *MacNeil/Lehrer Newshour,* ABC's *20/20,* NPR's *Talk of the Nation,* and the *G. Gordon Liddy Show,* among many others. A prolific writer, his writings can be seen in leading newspapers and journals such as the *Wall Street Journal, National Review, Economic Affairs,* and the *Washington Times.* Smith is also a columnist for the journal *Regulation,* and a contributing editor to *Liberty.* Smith is co-editor (with Michael Greve) of *Environmental Politics: Public Costs, Private Rewards,* and has contributed chapters to over one dozen books, including *The True State of the Planet, Market Liberalism: A Paradigm for the Twenty-First Century,* and *Assessing the Reagan Years.* Before founding CEI, Smith served as the director of government relations for the Council for a Competitive Economy, as a senior economist for Association of American Railroads, and for five years as a senior policy analyst at the Environmental Protection Agency. Smith has a degree in mathematics and political science from Tulane University where he earned the Arts and Sciences Medal. He has also done graduate work at Harvard, SUNY at Buffalo, and the University of Pennsylvania.

Mark Storrie is the chief technology officer of Risktoolz, an international corporate finance consulting and software firm (www.risktoolz.com).

Mark E. Zmijewski is the Leon Carroll Marshall professor of accounting and deputy dean of the University of Chicago Graduate School of Business where he has been a member of the faculty since 1984. Zmijewski earned his doctorate at the State University of New York at Buffalo, where he also earned his BS and MBA degrees. Zmijewski has taught courses in financial analysis, valuation, mergers and acquisitions, and entrepreneurship. Zmijewski has authored several articles and papers for professional and academic research journals related to his academic fields of study in journals such as the *Journal of Accounting Research* and the *Journal of Accounting and Economics*. He won the American Accounting Association's *Competitive Manuscript Award* (1984). He has also served on the editorial boards of various academic journals. Zmijewski is also a founding partner of Chicago Partners LLC. Chicago Partners provides a multidisciplinary approach to consulting services on matters of economics, finance, accounting, and technology. Through its subsidiary, CP Risk Management LLC, the firm offers specific consulting services for measuring and managing financial risks. Chicago Partners has expertise in a wide range of issues including antitrust and regulation, securities and investment matters, labor economics, international trade, intellectual property, and business torts.

PREFACE

Dashing into the wreckage of a building following an earthquake may seem both the honorable thing to do and perhaps the best way to save lives. But the threat of aftershocks makes this a risky business. Taking time to consider carefully the structural damage caused by the earthquake not only helps protect the rescuers, but also may better protect the survivors. Moving the wrong brick even a little, however, can bring the rest of the building down. In other words, without proper analysis before mounting a rescue effort, manmade aftershocks can cause more damage than the original earthquake.

This book provides a public policy analysis of the Enron failure in an effort to avoid unnecessary manmade aftershocks. Specifically, Enron's failure begs questions in at least four policy areas that should be analyzed before rushing into political action:

1. Was Enron an innovator, a sham, or a bit of both? What kinds of social institutions and corporate governance mechanisms can best distinguish legitimate but aggressive business and financial innovation from fraudulent, deceptive, and unethical business practices?
2. Given that Enron was primarily an energy services firm that was both active and successful in energy and derivatives activities, what can we learn from Enron's failure that might impact the future operation and regulation of energy and derivatives markets?
3. Is "structured finance" and the use of special purpose entities a legitimate form of financial and risk management? What role did accounting and disclosure policies play in Enron's apparent abuses of otherwise-legitimate structured finance activities? What changes might be adopted to mitigate the potential for similar abuses in the future?
4. Did the widespread proliferation of financial contracts and techniques designed to help firms manage their credit exposure to ailing counterparties exacerbate or mitigate the impact of Enron's

failure? What lessons can be learned from Enron about credit risk management practices and products prospectively?

These questions are addressed in the five parts of this book.

STRUCTURE OF THE BOOK

Enron was, in many ways, an innovative firm, both in its primary business activities and in the process by which Enron raised funds. As the chapters in this book further explain, Enron often walked a tight line between legitimate and beneficial innovation and excessively "creative" schemes that ultimately were designed more to confuse outsiders than inform them of Enron's true activities. But even in its legitimate business practice, Enron was often engaged in activities that were novel and had not been attempted before. Apart from complicating any analysis of Enron, this also makes it critically important to distinguish between Enron's role as a legitimate, albeit maverick, innovator and its role as a fraudulent propagator of half truths and financial deceptions. All the chapters in this book attempt to draw this distinction carefully.

Part One of the book explores the very broad theme of the role of the corporation in the process of innovation, and how corporations in the innovation business are monitored and governed. In Chapter 1, Culp and Hanke contend that Enron's basic business strategy was not only legitimate, but actually quite beneficial for the marketplace. Although not the first firm to pursue this "asset lite" business strategy, Enron will certainly not be the last to do so—nor should it be. At the same time, the authors argue that Enron's innovative business activity was inherently risky, and predicting which firms will succeed and which will fail *ex ante* is essentially impossible. The competitive market is the best adjudicator of such decisions. Culp and Hanke further argue that analyzing firms like Enron through the traditional lens of "neoclassical" price theory paints only a partial picture. A "neo-Austrian" approach in which variables like time, knowledge, and disequilibrium are explicitly considered delivers a better method of analysis.

In Chapter 2, Bassett and Storrie explore some of the corporate accounting and disclosure implications of Enron's failure. Their analysis and commentary on the importance of cash flow accounting is relevant to any corporation, but especially those involved with developing financial products and strategies that might be considered novel and may not be easily understood by outsiders. They argue that earnings represent opinions, whereas cash flow is a fact. From that perspective, Bassett and Storrie argue that much more information was contained in Enron's financials about its delicate financial situation than many people realized. The authors further argue that accounting based on principles may provide a more accurate picture of a firm's true financial condition than accounting based on rules.

Harris and Kramer conclude Part One with a comprehensive survey of the history of the consensus model of corporate governance in the United States and analyze the trend toward relying more and more on monitoring boards—a trend that the Enron failure seems to have reinforced, but in no way initiated. Harris and Kramer question the efficacy of these proposals for strong independent boards and argue that the time has come for a fundamental change in the rules of corporate governance in this country.

In Part Two of the book, the contributors take a closer look at the energy and derivatives markets in which Enron was an active participant. As Neves explains in Chapter 4, wholesale power trading remained a primary profit center for Enron right up to the end. Recent attention to power markets is not because they "sank Enron," but rather because of the regulatory concerns that Enron may have abused its position in the market. Neves' chapter is an invaluable introduction to this complex market, whose uniqueness and opacity make it otherwise difficult for outsiders to assess the merits and costs of proposed regulatory changes. Chapter 4 also summarizes the development of electricity markets under partial deregulation, the special problems that arose in those markets in 1998 and 2000, and the market response to the collapse of Enron.

Kramer, Pantano, and Ezickson are among the top electricity regulation experts in the United States. In Chapter 5, they discuss the legal and regulatory implications of Enron's failure for wholesale electricity market participants. They contend that Enron's demise added to existing jurisdictional and regulatory uncertainty, and that prompt resolution of this regulatory uncertainty is required for active volume to be restored to U.S. wholesale power markets.

In Chapter 6, Herron examines Enron's Internet trading venture, EnronOnline, and the consequences of Enron's failure for the markets in which EnronOnline was a dominant trading platform. He argues that the market response to the failure of Enron was remarkably resilient. Although a short-term migration of trading volume has occurred back toward more traditional futures and commodities exchanges, Herron argues that there is still an important market function to be provided by electronic and virtual trading platforms like EnronOnline, *if* they are adequately capitalized and prepared to address credit risk for their participants in a responsible manner.

Mengle concludes Part Two by arguing in Chapter 7 that no aspect of Enron's failure calls into question the current regulatory framework for over-the-counter derivatives. On the contrary, the swaps market absorbed the Enron failure and should provide a model for other markets in a crisis management context.

Part Three of this book pertains to structured finance, or the use of special purpose entities (SPEs) by corporations to facilitate asset-divestiture, fund-raising, and risk-management decisions. Kavanagh provides a useful introduction to and summary of structured finance in Chapter 8. She argues that the vast majority of structured financing activities are legitimate, legal, and economically beneficial. She further explores how Enron abused structured finance in certain areas, emphasizing that accounting for and disclosing SPEs were much more the problem than the SPEs themselves.

In Chapter 9, Culp and Kavanagh explore the world of structured commodity finance, paying particular attention to prepaid forward and swap contracts. Many have alleged that these products serve no useful purpose and were used by Enron only to conceal the firm's true long-term borrowings from banks. But as Culp and Kavanagh explain, prepaid commodity contracts have a long history playing an important—and quite legal—role in facilitating project finance. Although these structures can be abused in principle, they are not inherently problematic in practice.

Chapter 10 analyzes the existing accounting and disclosure framework for structured financial transactions, concentrating on SPEs and prepaid commodity contracts. Bockus, Northcut, and Zmijewski provide a useful overview of criteria that govern when SPEs must be consolidated on the balance sheets of participants. The authors also argue that in some cases, Enron may well not have broken accounting rules, but, on the contrary, simply learned the rules *so well* that Enron knew where the loopholes were to get the accounting results they most wanted to see. Like Bassett and Storrie, they conclude that a more principles-based accounting system might discourage such abuses more than the current rules-based approach.

Part Four considers who actually lost money on Enron's failure and what lessons can be drawn from Enron about how firms can and should manage their credit exposures. In Chapter 11, Culp explores the different tools that have evolved in the last several years that enabled many of Enron's direct creditors and counterparties to manage or transfer the risk of an Enron default to other firms. Given the widespread use of these instruments, Culp then explores where actual Enron credit losses seem to have occurred, arguing that the prevalence of credit risk transfer tools spread Enron's default risk fairly evenly across all major sectors of the global economy, thus helping ensure that Enron's failure was not more of a systemic disaster than it was. Distinctions between insurance and derivatives solutions for credit risk transfer are also examined in the chapter in the context of the Mahonia debate concerning the efficacy of insurance versus derivatives solutions for credit risk management.

Having set forth a cogent history and analysis of governance in Chapter 3, the Kramer/Harris team return in Chapter 12 to explore how Enron affected the vast and growing market for credit derivatives. They provide a comprehensive introduction to this new and emerging marketplace and examine how firms used these novel transactions to address their concerns with Enron's credit risk. A summary of some of the important distinctions between insurance-based credit risk management solutions and credit derivatives is included, along with a discussion of some recent legal issues that have been raised concerning credit risk mitigation tools.

In Chapter 13, Palmer explores the importance of a credit culture in the analysis and management of credit risk—especially noninvestment-grade or complex credit risk. He argues that insurance companies and banks have generally well-developed credit cultures, but the former are too heavily influenced by rating agencies and the latter by the Basel Accord capital requirements. As a result, firms like investment banks with fewer institutional hindrances but less of a credit culture have become major players in credit intermediation. Yet, Palmer cautions against credit risk management solutions that rely too heavily on firms lacking the appropriate credit culture to identify the most efficient and effective solutions.

In Part Five of the book (Chapter 14), Smith provides a comprehensive framework in which to view the Enron saga and, in particular, the calls for greater regulation that Enron's failure has engendered. Smith argues that on the frontiers of innovation, distinctions between "cowboys" and "cattle thieves" are hard to draw. As institutions evolve to help society manage the risks of innovation, cattle thieves must be punished, but without also punishing the cowboys whose purpose is a legitimate one on the frontier. Although the natural tendency of society is to revert to hierarchical and political forms of risk management, Smith compellingly argues that more competitive and decentralized institutional responses are preferable. He reminds us that in trial-and-error-based capitalism, errors are both inevitable and essential, and caution must be exercised before blaming innovative practices for those errors. As the Enron case illustrates, traditional management failures are often still to blame, even for failures involving innovative products and strategies on the economic frontier.

CHRISTOPHER L. CULP

Chicago, IL
November 2002

ACKNOWLEDGMENTS

T hanks to all the contributors to this book for their time, effort, and, in many cases, scheduling sacrifices. More than one family's Thanksgiving turkey was disrupted by our efforts to make the final production deadline. The contributors represent the absolute "best of the breed" in many of the issue areas explored, and the quality of the book is entirely a result of their hard work. Special thanks to Al Harris and Andie Kramer, who not only contributed multiple chapters, but who also helped Bill Niskanen and me plan the contents of the book.

I am particularly grateful to Bill Niskanen and the Cato Institute for making all of this possible. Dr. Niskanen is an excellent co-editor, full of ideas about shaping the book's content. He has also been an excellent content and text editor. I have long admired his path-breaking work on bureaucracy and his legacy of important intellectual contributions to economics, as well as his articulate defense of the principles of a free society. It has been a pleasure to work with him and, as expected, I have both learned much and enjoyed the process. More generally, Cato's long-standing struggle to preserve liberty and individual freedom has played a critical role in the modern political process. I am extremely grateful to have had this opportunity to work with Cato and for all the energy and resources that Cato has dedicated to this project and to the defense of free markets in general.

At Wiley, Bill Falloon once again proved a more than capable editor, and Melissa Scuereb is the glue that holds the work together. Their skills are exceeded only by their patience. This is my fourth book with Bill and my second with Melissa, and I hope not the last.

Thanks also to my Autumn 2001 derivatives class at the Chicago GSB. I gained much from discussing the Enron failure with the class as it occurred. Special thanks to "The Capitol Grill team" in that class, whose updates and insights that quarter were especially appreciated. The next steak is on me, gentlemen.

Finally, a personal word of thanks and admiration go to Heinz Schimmelbusch, the former chairman of the management board of Metallgesellschaft AG (MG AG). But first, a little background is required. As many readers may recall, MG AG earned its place as one of the largest so-called derivatives disasters of the mid-1990s after booking over $1.3 billion in losses on its U.S. oil marketing subsidiary, MG Refining and Marketing (MGRM). The decision by the MG AG supervisory board to end MGRM's marketing program early—against loud protests from Schimmelbusch and the management board—precipitated massive international controversy.

Among the many who analyzed the MGRM debacle were the late Nobel laureate Merton Miller and I. Together we wrote seven articles and co-edited one book attempting to explain what was really going on at MGRM.[1] It is fair to say in retrospect that the Miller and Culp articles were highly sympathetic to Schimmelbusch and his team.[2] This is not, of course, why we wrote them. In fact, Professor Miller and I resolved early in our analysis of MGRM that to preserve our credibility in the face of growing controversy, we would neither accept any payment for any of our work nor would we communicate with any of the principal players at MGRM or MG AG. Professor Miller and I were merely analyzing the facts and the economics of the case. That this proved to be a defense of Schimmelbusch's actions was a consequence of the facts, not a deliberate effort on our parts.

The first time I actually met Heinz Schimmelbusch was in July 2001, when we shared lunch at La Pavillion restaurant in Zürich's Baur Au Lac Hotel. I shall never forget what Dr. Schimmelbusch said to me at that lunch, six months before Enron's bankruptcy and three months before public signs of trouble: "Enron will fail by the end of the year."

Even as Dr. Schimmelbusch pulled spreadsheets and financials from his briefcase onto the table, I was skeptical and attributed this comment to the two bottles of excellent Montrachet we had consumed with our veal and rösti. Yet, Schimmelbusch persisted and proceeded to make a compelling case that Enron was in serious trouble. He pointed out quarter after quarter of huge negative cash flows coincident with huge positive earnings statements—itself a major red flag (see Chapter 2)—together with a consistent pattern of too much R&D spending in markets where Enron had no prior experience, and a number of other questionable entries in Enron's published financials.

The showstopper for Schimmelbusch was Enron's acquisition of MG PLC in mid-2000. MG PLC, a spin-off from MG AG, was at that time a global leader in the metals trading business. Enron acquired the whole operation (including some 330 people in 14 countries) for $413 million in cash and $1.6 billion in assumed MG PLC debt (Fox, 2002, p. 188). But the integration was a disaster. Fox reports that it took 50 to 70 people to oversee the information technology systems integration alone. Schimmelbusch further claimed that MG PLC was too cash intensive, research dependent, and industry specific for Enron to make it work. He felt strongly that Enron had vastly over-paid for this acquisition—and yet had figured out a way not to show that in its financials.

Unfortunately, for me, I left lunch that day and went back to work on my previous book instead of promptly shorting Enron's stock—then still trading around $45 per share. As a result, I still have to work for a living.

But as for Dr. Schimmelbusch, honor is due. He proved to be exactly right—*again*.

C. L. C.

NOTES

1. The articles are reprinted in the book by Culp and Miller (1999).
2. In fact, MG Refining and Marketing was functioning as a basis trader and pursuing a strategy quite similar to Enron's asset lite as Hanke and I discuss in Chapter 1 of this book.

INTRODUCTION

This is the first of two books sponsored by the Cato Institute that address the policy lessons from the collapse of Enron. This book, organized by Christopher L. Culp and edited by the two of us, focuses primarily on the policy lessons specific to the energy and other markets in which Enron traded and on the specialized financial instruments that it used. The contributors to this book are among the leading practical specialists in these markets and with these financial instruments, and we are grateful for the contribution of their valuable time to inform the broader community about these issues. The target audience for this book includes the academics who specialize in these issues, the others who trade in these markets, the many others who use these financial instruments, the regulators of these markets and financial instruments, and the policy officials who approve the rules by which these markets operate. Some of the policy lessons from these careful analyses of the collapse of Enron are also important to a broader audience—such lessons as the problems of conventional accounting and the limitations of the developing consensus model of corporate governance.

The second book, which I organized and edited, addresses the major policy lessons affecting the broader corporate sector from the collapse of Enron and several other large corporations. That book focuses primarily on the government policies that contributed to the collapse of these several large corporations, the reasons why their weak financial conditions were not revealed and possibly corrected earlier, and the major policy changes that would reduce the frequency and magnitude of future corporate failures. The major sections of that book, thus, focus on the policy lessons affecting accounting, auditing, taxes, and corporate governance that were highlighted by the collapse of these large firms. Most of the contributors to that book are academics who, in turn, have drawn on the extensive academic literature on these several subjects. The target audience for that book is the larger community of academics, the media, and policy officials who have been motivated to address the implications of the collapse of Enron and several other large firms for the broader policies affecting American corporations.

Both of these books have tried to focus on the rules by which people operate and how to improve these rules, rather than on the heroes and villains of these stories. There is ample evidence of outrageous and, in some cases, illegal behavior by some corporate managers and an unforgivable lack of attention by many people in the audit chain, and these cases should be acknowledged and addressed. On the other hand, as is characteristic of prior periods following a large decline in the equity markets, there is a severe danger that the populace, the press, and politicians will overreact, making scapegoats of people for innocent behavior and responding by misguided rules that do not address the basic problems. Our objective is to identify changes in the rules such that the normal incentives of people in both the market and government lead to better outcomes.

The Cato Institute is a private, nonprofit, and nonpartisan policy institute committed to individual liberty, free markets, and limited constitutional government. We choose our own research agenda, do no work under contract, and receive no funding from the government; most of our funding is from around 15,000 individual contributors to whom we are always grateful.

WILLIAM A. NISKANEN

Washington, DC
November 2002

EDITORS' NOTE

The manuscripts for this volume were submitted in November 2002, and most were updated to be current as of early March 2003. Apart from a few more Enron executives that may have pled guilty to various offenses, little has changed since late 2002 in the various regulatory and legal proceedings. They continue to move forward, but at a snail's pace.

The markets, however, have been hit with several aftershocks. Electricity prices in California soared up to the $150/MWh mark—Who will Gray Davis blame this time?—and natural gas prices have skyrocketed. At the same time, electricity markets continue to exhibit malaise and illiquidity, and more firms encounter credit problems every week. Asset divestitures have been significant, and hedge funds have now begun buying up many of the assets that power companies have been forced to sell off. Despite the clear economic benefits of a power trading market, only time will tell if market participants will escape from beneath the rubble of the Enron quake. Even those who do will not likely emerge undamaged.

Especially given the slow pace of most proposed public policy responses to Enron, we believe that the vast majority of this book's content will remain topical for a fairly long time. Nevertheless, no hardcover book can ever be *completely* current on its publication date. We hope readers will take that into account in reading what follows in the context of whatever may be "current news" at that time.

C.L.C.
W.A.N.

Interlaken, Switzerland
Washington, DC
March 2003

PART ONE

Corporate Innovation and Governance

1

EMPIRE OF THE SUN

A Neo-Austrian Economic Interpretation of Enron's Energy Business

CHRISTOPHER L. CULP AND STEVE H. HANKE

B y the time the Enron Corporation filed for Chapter 11 bankruptcy
protection on December 2, 2001, virtually everyone with a television set knew that things were not as they had once seemed in Houston. How could a company go from a market capitalization of almost $100
billion and the number seven ranking in the *Fortune 500* to bust within
two years? How could a stock that had seen highs of nearly $90 per share
become a penny stock in record time? How could the six-time consecu-
tive winner (1996 to 2001) of *Fortune's* "most innovative company in the
United States" have engineered its own financial destruction? *What can we
do to make sure this never happens again?*

We must be careful when we define *this* in the phrase "make sure this
never happens again." Not everything Enron did, after all, was illegal, unethical, or even questionable. What actually caused Enron to fail is still
subject to contentious debate. As Part Two of this volume describes,
Enron did *not* fail because it was engaged in commercial and merchant
commodity businesses. Nor did a "rogue trader" or Enron's use of creative and sometimes-complex financial contracts bring Enron to its knees.
And, as the chapters in Part Three explain, Enron's corrupt financial activities—concealing its true indebtedness, lining the pockets of select senior managers at the expense of shareholders, hiding major losses, and
so on—are also not what caused Enron to fail. Enron's financial deception
undoubtedly allowed it to remain in business for longer than an otherwise similar firm engaged in accurate financial disclosures, but this is a
question of timing alone and not causality.

3

We argue in this chapter that Enron's ultimate financial failure most likely occurred for the same reason that WorldCom, Global Crossing, and many other firms periodically have run into trouble. In short, these firms all lacked the ability to identify their true *comparative advantage*. In some cases, this meant overinvesting in new markets and technologies that never took off. In other cases, the firms simply overestimated the value that they could add. But is *this* something that new policies and regulations should strive to ensure "never happens again"? Or, as we argue here, is this aspect of Enron's failure nothing more than a testimonial to the fact that competitive markets are effective judges of success and failure?

We begin this chapter with an overview of Enron. In doing so, we stress that it was first and foremost an energy business that employed an innovative *asset lite strategy* that accounted for many of Enron's genuinely successful years. We then briefly discuss those businesses in which Enron failed because it departed from the successful asset lite strategy employed in the energy business. The next section formally frames Enron's asset lite strategy in the context of competitive economic theory. We argue that the standard "neoclassical" economic models do not explain firms such as Enron and that a more "disequilibrium-oriented" or "neo-Austrian" approach is required. A concluding section considers whether Enron's failure *as a business* either offers lessons for other firms or provides a proscriptive case for greater regulation.

Apart from providing an analysis of Enron's business strategy through the lens of economic theory, our chapter also illustrates the limitations of the traditional neoclassical theory of the price system for explaining *entrepreneurship* and *innovation*—terms we feel that, despite Enron's illegal and fraudulent activities in some areas, nevertheless, do describe this company in other areas. From a neoclassical perspective, markets are viewed as being in a stationary state in which the relevant knowledge about demand and supply is known and market prices are static, or given, data to be taken and used by individuals and firms. In this world without change, we need not ask how this state of affairs came about. This knowledge simply falls into the category of irrelevant bygones.

Neoclassical economics also deals with change. It does so by employing comparative statics. For example, we can conceive of a quasi-stationary state in which changes in the relevant knowledge in a market are few and far between, and the analysis of the full repercussions are dealt with by evaluating and comparing the stationary states before and after the changes in relevant knowledge occur. In the neoclassical world, prices act as signposts, guiding consumers to substitute goods for one another and producers to learn which lines of production to abandon or which to turn toward. In this neoclassical conception, the price system acts as a network of communication in which relevant knowledge is transmitted at once throughout markets that jump from one stationary state to the next.

In the neo-Austrian or disequilibrium-oriented context, by contrast, the market is viewed as a process that is in a constant state of flux.[1] As a consequence, there are no stationary or quasi-stationary states. Indeed, expectations about the current and future state of affairs are always changing because the state of relevant knowledge is always changing. With those changing expectations, market prices are also changing. The price system is functioning as a network for communicating relevant knowledge. It is also a discovery process that is in continuous motion, working toward creating a unity and coherence in the economic system. The speed of adjustment and the dissemination of knowledge in the price system depend on the scope and scale of the markets, however.

As it relates to our discussion here, the full force of market integration is realized when both spot and forward markets exist. Indeed, one important function of forward or derivatives markets is to spread relevant knowledge about what market participants think the future will be. Forward markets connect and integrate those expectations about the future with the present in a consistent manner. Although the future will always remain uncertain, it is possible for individuals to acquire information and knowledge about the expected future and adjust their plans accordingly. In addition, they can—via forward markets—express their views about the future by either buying or selling forward. Forward markets, then, bring expectations about the future into consistency with each other and also bring forward prices into consistency with spot prices, with the difference being turned into "the basis."

In a neo-Austrian world, the state of relevant knowledge and expectations is in a constant state of flux. And not surprisingly, spot and forward prices, as well as their difference (the basis), are constantly changing, too. Ever-changing expectations, therefore, keep the market process in motion. In consequence, disequilibrium is a hallmark of the neo-Austrian orientation. While the neo-Austrian market process is in a constant state of flux, it is working toward integrating and making consistent prices, both spot and forward.[2]

As the analysis in this chapter demonstrates, the explicit incorporation of neo-Austrian variables such as time, knowledge, and market process into the traditional price theoretical framework for microeconomic analysis is fundamental to understanding fully the financial and commercial market strategies of a company such as Enron.

ENRON'S ENERGY BUSINESS

To understand Enron's business model for its core activities requires a brief explanation of how *commodity markets* function. The usefulness of many physical commodities to producers (e.g., wheat that can be milled into flour) and consumers (e.g., bread) depends on the *supply chain* through which the commodity is transformed from its raw, natural state into something of practical use. Figure 1.1 shows a typical supply chain for a variety of commodities.

When a commodity moves from one part of the supply chain to the next, transportation, distribution, and delivery services are almost always involved. These services are the glue that keeps the supply chain linked. To put it simply, Enron specialized in these transportation, distribution, and transformation services—often called *intermediate supply chain* or *midstream* services. Accordingly, Enron acted as a wholesale merchant. It acquired the latest information about alternative sources of supply and set prices for goods in a process that would maximize Enron's turnover. Enron was an ideal vehicle for the discovery and transmission of relevant knowledge.

In its 2000 annual report, Enron described itself as "a firm that manages efficient, flexible networks to reliably deliver physical products at predictable prices" (Enron, 2001, cover).[3] This involved four core business areas for the firm: wholesale services, energy services, broadband services, and transportation services.

Enron Wholesale Services was the corporation's largest—and generally the most profitable—operation. The bulk of that business was the transportation/transmission and distribution of natural gas and electricity. On a volume basis, Enron accounted for more than twice the amount of gas and power delivery in the United States of its next-largest competitor (Enron, 2001, p. 9). In addition, Enron maintained an active (and, in several cases, growing) market presence in the supply chains

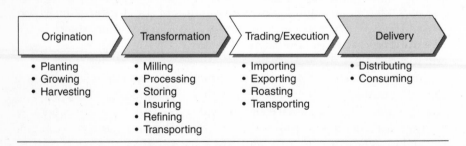

FIGURE 1.1   The Supply Chain

for other commodities, including coal, crude oil, liquefied natural gas (LNG), metals, steel, and pulp/paper. Enron Wholesale Service's customers were generally other large producers and industrial firms.

Enron Energy Services dealt mainly with the retail end of the energy market supply chains. Enron Wholesale Services might deliver electrical power to a utility, for example, whereas Enron Energy Services might contract with a large grocery store chain to supply their power directly.

Enron Broadband Services was focused on the nonenergy business of broadband, or the use of fiber optics to transmit audio and video. Capacity on fiber-optic cables is known as *bandwidth*. Enron Broadband Services had three business goals. The first was to deploy the largest open global broadband network in the world, called the *Enron Intelligent Network*, consisting of 18,000 miles of fiber-optic cable. The second commercial objective was for Enron to dominate the market for buying and selling bandwidth. Finally, Enron sought to become a dominant provider of premium content, mainly through streaming audio and video over the Internet.

Enron's fourth operating division was Enron Transportation Services, formerly the Gas Pipeline Group. Long a core competency of Enron, Transportation Services concentrated on operating interstate pipelines for the transportation of natural gas. Albeit highly specialized and narrowly focused, gas transportation was perhaps *the* core brick on which the Enron Corporation foundation was laid.

The Houston Natural Gas Production Company was founded in 1953 as a subsidiary of Houston Natural Gas (HNG) to explore for, drill, and transport gas. From 1953 to 1985, the firm underwent a slow but steady expansion, respectably keeping pace with the gradual development of the gas market.

Natural gas was deregulated throughout the late 1980s and early 1990s. During this time, supplies increased substantially, and prices fell by more than 50 percent from 1985 to 1991 alone. As competition increased, the number of new entrants into various parts of the natural gas supply chain grew dramatically, and many existing firms restructured.

One such restructuring was the acquisition in 1985 of HNG by InterNorth, Inc. The takeover of HNG was largely the brainchild of Kenneth Lay, who had joined HNG as its CEO in 1984. Working closely with Michael Milken, Lay helped structure the InterNorth purchase of HNG as a leveraged buy-out relying heavily on junk-bond finance.[4] Lay wrested the position of CEO of the merged firm from InterNorth CEO Samuel Segnar in 1985.

In 1986, InterNorth changed its name to Enron Corporation and incorporated Enron Oil & Gas Company (EOG), reflecting its expansion into oil markets to supplement its gas market presence. By then, most firms active in oil markets were also involved in gas—and conversely—given complementarities in exploration, drilling, pumping, distribution, and the like. With the exception of a brief hiatus toward the end, Lay remained CEO of Enron Corporation until the firm failed.[5]

In 1985, the Federal Energy Regulatory Commission (FERC) allowed open access to gas pipelines for the first time. As a consequence, Enron was able to charge other firms for using Enron pipelines to transport gas, and, similarly, Enron was also able to transport gas through other companies' pipelines.

Around this time, Jeffrey Skilling, then a consultant for McKinsey, began working with Enron. He was charged with developing a creative strategy to help Enron—recall, it had just been created through the InterNorth/HNG merger—leverage its presence in the emerging gas market. Skilling argued that the benefits of open access might be more than offset by the declining revenues associated with the general drop in prices and margins that greater competition would bring. Add to that Enron's mountain of debt, and Skilling maintained that Enron would not last very long unless a creative solution was identified.

Skilling argued, in particular, that natural gas would never be a serious source of revenues for the firm as long as natural gas was traded exclusively in a "spot" physical market for immediate delivery. Instead, he argued that a key success driver in the coming era of postderegulation price volatility would be the development of a *natural gas derivatives market* in which Enron would provide its customers with various price risk management solutions—forward contracts in which consumers could control their price risk by purchasing gas today at a fixed price for future delivery and option contracts that allowed customers the right, but not the obligation, to purchase or sell gas at a fixed price in the future.

Viewed from a neo-Austrian perspective, Skilling was functioning as a classic entrepreneur. Once FERC changed the rules of the game and natural gas became deregulated, Skilling spotted an entrepreneurial opportunity to develop new markets. By introducing forward markets, individuals could acquire information and knowledge about the future and express their own expectations by either buying or selling forward. Moreover, with both spot and futures prices revealed, the basis—the difference between spot and futures prices—could be revealed and a more unified and coherent natural gas "market" could be created. While such a new setup would not eliminate risk and uncertainty, it promised to allow much more relevant knowledge to be discovered and disseminated, allowing firms to adjust their expectations and plans accordingly and to manage their risk more effectively (Lachmann, 1978).

To create this market in natural gas derivatives, Skilling urged that Enron set up a "gasbank"—called GasBank. Much as traditional banks intermediate funds, Enron's GasBank intermediated gas purchases, sales, and deliveries by entering into long-term, fixed-price delivery and price risk management contracts with customers. Soon thereafter, other natural gas firms began to offer clients similar risk management solutions. And those producers, in turn, also came to Enron for their risk management needs.

Enron acted as a classic *market maker,* standing ready to enter into natural gas derivatives on both sides of the market—that is, both buying and selling gas (or, equivalently, buying at both fixed/floating prices or swapping one for the other). Enron thus became the primary supplier of liquidity to the market, earning the spread between bid and offer prices as a fee for providing the market with liquidity. In addition and in a broader sense, Enron was functioning to spread knowledge about what market participants expected prices to be.

Did this mean Enron was exposed to *all* of the price risks that its trading counter parties were attempting to avoid? No, because many of the contracts into which Enron entered naturally offset one another. True, a consumer seeking to lock in its future energy purchase price with Enron would create risk exposure for Enron. If prices rose above the fixed price at which Enron agreed to sell energy to a consumer, Enron could lose big money. But that might be offset by a risk exposure to *falling* prices that Enron would assume by agreeing to *buy* that same asset from a producer at a fixed price, thus allowing the producer to hedge its exposure to price increases. (See Chapters 4, 5, and 9 for more discussion of these different types of contracts.) Enron was left with only the *residual* risk across all its customer positions in its GasBank, which, in turn, Enron could manage by using derivatives with other emerging market makers, generally known as *swap dealers,* or on organized futures exchanges.[6]

For a long time, Enron was not merely *a* market maker for natural gas derivatives—it was *the* market maker, having virtually *created* the market. This meant wider spreads, higher margins, and more revenues for Enron as the sole real liquidity supplier to the market. But this also meant few counter parties existed with which Enron could trade to hedge its own residual risks.

Here is where Enron's *physical* market presence comes back into the picture. In addition to allowing Enron to discover and reveal a great deal of "local" knowledge, Enron's presence in the physical market meant that it could control some of the residual price risks from its market-making operations. This could be accomplished because of *offsetting positions in its physical pipeline and gas operations.* Consider, for example, a firm that is buying natural gas in Tulsa, Oklahoma, from a pipeline with a supply source in San Angelo, Texas. If that firm seeks to lock in its future purchase price for gas to protect against unexpected price spikes, it might enter into a forward purchase agreement with Enron, thus leaving Enron to bear the risk of a price increase. But if Enron also *owns the pipeline* and charges a price for distribution proportional to the spot price of gas, the *net* effect will be roughly offsetting.

Operating this kind of gasbank also gave Enron valuable information about the gas market itself. Knowing from its pipeline operations that congestion was likely to occur at Point A, for example, Enron could anticipate price spikes at delivery points beyond Point A arising from the squeeze in available pipeline capacity. And Enron could very successfully "trade around" such congestion points. Conversely, when prices in derivatives markets signaled surplus or deficit pipeline capacity in the financial market, Enron could stand ready to exploit that information in the physical market.

Gradually, thanks to Enron's role as market maker, the natural gas derivatives market became increasingly standardized and liquid. Accordingly, relevant knowledge was spread more rapidly and the natural gas market became more integrated and coherent. Enron still offered customized solutions to certain consumers and producers, but much of the volume of the market shifted to exchanges such as the New York Mercantile Exchange (NYMEX), which began to provide standardized gas futures. Nevertheless, Enron's role as dominant market maker left the GasBank well situated to profit from supplying liquidity to *those* standardized markets, as well as retaining much of the custom over-the-counter (OTC) derivatives dealing business.

The Enron GasBank division eventually became Enron Gas Services (EGS) and later Enron Capital and Trade Resources (EC&TR). In 1990, Skilling left McKinsey to become a full-time Enron employee, and Skilling later became CEO of both EGS and EC&TR. In 2001, Skilling ultimately replaced Lay as CEO for the whole firm, marking the only time in the history of Enron that Lay was not at the helm.

When Skilling joined Enron formally in 1990, he maintained that the future success of the firm would come from repeating the GasBank experience in other markets. To accomplish this, Skilling developed a business concept known as *asset lite*, in which Enron would combine small investments in capital-intensive commodity markets with a derivatives trading and market-making "overlay" for that market. The purpose was to begin with a relatively small capital expenditure that was used to acquire portions of assets and establish a presence in the physical market. This allowed

Enron to learn the operational features of the market and to collect information about factors that might affect market price dynamics. Then, Enron would create a new financial market overlaid on that underlying physical market presence—a market in which Enron would act as market maker and liquidity supplier to meet other firms' risk management needs. As Skilling described it, "[Enron] is a company that makes markets. We create the market, and once it's created, we make the market" (Kurtzman and Rifkin, 2001, p. 47). Needless to say, this encapsulates the essence of one of the central roles of a neo-Austrian entrepreneur.

One reason for the appeal of asset lite was that it enabled Enron to exploit some presence in the physical market without incurring huge capital expenditures on bulk fixed investments. Enron quickly discovered that this was best accomplished by focusing on investing in *intermediate* assets in commodity supply chains. In natural gas, this meant that Enron could get the biggest bang for its buck in midstream activities such as transportation, pipeline compression, storage, and distribution. Enron's Transwestern Pipeline Company eventually became the first U.S. pipeline that was *exclusively* for transportation, neither pumping gas at the wellhead *nor* selling it to customers (Clayton, Scroggins, and Westley, 2002).

Other markets in which Enron applied its asset lite business expansion strategy with a large degree of success included coal, fossil fuels, pulp, and paper. But after its successful experience with gas, Enron remained much more interested in markets that were being deregulated. Electricity thus became a major focus of the firm in the mid-1990s and was a key success driver for Enron, as Neves explains in Chapter 4.

OIL AND WATER DO NOT MIX

Throughout its history, Enron's consistent financial and market successes occurred only in the energy sector. This was not for lack of effort, however. On more than one occasion, Enron tried to expand its business outside the energy area, albeit rarely with any success.

Asset Heavy at Enron International

When it became clear that Lay was preparing to turn over the reins in the latter half of the 1990s, an extremely contentious struggle for the leadership of Enron ensued (Fusaro and Miller, 2002). In no small part, this occurred because of the success of Enron GasBank and the power marketing operations of EC&TR. When the dust settled, Lay named EC&TR CEO and asset lite inventor Skilling as the new CEO of Enron Corporation in

February 2001. That Skilling would rise to this level, however, was not at all a foregone conclusion. Right up to the announcement date, debates about whose shoulder Lay would tap were popular coffee shop banter. Skilling's chief competitor was Rebecca Mark.

In 1993, Mark prevailed on Lay to establish Enron International (EI), of which she became the first president. Mark did *not* adhere to an asset lite strategy. Instead, she pursued an *asset heavy* strategy of attempting to acquire or develop large capital-intensive projects *for their own sake.* In other words, there was no financial trading activity overlay component for most of her initiatives, nor was there intended to be. She tried instead to identify projects whose revenues promised to be sizable purely based on the capital investment component with no need for a market-maker component. Unlike asset lite, this did not prove to be an area in which Enron Corportion had much comparative advantage.

Water Trading Rights

The EI operations delved into the asset-heavy water supply industry. At least here, there was some pretense of eventually developing a "water rights trading market," but it was so far down the road that the firm's water investments had to be regarded as largely self-contained capital projects, the largest of which was Azurix and its Wessex Water initiative.

In 1998, Enron spun off the water company Azurix. Enron retained a major interest in the firm, which focused its efforts on water markets in a single purchase—the British firm Wessex Water, for which Enron paid about $1.9 billion. But in this case, deregulation did not help Enron. There was no market-making function and no trading overlay—there was only a British water company serving a market with plummeting prices. (This experience also underscores the fundamentally correct view that Skilling advanced when he was still at McKinsey—namely, expanding in a deregulating market makes little sense if you are limited to selling a spot commodity, whose price is falling out of bed.)

At the same time that the falling prices of deregulation in Britain were eating away Wessex's margins, Azurix itself was hit with staggering losses on several of its other operations, mainly in Argentina. In the wake of this failed venture, as well as the spectacular failure of EI's Dhabhol, India, power plant project, which may have cost Enron as much as $4 billion, Mark resigned as CEO in the summer of 2000. Enron eventually sold Wessex in 2002, just about three years after financing its acquisition by Azurix to a Malaysian firm for $777 million, or $1.1 billion less than it paid for the firm (Fusaro and Miller, 2002).

The Broadband Black Hole

Like its forays into the water industry, Enron's broadband efforts were plagued with problems from the start. In gas and power markets, Enron acquired its physical market presence by investing in assets sold mainly by would-be competing energy companies. It then used those investments to help create and develop a financial market, the growth of which, in turn, helped *increase* the value of Enron's physical investments. But that increase did not come at the expense of Enron's competitors, which in turn were benefiting from the new price-risk management market. In broadband technologies, by contrast, Enron's asset lite effort required the firm to acquire assets not just from competitors, but from the *inventors* of the technology. Even then, Enron was paying for a technology that was essentially untested with no guarantee that the emerging bandwidth market would bolster asset values. As such, Enron had to pay dearly to acquire a market presence from firms that viewed Enron's effort not as a constructive market-making move, but as essentially intrusive.

Several other drags on Enron's broadband expansion efforts contributed to its ultimate failure. One was the simple lack of demand for the technology to materialize as expected. Enron is also alleged to have been using the bandwidth market to mislead investors—and possibly certain senior managers and directors—about its losses on underlying broadband technologies. On the one hand, Enron touted optimism about the eventual success of the broadband strategy in part by pointing at significant trading in the bandwidth market. On the other hand, few other market participants were observing any appreciable trading activity, and Enron was openly disclosing millions of dollars of losses on its quarterly and annual reports on its broadband efforts. Much of that market activity now seems to have come from Enron's "wash" or "round-trip trades" or transactions in which Enron is essentially trading with itself.[7] To take a simple example, a purchase and sale of the same contract within a one- or two-minute period of time in which prices have not changed shows up as "volume," but the transactions wash out and amount to no real bottom-line profits.

Apart from using wash trades to exaggerate the state of the market's development, Enron was also alleged to have used some of its bandwidth derivatives for "manufacturing" exaggeratedly high valuations for its technological assets. Enron and Qwest are under investigation for engaging in transactions with each other that are alleged to have been designed specifically to create artificial mark-to-market valuations. Enron and Qwest engaged in a $500 million bandwidth swap negotiated just before the end of the 2001 third-quarter financial reporting period. Many would argue that Enron and Qwest were swapping one worthless thing for another worthless thing, given the lack of a market for bandwidth and the lack of *interest* in bandwidth. Nevertheless, both firms apparently used the swaps to justify having acquired a much more valuable asset than they were getting rid of. With essentially no market, no market prices were available to evaluate the validity of those claims at the time.

THE ECONOMICS OF ASSET LITE AND BASIS TRADING

Through its investments in the underlying commodity supply chains, the trading room overlay on the physical markets allowed Enron to generate substantial revenues as a market maker. But this was not the only source of profits associated with the asset lite strategy of combining physical and financial market positions. Specifically, Enron engaged in significant *basis trading.* Understanding what this is and when a company might be able to do it profitably is essential for recognizing the differences between businesses on which Enron made money and those on which it did not.

Synthetic Storage with Derivatives

To understand the economics of spread/basis trading, you must first recognize the important finance proposition that commodity derivatives—contracts for the purchase or sale of a commodity in the future—are economic substitutes for physical market operations.[8] Buying a forward oil purchase contract, for example, is economically equivalent to buying and storing oil (Culp, 2003; Williams, 1986). In a competitive equilibrium of the physical and derivatives markets, the forward purchase price—denoted $F(t, T)$ and defined as the fixed price negotiated on date t for the purchase of a commodity to be delivered on later date T—can be expressed using the famed *cost-of-carry model* as[9]

$$F(t, T) = S(t)\big[1 + b(t, T)\big]$$

where

$$b(t, T) \equiv r(t, T) + w(t, T) - d(t, T)$$

and

$S(t)$ = Time t spot price of the commodity to be delivered at T
$r(t, T)$ = Interest rate prevailing from t to T
$w(t, T)$ = Cost of physical storage of the commodity from t to T
$d(t, T)$ = Benefit of holding the commodity from t to T

such that w and d are expressed as a proportion of $S(t)$ and are denominated in time T dollars.

The term $b(t, T)$ is often called the *basis* or the *net cost-of-carry* to reflect the fact that its three components together comprise the cost of "carrying" the commodity across time and space to the delivery location on future date T. The term $d(t, T)$ that reflects the benefit of physical storage is called the *convenience yield,* a concept developed by Keynes (1930), Kaldor (1939), Working (1948, 1949), Brennan (1958), and Telser (1958). The convenience yield is driven mainly by what Working (1962) calls the "precautionary demand for storage," or concerns by firms that unanticipated shocks to demand or supply could precipitate a costly inventory depletion or stock-out. Airlines store fuel at different airports, for example, to avoid the huge costs of grounding their local fleets in the case of a jet fuel outage. Gas pipeline owners store fuel to help ensure there is always an adequate supply of gas in the lines to maintain the flow and avoid a shutdown.

Keynes (1930), Working (1949), Williams (1986), and others have observed how the *supply of storage* (i.e., the amount of a commodity in physical storage) is related to the convenience yield and, by extension, to the *term structure of futures prices.* More important, this relation defines the economic linkage among derivatives, physical asset markets, and the allocation of physical supplies across time (Culp, 2003). Specifically, the supply of storage is directly related to the premium placed on selling inventory *in the future* relative to selling spot *today.* When inventories are high, the *relative* premium that a commodity commands in the future vis-à-vis the present is reasonably small; plenty of the commodity is on hand today to assure producers and intermediaries that a stock-out will not occur, leading to a very low convenience yield. As current inventories get smaller, however, the convenience yield rises (at an increasing rate) and the spot price rises relative to the futures price to induce producers to take physical product *out* of inventory and sell it in the current spot market. A high spot price *alone* would not do that. But a high spot price *relative to* the futures price signals the market that inventories are tight *today* relative to the future.

We can now see more meaningfully where cost-of-carry pricing comes from. Namely, it is the condition that must maintain equilibrium to make market participants indifferent between physical storage and "synthetic storage" using forwards or other derivatives. Here's how it works. Suppose a firm borrows $S(t)$ in funds at time t and uses the proceeds to buy a commodity worth $S(t)$. At time T, the firm is holding an asset then worth $S(T)$ and repays the money loan. In the interim, the firm incurs physical storage costs w but earns the convenience yield d. Table 1.1 shows the net effect of this physical storage operation.

Table 1.1   Physical Commodity Storage

Time:	t	T
Money Loan:		
Borrow dollars	$S(t)$	—
Repay dollars and interest	—	$-S(t)(1+r(t,T))$
Buy and Store the Asset:		
Buy commodity	$-S(t)$	—
Pay storage costs	—	$-S(t)w(t,T)$
Earn convenience yield	—	$S(t)d(t,T)$
Still own the commodity	—	$S(T)$
NET	0	$S(T)-S(t)(1+r(t,T)+w(t,T)-d(t,T))$

Because not every firm has the same convenience yield or storage costs, commodity forward prices are driven to the cost-of-carry expression by the dynamics of a competitive equilibrium.[10] To see how it works, suppose the forward purchase price is

$$F^\circ = S(t)\left(1+b^\circ\left(t,T\right)\right)$$

where $b^\circ(t, T)$ denotes any arbitrary net cost-of-carry. All firms for which $S(t)(1 + b(t, T)) < F^\circ$ can earn positive economic profits by going short the forward and simultaneously buying and storing the commodity. They continue to do this until the forward price falls and $S(t)(1 + b(t, T)) = F^\circ$. As long as *any* firm can make positive profits from this operation, the selling continues, until $S(t)(1+b(t, T)) = F^*$ where

$$F^* = S(t)\left(1+b^*\left(t,T\right)\right)$$

where $b^*(t, T)$ denotes the *marginal* net cost-of-carry for the *marginal storer* from t to T. This marginal entrant earns exactly zero economic profits because its own net cost-of-carry is equal to b^*.

Things work in the other direction for any firms where $S(t)(1+b(t, T)) > F^\circ$. Those firms will go long the forward and then engage in a commodity repurchase agreement (i.e., lending the commodity at time t and repurchasing it at time T).[11] Again, entry occurs until F° exactly equals F^* and reflects the marginal basis of the marginal storer.

In the short run, the basis b^* thus reflects the marginal cost of carrying an incremental unit of the commodity over time. In the long run, b^*

also corresponds to the minimum point on a traditional U-shaped long-run average cost curve.[12] Suppose all firms have b^* below this minimum long-run average cost. In this case, at least one firm will expand output until marginal cost rises to minimum average cost and equals the marginal price of the cost-of-carry and the new b^* is also reflected in the forward price.

The process by which commodity derivatives and the underlying asset market simultaneously grope toward a competitive equilibrium helps illustrate an important point. Namely, the *relation* between forward and spot prices—the *basis*—is really a *third market* implied by the prices of the two explicit ones (Williams, 1986). In the previous example, the two explicit markets are the spot and forward markets, and the relation between the two implicitly defines *the price of physical storage*. Such third markets are also called *basis* relations. The implicit market for storage over time is called the *calendar basis*, the implicit market for transportation is called the *transportation basis*, and so on.

Firms can also use derivatives *based on different assets* to conduct "spread" trades to synthesize a third market. Going short crude oil and simultaneously long heating oil and gasoline, for example, is called trading the *crack spread* and is economically equivalent in equilibrium to synthetic refining. Short soybeans and long bean oil and meal is likewise *synthetic crushing*. Trading the *spark spread* through a short position in natural gas and a long position in electricity is called *synthetic generation* because the derivatives positions replicate the economic exposure of a gas-fired electric turbine.

A Neo-Austrian Explanation for Basis Trading

Armed with an understanding of how commodity derivatives are priced *in* equilibrium, we now consider the economic rationale for why Enron and firms like it sometimes dedicate substantial resources to basis trading. More important, we now want to recognize what can happen *out of equilibrium*—a state of affairs that typically prevails. Indeed, expectations and relevant knowledge (data) are in a constant state of flux. Accordingly, a neoclassical stationary state—one that treats the data as constant—is of limited use in explaining the market process.[13]

We have seen how equilibrium emerges from the interactions of numerous firms competing to drive prices to their marginal cost. Specifically, suppose b^* is the marginal net cost-of-carry reflected in the prevailing natural gas forward price. This is the price of transportation and delivery *in equilibrium*. The net cost-of-carry b^* may conform only to the *actual* physical and capital costs-of-carry less the convenience yield for one firm—the marginal entrant into the gas transportation market. Or b^* may be shared by all firms in the short run, but aggregate output may need to adjust in the long run if b^* does not also reflect the minimum average long-run cost-of-carry. The point is: The cost-of-carry reflected in the forward price may or may not be the optimal cost-of-carry for any given firm at any given time. As is standard in neoclassical microeconomic theory, the price that "clears the market" in the long run equals short-run marginal cost for any given firm only by pure coincidence.

Suppose we begin in a situation where b^* is the cost-of-carry reflected in the forward price and that b^* is equal to the short-run marginal costs of all market participants at their production optima. Now consider a new entrant into the market, and suppose that new entrant is Enron with its large number of pipelines and strong economies of scale that lead to cost of distributing and transporting natural gas at some point in time of $b^e < b^*$. In this case, Enron can *physically* move gas across time and space at a lower cost than gas can be moved "synthetically" using derivatives.

By going short or selling gas for future delivery using forwards or futures, Enron is selling gas at an implied net cost-of-carry of b^*. But its *own* net cost-of-carry—a cost that is relevant in Enron's ability to move the gas across time and space to honor its own future sale obligation created by the forward contract—is less. Accordingly, *in disequilibrium*—or, more properly, on the way to equilibrium—Enron can make a profit equal to the difference between its own net cost of storage and the cost reflected in the market.

The reason that this is a short-run profit inconsistent with a long-run equilibrium is that Enron's sale of the forward contract drives the b^* reflected in forward prices closer to b^e. If Enron is the lowest cost producer and other firms can replicate its production techniques (i.e., Enron owns no unique resources), ultimately b^* becomes b^e, which also eventually approaches the long-run minimum average cost-of-carry. Enron's capacity to earn supranormal profits will vanish in this new equilibrium—in fact, zero economic profits earned by every producer is basically the very meaning of a long-run equilibrium.

Because markets are constantly adjusting to new information, new trading activity, and new entrants, however, it is hard to determine when a market actually is in some kind of final equilibrium resting state, as opposed to when it is adjusting from one state to another. The inevitability of a long-run competitive equilibrium in which profits are *not* possible thus must be considered relative to the inability of market participants to identify slippery concepts such as *long run* and *in equilibrium*. Strictly speaking, a market is in equilibrium as long as supply equals demand. But we use the term here in a more subtle fashion, where *equilibrium* refers to the steady state in which firms earn zero supranormal economic profits in the long run. Firms may engage in basis trading to try to exploit the differences in prices reflected in derivatives and their own ability to conduct physical market "pseudo-arbitrage" operations that are economically equivalent to those derivatives transactions.[14]

Now consider a situation when the market is *always* adjusting and *never* reaches a long-run competitive equilibrium.[15] In this situation, the tendency is still toward the archetypical neoclassical long-run competitive equilibrium, but we never quite get there. Why not? Certainly economic agents are responding in the manner we have described, and this behavior should ultimately lead to a steady-state long-run equilibrium. The only reason it does not is that too much is happening at any given moment for us to make the leap from short run to long run.

In this situation, all firms are always inframarginal in some sense of the term. The kind of pseudo-arbitrage between physical and synthetic storage that we described previously thus can be expected to occur *regularly*. And at least some firms will earn supranormal profits regularly. More important, these profits are not riskless, but at least some firms are sure to be right at least some of the time.

Does this mean that physical and synthetic storage are not really equivalent? Technically, it does. But we never said otherwise. We claimed only that the two are equivalent *in equilibrium*. When a market is in disequilibrium, what you actually pay to store a commodity physically may differ from what you actually pay to store it synthetically. But this is not important.

What is important is that, even if new information and other market activities drive a wedge between $b°$ and $b*$, maximizing decisions by firms *always* leads *toward* the convergence of the two prices of storage. Conversely, the price mechanism *never* sends a signal that will lead maximizing firms to engage in physical or derivatives transactions that drive $b°$ and $b*$ further apart. The very fact that maximizing firms are constantly seeking to exploit differences between $b°$ and $b*$ is what gives the theory meaning. That the two might never end up exactly equal is really not very relevant because, as we now explain, information changes before the long-run equilibrium is ever reached.

Asymmetric Information

Now suppose that the net cost of storage is a random variable about which some firms are better informed than others—for example, the impact of supply or demand shocks on particular locational prices, the impact of pipeline congestion on the transportation basis, and the like. Suppose further that we assume a competitive long-run equilibrium *does* hold. Because of the information asymmetry, a rational expectations equilibrium (REE) results in which *expected* supranormal profits are zero in the long run. But *expected* by whom?

In this case, firms such as Enron may engage in basis or spread trading in an effort to exploit their perceived comparative informational advantage. If a firm owns physical pipelines, for example, it may have a superior capability for forecasting congestion or regional supply and demand shocks. This creates a situation similar to a market that is out of, or on the way to, equilibrium—that is, the net cost-of-carry that the *firm* observes may be *different from* the net cost-of-carry market participants expect, given the different information on which the two numbers are based. Just as in the disequilibrium case, firms may engage in basis trading to exploit these differences.

In a traditional rational expectations equilibrium, this type of behavior is akin to inframarginal firms attempting to exploit their storage cost advantage relative to the marginal price of storage reflected in forwards. And, as noted, this cannot go on for very long because the trading actions of the lower cost firm eventually lead them to *become* the marginal entrant, thus driving b^* to b° for that firm. The same is true in a REE, where trading *itself* is informative. Every time a well-informed trader attempts to exploit its superior information through a transaction, it reveals that superior information to the market. So, the paradox for the firm with better information is that the firm must either *not trade* based on that information to preserve its informational advantage or must *give away* its informational advantage while simultaneously trying to exploit it in the short run through trading.

Culp and Miller (1995b) argue, however, that this sort of classic equilibrium assumes that the trading activities of the better-informed firm are, indeed, informative. But what if other market participants cannot *see* all the firm's trades? And what if the trades are occurring in highly opaque, bilateral markets rather than on an exchange? In this case, better informed firms *can* profit from their superior information without necessarily imparting all of their valuable information into the new marginal price. Anecdotal evidence certainly seems to support this in the case of Enron, given how heavily the firm focused on less liquid and less transparent markets.

Why Not Speculate Outright?

Trading to exploit disequilibrium, market imperfections, or asymmetric information is hardly riskless. On the contrary, it can be *very* risky. This helps explain why many firms engaged in such trading do so with *relative* or *spread* positions in third markets rather than taking outright positions in one of the two explicit markets. Suppose, for example, that a firm perceives the "true" net cost of storage of gas to be b^* (which is equal to the firm's own net cost-of-carry) but that the current net cost-of-carry reflected in listed gas futures prices is $b' > b^*$. It is a good bet that b' will fall toward b^*. As such, an outright short position in forward contracts would make sense. But this is *extremely risky*.

A position that exploits the same information asymmetry *without* the high degree of risk is to go short futures *and simultaneously* buy and hold gas. In this manner, the firm is protected from wild short-term price swings and, instead, is expressing a view solely on the *relative* prices of storage as reflected in the futures market and storage by the firm itself.

In essence, asset lite is a basis trading or third-market trading strategy in which physical assets are traded vis-à-vis derivatives positions. A physical market combined with the *residual risk* of a market-making function is essentially one big spread trade.

Putting Enron in Context

Reading the marketing and business materials of Enron's energy business lines is eerily similar to reading an example of a firm putting all the theories of basis trading just discussed into practice. And, in this sense, Enron was hardly the first firm to leverage its physical market presence into financial and basis trading opportunities. Perhaps the best-known example of a firm engaged in the same practice is Cargill (see, e.g., Broehs, 1992). Cargill is the largest private company in the world, with $50 billion in annual sales and 97,000 employees deployed in 59 countries. For 137 years, Cargill has employed an asset lite strategy that has allowed it to basis trade and manage risks for a wide variety of agricultural commodities, among other things. For the commodities it deals in, Cargill is involved in every link of the supply chains. As a result of its commodity trading, processing, freight shipping, and futures businesses, Cargill has been able to develop an effective intelligence network that generates valuable information. Indeed, via its people on the ground, Cargill knows where every ship and rail car hauling commodities are in real time and what that implies about prospective prices over time and space. By being able to ferret out valuable local information, Cargill has been able to obtain an edge, one that accounts for much of its success. (See, e.g., Weinberg and Capple, 2002.)

Basis trading can make economic sense to a firm *ex ante* without making profits *ex post*. The key driver underlying most basis traders' behavior is the *perception* that they have some comparative informational advantage about some basis relation. But perception need not be reality. Markets are, after all, relatively efficient. Indeed, most of the inefficiencies that give rise to profitable trading opportunities can be linked to taxes, regulations, and other institutional frictions that essentially prevent markets from reflecting all available information of all traders at all times.

Enron did indeed attempt to focus its efforts on markets riddled with inefficiencies, often created by overregulation, ill-specified property rights, or a slow deregulation process. But this did not mean Enron had a comparative informational advantage in all of those markets.

Structural inefficiencies that prevent prices from fully reflecting all available information is only *part* of what it takes to run a successful basis trading operation. The other requisite component is for a firm to perceive itself as (and, hopefully, actually to be) *better informed.* In oil and power, Enron achieved this informational superiority like many other firms do in their own industries—by dominating the financial market. This allowed Enron to develop informationally rich customer relationships that, in turn, could be extrapolated into superior knowledge of firm-specific supply and demand considerations, congestion points along the supply chain, and the like.

Now consider, by contrast, a market such as broadband in which Enron was *not* the primary inventor of the technology, not the primary buyer or seller of the supply chain infrastructure, and not a regular player in the consumer telecommunications arena. The mere existence of market frictions in broadband attracted Enron, but without the requisite information, Enron could not achieve the market dominance required to make asset lite profitable.

BUYING TIME AND THE END OF ENRON

As Culp and Miller (1995a, 1995b, 1999) explain, firms best suited to the asset lite kind of strategy that Enron pursued typically require fairly significant amounts of capital—not invested capital assets necessarily, but rather *equity capital* in a financial market sense. Equity capital is a necessary component to successful basis trading and the asset lite strategy for several reasons. First, equity is required to absorb the occasional loss inevitably arising from the volatility that basis trading can bring to cash flows. Second, maintaining a strong market making and financial market presence requires at least the perception by other participants of financial integrity and creditworthiness. Especially in long-dated, credit-sensitive OTC derivatives, financial capital is essential to support the credit requirements that other OTC derivatives users and dealers demand (see Chapters 7 and 11).

Unfortunately, Enron's cash management skills were no match for its apparent trading savvy. Despite being asset lite, Enron's expenditures on intermediate supply chain assets were still not cheap. Add to this EI's asset-heavy investment programs *and* a corporate culture under Skilling and Lay that emphasized high and stable *earnings,* often at the expense of high and stable *cash flows* (Bassett and Storrie issue warnings about this in Chapter 2), and the net result was financial trouble for the firm.[16]

Enron's Deceptions

Much of the public controversy about Enron—and much of the remainder of this book—focuses on how Enron abused accounting and disclosure policies. In short, Enron's abuses in these areas included the following:

- Using inappropriate or aggressive accounting and disclosure policies to conceal assets owned and debt incurred by Enron through special purpose entities (SPEs)—see Chapters 2, 8, and 10.
- Using inadequately capitalized subsidiaries and SPEs for "hedges" that reduced Enron's earnings volatility on paper, despite, in many cases, being dysfunctional or nonperforming in practice—see Chapters 2 and 8.
- Allegedly engaging in wash trades with undisclosed subsidiaries designed to increase trading revenues or mark-to-market valuations artificially—see Chapters 2, 4, 5, 6, 8, and 10.

At first, Enron's abuses of these structures seem to have been driven more by a desire to manage earnings than anything else. But as time evolved, Enron used aggressive accounting and disclosure policies to buy time for itself. Especially as Enron moved into new markets in which its comparative advantage was more questionable (e.g., broadband) or in which Enron's success depended strongly on the rate of government deregulation (e.g., water), Enron's financial shenanigans amounted to robbing Peter to pay Paul. In other words, as Enron's cash balances got lower and lower, concealing its true financial condition was the only way that Enron could sustain itself long enough to hope that its next big investment program paid off. That might have worked had Enron stuck to markets in which its success with asset lite had been more assured. Unfortunately, as we have argued, the firm's end became inevitable once it decided to start moving into areas that deviated from its core business strategy.

There is also the question of whom Enron was actually deceiving with its accounting and disclosure policies. Over the course of many years, you could argue that Enron seduced investors, monitors (e.g., rating agencies and accounting firms), creditors, and even its own employees into believing that the firm was stronger financially than it actually was through a mixture of aggressive marketing, cultural arrogance, and, in some cases, outright deception. But especially as the end of Enron neared, many institutions had begun to view the company with deepening suspicion (see Chapter 2). By the time Enron failed, a surprisingly large number of firms dealing with Enron commercially had come to fear that the worst for Enron might lie ahead (see Chapter 11). In the end, those who seem to have been the most deceived—and for the longest time—were perhaps Enron's own employees, who, unlike other firms dealing with Enron, had more cause to be inherently optimistic and were doubtless taken almost completely off guard.

CONCLUSION

Enron's main business was asset lite—exploiting the synergies between a small physical market presence, a market-making function on derivatives, and a basis trading operation to "arbitrage" the foregoing. Many have questioned the wisdom of Enron's asset lite strategy. Most of these criticisms are hard to address without getting into the details of Enron's financial situation. In short, people argue that although asset lite did not require much capital expenditure and investment in fixed capital, the strategy *did* require Enron to have a fairly large chunk of equity capital—enough to convince its numerous financial counter parties that it was creditworthy. If indeed Enron was camouflaging its capital structure to hide a massive amount of debt, Enron probably *was* undercapitalized to exploit asset lite effectively. But this is not a criticism of asset lite—it is a criticism *of Enron.*

Asset lite has become a very common practice for many firms engaged in energy market activities, especially at intermediate points along the various physical supply chains—transmission and distribution in power, midstream transportation and distribution in oil and gas, and the like. One firm that has been consistently successful at playing the asset lite game, for example, is Kinder Morgan, founded by Enron's former president, Richard Kinder, when he left Enron in 1996. Kinder Morgan was started in part by Kinder's successful acquisition from Enron of Enron Gas Liquids, for which he outbid six other firms, including Mobil Oil (Fusaro and Miller, 2002).

In nonenergy markets, firms such as Cargill and André have also long practiced their version of asset lite, often going the way of Enron in electricity and becoming asset heavy over time. The key common denominators are twofold: the use of a physical market presence to acquire specific

EMPIRE OF THE SUN 25

information about the underlying market and the use of a financial trading operation to make markets and engage in basis trading to leverage off that underlying asset infrastructure.

Unfortunately, there is no exact answer to the question of when asset lite and basis trading might work for a firm versus when it might fail dismally. The comparative informational advantage that allows some firms to earn positive economic profits is exceedingly hard to analyze or identify except through trial and error. This process of trial and error is what Schumpeter meant by the "creative destruction" of capitalism, and great economists such as Knight and Keynes went on to emphasize further that the success or failure of a given firm cannot ever really be predicted. "Animal spirits," as Keynes put it, ultimately dictate the success or failure of a business as much as any other variable.

Economists are uneasy with this notion. As noted earlier, the neoclassical model postulates that markets tend to *be* in equilibrium, whereas the neo-Austrian perspective merely argues that markets lean in that direction. To be in equilibrium implies some steady state of profits resting on an identifiable cost advantage or structural informational asymmetry. But concepts such as *information asymmetry* are completely nontestable. This makes theoretical economists nervous because it means that the success or failure of a firm cannot be related to a defined set of assumptions and parameters *ex ante*. And empirical economists get even more disgruntled because the success or failure of a firm cannot be explained *ex post*.

Nevertheless, this is the state of affairs. Economic theory says merely that firms strive to exploit perceived comparative informational advantages in disequilibrium situations where prices do not reflect every market participant's information equally. Theory says nothing about firms' being correct in their perceived advantages, nor does theory help us pinpoint precisely what those advantages are. These things are what the market is for.

Can Enron be generalized to suggest a "failure" of the theory underlying basis trading? In fact, Enron cannot be generalized *at all*. Looking purely at the firm's *legitimate* business activities, Enron perceived a comparative informational advantage, pursued it, and was wrong. This makes neither the underlying economic model nor even Enron's managers and shareholders wrong. If we could generalize the economic factors that explain why one firm succeeds and another fails, competition in the open market would serve no purpose. Instead, competition and the market are both judge and jury to a company's perceived informational advantage. Unless a firm takes the risk of failure, it will never earn the premium of success (Knight, 1921).

There can be little doubt that Enron did many things wrong. Indeed, where it deviated from its asset lite strategy, Enron tended to engage in businesses that were unprofitable. In addition, many of the firm's senior managers were basically unethical. But amidst all these legitimate criticisms of Enron, we must be careful not to indict *everything* the firm did. In some instances, Enron got it right. And, at a minimum, the firm entrepreneurially moved into new areas and put itself to the ultimate test of the market. Finally, Enron failed that test, but we must at least tip our hats to the part of Enron that was at least willing to try. (See Chapter 14.) Without that spirit of innovation, the process of capitalism would grind to a screeching halt.

NOTES

1. The Austrian school of economics was developed in the nineteenth and twentieth centuries by a group of principally Austrian economists in response to several noted shortcomings in the neoclassical theory of the price system. The approach we adopt here, however, is more properly called *neo*-Austrian. Following Sir John Hicks' (1973) use of the term, a neo-Austrian approach recognizes some of the deficiencies of the neoclassical school and seeks to address those problems with a more Austrian perspective. We do not consider, as some do, the pure Austrian school to be a viable stand-alone theory of the price system. Rather than forcing a choice of theories in either/or fashion, the neo-Austrian approach recognizes instead that a little bit of Austrian insight can go a long way toward salvaging the neoclassical paradigm. See Hicks (1973) for another example of this theoretical approach.
2. For a full elaboration of these concepts, see Lachmann (1978).
3. Perhaps we should have all taken it as a bad omen that in its core one-sentence description of itself, Enron used a split infinitive.
4. A typical use of junk bonds during this period was providing funds to companies with otherwise questionable access to capital given their credit risk. Highly leveraged transactions such as leveraged buy-outs were thus a natural candidate for junk-bond financing.
5. EOG continued for two decades to spearhead all of Enron Corportion's exploration and production activities in oil and gas. In 1999, EOG exchanged the shares in EOG held by Enron for its operations in India and China. In so doing, EOG became independent of Enron Corportion and, changed its name the same year to EOG Resources, Inc. This firm still exists today.
6. In the huge interest rate swap market, dealers did essentially the same thing as the Enron GasBank—they used other swaps and futures contracts to manage the *residual* risks of running a dealing portfolio, called a *swap warehouse*.
7. This can be accomplished in various ways—see Chapters 5 and 13 for examples.
8. Early discussions of the economic rationale for basis or spread trading can be found in Johnson (1960) and Working (1948, 1949, 1962).

9. Alternative versions of this rely on different types of discounting and compounding assumptions, as well as allowing certain variables in the equation to be stochastic. But the spirit of all versions of the model is well captured by the representation here. See Culp (2003) for more detail.

10. Cost-of-carry pricing for forwards on financial assets, by contrast, is enforced by direct cash-and-carry arbitrage because financial assets pay *observable* and *explicit* dividends that are the same regardless of who holds the asset. See Culp (2003).

11. Commodity lending *does* occur, so this example is not unrealistic. See Williams (1986).

12. The classical U-shape is consistent with a production technology that demonstrates increasing returns to scale up to b^* and diminishing returns thereafter.

13. For a more general discussion, see Cochrane and Culp (2003a).

14. This is pseudo-arbitrage because it has the flavor of an arbitrage transaction but is far from riskless.

15. This seems heretical in the neoclassical microeconomic paradigm but is typical of the notion of *equilibrium* developed by economists in the Austrian and neo-Austrian tradition, such as Menger (1871), Hayek (1937, 1945, 1949, 1978a), Hicks (1973), and Lachmann (1978).

16. Cash flow mismanagement was not always the norm at Enron. Jeffrey Skilling's predecessor, Richard Kinder, was actually known for being a cash flow tightwad and kept the firm's financial health relatively strong during his tenure at the operational helm of Enron.

2

CORPORATE ACCOUNTING AFTER ENRON

Is the Cure Worse Than the Disease?

RICHARD BASSETT AND MARK STORRIE

T he collapse of Enron in December 2001 amid a flurry of accusations of misleading accounting, unreliable financial disclosure,
and probable criminal behavior has rocked the wholesale energy
markets and contributed to a downturn in worldwide equity markets.
Were these global market reactions predicated on the notion that Enron
was just the tip of the iceberg? Are Enron, WorldCom, Adelphia, Global
Crossing, and a few others just the first of many to be caught "cooking
the books," with many more to follow? If so, falling equity prices may be
a reflection more of the expectation by investors of a correction in en-
demically misleading U.S. corporate accounting and disclosure policies.
Alternatively, if the problem is *not* one of systemic corporate corruption
and the vast majority of business people and corporations are honest and
responsible, the systemic fault crushing American equity markets is actually the fear of too many government interventions in a market already
working diligently to right itself.

In this chapter, we focus on the accounting and disclosure issues that
Enron has created with the ultimate goal of attempting to answer the previous question: Are current equity market woes driven by a fear of "more
Enrons" and "too little post-Enron action," or rather by the fear of too
much Enron *over* reaction? To answer that question, we begin by examining what Enron itself allegedly did wrong—what, exactly, were Enron's
accounting and disclosure sins believed to be lurking out there at so many
other companies?

28

After summarizing what went wrong *at* Enron, we then turn to the bigger issue of what is wrong *with mandated accounting rules* themselves. We argue that *earnings* can never be more than opinion, whereas *cash flows* are the real basis for corporate valuations. We examine some commonly misleading accounting aggregates and explore the central role played by cash flows in modern corporate finance. We then examine what a cash flow analysis of Enron would have shown in 2001, as compared to the firm's stated and misleading earnings releases.

Next, we turn to the issue of how estimates of future cash flows are reflected in equity prices. Specifically, we consider how Enron's stock price processed information in a manner very different from Wall Street analysts, rating agencies, regulators, and other spectators of Enron. The Political Reaction and Corporate Reform section then analyzes the political response to Enron. We first evaluate whether the accounting and disclosure problems that beset Enron appear to be systemic in the United States, and after concluding the problem is *not* a systemic one, we turn to consider some of the problems and risks of political overreaction to Enron before making our final conclusions.

ACCOUNTING AND DISCLOSURE AT ENRON

The current debate over the adequacy of accounting and disclosure in the United States crosses both industry lines and company types and traces not just to Enron, but to WorldCom, Global Crossing, Tyco, and several other corporate disasters. But Enron was the first and, arguably, by far the most important and complex.

The black cloud Enron has created now hangs over all U.S. corporations, but there is little doubt that energy companies have borne the greatest impact on their equity value, debt ratings, costs of funding, and liquidity issues. Accordingly, we begin this chapter by analyzing Enron's sins.

In brief, Enron's senior management and others engaged in a systematic attempt to use various accounting and reporting techniques to mislead investors. The primary areas of abuse in which Enron misled investors can be separated into four categories, most of which pertain to the company's energy market activities. We merely state these problems here, offering a more detailed explanation later:

- *Wash and round-trip trades:* In these transactions, there is no real counter party. Mainly in electricity markets, Enron appears to have essentially been "trading with itself" in a number of cases, seemingly to inflate its revenues and possibly its asset values without generating any tangible economic benefits.

- *Mark-to-market accounting:* At least in some cases, Enron improperly applied the useful and well-accepted principle of marking certain open energy transactions to their current market values to create false accounting results.
- *Revenue recognition:* Enron apparently booked trading revenues on many energy transactions when the deals were first consummated, rather than waiting for the actual economic profits to be earned as the life of the transaction evolved.
- *Special purpose entities:* Enron used certain special purpose entities (SPEs) inappropriately to facilitate improper wash trades and mark-to-market accounting. In addition, Enron appears to have used these types of structures outside its energy activities to hide its total indebtedness and to inflate certain asset values.

To illustrate how Enron could have used these techniques to enhance earnings and inflate its balance sheet, we have constructed a simple example. Suppose Enron entered into a seven-year weather derivatives transaction with a firm at an agreed price of $120 million when the true value of the same transaction is $100 million.[1] Suppose the counter party firm is an SPE owned by Enron and established solely for the purpose of conducting transactions *with Enron.* Then, the transaction is a wash trade—the total cash flows and risks to Enron when considered across the company *and* the SPE are unaffected by the transaction. The SPE thus does not care whether the $120 million price is correct—it is taking no risk. Enron, however, could book a profit of $20 million to reflect the immediate realization of the increase in the contract's value above its fair value. Note that because this $120 million is an actual transaction price, this profit would be based on the market value of the transaction and not just on its mark-to-market revaluation.

This transaction only makes sense in several circumstances. First, the SPE must be essentially a part of Enron. Otherwise, the shareholders of the SPE will never agree to the terms of the initial transaction. Because derivatives transactions are a zero sum game, an immediate gain of $20 million for Enron implies an immediate loss for the SPE. Second, Enron must not be consolidating the financial statements of the SPE up onto its own balance sheet, else the $20 million gain for Enron would just wash with the $20 million loss the SPE takes. Finally, this transaction makes sense only for highly illiquid and customized transactions in which the "true" value of the deal is not easily observable. If no one else was actively trading seven-year weather derivatives, Enron's internal or external auditor or internal risk managers might well have accepted that this was a reasonable market price. But if a liquid market quote revealed the true value of an otherwise identical trade to be $100 million, the $120 million valuation likely would have been questioned.

The next step would be for Enron to extrapolate from this single trade to revalue its *whole book* of seven-year weather derivatives. If this book or portfolio had a prior value of $1 billion, the whole book could now be marked-to-market at $1.2 billion based on the transaction price of $120 million observed between Enron and the SPE. This would create a *notional* profit of $200 million for Enron.

This illustrative transaction would create an accounting profit of $200 million for Enron, but it would actually be cash negative. Enron or others would normally have a minimum of two cash costs to achieve this notional profit—a bonus to the people involved in creating the notional profit and the transaction costs of the deal itself. In an accounting framework, this could be depicted as a success at a certain point in time, usually at the end of an accounting period. However, in an economic/cash flow framework, this would be value destroying. Although the only people harmed by this fiction are the Enron shareholders and not the overall market, this type of behavior that rewards people for accounting fiction instead of economic value creation would send a signal to others at Enron to create further transactions with similar value-destroying characteristics.

Powers et al. (2002) describes the accounting-driven behavior at Enron as follows:

> Many of the most significant transactions apparently were designed to accomplish favourable financial statement results, not to achieve bona fide economic objectives or to transfer risk. Some transactions were designed so that, had they followed applicable accounting rules, Enron could have kept assets and liabilities (especially debt) off its balance sheet; but the transactions did not follow those rules.
>
> Other transactions were implemented—improperly, we are told by our accounting advisors—to offset losses. They allowed Enron to conceal from the market very large losses resulting from Enron's merchant investments by creating an appearance that those investments were hedged, that is, that a third party was obliged to pay Enron the amount of the losses—when in fact, that third party was simply an entity in which only Enron had a substantial economic stake. We believe these transactions lead to Enron reporting earnings that were almost $1 billion higher than should have been reported.
>
> Asset Sales—Enron sold assets to [an SPE called LJM][2] that it wanted to remove from its books. The sales were often close to the end of the reporting period and 5 of 7 were repurchased at a profit to LJM by Enron within months of the original transaction even when the value of the asset appeared to have declined. (p. 4)

This quote reveals the accounting mind-set that continues to dominate discussions about Enron. Notably, "Some transactions were designed so that, had they followed applicable accounting rules, Enron could have kept the assets and liabilities (especially debt) off its balance sheet, but the transactions did not follow those rules" (p. 4). In other words, all of this deception could have worked if Enron had followed the accounting rules. However, by following the rules, Enron would still not have achieved a bona fide economic result. The company would have still achieved only an *accounting* result.

This is indicative of how the rules-based system that guides U.S. generally accepted accounting principles (GAAP) has conditioned people not to look at whether information presented to the market is a "true and fair" characterization of the condition of the company, but whether it was compliant with the rules. By contrast, if the overriding guidance was "principles-based"—as in some other countries such as England—it is more likely that managers and professionals would simply have seen Enron's behavior for what it was: a deceptive and fraudulent practice. More importantly, if the measure of success is not adherence to accounting rules and government regulation but rather adherence to investor concerns, we would measure success in terms of delivering the highest sustainable risk-adjusted returns, not on merely a pure compliance standard.

ACCOUNTING VERSUS CASH FLOWS

Accounting is not an exact science. Current accounting standards are a combination of rules and guidelines that run to many thousands of dense pages. A great deal of the complexity inherent in current accounting practice is the result of legislation at the state, federal, and international levels concerning taxes, capital markets regulation, corporate governance, social programs, health and safety, environmental and pension issues, among many others. For accounting standards to incorporate all of the variables inherent in this constantly changing landscape while still providing a framework that can fulfill its original role of reporting historic information to investors is not a simple task.

Inherently Subjective Art, Not Science

Different companies have different needs, and, as a result, all accounting rules cannot be universally applied in lock-step to all firms—that is why the rules in the United States are referred to as *generally accepted* accounting principles (GAAPs). For example, a rule that all fixed capital assets must be depreciated over 10 years would not suit a steel mill where 20 years may be more appropriate, and depreciating laptop computers over 10 years would be equally unrealistic. From an economic (i.e., cash flow) viewpoint, depreciation is a noncash charge and does not affect the cash flow, unlike an accounting viewpoint where depreciation choices can make a significant difference to the accounting bottom line.

Depreciation schedules are one simple example where companies and accounting practitioners are left to make some reasonable judgments. Managers and auditors know that in making most of these judgments, they alter the earnings result, and many alter the balance sheet, as well. However, most of these do not alter the cash flow of a business; hence, the increasingly well-known phrase, first recorded in the 1890s: *Earnings are an opinion; cash flow is a fact.*

A sample list of standard accounting issues, with a description of how these issues affect earnings and cash flows, is shown in Table 2.1.[3] Most of these issues require managers and auditors to make judgments, and some of these judgments are based on assumptions about the future—for example, outcomes from litigation matters, health and pension liabilities, foreign asset values, environmental costs, and many others. These assumptions are virtually always detailed in the notes to the annual report and in various regulatory filings and have been for decades. The difficulty arises in that as the complexity of legislation and regulation has increased, this analysis has become more difficult and time-consuming. The unfortunate consequence is the continuing use and growth of certain types of investor shorthand, of which the most prominent are price-to-earnings (P/E) multiples, earnings per share (EPS) numbers, and earnings before interest, taxes, depreciation, and amortization (EBITDA).

The shortcomings of P/E and EPS as true measures of value have been well documented over the past 40 years (see, especially, Rappaport, 1998). EBITDA warrants more up-to-date attention because of the prevalence it played in recent years in promoting the telecoms, media, and technology sectors and the false assertion that it is a cash flow equivalent measure. The reliability of EBITDA as a measure was recently summed up by Warren Buffett: "Among those who talk about EBITDA . . . and those who don't, there are more frauds among those who do. Either they're trying to con you, or they're conning themselves" (Buffett, 2002).

Buffett, like many other investors, recognizes that the variability of earnings makes EBITDA an unreliable measure. Using Enron's figures as an example, Table 2.2 contrasts EBITDA with free cash flow. The wide disparity in these results just serves to remind us that accounting is the starting point of an investment analysis and not the end point.

Table 2.1 Impact of Accounting Variables on Earnings and Cash Flows

Issue	Change in Earnings	Change in Cash Flow
1 Depreciation: at least three choices and variations within these	Yes	No
2 Revenue recognition: on long-term contracts, prepayments, advances, and so on	Yes	No
3 Mark-to-market: in liquid markets straightforward, but in illiquid markets requires application of formulas and a range of assumptions	Yes	No
4 Affiliated transactions: transfer pricing and royalties, implications for tax and international issues	Yes	Possibly because of tax issues
5 Pensions: the asset and liability sides of this can both be overstated/understated, requires a judgment on future returns of the fund and future liabilities of the fund	Yes	No
6 Valuation of foreign assets: considerations of useful life, exchange rates, and taxation issues	Yes	No
7 Securitization of receivables or other items: revenue, risk, horizon, and liability issues	Yes	Yes
8 Foreign exchange: beginning-, mid-, and end-periods are all usually different and the managerial decisions about how and when to recognize gains and losses are often material	Eventually, but the changes in the balance sheet may be more significant	Yes, in terms of repatriation of cash but not necessarily in terms of local currency
9 Treatment of stock options: expensing, valuing, recording	Yes	No
10 Goodwill: the accounting rationale for the difference between the book and the economic value	Yes	No
11 Amortization of goodwill	Yes	No
12 Income taxes: deferred, in dispute, tax credits	Yes	Yes

Table 2.1   Continued

Issue	Change in Earnings	Change in Cash Flow
13 Litigation: estimates and provisions of liability/outcomes	Yes	Not until realized
14 Customer returns/product defects	Yes	Not until realized
15 Leases: capitalized versus operating	Yes	No
16 Allowance for bad debts: customers	Yes	No
17 Provisions and write-downs: in banks for loan losses	Yes	No, the money is already gone
18 Reserves: in insurance companies	Yes	Possibly
19 Product liability and other contingent liabilities	Yes	No
20 Impairment of long-lived assets (i.e., you paid too much and now you need to write it down)	Yes	No, you already paid the money; this is just the accounting reconciliation of failure

Modern Corporate Finance and Discounted Cash Flow Analysis

Academics and market practitioners have dramatically advanced our understanding of how markets work and investors behave, which makes it dismaying that the contributions of financial economists have played little or no role in the current public debate. Contributions by Nobel Prize-winning economists such as Harry Markowitz (diversification theory),

Table 2.2   Enron's EBITDA versus Free Cash Flows (in Millions)

	1997	1998	1999	2000
EBITDA	615	2,205	1,672	2,808
Free cash flow	(5,717)	1,986	(1,108)	(5,256)

William Sharpe and John Lintner (the Capital Asset Pricing Model), and Merton Miller and Franco Modigliani (the relation between the value of the firm and its capital structure) have been largely ignored in the public post-Enron debate. Yet, as we discuss later, the markets performed much as financial economists would have expected by consistently reducing the value of Enron, WorldCom, and others to reflect their worsening future prospects, deteriorating cash generation, and increasing risks.

Financial economists observe and measure market behavior over long periods and have developed and tested a range of tools to analyze investments with explicit measures of risk and return. The financial economics definition of the value of a business or an investment is *the present value of a stream of expected future cash flows discounted at an appropriate rate.* This is not the same as a stream of earnings, a multiple of the balance sheet, or a multiple of past results. Valuation is future-oriented and based on expected results—keep in mind that investors cannot earn last year's dividends or cash flows, only future years'.

This is not just an academic measure but also a description of how "the market" actually values investments. For example, Warren Buffett, when asked how to value a company at the April 2002 Berkshire Hathaway annual meeting, gave the same answer he has been giving for decades: "You just want to estimate a company's cash flows over time, discount them back, and buy for less than that" (Buffett, 2002).

Every mainstream corporate finance textbook chooses discounted cash flow (DCF) analysis as its preferred measure of valuation or investment analysis. However, there is no alchemy in this formulation that implies an equivalence between applying this framework and being stock market geniuses—forecasts always require judgments and some people are better at forecasting than others. However, DCF does provide us with a valid economic framework to consider our forecasts of an investment or company's expected future returns so that we can price the opportunity.

A DCF analysis has two requirements: establishing a financial framework for the analysis and generating the inputs to populate the framework. Setting the framework requires a reasonable understanding of finance and includes the following:

- Creating a free cash flow format (the first step is normally translating income statement and balance sheet information into free cash flow).
- Estimating an appropriate discount rate (the minimum expected risk-adjusted return).
- Selecting a forecast horizon (the length of the forecast reflects the company's competitive advantage and the forecast horizon affects the value).

- Selecting a residual value method (the most conservative—normally a perpetuity—is usually the most appropriate given the total percentage of the value that this calculation represents).
- Choosing a capital structure (ideally by iterating to an "optimal" capital structure) and reflecting this target capital structure in the discount rate estimate.

The art of the analysis involves making the forecast of sales, costs, fixed and working capital investments, and taxes.

In the past 20 years, the growth of computer models makes the first part of this effort comparatively easy.[4] The second stage of the analysis, however, involves the quantification of strategic assumptions. A standard strategic analysis can often be gleaned from an analyst report or a five-year forecast can simply be taken from a "Value Line" tear sheet and used for a quick and dirty valuation.

Do investors use these approaches? We think that WorldCom provides a clear example of the difference between, on the one hand, investor expectations and the cash flow-driven analysis that drives equity markets, and, on the other hand, the accounting reports that drive regulators and ratings agencies. For example, in January 1999, WorldCom stock was worth $75 per share. On the day *before* the firm announced a $3.9 billion restatement of revenues, the shares were worth $0.83.

While the announced earnings restatement dramatically altered WorldCom's reported earnings and EBITDA, the accounting restatement did not change its cash flows by a single dollar. Similarly, the incremental announcements of more wrongdoing at WorldCom look suspiciously like efforts by the insolvency practitioners to overstate the difficulties of the firm because virtually none of these make a material difference to the cash balances or cash generation of the remainder of WorldCom. The market reality is that investors had been anticipating and reacting to the value destruction in WorldCom's operating strategy for years before the accounting restatement or the arrival of the insolvency "experts."

Cash Flows at Enron

Table 2.3 was constructed from Enron's public cash flow statements in its 2000 annual report (Enron Corporation, 2001) and from several of the firm's 2000 filings with the U.S. Securities and Exchange Commission (SEC). From a reading of the notes in the annual report, we made judgments based on the information provided about cash and noncash revenues and transactions. The impact of *noncash revenues* recorded and accepted by Arthur Andersen, Enron's external auditor, are shown in Table 2.3.

Table 2.3   Enron's Cash Flow Analysis (in Millions)

	1998	1999	2000
Revenues			
Natural gas and other products	13,276	19,536	50,500
Electricity	13,939	15,238	33,823
Metals	—	—	9,234
Other	4,045	5,338	7,232
Total revenues	31,260	40,112	100,789
Less: noncash revenues (see footnotes)	(1,984)	(2,533)	(4,794)
Cash revenues	29,276	37,579	95,995
Cash cost of sales	26,381	34,761	94,517
Cash gross margin (deficit)	2,895	2,818	**1,478**
Operating expenses	2,473	3,045	3,184
Cash operating income (loss)	422	(227)	**(1,706)**

Source: Prepared from information provided in the Enron 2000 *Annual Report,* selected filings by Enron with the Securities and Exchange Commission, and with the assistance of Charles Conner, formerly an executive at Enron. The data was synthesized by Charles Conner, Mark Storrie, and Richard Bassett.

Further, for the years ended December 31, 1998, 1999, and 2000, Enron disclosed pretax gains from sales of merchant assets and investments totaling $628 million, $756 million, and $104 million, respectively, all of which are included in "Other Revenues" (Enron Corporation, 2001, Note 4). Proceeds from those sales were $1,838 million, $2,217 million, and $1,434 million, respectively. In each year, these gains on sales from merchant assets and investments *exceeded the whole of Enron's annualized earnings figures.* The combination of the notes and the reported statements led us to the results in Table 2.4.

The steady growth in the net income year-on-year may look good to accountants, but investors follow cash flow. The more erratic and deteriorating cash position at Enron gave a truer picture of the firm's performance.

Table 2.4   Enron's Net Income and Cash Flows (in Millions)

	1998	1999	2000
Net income	703	893	979
Enron cash flows	(205)	(815)	(2,306)

Investors could also have read the following in note 1 from Enron's year 2000 annual report:

Accounting for Price Risk Management. Enron engages in price risk management activities for both trading and nontrading purposes. Instruments utilized in connection with trading activities are accounted for using the mark-to-market method. Under the mark-to-market method of accounting, forwards, swaps, options, energy transportation contracts utilized for trading activities and other instruments with third parties are reflected at fair value and are shown as "Assets and Liabilities from Price Risk Management Activities" in the Consolidated Balance Sheet. These activities also include the commodity risk management component embedded in energy outsourcing contracts. Unrealized gains and losses from newly originated contracts, contract restructurings and the impact of price movements are recognized as "Other Revenues." Changes in the assets and liabilities from price risk management activities result primarily from changes in the valuation of the portfolio of contracts, newly originated transactions and the timing of settlement relative to the receipt of cash for certain contracts. The market prices used to value these transactions reflect management's best estimate considering various factors including closing exchange and over-the-counter quotations, time value and volatility factors underlying the commitments. (Enron Corporation, 2001, p. 36)

This note attracted the attention of some analysts in 2000 and 2001 who recognized that there was a risk that the values of some of Enron's positions could have been overstated. As noted previously, one reason was the lack of any real market for some of the financial instruments in which Enron traded. Enron's own assumptions, estimates, calculations, and questionable wash trades thus allowed Enron to manufacture valuations.

In addition, as the note suggests, unrealized gains or losses on newly recognized transactions were booked by Enron into Other Revenue. Even for a *fairly* priced derivatives transaction, such upfront "gains" would actually represent a risk premium paid to Enron for bearing the risk that the transaction could move substantially against them. Nevertheless, Enron still treated these risk premiums as gains when transactions were first initiated.

Stress Testing the Balance Sheet

If analysts become uncomfortable with discrepancies between reported accounting profits and the risk that there is no underlying operating cash generation in some of these transactions, they would normally turn to the balance sheet to "stress test" the result. Stress testing the balance sheet—particularly one composed largely of financial assets—is done from a cash liquidation viewpoint. Adopting this stance, together with more principles-based accounting philosophy as opposed to a pure compliance philosophy, should have led to a different interpretation of Enron's numbers.

First, of the $9 billion in current assets listed as "assets from price risk management activities," note 1 implies the risk that these assets may have been overstated by as much as 25 percent ($2 billion).

Second, of the $7.1 billion of long-term investments in the form of advances to unconsolidated affiliates, it would have been reasonable to assume that in a position of financial distress, these assets—probably largely illiquid—would become unrecoverable. Accordingly, the cash value could have been marked down by as much as 50 percent from book value ($3.5 billion). Indeed, early in 2001 analysts were questioning Enron on the value of these assets because they suspected that a significant portion of these assets were in failed dot-coms, fiber optic capacity, or other technology-related investments where 90 percent drops in value during 2000 were not uncommon. Enron remained true to its accounting view of the world, however, and resisted market suggestions to write these positions down. But the market, in turn, remained true to its economic view of risk and return and wrote down the value of Enron's stock to reflect the deterioration in these and other assets.

Third, $9.7 billion in long-term investments were "assets from price risk management activities." Those were the assets most likely to have been overstated because of false marks-to-market or wash trades. These assets also were presumably less liquid than other assets and probably represented the highest proportion of assets in which no other firm was making a market. In the extreme case of a short-term asset liquidation, the cash realized could have been as little as 50 percent less than the amount stated on the balance sheet ($4.5 billion). As a rule of thumb, assuming a 50 percent discount for the liquidation value of contracts in which the firm is essentially the sole market maker seems reasonable.

Fourth, Enron booked $3.5 billion of goodwill. Goodwill is largely a meaningless number to anyone other than an accountant because it represents cash that has gone out the door to purchase a company for more than its net asset value. As virtually no company has a value that is equal to or less than net asset value, merger and acquisition (M&A) transactions almost always create goodwill. As studies by McKinsey, BCG, KPMG, and Deloitte have shown, more than 65 percent of M&A transactions fail to deliver value to the buyer (Sirower, 1997) Given this backdrop of probable economic failure, listing goodwill as an asset, particularly in a distress situation, produces highly suspect figures for goodwill, which is in itself a somewhat spurious concept.

Notwithstanding the evidence, in the United States, the buyer in a corporate transaction can list goodwill on its balance sheet as an asset. Managers at Enron, WorldCom, and Global Crossing clearly thought this important because it inflated their balance sheets. However, while accountants, regulators, and ratings agencies get worked up about this, markets do not pay as much attention to these figures as do accountants. Table 2.5 shows the scores of billions of dollars written off the asset values of JDS Uniphase, AOL, Nortel, WorldCom, Lucent, and many others in recent years. In each of these cases and others, the fall in the equity value reflecting the loss of goodwill always occurred far in advance of the actual accounting write-down.

JDS Uniphase provides the strongest indication that the market recognizes value destruction faster than accountants, ratings agencies, or investment bankers. At the time of the firm's $50 billion write-down, its market capitalization was only $12 billion, less than one-sixth the book value of the equity; the change in value at the announcement of the $50 billion write-down was less than $1 billion.

Enron, with its accounting-oriented mind-set, strongly resisted making these write-downs, but the market did it for Enron anyway by reducing the firm's share value. In our view, goodwill should have a zero cash value in a distress situation. So, when looking at the $3.5 billion in goodwill on Enron's balance sheet, we would reduce this to zero.

Finally, the cash value of the $5.6 billion of "Other" could have been overstated by as much as 25 percent, depending on the assumptions used ($1.4 billion) to value "Other." In the period 1997 to 2000, it appears that less than 25 percent of the "Other" actually had a cash value. A reduction of only $1.4 billion thus may be too generous.

The previous five points certainly do not constitute an exhaustive balance sheet stress test, notably because we have not considered the liabilities

Table 2.5   Goodwill Write-Offs and Changes in Market Caps

Company	Market Capitalization (in Billions)	Goodwill Write-Off (in Billions)	Change in Market Cap (in Billions)*	Change in Market Cap (%)*
AOL	$103	$54	$3.18	3
JDS Uniphase	12	50	0.82	6.8
Lucent	22	10	0.73	3.3
Vivendi	35.5	13	2.84	8

Source: The data in this table was derived from market data provided through links to the respective exchanges for the individual share price performance of the companies noted.

*Change from one day before write-off to one day after the announcement.

at all. But even with this simple analysis, it is easy to see how pessimistic assumptions about Enron's balance sheet could lead to a reduction in assets of $15 billion that would have eliminated 100 percent of its equity book value and made the firm technically insolvent long before the company went into Chapter 11.

ROLE OF THE EQUITY MARKET

Some may contend that the analysis of Enron's cash flows in the prior section is easy to do *ex post* but would have been hard to undertake *ex ante*. Hindsight, after all, is 20/20 vision. Some further argue that the DCF approach is just one of many valuation methods. But in fact, there is a compelling reason to believe that the most important processor of information about corporate performance—the stock market—does indeed reflect a cash flows-based approach.

Indeed, movements in Enron's share price strongly suggest that the equity market saw through many of Enron's accounting machinations many months before its illegal operating and accounting practices were formally acknowledged. While the accountants, regulators, and rating agencies were on the sidelines, the equity market was anticipating a steep fall in Enron's fortunes.

By August 14, 2001, the stock market value of Enron had declined by almost 40 percent from $62 billion to $38 billion. By contrast, other stocks in the U.S. energy sector were basically unchanged to slightly higher for the year to date. By the date of the accounting restatement—November 8, 2001—the share price was down 90 percent (down $56 billion) from January 1, 2001. When Enron lost its investment-grade credit rating in late November 2001, the equity was virtually worthless.

Throughout 2001, investors in Enron appear to have been more concerned about the firm's future prospects than about current results. Enron continued to post double-digit growth and EPS numbers throughout 2001, but the shares continued to fall. Investors appear to have been particularly concerned about the following Enron-specific issues:

- The firm's cash negative position, despite Enron's reported double-digit earnings growth in each quarter of 2001.
- Declines in sales profit margins from 5 percent to 1 percent over the prior five years.
- The potential overvaluation of some assets on Enron's balance sheet and suggestions that debt was understated.
- The possibility of conflict of interest issues with the firm's SPEs.[5]
- The overall risk/return characteristics of the business, given the failures in dot-coms and fiber optic markets, suggesting that the

firm was actually making investment returns below its cost of capital and had been for some time.

Yet, while the market was sending clear signals of concern about Enron and its future prospects, Enron's external auditor—Arthur Andersen—did not qualify any of the quarterly reports nor resign as the company's auditor. Nor did the SEC launch an informal inquiry into third-party transactions until October 22, 2001, or a formal inquiry until October 31, 2001. The rating agencies, moreover, did not downgrade Enron below investment grade until November 28, 2001, only days before its bankruptcy.

Equity investors were focused largely on future prospects while regulators appeared to be focused on past events and how they were reported. Enron's management continued with its "laser like focus on earnings per share" while investors reduced the value of the shares (Enron Corporation, 2001, p. 1). In short, there is strong reason to believe that despite Enron's attempts to fool the market, the firm had not entirely succeeded in that endeavor.

POLITICAL REACTION AND CORPORATE REFORM

"When Dr Johnson said that patriotism was the last refuge of the scoundrel," an American senator once remarked, "he overlooked the immense possibilities of the word 'reform'" (Parris, 2002, p. 16). Despite the sound performance of equity markets in accurately processing the information available and pricing the risk in Enron or WorldCom, while the compliance-driven accounting and disclosure rules failed to reflect these risks, the *political* focus has remained squarely on the measures and bodies that failed, rather than on reinforcing the measures and groups that processed the available information in the most timely fashion—that is, the equity and debt markets.

On the day after the WorldCom's $3.9 billion revenue restatement announcement (June 27, 2002), the SEC issued an order that required officers at almost 1,000 of the largest publicly traded companies to file sworn statements attesting to the truthfulness of their accounting and disclosure policies by August 14, 2002. In addition to increasing market volatility and imposing huge legal and accounting costs on shareholders, this misguided action effectively retrenches the measures and positions of the bodies that failed the shareholders at Enron, WorldCom, and others. Perversely, accounting is now more important than ever, and auditors will be significant beneficiaries from the reform process as the cost of audits and internal management increases, all at the expense of shareholders.

Further, this action reinforces the widespread perception among many politicians, commentators, and the public alike that the problems at

Enron, WorldCom, and others are somehow "systemic" in nature—that is, broadly representative of a much bigger problem endemic to U.S. corporate governance. Can this proposition be supported?

Is There a Systemic Problem in the United States?

The notion that "corporate irresponsibility" is relatively more widespread in the United States than elsewhere is based more on assertion than on any hard empirical evidence. Indeed, many would consider existing U.S. laws to be already on the conservative side when compared to other international corporate law regimes. One recent study, for example, examined the accounts of more than 70,000 companies from 31 countries over the period from 1990 to 1999, specifically to evaluate the relations among accounting practice, legal protections, and quality of investor protection. In this study, Leuz, Nanda, and Wysocki (2001) concluded that the United States and United Kingdom experienced the lowest deviations between corporate cash flows and reported earnings. In other words, companies in the United States and United Kingdom appear to engage in "earnings management" *the least* when compared to the companies in the other 29 countries.

In addition, on the question of rights afforded to outside investors, the United States, United Kingdom, Canada, Hong Kong, India, Pakistan, and South Africa all scored top marks. While there is always room for improvement, this study and a number of similar ones suggest that the problem may not be quite as widespread in the United States as some commentators would have us believe (see LaPorta, Lopez-de-Silanes, Schliefer, and Vishny, 2000).

When considering the implications of actions such as the recent forced officer disclosures, it is useful to think about the reporting requirements a typical *Fortune 1000* company *already faces*. On average, each of these companies has more than 100 legal entities or business units and operates in more than 50 countries. The ownership of each entity is often less than 100 percent, which means that the decision on certain accounting issues is not solely the domain of the U.S. partner—and all of the non-U.S. countries have different accounting standards. Even the translation from Canadian or English GAAP to U.S. GAAP is a nontrivial task.

As noted earlier, hundreds, if not thousands, of judgments are made about revenue recognition, cost allocations, capital structures, and other issues in each of these individual entities and again at a consolidated or holding company level. Frankly, the notion that a CEO or CFO at a large company could reasonably "certify" a company's accounts on pain of imprisonment could only be propagated by someone with no practical knowledge of accounting, reporting, nor any practical understanding that this type of order costs real time and real money—all of which achieves, at best, a spurious result.

As the new disclosures are being required under the pain of severe personal penalties for noncompliance, the most likely result will be a significant number of restatements as CEOs and CFOs move from an accounting stance that may have been overly optimistic to one likely to be overly cautious. That does *not* mean that they lied or misrepresented their accounts before; it is simply a recognition that accounting requires, by definition, managerial choices, and the bias on these choices will have shifted.

Regulatory moves such as the required SEC disclosures have already imparted significant volatility into U.S. equity markets. A further downturn in the market seems likely, moreover, after the results of the mandated officer disclosures are published. Companies will be extremely cautious about what they say, and this could further undermine investor confidence in the future performance of the firms—for no good reason, alas. Unfortunately, this in turn could reinforce claims that there is a systemic failure in corporate governance and have the undesirable result of reinforcing in the public mind-set that political intervention is the only answer.

Voluntary versus Political Responses

Legislative or regulatory efforts to mandate "more responsible corporate behavior," are *not* the only way to restore confidence in corporate America. In fact, many proposals—including the Sarbanes-Oxley Corporate Reform Act of 2002 (HR 3763)—will probably achieve the opposite result.

At a series of SEC roundtable functions held before the adoption of the Sarbanes-Oxley Act,[6] the clear and overriding opinion of the participants was that market participants—not government—should make credible changes. Numerous such changes were, in fact, underway even before the Sarbanes-Oxley Act was passed. Consider some examples:

- Many corporations had already passed resolutions restricting the granting of contracts to their auditors for nonaudit-related consulting work.
- The boards of the New York Stock Exchange and the Nasdaq Stock Market proposed changes, received feedback, and adopted a series of new rules on the independence of corporate directors, the operation and organization of audit committees, and other pro-shareholder power-oriented initiatives.[7]

- Many securities firms had already adopted the practice of declaring on their reports when they acted for a company in an investment banking or other capacity.
- The ratings agencies—notably S&P—had already moved to bring their data on company accounts closer to a cash flow result. Moody's went further with its February purchase of KMV for a reported $200 million. KMV models and databases are intended to aid in the credit rating process by providing explicit guidance to debt issuers and lenders on expected default rates, based on equity market movements.[8]

In short, the market was already working to heal itself in response to its constituents—shareholders.

By contrast, the Sarbanes-Oxley Act has created a series of actions that will measurably *harm* investors:

- The Act will reduce the *quality* of reports in favor of increasing the *quantity.* Because accounting is not a precise science and judgments must be made, for executives to avoid any personal risk, the quality of the information they provide in their filings may be reduced and the language may become even more guarded to reduce the threat of legal action to senior executives, all of which will increase the quantity of reporting and make the reports less accessible to the average reader.
- The legislation will exacerbate the divide between shareholders and managerial custodians of their business. Managers may be forced to choose between the desires of the shareholders for information and the shareholders' demand for improving ongoing operating performance. The severity of the regulatory demands with their threats of jail and personal bankruptcy are tilting the scales in favor of form filing over value creation. Inevitably, senior managers will spend less time running the business and more time with their lawyers than with their shareholders.
- The new accounting oversight body will impose direct costs on publicly traded companies, as well as indirect costs through increased and unnecessary compliance costs and the cost in management time—all of which will ultimately be shouldered by the shareholders. In addition, efforts by U.S. companies to compete with one another through creative voluntary disclosures will stagnate in the face of a superregulator dictating accounting policy. In other words, the current compliance system will become *even more compliance-based,* despite the obvious benefits presented earlier to a more principles-based approach.

- The legislative initiative gives a new weapon to the friends of anarchy, opponents of capitalism, and enemies of global free trade. Public interest groups representing the opinion of small minorities of the public, for example, will be able to buy small quantities of shares and use these as the basis to launch nuisance suits. These suits will be used to blackmail companies into actions not in shareholders' best interests, smear the company's reputation in the public eye, and distract senior executives from managing in shareholders' interests.

- Global capital flows into the United States will be inhibited by the new law. The vagaries of accounting interpretation and ambiguities in the American legal system will surely lead prudent non-U.S. issuers to review the status of their U.S. listings. The overwhelming business opinion outside the United States before the passage of this Act was *already* that the U.S. legal system is highly politicized and actively discriminates against non-U.S. defendants (note U.S. asbestos, trade, and environmental rulings). According to the international relations department at the NYSE, more than 10 percent of the securities on the NYSE—$1.2 trillion of securities—are from non-U.S. firms. In light of Sarbanes-Oxley, all non-U.S.-domiciled company boards should reconsider the value of any U.S. listing because the legal risk and shareholder costs to maintain these listings are probably too high to justify continuing their U.S. listings.

- The Act is also the twenty-first century equivalent of economic imperialism in the manner that it arbitrarily dictates the standard of behavior to non-U.S. accounting bodies, foreign-owned companies, and non-American executives.

- The worst aspect of the Sarbanes-Oxley Act is that it, through Section 401 on disclosures, actually reduces the ability of companies to provide reasonable guidance on their future prospects to investors and potential investors. The fear of up to a 25-year jail sentence is a major disincentive to provide any information that could be refuted later. Valuing the firm by forecasting the cash flows and discounting them back at an appropriate rate to a present value just got harder. Investors will have less information about a firm's long-term prospects, which, in turn, reduces their ability to price investments, makes investors more short-term focused, increases the volatility of stock prices, and, most perversely, increases the power of Wall Street analysts.

ENERGY MARKET IMPACT

In the pursuit of short-term accounting targets and annual bonuses, Enron executives harmed the wholesale energy markets, damaged the credibility

of the derivatives markets, and handed the friends of regulation a powerful political weapon—"corporate sleaze." This has had the combined impact of reducing the attractiveness of new energy projects and, as such,
increasing U.S. dependency on external providers of energy. It has damaged the credit ratings of all energy traders and precipitated ratings downgrades and liquidity problems that undermine the efficiency in energy
trading and, therefore, consumer prices.

Fortunately, this situation may be short-lived as the markets and the
reality of U.S. energy demands reassert themselves. Unfortunately, this is
at best a 50/50 proposition because the ratings agencies, in particular,
are as concerned about their own reputation risk as they are about the
energy providers.

What may not be short term is the damage done to the trust in business leaders and the regulatory overreaction inflicted on the broader markets. This combination is likely to increase *permanently* market volatility
and the cost of capital for all U.S. firms to the detriment of everyone with
a pension plan, savings plan, insurance, or direct investment portfolio.

NOTES

1. Assume here that *fair value* is what the transaction would be worth if negotiated freely on the open market between two competitive firms. For the
   purpose of this example, suppose this fair value is uncontroversial and readily available.
2. LJM and other SPEs are discussed in Chapter 8, and certain accounting issues concerning SPEs are discussed in Chapter 10.
3. The accounting issues listed in this table are generalized and based on U.S.
   GAAP; in other jurisdictions, other treatments may produce a cash event,
   primarily because of tax issues.
4. We have provided a PDF file with a full set of Enron financial statements
   that allows interested parties to review the historic performance as well as
   the forecasts that we developed for our analysis. This is available from www
   .risktoolz.com/enron.
5. See Part Two of this volume.
6. SEC Roundtables were announced in 2001 for 2002 and included issues on
   disclosure, regulation, and related market issues. Transcripts are available
   on the SEC Web site, www.sec.gov.
7. The complete list of actions is available on their Web sites, www.nyse.com
   and www.nasdaq.com.
8. The authors are not suggesting support for the KMV model but rather are
   simply noting the reaction of one of the rating agencies to recognize the superiority of market information to filed reports.

3

CORPORATE GOVERNANCE

Pre-Enron, Post-Enron

ALTON B. HARRIS AND ANDREA S. KRAMER

C*orporate governance* is the process by which a corporation's management is held accountable to its residual owners—the stockholders. Because of Enron and scores of other corporations currently embroiled in accounting and managerial scandals, the New York Stock Exchange (NYSE) and the NASDAQ Stock Market (NASDAQ) have approved sweeping new listing standards; and Congress has enacted wide-ranging federal legislation—the Sarbanes-Oxley Act of 2002[1]—that will profoundly affect the nature of and control over corporate governance in the United States.

While the implosion of Enron was unquestionably the decisive event that shaped the content and timing of the new corporate governance paradigm, Enron's significance in this regard cannot be fully appreciated except in the context of the changes in expectations as to *best practice* for corporate governance over the prior 30 years. In this chapter, we examine the unique nature of the corporate governance problem, trace the development of a consensus model of best practice expectations, discuss the changes that the new listing standards and Sarbanes-Oxley will force on major corporations, and, finally, offer a few tentative comments on the sensibleness of the entire best practice enterprise.

We wish to make clear that, in what follows, we touch only very briefly on an alternative to the consensus model of corporate governance, what Henry G. Manne has called "the market for corporate control."[2] We have largely chosen to ignore this alternative model, not because of our personal views as to its potential effectiveness, but because recent legislative and judicial decisions have stripped it of much, if not all, of its usefulness as a management control mechanism. How and why that came about is an interesting and important story, but it is not the story we tell in this chapter. Our story is decidedly immediate and practical: What is the current *consensus* model of *best practice* for corporate governance, how did it become such, and is it likely to accomplish its intended objectives?

THE FOREIGN CORRUPT PRACTICES ACT

The sea of change in corporate governance now upon us did not begin with Enron[3] or Cendant[4] or Sunbeam[5] or even Bausch & Lomb.[6] Rather, it began with a series of corporate misadventures in the 1970s that have an unsettling familiarity to those of today. In 1973, the Watergate special prosecutor announced that Lockheed, Northrop, Gulf Oil, and other prominent corporations may have used corporate funds to make illegal domestic political contributions.[7] The Securities and Exchange Commission (SEC) immediately commenced an extensive investigation, the result of which was the revelation that scores of American corporations had violated U.S. election laws and hundreds more had made payments abroad in circumstances suggesting indifference, or worse, to domestic and foreign laws prohibiting bribery and other questionable methods of securing business.[8] When the dust settled, many of the largest and most respected U.S. corporations were found to have used phony subsidiaries and off-book accounts to channel millions of dollars to government officials and others to influence the purchase of goods and the awarding of lucrative contracts. All told, more than 500 publicly held American companies, including 117 of the Fortune 500, were either charged by the SEC or voluntarily confessed to have engaged in serious misconduct, almost all involving accounting irregularities.[9]

For the SEC, the widespread occurrence of questionable and illegal corporate payments—facilitated by the falsification of basic financial records—constituted evidence of a pervasive "frustration of our system of corporate accountability."[10] For Congress, it was apparent that this seemingly epidemic corporate misconduct had "erod[ed] public confidence in the integrity of the free market system."[11] In December 1977, following specific recommendations of the SEC, Congress enacted the Foreign Corrupt Practices Act (FCPA),[12] which criminalized foreign bribery and, for the first time in U.S. history, imposed on public companies a federal obligation "to maintain books and records that accurately and fairly reflect transactions and dispositions of [their] assets." Shortly thereafter, the SEC adopted supplemental rules making it illegal for anyone to falsify (or cause to be falsified) any corporate accounting record or to misrepresent (or cause to be misrepresented) to a corporation's independent accountant any material fact.[13]

HAROLD WILLIAMS' THREE-ACT PLAY

In 1978, in the midst of the public and congressional outrage over questionable and illegal payments, then SEC Chairman Harold M. Williams gave an extraordinarily prescient speech on the likely future course for corporate governance. Williams began by outlining what he referred to as a "familiar" three-act play titled "Federal Regulation of Business." In Act I of this play, a series of apparently isolated events involving corporate excess or insensitivity attracts press coverage under the rubrics of "scandals" and "flagrant abuses." Next, there are "thinly scattered comment by public interest types" and occasional arguments that "the government should do something to prevent these 'outrages' from happening again." The public, however, is apathetic, and, at this point, the play's plot seems weak, insignificant, and easy to ignore.[14]

Act II is the longest act in the play. More corporate misdeeds occur, but at first only sporadically and in apparent isolation. After the passage of time—unspecified as to duration—the offending events begin to occur more frequently and the sense of their separateness dissipates. Public sentiment is fanned by the multiplication of scandals and flagrant abuses. Congress then shows interest, and legislation is introduced "but [initially] attracts little support." Act II, however, closes with a bang. "Inflamed by a single dramatic and widely publicized occurrence," Congress is spurred "to a full-blown and broadly based legislative effort."[15]

Act III is straightforward. Congress enacts legislation designed to prevent the reoccurrence of the corporate misconduct at issue. "A chorus of businessmen deplor[e] the further intervention of government into business affairs." And the audience is left with the moral: "It takes a law to get business to behave responsibly."[16]

In outlining this familiar play, Williams reminded his listeners that over the prior 10 or 15 years, it had been frequently revived under a variety of subtitles including "auto safety," "truth in packaging," "occupational health and safety," "ERISA," and, most recently, "questionable and illegal payments."[17] Williams' concern was that without reform of the mechanisms of corporate governance itself, the next revival of this play was likely to be titled "federal legislation on corporate accountability."[18] Williams wanted to avoid such a revival, but he saw clearly that if America's public corporations were to preserve their ability to control their own structures and governance, "they must be able to assure the public that they can discipline themselves. . . . Mechanisms which provide that assurance must become structural components of the process of governance and accountability of the American corporation."[19] The point of Williams' exhortation was, thus, that the American business community could not ignore, stonewall, or adopt a head-in-the-sand attitude toward the corporate governance crisis if federal legislation was to be avoided.[20]

ENRON, WORLDCOM, AND FEDERAL LEGISLATION

When Williams spoke in 1978, he thought that the United States was in "the early stages of Act II" of the familiar play.[21] If that was the case, Act II was very long, indeed, lasting from the middle of the 1970s until early 2002. But Act II ran its course just as Williams had predicted. Toward its end, the revelations of flagrant abuses at Enron, following as they had on a series of accounting and managerial scandals over the prior 10 years, resulted in the introduction of federal legislation designed to impose significant federal control over public accounting and the governance processes at all public companies.[22] Public outrage at persuasive management self-enrichment was high.[23] Executive compensation by 2000 had, on average, reached 411 times the amount of the average factory worker's salary, which was up from only 42 times in 1982.[24] Executive stock sales during the telecom bubble had resulted in "one of the largest transfers of wealth from investors—big and small—to corporate insiders in American history."[25] Questionable and sometimes unapproved loans by corporations to top executives totaled billions of dollars.[26] And in 2000, executives at America's 325 largest corporations had been awarded options worth 20 percent of their corporations' total pretax profit.[27] The public's view of corporate management seemed to be accurately captured by Alan Greenspan's characterization of the business community as having been gripped in the late 1990s and early 2000s by "infectious greed."[28]

Within six months after Enron's collapse, however, the "wave of enthusiasm for overhauling the nation's corporate and accounting laws ha[d] ebbed and the toughest proposals for change [were] all but dead."[29] Yet, just as Williams had predicted in 1978, Act II closed with a bang. WorldCom's announcement of a $3.8 billion accounting restatement provided the "single dramatic and widely publicized occurrence" that energized both the public and Congress to undertake "a full blown and broadly based legislative effort."[30]

Act III then followed in straightforward and predicted fashion. The wave of enthusiasm for overhauling the nation's corporate and accounting laws that only weeks before had been "all but dead" became an unstoppable tidal wave.[31] Thirty-six days after WorldCom's first public announcement of its accounting irregularities, President Bush signed into law Sarbanes-Oxley, the most sweeping federal legislation addressing public accounting and corporate governance since the 1930s.

The play that Williams named "federal legislation on corporate accountability" has now come to an end.[32] Its moral appears to be as predicted: "It takes a law to get business to behave responsibly."[33] But the predicted businessmen's chorus deploring government intervention has been largely missing. When President Bush signed Sarbanes-Oxley, The Business Roundtable (BRT), unquestionably the most prominent and outspoken defender of private corporate prerogatives, did not deplore government intervention in the area of corporate governance, historically left to contract and private initiative, but rather announced that it "welcomes these reforms and will quickly implement the changes to strengthen our companies' governance. We believe the law will go a long way toward establishing new higher standards for America's corporations."[34]

A cynic no doubt would explain the business community's position on Sarbanes-Oxley as a ploy designed to deflect public anger away from the "good" corporations. There is surely something to that explanation. But without yet turning in our cynic membership cards, we want to suggest that the business community's attitude toward federal intervention in the area of corporate governance results, at least in part, from its realization as a result of Enron, WorldCom, Tyco, and their fellow travelers that relying on individual corporations voluntarily to implement appropriate and effective corporate governance mechanisms has not and is not likely to stop the corporate scandals and flagrant abuses that have been so devastating for public confidence and corporate prosperity. Indeed, there now appears to be a general perception, even on the part of the major corporation community, that some form of collective action is needed—whether direct legislation, mandatory listing standards, or otherwise—to ensure that all corporations behave responsibly toward their stockholders. In what follows, we trace the evolution, on the one hand, of the consensus view of the appropriate mechanisms for effective corporation governance and, on the other, of the agreement as to how those mechanisms are to be imposed.

WHY CORPORATE GOVERNANCE?

The Unique Status of Stockholders

The modern corporation has many constituencies in addition to its stockholders: employees, suppliers, consumers, communities in which it operates and that it can affect, the public generally when the national interest is implicated, and undoubtedly many others. At various times since the late 1800s, the corporation has been faulted for its failure to fulfill its responsibility to one or another of these constituencies. As the frequent revivals of Williams' familiar play make clear, the federal government periodically steps in to control what is perceived to be corporate greed, to demand corporate attention to an asserted public interest, or to protect one or more of the corporation's "vulnerable" constituencies. Whatever the justification for any one of these interventions in particular or government intervention of this sort in general, such legislative efforts relating to one or more of these corporate constituencies are not addressed at corporate governance.

Corporate governance addresses a corporation's relationship with only one of its constituencies: its residual owners or stockholders. However egregious a corporation's greed or blatant its disregard of an asserted public interest, the conduct in question, in all likelihood, has been pursued to enhance the corporation's profits and hence to benefit (ill gotten perhaps, but benefit no less) its stockholders. As Peter Drucker remarked about Lockheed and the foreign bribery scandals of the 1970s:

> Here was not a management looting a company; on the contrary, what the management did was intended to advance the interests of the company and of its employees—and, in respect to sales of military aircraft, even the interest of the country, of its foreign policy and of its balance of payments.[35]

Harm to stockholders occurs for reasons different from harm to the corporation's other constituencies. When harm to stockholders is alleged, it is not because of the corporation's greed or the corporation's indifference to stockholder interests but rather because corporate management of the corporation is shirking its responsibilities, has fallen victim to extraordinary miscalculation, or is pursuing its personal self-interest at the stockholders' expense. Corporate governance, thus, is concerned with the control of corporate managers to ensure that they do not enrich themselves at the expense of the stockholders or act (as was surely the case in the corporate bribery scandals and, we believe, to a considerable extent in Enron) in such a grossly irresponsible manner as to seriously damage the corporation, if not wreck it entirely.

The Berle and Means Corporation

The Modern Corporation and Private Property by Adolf Berle and Gardiner Means, published in 1932, constitutes the paradigmatic articulation of the reason that effective corporate governance is both so needed and so elusive. Berle and Means' fundamental insight was that "the separation [in the modern corporation] of ownership from control produces a condition where the interests of owners [of the enterprise] and of [the enterprise's] ultimate manager may, and often do, diverge."[36] A mechanism to ensure the attention and faithfulness of corporate management—that is, an effective scheme of corporate governance—is needed if the divergence of such interests is to be prevented or, at least, the adverse consequences of such divergence minimized.

For Berle and Means, the large public corporation became in the twentieth century "the dominant institution in the modern world."[37] As the wealth of innumerable individuals was concentrated "into huge aggregates," control over that wealth shifted from the hands of its owners to the hands of those able to provide a unified direction to these new corporate enterprises.[38] This separation of ownership from control constituted a fundamental departure from the classic economic model under which the right of individual property owners to use their property as they saw fit could be "relied upon as an effective incentive to [the] efficient use of [that] property." But as individual, self-interested, property owners moved from active market participants to passive investors, their capacity to direct the deployment and disposition of their property "declined from extreme strength to practical impotence."[39] As a consequence, owners are exposed to a continual risk "that a controlling group may direct profits into their own pockets [and fail to run] the corporation . . . primarily in the interests of the stockholders."[40]

Berle and Means saw the separation of ownership from control as posing an extraordinarily difficult economic problem because the identification and implementation of mechanisms (beyond reliance on market forces and the goodwill and ethical probity of managers) that will ensure the alignment of the interests of those who control the corporation with those who own it are neither obvious nor easy. Yet without this separation of ownership from control, there is no efficient solution to the problems of decision making in a large organization.[41] The separation of ownership from control is, thus, a very sharp two-edged sword: Without the separation of ownership from a centralized management having virtually absolute authority, the essential wealth-enhancing corporate decisions essential for the growth and well-being of our capitalist economy would not and could not be made; yet as a result of such separation, management holds "the power of confiscation of a part of the profit streams and even of the underlying corporate assets."[42]

Since at least the 1970s, the presumed resolution of this dilemma has been seen by a consensus of establishment lawyers, corporate representatives, and academics to lie in a system of corporate governance whereby, on the one side, management, primarily in the form of a strong CEO, controls the direction and initiatives of the corporation, and, on the other side, a board of directors, independent of management and the CEO, has the knowledge, incentive, and authority to monitor management's performance and curb its temptations for opportunism.[43] The formulation, sharpening, and testing of this consensus view of corporate governance over almost 30 years sets the stage for approval of the new NYSE listing standards and passage of Sarbanes-Oxley.

PRIVATE INITIATIVES TO IMPROVE CORPORATE GOVERNANCE

The Strong Corporate Board

Because of collective action problems, free-riding temptations, and the so-called *Wall Street Rule*—it's always easier to sell than fight—the modern corporation's stockholders have neither the incentive nor the practical ability to act as the enterprise's ultimate monitors.[44] Thus, the consensus view that has developed is that this monitoring function can be, and can best be, performed by the board of directors. As one leading corporate scholar expresses the point, the monitoring of management is "of critical importance to the corporation and uniquely suited for performance by the board."[45] For William Allen, then chancellor of the Delaware court of Chancery, the basic responsibility of the board is "to monitor the performance of senior management in an informed way."[46] And yet another prominent corporate scholar states flatly that "the heart of corporate governance has been the imposition of the so-called monitoring model [on the board of directors]."[47]

In this consensus view, best practice for dealing with the problems caused by the separation of ownership from control, or, as contemporary corporate scholars would put it, of reducing corporate agency costs,[48] is the establishment of what is variously called a *monitoring board*,[49] *certifying board*,[50] or *empowered board*.[51] However labeled, the basic characteristics of this strong board of directors have come to be generally understood to include directors that are all, or a majority of whom are, independent; an active audit committee composed entirely of independent and adequately informed directors; other specialized committees (nomination and compensation, in particular) also composed entirely (or almost entirely) of independent directors; a formal charter setting out the board's authority and responsibility to monitor the corporation's performance, compliance, and financial reporting; and a style of operation characterized by independence from management, skepticism with respect to unsupported assertions made to them, and dogged loyalty to shareholder interests.[52]

Evolution of the Consensus

The *consensus* view that a strong board of directors constitutes best practice with respect to corporate governance is of relatively recent origin. When Myles Mace published his landmark study of boards of directors in 1970, he concluded that boards did not manage corporations or monitor corporate management but served solely as advisors and counselors to the CEO.[53] And as Ira Millstein has observed, at this time "[corporate] boards were the parsley on the fish . . . usually composed of a group of friends or acquaintances of the CEO who could be counted on to support management."[54] Audit committees, despite having been recommended by the SEC in 1940[55] and the NYSE in 1939,[56] had spread slowly and had received relatively little public attention.[57] Yet, between 1970 and 1980, the United States witnessed what can only be described as a revolution in the concept of *best practice* for corporate governance.

In May 1976, then SEC Chairman Rodrick Hills wrote to then NYSE Chairman Melvin Batten suggesting that the NYSE revise its listing standards to require that all listed companies have an independent audit committee.[58] The NYSE accepted the suggestions, and effective June 30, 1978, all NYSE listed companies were required to "maintain . . . an audit committee comprised solely of directors independent of management and free from any relationship that, in the opinion of the board of directors, would interfere with the exercise of independent judgment as a committee member."[59]

In November of that same year, the Subcommittee on Functions and Responsibilities of Directors, Committee on Corporate Laws, American Bar Association (ABA) published the first edition of the *Corporate Director's Guidebook*.[60] Revised and adopted by the full ABA Committee on Corporate Laws seven days before the adoption of the FCPA, the *Guidebook* represented the establishment bar's first attempt to set forth "a structural model for the governance of a publicly owned business corporation."[61] At the heart of this model was a "board of directors [that] function[ed] effectively in its role as reviewer of management initiatives and monitor of corporate performance."[62] The effective performance of this role required, in the ABA's view, that "a significant number of [the] board's members should be able to provide independent judgment regarding the proposals under consideration."[63]

Shortly thereafter, the BRT, a consistent and steadfast defender of CEO prerogatives, issued a statement titled "The Role and Composition of the Board of Directors of the Large Publicly Owned Corporation."[64] While, in hindsight, certain parts of this statement are embarrassingly defensive,[65] the BRT's statement is remarkably consistent with that of the ABA, particularly in its acknowledgment of the board's monitoring role[66] and its firm recommendation that all boards should have a sufficient number of "outside" directors "to have a substantial impact on the board['s] decision process."[67]

In 1980, when its "Staff Report on Corporate Accountability" was issued,[68] the SEC saw:

> a new consensus . . . emerging with respect to the vital monitoring role to be played by the board of directors in the corporate accountability process and the most desirable and appropriate composition and structure of a board designed to play such an enhanced oversight role. The consensus is moving strongly toward greater participation by directors independent of management, currently calling for a board composed of at least a majority of independent directors, with properly functioning independent audit, compensation, and nominating committees, as essential to enhanced and effective corporate accountability.[69]

This consensus as to best practices for corporate governance included, according to the SEC, the following:

1. "A strong board of directors is the key to improved accountability."[70] For this to occur, the "board's primary function [must be] to monitor management."[71] And if this monitoring process is to be successful, "the board of directors [must be] an independent force in corporate affairs rather than a passive affiliate of management."[72]
2. Because the traditional board dominated by insiders cannot adequately monitor the performance of management, "a majority of the board of directors should be nonmanagement directors."[73] While corporations may differ as to the appropriate mix of insiders and outsiders on their boards, as well as the affiliations of their outside directors, "a majority of nonmanagement, preferably independent, directors is necessary for the board to successfully perform its monitoring function."[74]
3. While "there appear[ed] to be an emerging consensus that those directors with significant business relationships with the corporation should not be considered independent of management when. . . . determining if [the board] has a sufficient critical mass of independence,"[75] the primary emphasis was on independence as "a state of mind" rather than a formal specification of affiliations that would disqualify someone from being viewed as independent.[76]
4. Because of NYSE requirements and American Stock Exchange (AMEX) and National Association of Securities Dealers (NASD) recommendations, a significant majority of public companies had audit committees. Although many of these audit committees had

members that were not "independent,"[77] the consensus view was that "audit committees should be composed exclusively of directors independent of management."[78]

5. Despite the recommendations in the *Corporate Director's Guidebook,*[79] there was no consensus that the audit committee should have the authority to engage or discharge the outside auditors. Likewise, despite the audit committee's "important role . . . in assuring the independence of the accounting firm," very little evidence existed that this role was assumed by audit committees generally.[80]

6. The existence of a compensation committee—charged with review of compensation arrangements for senior management—composed of nonmanagement directors, some of whom were "independent" of management, was viewed as desirable.[81]

To summarize, by 1980, the strong corporate board had come to be seen by most observers as the critical and only realistically available check on management opportunism. Over the next 20 years, this consensus view grew sharper; the concept of *independence,* for example, became increasingly specific—and far less flexible in its application—and one size of corporate governance was increasingly seen to fit all corporations. Yet, through this entire period, the changes in the consensus view were mostly evolutionary and incremental—except, that is, in the crucial area of the appropriate relationship between the strong board and corporate management. At the end of the 1970s, the BRT, speaking for the "consensus," described that relationship as appropriately one "of mutual trust . . . challenging yet supportive and positive . . . arm's length but not adversary."[82] After Enron, the BRT, speaking now for a substantially evolved consensus, described the board's appropriate attitude toward management as one "of constructive skepticism [, of] ask[ing] incisive, probing questions and requir[ing] accurate, honest answers."[83]

The story of the shift from mutual trust to constructive skepticism is also the story of the ultimate failure of Harold Williams' hope that the response of corporate America to the continuing scandals and flagrant abuse would eliminate the need for federal legislation on corporate accountability and avoid the performance of Act III of the familiar play.

The Market for Corporate Control

But before telling that story, it is worth pausing briefly to note the United States' flirtation with, and ultimate rejection of, the "market for corporate control"[84] as a model for control of managerial opportunism. The concept, in brief, is that there is a high positive correlation between corporate managerial efficiency and the market price of that corporation's shares. If there is a relatively unimpeded market for corporate control, inefficient and overcompensated management is, thus, subject to ouster through the mechanism of the hostile takeover. According to Henry G. Manne, "only the takeover scheme provides some assurance of competitive efficiency among corporate managers and [thus] strong protection to the interests of vast numbers of small, noncontrolling shareholders. Compared with this mechanism . . . [the benefits] of a fiduciary duty concept [associated with independent directors] seem small indeed."[85]

The merits of Manne's claim that the "market for corporate control" provides the best approach for resolving the dilemma confronting the Berle and Means corporation is provocative but certainly arguable. For example, both Enron and WorldCom declared bankruptcy within months of their stocks' trading at what can only be regarded as extremely high multiples. Further, until they collapsed, these corporations were active acquirers rather than likely prospects for a hostile takeover. Nevertheless, whatever your view of the benefits of a robust market for corporate control, several developments have imposed severe impediments to this market's effective operation. First, following more than 100 hostile cash tender offers in 1966,[86] Congress passed the Williams Act in 1968.[87] This statute significantly limits the ability of a corporate raider to mount a hostile takeover without advance warning to the target corporation and extensive disclosure of the raider's intentions and financing.[88] Second, as a result of a series of highly publicized takeover battles, in 1985 the Delaware courts decided four cases that gave existing management unprecedented power to resist hostile takeover attempts.[89] Third, by 1992, under intense lobbying from the BRT and other business groups, more than two-thirds of the states had enacted highly effective antitakeover laws.[90] As a consequence of these developments, while hostile takeover activity continues in various forms,[91] by the early 1990s the "market for corporate control" as Manne had envisioned it had effectively ceased to exist.[92]

The Consensus Sharpens

The elimination of the hostile takeover as a useful mechanism for protecting stockholders from management opportunism renewed interest in the role and responsibility of the strong corporate board. In 1992, the American Law Institute (ALI) completed its 14-year project, *Principles of Corporate Governance: Analysis and Recommendations.*[93] While the gestation of the ALI's *Principles* was difficult and controversial,[94] in the end, the *Principles,* at least in the areas with which we are concerned, sharpened, but remained solidly within, the consensus tradition. Under the *Principles,* the board is assigned "ultimate responsibility for oversight"[95] of "the conduct of the corporation's business to evaluate whether the business is being properly managed."[96] Public corporations with $100 million or more of total assets "should have a majority of directors who are free of any significant relationship with the corporation's senior executives."[97] The audit committee should be composed entirely of persons who are not present or former employees, a majority of whom should "have no significant relationship with the corporation's senior executives."[98] And while the board itself should have responsibility for determining "the appropriate auditing and accounting principles and practices" for the corporation,[99] the audit committee should "recommend the firm to be employed as the corporation's external auditor and review . . . the external auditor's independence."[100] In performing the latter function, the audit committee "should carefully consider any matter that might affect the external auditor's independence, such as the extent to which the external auditor performs nonaudit services."[101]

Two years after the ALI adopted the *Principles,* the ABA amended its *Corporate Directors Guidebook,* emphasizing "the board's role as an independent and informed monitor of the conduct of the corporation's affairs and the performance of its management."[102] The second edition of the *Guidebook* changed the ABA's original recommendation for composition of the board of directors from a "significant number" who are "nonmanagement directors" to "at least a majority" who are independent of management;[103] and it formalized the concept of a board member's "independence"[104] and changed the previous ABA recommendation of an audit committee composed of "nonmanagement directors, a majority of whom are unaffiliated nonmanagement directors"[105] to a committee composed solely of "independent directors."[106]

And in 1997, the BRT published a white paper titled "Statement on Corporate Governance."[107] Sharpening its 1978 recommendations, the BRT emphasized that the board of directors must have "a substantial degree of independence from management" and that the members of the audit committee should meet "more specific standards of independence."[108] While the BRT's statement is less specific in a number of respects than those of the ALI or ABA, its recognition that "the absence of good corporate governance . . . may imply vulnerability for stockholders" and that the failure of "knowledgeable directors . . . to express their views" places a corporation at "risk" give the BRT's statement a decided air of serious practicality.[109]

The corporate governance recommendations of the ALI, ABA, and BRT made in the 1980s differ in emphasis, specificity, and tone, but largely they all build on the earlier consensus in apparently constructive ways. Although only the ALI's recommendations continue to approximate the current consensus as to best practice, it is by no means an exaggeration to state that a corporation that had, in 1990, modeled its corporate governance mechanisms, in both process and spirit, on any one of these sets of recommendations, would have been a highly unlikely candidate for a corporate governance scandal or flagrant abuse. Unfortunately, however, all of these best practice recommendations were just that—recommendations—and a sharpened consensus with respect to corporate governance did not mean that most or any of the major corporations in the United States were following, in more than form, best practice.

The Need for Cultural Change and the Blue Ribbon Committee

Almost 20 years to the day after Harold Williams had delivered his speech on the familiar three-act play, Arthur Levitt, then chairman of the SEC, gave another prescient commentary on the future course for corporate governance. For Levitt, corporate America had done too little to implement the recommended corporate governance mechanisms for control of managerial opportunism. Levitt saw "too many corporate managers, auditors, and analysts [as] participants in a game of nods and winks."[110] The managerial motivation to meet Wall Street earnings expectations was "overriding common sense business practices." Indeed, Levitt was concerned that "managing may be giving way to manipulation. Integrity may be losing out to illusion."[111] It is hard to imagine a harsher critique of corporate America, but Levitt, like Williams before him, apparently still believed that the situation could be corrected without government action if there was a voluntary reexamination by "corporate management and Wall Street [of] our current environment [and an] embrace [of] nothing less than a cultural change."[112]

On the same day that Levitt spoke, the NYSE and NASD announced that "in response to recent concerns expressed by . . . Levitt about the adequacy of the oversight of the audit process by independent corporate directors," the two self-regulatory organizations were sponsoring a blue ribbon committee charged with recommending ways to improve the effectiveness of corporate audit committees.[113] In February 1999, this Blue Ribbon Committee issued its report with 10 recommendations "geared toward effecting pragmatic, progressive changes . . . [in] financial reporting and the oversight process."[114] The committee acknowledged that the substantive matters covered by its recommendations had been "studied and commented upon . . . for years," but the committee "anticipate[d]" that "this time" there would be "prompt and serious considerations."[115] And, indeed, before the year was over, the NYSE and NASD had proposed, and the SEC had approved, significant changes to their audit committee listing standards.[116]

Levitt had emphasized the need for more reliable financial reporting to ensure that public confidence was maintained in the integrity of corporate America. The Blue Ribbon Committee concluded that this could be accomplished by making mandatory for listed companies more of the consensus model of corporate governance. The committee, as well as the vast majority of commentators over the past 30 years, saw the board of directors as having the responsibility "to ensure that management is working in the best interests of the corporation and its shareholders" and the independence of a majority of these directors as "critical to ensuring that the board fulfills [this] objective oversight role and holds management accountable to shareholders."[117] The most serious problem the committee found in the existing listing requirements for public companies was that the standards for determining "independence" allowed for "too much discretion and [, therefore,] should be fortified."[118]

Since 1978, the NYSE had required that all listed companies have an audit committee composed of at least three directors, all of whom "in the opinion of the board of directors" are independent of management. Following the recommendation of the Blue Ribbon Committee, the NYSE amended its listing standards by specifying four specific criteria for determining the independence of audit committee members. Also on the recommendation of the Blue Ribbon Committee, the NYSE amended its listing standards to require that each board of directors adopt for its audit committee a formal written charter, which, among other matters, specified that the board and audit committee have the "authority and responsibility" to select, evaluate, and determine the independence of the outside auditor. In addition, the NYSE included in its amended listing standards a requirement that every listed corporation provide to the exchange annually a written confirmation (1) of "the financial literacy" of all audit committee members, (2) that at least one committee member "has accounting or related financial management expertise," (3) that the committee's charter is adequate, and (4) that any board determination regarding director "independence has been disclosed."[119]

In approving the new NYSE audit committee requirements, the SEC stated that these requirements "will protect investors by improving the effectiveness of audit committees. . . . [and] enhance the reliability and credibility of financial statements. . . . by making it more difficult for companies to inappropriately distort their true financial performance."[120] It would have been tempting in 2000 to believe that with the adoption of these amended listing standards, the sharpening of best practice recommendations by the ALI, ABA, and BRT, and the promulgation by the SEC of various new corporate disclosure requirements,[121] corporate governance for America's public companies had finally been gotten right, or at least, was about to be gotten right. As the BRT somewhat immodestly stated in its 1997 white paper:

> The Business Roundtable notes with pride that . . . many of the practices suggested for consideration by The Business Roundtable have become more common. This has been the result of voluntary action by the business community without new laws and regulations. . . . The Business Roundtable believes it is important to allow corporate governance processes to continue to evolve in the same fashion in the years ahead.[122]

Unfortunately, in 2000, corporate governance was not even close to having been gotten right, and the processes for its development were certainly not to be allowed to evolve "in the same [voluntary] fashion" in the years ahead. Despite the recommendations of the Blue Ribbon Committee and the SEC's brave assurances that "the reliability and credibility of financial statements [thereby] would be enhanced," public revelations of corporate scandals and flagrant abuses were to continue at an accelerating pace.

ENRON

The Run-Up

Within months of the issuance of the Blue Ribbon Committee's Report, Rite Aid Corporation, a more than $3 billion corporation listed on the NYSE, restated its operating results for 1997, 1998, and 1999, eventually writing off more than $2.3 billion in pretax profits. Before resigning, Rite Aid's outside auditor publicly announced that the corporation's financial controls were so inadequate that it could not "accumulate and reconcile information necessary to properly record and analyze transactions on a timely basis."[123] Eventually, the SEC charged four former Rite Aid executives, including its former president, with "one of the most egregious accounting frauds in recent history."[124]

Three weeks after the SEC approved the new audit committee requirements, Cendant Corporation, another multibillion dollar company listed on the NYSE, announced that it had agreed to pay stockholders $2.8 billion to settle accusations of widespread accounting fraud.[125] The SEC subsequently brought charges against six former executives, including Cendant's former chairman, for "a long-running financial fraud" that "originate[d] at the highest level of [the] company."[126] According to the FBI agent in charge of the Cendant investigation, "this case boils down to greed, ego, and arrogance."[127]

On June 13, 1998, Sunbeam Corporation, another NYSE listed company, fired its CEO after the corporation's directors began questioning the integrity of the reports they had been given on the financial condition of the company.[128] On August 6, 1998, Sunbeam announced a restatement of its financial statements back to 1996.[129] The SEC eventually charged the former CEO and four other former Sunbeam executives with fraud,[130] alleging that they had "orchestrated a fraudulent scheme to create the illusion of a successful restructuring of Sunbeam [to] facilitate the sale of the company at an inflated price [with enormous gains for its executives]."[131]

In February 1998, Waste Management, Inc., yet another NYSE listed company, acknowledged that it had misstated its pretax earnings by approximately $1.7 billion, the largest corporate restatement in history—until that time.[132] In June 2000, the SEC charged Waste Management with fraud and violations of internal financial control requirements for its failure to "maintain effective and accurate billing, accounting, and management information systems."[133] The SEC subsequently charged Waste Management's former CEO and five other former executives with perpetrating "a massive financial fraud lasting more than five years."[134] Waste Management, it appears, had used a veritable "catalog of ways to cook the books," assuring the executives tens of millions of dollars in stock options and bonuses that would never have been paid out without the accounting fraud.[135]

Perhaps ultimately more important than any of these high-profile scandals and flagrant abuses was the fact that 156 public companies restated their financial statements in 2000,[136] compared with an average of fewer than 50 per year over the previous 10 years.[137] And of the 201 securities fraud class action lawsuits filed in 1999 and 2000, more than half were based on allegations of accounting fraud.[138] Despite these alarming developments, for corporate governance, the worst was yet to come.

Enron

Although by 2001 public belief in the integrity of corporate management and the ability of boards of directors to control managerial opportunism was extremely low,[139] nothing had prepared the public, the regulators, or Congress for the spectacular implosion of, and revelations of fraud by, Enron Corp., another NYSE listed company. Enron was classified as the seventh largest corporation in the United States, with more than $100 billion in gross revenue and more than 20,000 employees worldwide.[140] For the six years immediately before its collapse, *Fortune* magazine had named Enron the most innovative company in America.[141] And in February 2001,

Enron's Chairman, Kenneth L. Lay, and its CEO, Jeffrey K. Skilling, wrote to stockholders:

> Enron has built unique and strong businesses that have tremendous opportunities for growth. . . . The 10-year return to Enron shareholders was 1,415 percent compared with 383 percent for the S&P 500. . . . Our results put us in the top tier of the world's corporations. . . . We plan to leverage all of [Enron's] competitive advantages to create significant value for our shareholders.[142]

Less than eight months later, Enron announced a $544 million after-tax charge to earnings and a $1.2 billion reduction of stockholders' equity, both the result of transactions with an affiliated partnership that had been inappropriately accounted for. On November 19, 2001, Enron filed a further restatement of its financial statements with the SEC, which, among other matters, reduced stockholder equity by $258 million in 1997, $391 million in 1998, $710 million in 1999, and $754 million in 2000. Three weeks later, Enron filed for bankruptcy protection, the largest such filing in history—until then.[143] Thus, in "a span of less than two months during the autumn of 2001, [Enron] fell from business idol to congressional doormat, or somewhat more importantly, from the new business model to a model of business greed and ultimate failure."[144]

Discussions of Enron and its collapse are now legion.[145] According to the report released by Enron's special investigation committee of its board of directors, Enron's board of directors had "failed" in its duty of "oversight" with respect to "the related-party transactions" that brought the company down.[146] The Senate Permanent Subcommittee on Investigations found: "Much of what was wrong at Enron was not concealed from its Board of Directors. . . . The Subcommittee investigation . . . found a Board that routinely relied on Enron management and Andersen representations with little or no effort to verify the information provided, that readily approved new business ventures and complex transactions, and that exercised weak oversight of company operations."[147] And the BRT, hardly a corporate gadfly, ascribed Enron's failure to "a massive breach of trust" involving "a pervasive breakdown in the norms of ethical behavior, corporate governance, and corporate responsibility to external and internal stockholders."[148]

Our concern is not the vehement denunciations of Enron and its management, but the consequences of this massive corporate fraud for the consensus model of corporate governance. By looking at the responses to Enron of the principal spokesmen on issues of corporate governance, it may become easier to understand why Sarbanes-Oxley became an inevitability, particularly when the WorldCom scandal broke only six months after Enron had filed for bankruptcy.

Two Responses to Enron

In the four years immediately preceding Enron's implosion, the BRT and ABA had each issued comprehensive and confident recommendations with respect to best practices for corporate governance. Yet, within weeks of Enron's bankruptcy filing, both organizations convened task forces or special committees to reassess and further refine their positions on best practice for corporate governance.[149] The first to do so was the BRT.

The BRT issued its restatement of the "guiding principles of corporate governance" in May 2002.[150] Three things are striking about the BRT's new position in its *Principles of Corporate Governance*. First, although during 2000 and 2001 more than 300 corporations had restated their audited financial statements, the SEC had filed more than 200 actions alleging financial fraud in 2000, and the five largest corporate bankruptcies in United States history had been filed in the previous 18 months, the BRT continued to insist: "The United States has the best corporate governance [and] financial reporting systems in the world." As for Enron and its fellow travelers, BRT characterized them merely as "notable exceptions to a system that has generally worked well."[151]

Second, in its congressional lobbying efforts, the BRT sought to emphasize "the inherently self-correcting nature of our market system [as evidenced by the fact that] [c]orporate boards of directors are [already] taking steps to assure . . . that Enron-like failures will not occur at their corporations."[152] The BRT's pitch to Congress was that before proceeding with any new legislation, it should give consideration to the "SEC and private sector initiatives already underway [including BRT's] pending update [of] its 1997 Statement on Corporate Governance."[153]

Third, despite its refusal to acknowledge a systemic problem in corporate governance and its initial (pre-WorldCom) opposition to federal legislation in its new *Principles,* the BRT recommended a role and responsibilities for the board of directors that were clearly inconsistent with its 1978 statement and far beyond the position it had taken only five years earlier. For example, rather than urging a relationship between the board and corporate management characterized by "mutual trust . . . [that is] challenging yet supportive,"[154] the BRT's *Principles* describe "effective directors" as those who "maintain an attitude of constructive skepticism [and] ask incisive, probing questions and require accurate, honest answers."[155] Further, in 1997 the BRT had called on corporations to have a "substantial majority [of directors who are] outside (nonmanagement) directors" but had left to each board the determination of the independence of individual directors based on "individual circumstances rather than through the mechanical application of rigid criteria."[156] In its *Principles,* however, the BRT explicitly stated that to be independent, a "director should be free of any relationship with the corporation or its management that may impair, or appear to impair, the director's ability to make independent judgments."[157] And the audit committee's responsibilities, about which the BRT was silent in 1978, include, according to the *Principles,* "supervising the corporation's relationship with its outside auditors . . . [and] [b]ased on its due diligence . . . mak[ing] an annual recommendation to the full board about the selection of the outside auditor."[158]

On July 16, 2002, less than two months after the BRT issued its *Principles,* a specially appointed Task Force on Corporate Responsibility of the ABA (Task Force) issued its own preliminary report.[159] The two reports were poles apart. Unlike the BRT, the Task Force did not see Enron and its fellow travelers as aberrations. To the contrary, the Task Force forcefully acknowledged "the system of corporate governance at many public companies has failed dramatically."[160] Evidenced by "the disturbing series of recent lapses at large corporations involving false or misleading financial statements and misconduct by executive officers," it is apparent, in the view of the Task Force, that "the exercise by [independent directors and advisors] of active and informed stewardship of the best interests of the corporation has, in too many instances, fallen short."[161] Despite the ABA's three editions of the *Corporate Directors Guidebook,* the ALI's massive corporate governance project, the BRT and other business groups' numerous recommendations, the NYSE's listing requirements, and the SEC's jawboning over 20 years, the central feature of the corporate governance consensus to which all of these organizations subscribed—a monitoring board sufficiently independent of management to control managerial opportunism—had too often, the Task Force believed, failed in practice because:

> Many aspects of the outside directors' role have reflected a dependence on senior management. Typically, senior management plays a significant part in the selection of directors, in proposing the compensation for directors, in selecting their committee assignments, in setting agendas for their meetings, and in evaluating their performance. In addition, directors often defer to management for the selection of the key advisors to the board and its committees (e.g., compensation consultants), as well as the outside auditors for the company. Recommendations to create active independent oversight must address these realities and bring about actual change.[162]

For the Task Force, therefore, the solution to the failure of independent directors to perform the role assigned to them was a set of standards that will "establish active, informed, and objective oversight as a behavioral norm [and] create mechanisms that empower [directors] to exercise such oversight."[163] Specifically, all public corporations, in the view of the Task Force, should adhere to tough, new "standards of internal corporate governance," essentially identical to the new listing standards proposed by the NYSE and discussed in the next section of this chapter.

The problem for the Task Force was whether and, if so, how such standards should be imposed. In the third edition of its *Corporate Directors Guidebook,* the ABA had emphasized: "No one governance structure fits all public corporations, and there is considerable diversity of organizational styles. Each corporation should develop a governance structure that is appropriate to its nature and circumstances."[164] And the BRT, only weeks before the Task Force released its report, had asserted, as it had since its first statement on corporate governance in 1978: "Publicly owned corporations employ diverse approaches to board structure and operations, and no one structure is right for every corporation."[165] The Task Force, however, rejected this position, concluding that "substantial uniformity of governance standards applicable to public companies is desirable and would have the greatest impact on reliable corporate responsibility."[166] The trick, of course, was how to achieve that uniformity.

The BRT's approach of allowing corporate governance mechanisms to continue to evolve through "voluntary action by the business community"[167] was now out of the question. And the new listing requirements at the NYSE, by themselves, would not achieve uniform best practice mechanisms for all public corporations. Therefore, the Task Force suggested that the NYSE, NASDAQ, AMEX, and the regional exchanges jointly appoint a new Blue Ribbon Committee to recommend uniform corporate governance standards for adoption by all exchanges.[168] But the Task Force clearly recognized that if "the desired uniformity is not achieved through this approach . . . serious consideration" would have to be given to legislation amending the Securities Exchange Act of 1934 "to empower the SEC to amend the rules of a self-regulatory organization to assure uniformity in listing standards with respect to corporate governance matters."[169]

The Task Force saw the need for tough, uniform corporate governance standards for all public corporations, acknowledged that federal legislation might be necessary to achieve such uniform standards, and even suggested that Congress could achieve the needed uniformity through the intermediation of the SEC. And that is precisely what Sarbanes-Oxley did, at least with respect to audit committees. But one more event, what Harold Williams had called "a single dramatic and widely publicized occurrence," was still needed to spur Congress to the "full-blown and broadly based legislative effort" that would result in the passage of federal legislation.[170]

WORLDCOM

WorldCom, Inc., was the second largest long-distance carrier in the United States. It had 20 million consumer customers, thousands of corporate clients, and 80,000 employees on six continents.[171] Its CEO, Bernard J. Ebbers, was "an icon of the business world."[172] Its common stock, listed on NASDAQ, had hit its high of $96.75 in June 1999, giving it a market capitalization of $191 billion.

On April 22, 2002, WorldCom reduced its revenue projections for 2002 by "at least" $1 billion.[173] Seven days later, Ebbers resigned as President, CEO, and a director "under pressure from outside directors frustrated with the company's sinking stock price, controversy over Mr. Ebbers' $366 million [the May 20, 2000, WorldCom Proxy Statement revealed that the true amount was $408.2 million] personal loan from the company, and the wide-range investigation of the firm by the Securities and Exchange Commission."[174] On June 25, 2002, WorldCom announced that an internal audit had determined that approximately $3.8 billion of expenditures were improperly capitalized rather than expensed.[175] What then followed was the uncovering of "one of the largest accounting frauds in history."[176] The day of the announcement, WorldCom stock closed at $0.83, representing a decline from its high of over 98 percent and a loss of investor wealth of more than $188 billion. The next day the SEC filed suit against WorldCom alleging "a massive accounting fraud totaling more than $3.8 billion."[177] On July 21, 2002, WorldCom filed for bankruptcy protection, listing assets valued at $107 billion, making its filing by far the largest in United States corporate history. Enron, which had previously held that distinction, had listed assets of only $63.4 billion.[178] On August 8, 2002, WorldCom announced that its "ongoing internal review of its financial statements" had uncovered an additional $3.3 billion of "improperly reported earnings."[179] And on August 28, 2002, Scott Sullivan, the former CEO of WorldCom, was indicted in New York for engaging "in an illegal scheme to inflate artificially WorldCom's publicly reported earnings by falsely and fraudulently reducing . . . expenses."[180]

But the accounting misadventures and managerial self-dealing at WorldCom and other corporations that occurred after July 30, 2000, are really irrelevant to our story, for on that date President Bush signed Sarbanes-Oxley into law. It took only 28 days for WorldCom to collapse after its management's accounting fraud was discovered. It took only two days longer for the Senate to pass the new reform legislation, the Conference Committee to reach agreement, both houses of Congress to vote on the compromise bill, and the president to sign it. WorldCom was unquestionably the "bang" that Williams had predicted would end Act II of the familiar play, and Sarbanes-Oxley is obviously the "federal legislation on corporate accountability" that he had reluctantly predicted in 1978 would close Act III.[181]

CORPORATE GOVERNANCE POST-ENRON

Harold Williams' familiar play is now ended. Sarbanes-Oxley has been enacted, the first direct federal regulation since the 1930s of matters of internal corporate governance—matters historically governed by state law and private contract. Yet this legislation did not come about, as Williams feared it would, because the American business community (as represented by its most prominent spokesmen) ignored, stonewalled, or adopted a head-in-the-sand response to the corporate accountability scandals and flagrant abuses of the past 30 years.[182] To the contrary, over that period, a voluntary consensus view of best practice with respect to corporate governance was continually promoted and refined. Indeed, Sarbanes-Oxley, to the extent it addresses audit committee matters, is based directly on this consensus view and is an expression not of Congress's disagreement with the consensus recommendations but of its frustration with the corporate community's inability voluntarily and comprehensively to impose these consensus recommendations on itself.[183]

Yet, significantly, Sarbanes-Oxley imposes on all public corporations only a small part of the full set of best practice standards embraced by the now current consensus view that developed after Enron. This view, expressed in the proposed new listing standards at the NYSE[184] and endorsed by the Task Force[185] and the BRT,[186] goes well beyond the requirements in Sarbanes-Oxley and constitutes the most comprehensive, specific, and rigorous articulation to date of the consensus model of corporate governance best practices. But if the Task Force is correct and "substantial uniformity of governance standards applicable to [all] public companies is desirable,"[187] Sarbanes-Oxley will achieve that uniformity for only certain key consensus standards—primarily with respect to the composition and authority of the audit committee. Left unaffected and decidedly nonuniform are many other important components of the new consensus view, including the composition, selection, and authority of the board of directors as a whole, the composition and authority of other board committees, and the development and content of codes of business conduct and committee charters. In the last section of this chapter, we discuss our overview of the ultimate value of this consensus model and whether the SEC, which appears to be so inclined, should expend significant resources to achieve uniformity in these other areas as well. But before doing so, we conclude the current corporate governance saga with a summary of the principal provisions of Sarbanes-Oxley and the new NYSE listing standards.

Sarbanes-Oxley Act

Most of the press coverage of Sarbanes-Oxley has focused on its creation of a new Public Company Accounting Board[188] and its establishment of new standards of auditor independence.[189] One title of the Act, however, is *Corporate Responsibility,* and four features of Sarbanes-Oxley's approach to corporate governance are worthy of careful note.

As we pointed out previously, the only part of the consensus view of corporate governance that Sarbanes-Oxley enacted into federal law concerns the composition and authority of the audit committee. To an extent, this limited federalization of corporate structure is entirely understandable. Matters of internal corporate structure have been historically the province of state law and private contracts, and Congress is surely correct to legislate in the area only with great deference. Furthermore, the impetus for the Act was the "recent corporate failures [that highlighted the need] to improve the responsibility of public companies for their financial disclosure."[190] It was, therefore, logical for Congress to have limited its incursion into the area of corporate governance simply to assure that all public companies have "strong, competent audit committees with real authority."[191]

Nevertheless, despite the limited federalization of the consensus view of best practice, Congress was prepared to ignore entirely such best practice notions and rely on an entirely different model of corporate governance model when it saw a clear need to control specific types of management opportunism. Thus, for example, Sarbanes-Oxley:

1. Prohibits outright any publicly held corporation from making a loan to any of its directors or officers.[192]
2. Forces the CEO and CFO of any publicly held corporation that is required to file a financial restatement "due to the material noncompliance of the issuer, as a result of misconduct, with any financial reporting requirement under the securities laws" to reimburse the corporation for any bonuses received or profits from stock sales realized during the 12 months following the filing of the inaccurate financial report.[193]
3. Requires CEOs and CFOs to certify that all financial statements filed by their corporations with the SEC "fairly present in all material respects the financial conditions and results of operations of the issuer"[194] and makes it a federal crime to do so "knowing" that the financial statements do not.

4. Prohibits directors and executive officers from selling company stock during benefit plan "blackout periods."[195]
5. Makes it unlawful for any officer or director to take any action "to fraudulently influence, coerce, manipulate, or mislead" the corporation's auditor.[196]

In the consensus view, a strong independent board can and will protect stockholders from management's temptation, in Berle and Means' words, to "direct profits into their own pockets [and fail to run] the corporation . . . primarily in the interest of the stockholders."[197] But at least in these five areas identified, Sarbanes-Oxley reflects Congress's serious doubts as to the ability of the board of directors, however independent, effectively to perform that function.

In the audit committee area, Sarbanes-Oxley does follow the consensus model of corporate governance by requiring every publicly listed corporation[198] to have an audit committee composed entirely of *independent* directors, defined as individuals who are not in any way affiliated with the corporation[199] or receive "any compensatory fee" from the corporation other than for serving on the board of directors.[200] Every public corporation must disclose whether at least one member of its audit committee is a "financial expert" and, if not, why.[201] The audit committee must be "directly responsible for the appointment, compensation, and oversight" of the corporation's outside auditor[202] and preapprove any "nonaudit services" that the outside auditor provides to the corporation.[203] The audit committee is required to receive from the outside auditor reports as to "all critical accounting policies . . . and all alternative treatments of financial information . . . discussed with management."[204] In addition, the audit committee must have "the authority to engage independent counsel and other advisors" and to compensate these advisors through such corporate funding as it determines appropriate.[205]

The method by which Congress chose to impose the new audit committee requirements on publicly listed corporations is precisely that recommended by the Task Force.[206] That is, Sarbanes-Oxley does not impose these requirements directly, but rather requires the SEC to direct the exchanges and NASDAQ to "prohibit the listing" of a corporation that is "not in compliance with these requirements."[207] The significance of this apparently convoluted approach has generally gone unnoticed, but by structuring the audit committee requirements in this way, corporations, their boards of directors, and their audit committee members are not faced with liability in the event the audit committee requirements, for whatever reason, are not adhered to.[208]

Sarbanes-Oxley creates new financial crimes,[209] increases the criminal penalties for many existing financial crimes,[210] and gives the SEC substantial new enforcement authority.[211] It does not, however, except for extending the statute of limitations for fraud,[212] in any way facilitate stockholders' ability to sue for a breach of the securities laws or any new requirement imposed by the Act. Indeed, as noted previously, even an intentional breach of the new audit committee requirements will not be actionable because those requirements will be imposed by self-regulatory organization rules. And enforcement of the new prohibition against fraudulently influencing an auditor is specifically limited to the SEC.[213] Thus, while Congress sought through Sarbanes-Oxley "to increase corporate responsibility," it most clearly did not want to use increased stockholder litigation as a means for accomplishing that objective.

NYSE Listing Standards

In February 2002, at the request of the chairman of the SEC, the NYSE appointed a special Corporate Accountability and Listing Standards Committee (Accountability Committee) to review the NYSE's listing standards in light of Enron. On June 6, 2002, the Accountability Committee issued its report. Although the report of the Blue Ribbon Committee had been completed less than three years earlier, the Accountability Committee saw a need "in the aftermath of the 'meltdown' of significant companies due to failures of diligence, ethics, and controls, [for] the NYSE . . . once again [to use its authority] to raise corporate governance and disclosure standards."[214] Unlike the Blue Ribbon Committee's recommendations, there is little conventional and nothing timid about the recommendations of the Accountability Committee. These recommendations, which in all significant respects have been incorporated in proposed rule changes filed by the NYSE with the SEC on August 1, 2002,[215] are unquestionably the most far-reaching and rigorous expression of the consensus view of corporate governance ever promulgated.[216] A brief summary of certain key provisions of the new listing standards should illustrate their boldness.

The starting point is hardly surprising. All listed companies must have a majority of independent directors.[217] Interestingly, a director does not qualify as "independent" unless the board of directors affirmatively determines that the director has no material relationship with the corporation and that determination (and its basis) is "disclosed in the company's annual proxy statement."[218] In addition, regardless of any board determination, no director may be considered to be independent until five years after he or she ceases to be an employee of, affiliated with the auditor for, part of an interlocking directorate involving, or a member of the immediate family of someone who is not independent of, the listed company.[219]

It is, however, in the powers and authority of the independent directors that the recommendations of the Accountability Committee take the corporate governance paradigm of the strong board of directors to what must be regarded as its apotheosis. First, with the explicit objective of "empower[ing] nonmanagement directors to serve as a more efficient check on management," these directors must "meet at regularly scheduled executive sessions without management."[220] Second, each listed company must have three committees composed solely of independent directors: a nominating/corporate governance committee, a compensation committee, and an audit committee. The nominating committee must have the authority "to select, or to recommend that the board select," the future director nominees and the responsibility to prepare a written charter addressing, among any other matters, "a set of corporate governance principles applicable to the corporation."[221] The compensation committee must "review and approve corporate goals and objectives relevant to CEO compensation, evaluate the CEO's performance in light of those goals and objectives, and set the CEO's compensation level based on this evaluation."[222] With respect to the audit committee, no member of the audit committee may receive any compensation from the corporation other than director's fees; the committee must have "the sole authority to hire and fire independent auditors; and it must preapprove any significant nonaudit relationship with the independent auditors."[223] In addition, the audit committee is empowered "without seeking board approval" to "obtain advice and assistance from outside legal, accounting, or other advisors."[224]

The Accountability Committee's report and the NYSE's actual proposed new listing standards contain many more specific requirements designed to "give the legions of diligent directors better tools to empower them and encourage excellence."[225] Indeed, it is hard to think how independent directors could be more empowered than they will be under the new NYSE standards without seriously interfering with the need for strong, centralized management capable of efficiently making the adaptive decisions necessary for the competitive operation of the modern corporation.[226] The question, of course, to which we now turn, is whether the fully empowered, independent board of directors will have the disposition, incentive, and resolution "to serve as a more effective check on management."

CONCLUSION

Virtually all of the significant developments in corporate governance over the past 30 years flow from a paradigm shift in the general view of the role of the board of directors that occurred in the 1970s. At the start of that decade, boards of directors were seen as operating best through consensus, not conflict, and the outside directors' principal value was understood to be that of experienced, constructive advisors to the CEO, offering knowledgeable and objective perspectives on the company's competitive challenges. As the decade progressed, however, scholarly and regulatory concern was increasingly expressed that such collegial, conflict-avoiding boards were little more than rubber stamps for CEOs. Thus, a consensus of establishment lawyers, academics, and business leaders developed that such boards should be replaced by monitoring boards, characterized by independence, skepticism, and unflinching commitment to stockholders' interests. As corporate scandals and flagrant abuses continued through the 1980s and 1990s, this consensus view of the monitoring board as best practice spread and sharpened, culminating ultimately in Sarbanes-Oxley's audit committee requirements and the NYSE's new listing standards.

But the validity of the consensus view, in general, and of these recent corporate governance initiatives, in particular, rests on the assumption that increases in director independence and empowerment lead to decreases in instances of management opportunism. While it may be difficult to disprove (or prove) this assumption,[227] we offer in closing some brief but skeptical comments on the wisdom of the apparently ever increasing public reliance on it.

First, boards of directors in the late 1990s and early 2000s were undoubtedly far more independent than those in the early 1970s. But surely no one would argue that the managerial misdeeds leading to passage of the FCPA were worse than those leading to passage of Sarbanes-Oxley. Enron, WorldCom, Adelphia, Tyco, and Global Crossing were all listed on the NYSE or NASDAQ. These companies were in full compliance, formally at least, with all applicable requirements for board and audit committee independence, yet it would be hard to find any corporation in the 1970s whose management behaved with comparable piracy.

Second, if independent directors are to perform an effective monitoring role, they need "to bring a high degree of rigor and skeptical objectivity to the evaluation of company management and its plans and proposals."[228] But these characteristics are likely to be far different from the characteristics of directors valued by a CEO for their strategic insights and business acumen. At a minimum, therefore, the consensus demand for a monitoring board forces a tradeoff of strategic vision for skeptical objectivity—without any demonstration that a cost-benefit analysis favors a monitoring versus counseling board. More fundamentally, the success of the monitoring board would appear to depend on the recruitment of directors with profiles very different from those of the directors that now oversee our major corporations. Without exaggeration, the rhetoric used by the NYSE's Accountability Committee and the ABA's Task Force—and the apparent objective of Section 301 of Sarbanes-Oxley—suggests that in recruiting members for their boards of directors, public companies should be looking not for successful executives at other companies, investment bankers with broad industry expertise, or professional consultants with detailed knowledge of business processes and operations, but rather, for former staff members of the SEC's Division of Enforcement. Surely, this cannot be right.

Third, if the premise of the monitoring board is correct, that is, if the stockholders are, in fact, to rely on the independent directors to prevent management opportunism, you would expect that when such a board fails to prevent such opportunism, through negligence or worse, it should be possible to call the board to account for its failure. But that is not the case. "On the contrary . . . many prominent features of corporate law [are] designed for the express purpose of making it difficult for shareholders to hold the board . . . legally responsible, except in the most provocative circumstances. . . . [And it would be] dangerously optimistic [to] assum[e] that the level of judicial supervision of business can be dramatically increased without unforeseeable and incalculable consequences for the efficiency with which businesses make necessary adaptive decisions."[229] Yet, as we assign more and more responsibilities to the independent directors but do not in any way attend to the legal consequences of their negligent performance of these responsibilities, we are, in effect, putting cops on the beat without supervision or risk of sanction. Neither Sarbanes-Oxley nor the NYSE's new listing standards acknowledge this anomaly, but surely the disconnect between director responsibility and director accountability is far too large to remain unaddressed.

Fourth, and finally, the consensus model of best practice in the area of corporate governance represents an attempt to control corporate opportunism through private initiatives, thereby avoiding federal intervention into matters of internal corporate organization and management. Over the past 30 years, the pattern has been for the consensus to recommend independence on corporate boards to prevent further scandals or flagrant abuses. When more scandals and flagrant abuses occur, the consensus recommends even more independence, and then when scandals and flagrant abuses continue, it recommends yet more independence, and so on. In Sarbanes-Oxley, Congress showed its impatience with this continual ratcheting up of the standards for, and powers of, the independent directors by imposing federal bans on matters such as corporate loans to executives and forced executive repayments of bonuses and stock gains before corporate restatements. In doing so, Congress was testing a new approach to corporate governance.

Berle and Means focused corporate scholarship's attention on the risks of management opportunism given the separation of ownership and control. Berle and Means, however, never suggested that a monitoring board was the solution to that endemic corporate problem. At present, the consensus view as to corporate governance best practice is so dominant that it is difficult even to suggest that further empowerment of an independent monitoring board may not be the solution to the current round of corporate scandals and flagrant abuses. Nevertheless, after watching independence and empowerment ratcheted up and up and up for 30 years, our conclusion is that enough is now enough. It is time to recognize that other best practice models of corporate governance need to be evaluated. First, the costs and benefits of allowing an efficient market for corporate control to develop need to be reevaluated. Second, members of the consensus and, particularly, the establishment business community need to think seriously about the trade-offs between boards that *counsel* and boards that *monitor.* And third, attention needs to be paid to other approaches to controlling management opportunism. While more direct federal prohibitions on specific types of management misconduct and more substantive corporate governance authority in the SEC are not particularly attractive on their own, they nevertheless may need to be explored once the impact of Sarbanes-Oxley is thoroughly analyzed. More promising approaches may be carefully tailored oversight of executive compensation, mandatory holding periods for options, and limitations on executive stock sales. An increased role for trained internal monitors is not out of the question, and surely any number of other approaches could be explored. The point is that by turning the corporate board into the "monitor" of corporate management, we do not appear to have been able to stop the scandals and flagrant abuses, and we may well be losing the vision, advice, and competitive perceptiveness that a good board should be providing the CEO. Surely there must be better ways to deal with the consequences of the separation of ownership from control in the modern corporation. The time has come, we believe, to think outside the consensus box.

NOTES

1. Pub. L. 107-204, July 30, 2002, available at http://frwebgate.access.gpo .gov/cgi-bin/getdoc.cgi?dbname=107_cong_bills&docid =f:h3763enr.txt.pdf.
2. Manne (1965), p. 110.
3. On October 16, 2001, Enron announced a $618 billion reduction in third quarter profits and a $1.2 billion loss in shareholder equity (Hays, 2002).
4. In April of 1998, Cendant announced plans to restate its 1997 earnings because of major "accounting irregularities" that resulted in Cendant's

overstating income of up to $115 million. "Cendant to Restate Results," *CNNMoney,* available at http://www.money.cnn.com/1998/04/15/companies/cendant April 15, 1998.

5. In 1998, Sunbeam Corp. restated its 1996 and 1997 financials because of accounting discrepancies (Belstran and Rogers, 2002).

6. In late 1994, Bausch & Lomb announced that excess distributor inventories would reduce 1994 earnings by 54 percent (Maremont and Barnathan, 1995).

7. See *Presidential Campaign Activities of 1972: Hearings Before the Select Comm. on Presidential Campaign Activities,* 93rd Cong., 1st Sess. (1973).

8. See *Activities of American Multinational Corporations Abroad: Hearings Before the Subcomm. on International Economic Policy of the House Comm. On International Relations,* 94th Cong., 1st Sess. 36-37 (1976) (statement of Philip A. Loomis, Commissioner, SEC); SEC, Report of Questionable and Illegal Corporate Payments and Practices (May 12, 1976) (submitted to the Senate Banking, Housing, and Urban Affairs Comm.).

9. See S. Rep. No. 114 (1977); H.R. Conf. Rep. No. 831 (1977), reprinted in 1977 U.S. Code Cong. & Admin. News 4121; Note, Effective Enforcement of the Foreign Corrupt Practices Act, 32 Stan. L. Rev. 561 n.1 (1980).

10. SEC, 94th Cong., *Report on Questionable and Illegal Corporate Payments and Practices* (Comm. Print 1976).

11. Unlawful Corporate Payments Act of 1977, H.R. Rep. No. 95-640, 4 (September 28, 1977).

12. *Foreign Corrupt Practices Act,* Pub. L. No. 95-213, 15 U.S.C. § 78dd et. seq. (December 19, 1977).

13. SEC, Regulation 13B-2, 44 Fed. Reg. 10970 (February 23, 1979).

14. Williams (1978), p. 319.

15. See note 14.

16. See note 14.

17. See note 14.

18. See note 14.

19. See note 14, p. 327.

20. See note 14, p. 319

21. See note 14, p. 320.

22. Legislation was introduced in the House as H.R. 3763 on February 14, 2002, and in the Senate as S. 2673 on June 25, 2002.

23. The chairman and CEO of Goldman Sachs said he "cannot think of a time when business overall has been held in less repute" (McGeehan, 2002, p. A1). See also Morgenson (2002, p. C4), addressing a May CBS/Gallop poll finding that "84 percent feel that [the accounting impropriety] issue is punishing stock prices, ranking it ahead of conflict in the Middle East and terrorism."

24. Klinger et al. (2002), p. 1.

25. See Berman (2002).

26. See Lublin and Sandberg (2002).

27. See Wing (2002), p. 4.
28. Greenspan (2002). "If the past thirty years have demonstrated anything, it is that the avarice of America's corporate leaders is practically unlimited, and so is their power to run companies in their own interest" (Cassidy, 2002, p. 76).
29. Labaton and Oppel (2002).
30. See Williams (1978), p. 319.
31. See Labaton and Oppel (2002).
32. Sarbanes-Oxley was signed into law on July 30, 2002.
33. See Williams (1978), p. 320.
34. *BRT Strongly Supports President Bush's Signing of Accounting and Financial Reform Law* (July 2002), available at www.brtable.org/press.cfm/748.
35. Drucker (2001), p. 113.
36. Berle and Means (1991), pp. 6–7. Adam Smith made much the same point a little over 150 years earlier. In discussing joint stock companies, Smith wrote: "The directors of such companies, however, being the managers rather of other people's money than of their own, it cannot well be expected, that they should watch over it with the same anxious vigilance with which the partners in a private copartnery frequently watch over their own. Like the stewards of a rich man, they are apt to consider attention to small matters as not for their master's honour, and very easily give themselves a dispensation from having it. Negligence and profusion, therefore, must always prevail more or less, in the management of the affairs of such a company" (Smith 1976/1992, vol. 2, p. 741, Chapter v.i.e.).
37. See note 36, p. 313.
38. See note 36, p. 4.
39. See note 36, p. 131.
40. See note 36, p. 293.
41. See Arrow (1974), pp. 68–70.
42. See Berle and Means (1991), p. 219.
43. By *opportunism,* we mean not only management's pursuit of its self-interest at the expense of the stockholders, but also (1) what is generally referred to in the economic literature as the temptation for "shirking," that is, management's tendency to avoid responsibility, negligently perform assigned duties, and free ride on the efforts of others, and (2) the likelihood of systematic deviation from rationality when managers attempt to deal in complex situations and are "erroneously confident" in their knowledge and underestimate the odds that their information or beliefs will be proved wrong. See Bazerman and Messick (1996).
44. Clark (1986), pp. 390–392, and Alchian and Demsetz (1972), p. 777.
45. See Eisenberg (1976).
46. Allen (1992).
47. Bronson (2002).
48. Jensen and Meckling (1976).
49. See Eisenberg (1976), pp. 140–148.

50. Millstein (1993), p. 1485.
51. Lorsch (1995).
52. See, for example, Gordon (2002), Monks and Minow (2001), and Lipton and Lorsch (1992).
53. Mace (1970).
54. Millstein (1993).
55. SEC, Accounting Series Release No. 19 (December 15, 1940).
56. Report of the Subcommittee on Independent Audits and Procedure of NYSE Committee on Stock List (1939), p. 7.
57. Mautz and Newman (1977).
58. Letter from Hills to Batten, Exhibit D to 1976 Report (May 11, 1976).
59. *NYSE Company Manual* A-29 (1980).
60. American Bar Association (1978).
61. See note 60, p. 1619.
62. See note 36.
63. See note 36.
64. BRT (1978).
65. For example, "We enumerate all these legal, regulatory, and political constraints on U.S. business organizations with some mixed emotions because a number of them impose excessive and unnecessary costs [and] impair the effectiveness of U.S. business in a world increasingly characterized by transactional markets and transactional competition." See note 64, p. 293.
66. See note 64.
67. See note 64, p. 310.
68. *Staff Report on Corporate Accountability,* 96th Cong. 2d Sess. Senate Committee on Banking, Housing and Urban Affairs, (Comm. Print, September 4, 1980).
69. See note 68, pp. 8–9.
70. See note 68, p. 428.
71. See note 68, p. 431.
72. See note 68, p. 428.
73. See note 68, p. 437.
74. See note 68, p. 442.
75. See note 68, p. 448.
76. See note 68, p. 469.
77. See note 68, p. 495.
78. See note 68, p. 494.
79. See American Bar Association (1978), p. 32.
80. *Staff Report on Corporate Accountability,* 96th Cong. 2d Sess. Senate Committee on Banking, Housing and Urban Affairs, (Comm. Print, 1980), at 499.
81. See note 80, p. 519.
82. See note 64, pp. 304, 312, 315.
83. See BRT (2002), p. 3.
84. Manne (1965), p. 110.
85. See note 84, p. 113.

86. House Interstate and Foreign Commerce Committee, House Report No. 1711, to Accompanying S.510, 90th Cong. 2nd Sess. (July 12, 1968). Reprinted in 1968 U.S. Code Cong. & Admin. News, Vol. 2 at 2812.

87. Pub. L. 90-439, July 29, 1968.

88. See Securities Exchange Act of 1934 at Sections 13(d)(1) and 14(d).

89. In *Smith v. Van Gorkom,* directors were given the authority to make takeover-related decisions based not on a corporation's market value, but on its "intrinsic value." *Smith v. Van Gorkom,* 488 A.2d 858 (Del. 1985). In *Unocal Corp. v. Mesa Petroleum Co.,* takeover defenses were permitted provided they were "reasonable in relation to the threat posed" test. *Unocal Corp. v. Mesa Petroleum Co.,* 493 A.2d 946 (Del. 1985). In *Revlon v. MacAndrews & Forbes Holdings,* directors were held to have a duty to maximize the short-term value of the corporation once the decision had been made to sell, but they were under no duty to make the corporation available "for sale" at all times. *Revlon v. MacAndrews & Forbes Holdings,* 506 A.2d 173 (Del. 1986). And, in *Moran v. Household International, Inc.,* board authority to adopt "a poison pill" was affirmed, effectively blocking any takeover attempts unless shareholders replaced the directors with a takeover-friendly board. *Moran v. Household International,* 500 A.2d 1346 (Del. 1985).

90. Bainbridge (1995).

91. See Lipton and Steinberger (2001), pp. 1-5 to 1-10.1.

92. Manne (2002).

93. American Law Institute (1994).

94. See generally, *Symposium on Corporate Governance, The Business Lawyer* 48 (August 1993), p. 1267.

95. See American Law Institute (1994), at § 3.02(c).

96. See note 95 at § 3.02(a)(2).

97. See note 95 at § 3A.01.

98. See note 95 at § 3.05.

99. See note 95 at § 3.02(a)(4).

100. See note 95 at § 3A.03.

101. See American Law Institute (1994), at Vol. 1, p. 117.

102. American Bar Association (1994), p. 15.

103. See note 102, p. 16.

104. See note 102.

105. American Bar Association (1978), p. 1627.

106. See note 102, p. 27.

107. BRT (1997).

108. See note 107, pp. 10–11.

109. See note 107, p. 1.

110. Levitt (1998).

111. See note 110. While there were a number of accounting "scandals" that predated Levitt's speech, perhaps the most notorious was reported in 1994 when auditors discovered that Bausch & Lomb's Hong Kong division had inflated sales with a scheme of phony invoices and hidden inventory. Later in the same year, an SEC investigation revealed that the company's contact

lens division inflated 1993 profits by offloading enormous amounts of unwanted inventory to distributors at year-end under delayed payment plans. After these issues surfaced, Bausch & Lomb announced that excess distributor inventories would slash 1994 earnings by 54 percent. Further investigations disclosed a pattern of corporate misdeeds, including funneling products onto the "gray market"; threatening distributors unless they agreed to take excess inventory; preshipping products without obtaining orders and recording them as sales; and providing customers unusually long payment terms. See Maremont and Barnathan (1995). SEC investigations found that Bausch & Lomb had overstated income by $17.6 million. The company later settled a shareholder lawsuit for $42 million. See "Accounting Failures Aren't New—Just More Frequent" (2002).

112. See note 110.
113. SEC, News Rel. 98-96 (Sept. 28, 1998).
114. NYSE and NASD (1999).
115. See note 114, p. 4.
116. SEC, Rel. No. 34-42231 (December 14, 1999); SEC, Rel. 34-42233 (December 14, 1999).
117. See note 114, pp. 20, 22.
118. See note 114, p. 23.
119. NYSE Company Manual § 303.01. The NASD made similar but not identical changes to the NASDAQ listing standards.
120. See SEC, Rel. No. 34-42233 at 9–10; see SEC, Rel. No. 34-42231 at 12.
121. See, for example, revisions to the proxy rules relating to disclosure of executive compensation (SEC, Regulation 14A, Item 10) and audit committees operations (SEC, Regulation 14A, Item 7(d)).
122. See BRT (1997) at Foreword.
123. Norris (2000).
124. SEC, Litigation Release No. 17577 (June 21, 2002).
125. Treaster (1999).
126. SEC, Litigation Release No. 16910 (February 28, 2001).
127. Norris and Henriques (2000).
128. Fields (1998).
129. "Dunlap to Leave Sunbeam Board" (1998).
130. SEC, Litigation Release No. 17001 (May 15, 2001).
131. Norris (2001).
132. SEC, Litigation Release No. 17435 (March 26, 2002).
133. SEC, Release No. 34-42968 (June 21, 2000).
134. SEC, Litigation Release No. 17435 (March 26, 2002).
135. Eichenwald (2002).
136. Min (2001).
137. "Heard on the Street" (2002).
138. PricewaterhouseCoopers Securities Update (2001).
139. In December 2000, 30 percent of Americans had no, or very little, confidence in large corporations and only 9 percent had a great deal of confidence. By comparison, the comparable percentages for Congress were 24

percent and 10 percent. NBC News/Wall Street Journal Poll conducted by Hart-Teeter, available at online.wsj.com/documents/poll-20020724.html.

140. Enron Corp., Form 10-K for Fiscal Year Ended 2000.

141. Barroveld (2002).

142. Enron Corporation (2001).

143. Powers et al. (2002).

144. Clayton et al. (2002).

145. In addition to materials cited elsewhere in this paper, see Fusaro and Miller (2002), International Swaps and Derivatives Association (2002), Bratton (2002). News stories, court developments, reports, and SEC filings with respect to Enron are available at http://news.findlaw.com /legalnews/lit/enron/index.html.

146. See Clayton et al. (2002), p. 148.

147. *The Role of The Board of Directors in Enron's Collapse,* report prepared by the Permanent Subcommittee on Investigations of the Committee on Governmental Affairs, United States Senate, 107th Congress 2d Session, Report 107-70 (July 8, 2002).

148. BRT Press Release, The Business Roundtable Calls Enron Failure "Massive Breach of Trust"; Task Force Chair Raises Outlines Principles for Corporate Governance Before House Panel, March 3, 2002.

149. The BRT and the ABA were by no means the only organizations that issued statements on corporate governance. See, in addition, March 2002 Financial Executives International, Observations and Recommendation Improving Financial Management, Financial Reporting and Corporate Governance; Council of Institutional Investors Corporate Governance Policies available at http://www.cli.org/corp_governance.htm. On June 4, 2002, Institutional Shareholder Services announced the release of its "corporate governance quotient calculation" to "assist institutional investors in evaluating the quality of corporate boards and the impact their governance practices may have on performance." ISS, Press Release, available at http://www.issproxy.com /Press_ Release_CGO_launch percent20_Final.htm.

150. BRT (2002), p. iv.

151. See note 150, p. iii.

152. The Business Roundtable, "Statement of BRT on the Corporate and Auditing Accountability, Responsibility and Transparency Act of 2002 (H.R. 3763)," submitted on March 20, 2002, to the Comm. On Financial Services, H. of Rep., at 2.

153. See note 152, p. 9.

154. BRT (1978).

155. See note 150, p. 3.

156. See note 150, p. 11.

157. See note 150, p. 10.

158. See note 150, pp. 13–14.

159. American Bar Association (2002).

160. See note 159, p. 6.

161. See note 159, pp. 3, 10.

162. See note 159, p. 13.

163. See note 159.

164. American Bar Association (2001).

165. See note 150, p. 9.

166. American Bar Association (2002).

167. See BRT (1997), at foreword.

168. See American Bar Association (2002), p. 15.

169. See note 168, pp. 14–15.

170. See Williams (1978).

171. WorldCom, Form 10-K for the fiscal year ended December 31, 2001.

172. Blumenstein and Sandberg (2002).

173. Young (2002).

174. Blumenstein and Sandberg (2002).

175. WorldCom Announces Intention to Restate 2001 and First Quarter 2002 Financial Statements, WorldCom Press Release, June 25, 2002.

176. Sandberg et al. (2002).

177. SEC, Litigation Release No. 17588 (June 27, 2002).

178. Young et al. (2002).

179. WorldCom Announces Additional Changes to Reported Income for Prior Periods, WorldCom Press Release, August 8, 2002.

180. *United States of America v. Scott D. Sullivan and Buford Yates Jr.*, Indictment ¶ 20.

181. WorldCom was not the only corporate scandal to follow Enron. The Task Force cites the following: (1) On June 25, 2002, Adelphia Communications filed for bankruptcy protection three months after revealing that it had guaranteed loans of $2.3 billion to members of the Rigas family, Adelphia's controlling shareholders (Treaster, 2002, p. C2). Adelphia's common stock, which had reached a high of nearly $28 per share in December 2001, was now essentially worthless (Lauria, 2002). (2) The market capitalization of the stock of Tyco International has fallen by some $100 billion in 2002 after the indictment of its former CEO on charges of state sales tax evasion and because of concerns about the use of corporate funds for the personal benefit of the CEO and the general counsel of the company (see Berenson, 2002). (3) Gary Winnick, the former head of Global Crossing Ltd., sold over $700 million of his stock from 1999 (when the price reached $60 per share), through the end of 2001 shortly before the company's bankruptcy filing. Global Crossing's revenues were alleged to be inflated due to swaps without economic substance (see Stewart, 2002). Before these companies went into bankruptcy, their common stock was traded on the NYSE or the NASDAQ National Market.

182. See Williams (1978), p. 319.

183. Sarbanes-Oxley also contains provisions—blanket prohibitions of loans to corporate executives, recapture of profits from stock sales in the event of an earnings restatement, executive certification of financial statements, and prohibition of executive stock sales during blackout periods—that reflect substantial skepticism with respect to the consensus view that strong boards of directors can effectively control management opportunism.

184. Corporate Governance Rule Proposals Reflecting Recommendations from the NYSE Corporation Accountability and Listing Standards Committee as Approved by the NYSE Board of Directors, August 1, 2002, available at www.nyse.com. On August 21, 2002, NASDAQ's Board of Directors approved a comprehensive package of corporate governance reforms that basically tracks the NYSE's new listing standards. Because the full text of the NASDAQ proposals are not yet available, we will cite hereafter only to the NYSE Standards. A summary of the NASDAQ Corporate Governance proposal is available at http://www.NASDAQnews.com/about/corpgov /Corp_Gov_ Summary082802.pdf.

185. See American Bar Association (2002), pp. 16–21.

186. The Business Roundtable Praises the New Listing Standards of the New York Stock Exchange, BRT Press Release, August 1, 2002, available at http://www.brtable.org/press.cfm/751.

187. See American Bar Association (2002), p. 14.

188. See note 187 at Title I.

189. See note 187 at Title II.

190. Public Company Accounting Reform and Investor Protection Act of 2002, Report of the S. Comm. On Banking, Housing and Urban Affairs, to accompany S. 2673, 107th Cong., 2d Sess., Rep. 107-205, 23 (July 3, 2002).

191. See note 190.

192. See note 1 at § 402. This provision could well have far-reaching implications for several well-established corporate employee benefit programs. See Rozhon and Treaster (2002) and Treaster and Rozhon (2002).

193. See note 1 at § 304. Presumably, this provision can be enforced in the same manner as the current prohibition on short-swing profits in Section 16(b) of the Securities Exchange Act of 1934, that is, through stockholder derivative action.

194. See note 1 at § 302. The SEC has now adopted rules implementing section 302 of Sarbanes-Oxley as well as imposing extensive additional requirements concerning internal controls for both disclosure and financial reporting. SEC, Rel. No. 33-8124, Certification of Disclosure in Companies' Quarterly and Annual Reports, August 29, 2002.

195. See note 1 at § 306.

196. See note 1 at § 303.

197. Berle and Means (1991), pp. 6–7.

198. This is a narrower universe than that of all public corporations because it includes only corporations "listed" on NASDAQ or another exchange.

199. This is a defined term and includes any person directly or indirectly controlling, controlled by, or under common control with the corporation. See Securities and Exchanges Act of 1934, § 3(a)(19).

200. See note 1 at § 301.

201. See note 1 at § 407.

202. See note 1.

203. See note 1 at § 202.

204. See note 1.

205. See note 1 at § 301.

206. See American Bar Association (2002).

207. See note 1 at § 301.

208. The generally accepted legal doctrine is that there is no private right of action for violation of rule of a self-regulated organization.

209. See note 1 at §§ 802, 807, 1102, and 1107.

210. See note 1 at §§ 902, 903, 904, and 1106.

211. See note 1 at §§ 305, 602, and 1105.

212. See note 1 at § 804.

213. See note 1 at § 303.

214. *Report of New York Stock Exchange Corporate Accountability and Listing Standards Committee* (June 6, 2002).

215. Corporate Governance Rule Proposals Reflecting Recommendations from the NYSE Corporate Accountability and Listing Standards Committee as Approved by the NYSE Board of Directors, August 1, 2002, available at www.nyse.com.

216. While the NYSE's actual proposed rule changes were approved by its Board after enactment of Sarbanes-Oxley, the Corporate Accountability Committee's recommendations on which they were based were made almost two months before the Act was signed into law and several weeks before Senator Sarbanes' Senate Banking Committee reported the bill. The NASDAQ Stock Market has proposed somewhat similar requirements. NASDAQ Press Release, June 5, 2002.

217. See note 215 at ¶ 1. The NYSE had previously required a listed company to have only three independent directors, all of whom were to serve on the audit committee. NYSE Listed Company Manual, § 303.01 (B)(2)(a).

218. See note 215 at ¶ 2(a) and Commentary.

219. See note 215 at ¶ 2(b).

220. See note 215 at ¶ 3.

221. See note 215 at ¶ 4.

222. See note 215 at ¶ 5.

223. See note 215 at ¶ 7(a).

224. See note 215 at ¶ 7(b)(ii)(E) and Commentary.

225. See note 215 at 1.

226. See Arrow (1974).

227. But see Bhagat and Black (1999). "[Evidence suggests] the opposite—that firms with super majority-independent boards perform worse than other firms, and that firms with more inside than independent directors perform about as well as firms with majority (but not super majority) independent boards."

228. Langevoort (2001).

229. Dooley (1992).

PART TWO

Energy and Derivatives Markets after Enron

4

WHOLESALE ELECTRICITY MARKETS AND PRODUCTS AFTER ENRON

Andrea M. P. Neves

O f the numerous energy markets in which Enron Corporation was an active participant, electricity markets have received the most attention.[1] No doubt one reason for this is the conventional belief that power is a "public good," and that low-priced electricity and reliability are "rights" to which consumers are naturally entitled—like national defense.[2] Both the size of Enron's activity in global power markets and Enron's alleged complicity in contributing to (or exacerbating) the California energy crisis of 2000 have brought about the realization that an otherwise complex trading market and John Q. Public are innately connected. The unusual features of electricity (e.g., nonstorability) itself have also led to confusion about what exactly "wholesale power markets" are, what Enron did in these markets, and whether the firm's activities were on balance stabilizing or *destabilizing* for the market in general.

This chapter provides a brief primer on the U.S. power market to help explain the function and operation of this market and Enron's place in the market. The first section provides a brief history of Enron itself and its role in the development of energy markets. The second section presents basic concepts key to understanding electricity markets. In the third section, the types of participants in the wholesale power market are reviewed, followed by a discussion of the most common contracts that allow electricity to be traded both physically and *financially*. Next, some of the challenges that this market faced before Enron's failure are explored, including the credit crisis of 1998 and the California energy crisis of 2000.

The last section concludes with a comment on the likely consequences of Enron's failure on the future of this growing and important marketplace.

A BRIEF HISTORY OF ENRON

In July 1985, Houston Natural Gas, led by CEO Kenneth Lay, merged with InterNorth, another natural gas company based in Omaha, Nebraska. The newly formed company owned more than 37,000 miles of natural gas pipeline and became the first firm to own pipelines that crossed the nation. In 1986, Lay was named chairman and CEO of the new company, which was renamed Enron.

Enron faced credit difficulties early on in 1987 when oil traders from New York overextended the company's accounts by almost $1 billion. Over a short period of time, Enron reduced these losses to $142 million.[3] In doing so, Enron developed a set of services aimed at reducing the risk of price swings in commodities markets–the first sign of many financial innovations to come.

Jeffrey Skilling began advising Enron in 1985 as a consultant for McKinsey and joined Enron in 1989. During that time, the company launched a program called *GasBank* that allowed natural gas buyers to lock in fixed prices for gas purchases over long periods. In other words, Enron began trading *forward contracts* on gas (more on this later). In addition, Enron offered financing for gas and oil producers, acting as a sort of investment bank for the gas industry. Soon, Enron evolved into the largest natural gas merchant in North America and abroad.

In 1988, the United Kingdom deregulated its own power industry, and Enron opened its first overseas office there. Enron's decision to participate in this newly deregulated, emerging market was the sign of a major shift in strategy away from its existing pipeline business—a line of business that the company would continue to pursue over time—toward extending its GasBank model into the new, emerging power market.

Enron's growth internationally over the next several years was impressive. In 1992, Enron expanded its existing reach for pipeline business into South America through the purchase of Transportador de Gas del Sur. In the meantime, an Enron-owned power plant in England began operations. Both significant events illustrate the rising success of Enron's international strategy in the pipeline business. In addition, Enron Europe established a trading center in London in 1995, marking the company's first entry into the European wholesale power market and identifying Europe as the company's primary growth market in the overseas power markets.

During this period of international growth, Enron was also growing domestically. The company's strategy was equally wide-reaching but focused on the new power industry. Enron made its first electricity trade in 1994 and thus initiated what would eventually become the company's largest profit center. In late 1996, Skilling was named president and COO of Enron while maintaining his ongoing role as chairman and CEO of Enron Capital & Trade Resources.

In 1997, Enron decided to expand its role in the electricity business by buying Portland General Electric Corporation, the utility serving the Portland, Oregon, area. In addition, Enron Energy Services was formed to provide management solutions to commercial and industrial customers throughout the United States. Also during this year, Enron formed its broadband services group, another foray into a new commodity.

Perhaps the most significant development to take place for Enron occurred in late 1999 with the establishment of the company's Internet-based trading platform, EnronOnline, described as an Internet-based global transaction system that allows participants to view real-time prices from Enron's traders and transact instantly online.[4] With close to 2,000 products listed for trading at one point, this quickly became the largest e-business site in the world, averaging 6,000 transactions per day and worth about $2.5 billion.

By March 2000, the Energy Financial Group ranked Enron as the sixth largest company in the world based on market cap.[5] On December 28, 2000, Enron shares hit a record high of $84.87, making Enron the country's seventh most valuable company with a market value of more than $70 billion. Enron's participation in electricity markets was a large reason for this degree of success.

KEY CONCEPTS TO UNDERSTANDING ELECTRICITY MARKETS

Electricity can be generated from a variety of sources including water, coal, gas, and nuclear energy. Often the choice of generation asset depends on the availability of the natural asset as well as regulatory guidelines, hence the distinct geographical concentration of different generational facilities across the country as well as the disparity in prices depending on the costs of production.

After generation, electricity goes through two distinct but similar processes: transmission and distribution. Transmission occurs immediately after generation and consists of maintaining power current in a *grid system* where the electricity voltage or strength is adjusted using transformers. These grid systems are akin to our central nervous system, serving as an electron highway. Interconnection sites exist at strategic locations within the grid system such as the PJM hub covering Pennsylvania, New Jersey, and Maryland. Many utilities are tied into these interconnection sites, thus allowing a single utility to generate power that can be used by other utilities and consumers anywhere in the grid system.

Maintaining a proper voltage and frequency in a power transmission grid ensures that electricity "wheels," or regularly flows, through sub-transmission grids that route electricity to end users. Transmission typically occurs on a high-voltage grid—too high for end users to access directly. Accordingly, distribution is the process by which power is taken from the high-voltage transmission system and transformed into lower voltage current that is sent to end consumers through wires, plugs, and the like. End users may be categorized into three main types: residential, commercial (e.g., office buildings and retail stores), and industrial (e.g., large-process operations).

Two concepts are key to electricity generation and distribution: load and capacity. *Load* refers to the level of electricity demand in a given period, usually distinguished as day and night. *Peak* load refers to time when demand for electricity is at its highest—in the United States, usually over a sixteen-hour period from 7 A.M. until 11 P.M. *Load factor* is defined as the difference between the average demand and peak demand over a given period. *Capacity* refers to a utility's ability to meet its native load. Should peak demand exceed expected or average demand, a utility may be under capacity. This may occur for a variety of reasons, ranging from generation failures and equipment faults to the loss of electrons along a poor-quality transmission path.

DEREGULATION AND THE RISE OF INDEPENDENT POWER MARKETERS

In a 1970s effort to encourage electricity conservation and unconventional means of producing power, Congress passed the Public Utility Regulatory Policies Act. Besides increasing competition, this act laid the groundwork for deregulation by opening wholesale power markets to nonutility producers of electricity. Nevertheless, the power "market" remained largely segmented by region, and "trading" was limited to short-term power purchases and sales undertaken primarily to serve a load and ensure reliability.

In 1992, Congress passed the Energy Policy Act, which allowed individual utilities to expand their reach beyond previously designated supply regions. A utility in Texas, for example, thus could now also own generation facilities and produce electricity in California as long as the utility's original Texas customers were not disadvantaged. This act also required utilities to make their transmission systems available to other utilities. Electricity thus could now be freely purchased or sold before final delivery to the customer.[6]

In 1996, the Federal Energy Regulatory Commission (FERC) released Orders 888 and 889, whose stated objectives were to "remove impediments to competition in the wholesale bulk power market and to bring more efficient, lower cost power to the Nations' electricity consumers."[7] The orders went further to say that the purpose of lifting prior restrictions was to "facilitat[e] the State's restructuring of the electric power industry to allow customers direct access to retail power generation," thus laying the groundwork for states to deregulate *retail* electricity distribution and rates.[8]

The belief behind deregulation was that more competitive markets would lead to more efficient generation, increased technological innovation, and, eventually, reduced electricity prices for consumers.[9] The notion that market discipline should determine both prices and fair practice became the dominant theme in regulation during the 1980s.

Not everyone, however, supported electricity deregulation. Regulated utilities provided strong opposition by arguing that competition would not allow previously regulated utilities to recover their "sunk costs." To cover the costs they incurred in building generation plants and laying transmission lines, these utilities felt they needed to charge certain prices for electricity. They feared that new entrants that could move power from one region to another would be able to charge less for electricity, hence driving down electricity prices and making cost recovery impossible.

For example, consider a new wholesale generator that can buy a relatively inexpensive gas turbine generator fueled with cheap natural gas from the Southeast and sell that electricity in the same market as a utility that operates an expensive nuclear power plant in the Northeast.[10] In that case, the existing Northeast utilities would be stuck holding the sunk costs associated with expensive production facilities and even perhaps some long-term contracts with suppliers of generation assets that were all negotiated in the previously regulated business environment. In the meantime, however, any outstanding contracts to customers would be waived and renegotiated in the new, competitive business environment. In other words, there would be no "level playing field" in which old utilities and new providers could compete fairly.[11]

In the end, deregulation passed and laid fertile ground for the birth of the *power marketing* industry. Power marketers are different from utilities in that they have no ownership of generation assets or equipment to produce and distribute electricity. Instead, they simply buy energy and transmission services from traditional suppliers and resell the electricity to other utilities or power distributors. Power marketers thus treat electricity purely as a *commodity* defined in terms of megawatts per hour (MWh).

Power marketers emerged in two basic forms. The first were essentially trading houses, whose sole purpose was to make a profit on the spread between electricity bought and sold. The second were power marketers owned by and/or affiliated with utilities and other physical suppliers. Although trading for a profit is a common goal at many such operations, power marketers affiliated with power suppliers are also often intended to help ensure that power can be acquired at the lowest cost by the affiliated generator—a task actually at odds with maximizing trading revenues.

Power marketers of all types helped *liquefy* the wholesale power market by helping mix and match suppliers to achieve the best combination of prices with which electricity can be packaged and resold. For example, consider Utility A that sells peak electricity at $32/MWh and nonpeak electricity at $18/MWh and Utility B that sells peak electricity at $33.50/MWh and nonpeak electricity at $17.25/MWh. A power marketer could buy peak electricity from Utility A and nonpeak electricity from Utility B to resell to a municipality at a combined price lower than that customer could receive buying from just one utility supplying electricity. Power marketers transact among each other and the trading entities established by existing utilities. In other words, the seller does not have to generate the electricity being dealt, merely acquire it through a similar transaction.

Overall, power marketers are key players in achieving the stated goals of deregulation by reducing prices through competition. In addition, power marketers play an important role in diversifying the market in terms of the number of available players.

TRADING ELECTRICITY WITH WHOLESALE POWER MARKET PRODUCTS

Active trading of different contracts for the delivery of wholesale power began to boom in the mid-1990s following deregulation and the inflow of power marketers into the industry. Enron quickly became one of the key players in this market, acting mainly as a *market maker* to which electricity was both bought and sold by the firm in an effort to make a profit. Many of the products sold in this market—a number of which were conceived by Enron—were aimed at helping power suppliers manage the price risks associated with their future purchases of electricity.

Spot and Forward Contracts

Spot and forward power purchase agreements are the simplest types of contracts employed in wholesale power marketing. These are simple agreements where the purchaser agrees to buy a certain amount of electricity at a designated interconnection point for delivery over a certain period at a specified price from the seller. From an economic and trading perspective (in contrast to the legal/regulatory one explored in Chapter 5), a transaction calling for the delivery of power on the same day (a *real-time* transaction) or the next day (a *day-ahead* transaction) is called a *spot* power purchase agreement. Transactions for delivery further in the future are known as forward contracts. For example, Power Marketer Z could agree to buy 50 MWh of peak electricity (defined over a 16-hour period) for every weekday of the next month from Power Marketer Y in the PJM hub at a fixed price of $36 per MWh.

Now suppose that Power Marketer Y may have acquired this electricity by buying two separate forward contracts for 25 MWh of peak electricity to be delivered in the next month into the PJM hub, one with a price of $34 per MWh from Power Marketer Q and another at a price of $34.50 per MWh from Power Marketer R. Hence, by reselling this electricity to Power Marketer Z, Power Marketer Y stands to make $2 per MWh from electricity originally bought from Q and $1.50 per MWh on electricity originally bought from R. A $3.50 profit on 50 MWh over 16 hours per day for every weekday of the month adds up to $56,000 total profit (assuming 20 trading days per month and no commissions, for illustrative purposes).[12]

As the previous example shows, forward contracts can be negotiated for different amounts of electricity (although typically in units of 25 MWh) and over different periods (e.g., weeks, single or multiple months, or even annual). It is up to the power marketer to recombine incoming transactions to match the outgoing transactions so that there is never any excess or lack of electricity to meet contract specifications.

In addition, traders typically use electricity designated for one geographical hub or interconnection point to meet contracts at that same point because of high costs and inefficiencies associated with wheeling electricity from one hub to another. In fact, should a shortage occur during periods of normal market behavior, it is often cheaper and more reliable simply to buy electricity in the spot market within the same hub to meet a demand shortage than to arrange for interhub transfers.

Options Contracts

A *call* option gives the buyer the right, but not the obligation, to purchase electricity from the seller with specified terms of delivery location and quantity. Similarly, a *put* option gives its buyer the right, but not the obligation, to sell electricity with similar terms. An option's *strike price* is the prenegotiated purchase or selling price.

To demonstrate how options work, reconsider the forward contract transacted between Power Marketers Z and Y as a call option with strike price of $36 per MWh purchased from Y by Z. In this case, Z would buy electricity from Y only if market prices exceed $36 per MWh because, in any such case, it would be cheaper to exercise the option at $36 than pay more for the electricity in the spot market. If the price is below $36/MWh, Z lets the option expire worthless and buys electricity from the spot market. For the value of this right to choose, Z pays Y a premium at the beginning of the transaction; forwards, by contrast, involve no initial payment.

Options on wholesale power can be designated as daily or monthly strike options. If the option has a daily strike feature, the decision of whether to exercise the option for delivery of power can be made on a daily basis. Alternatively, if the option has a monthly strike feature, the exercise decision must be made before the start of the designated month (assuming it is a one-month option) for delivery of electricity during every specified day of that month.[13] In other words, the monthly strike option, once exercised, becomes the equivalent of a monthly forward contract with the fixed price set at the strike price of the option. Like forwards, options may be struck over a variety of time horizons, including for the next day or week, any future month or months, or even over the following year(s).

Many additional features may be found in wholesale power options, including options with flexible quantity known as *swing options,* options with strike prices set equal to average historical prices known as *Asian options,* options that allow for plays on the seasonal variations in electricity prices, and the like. Overall, the flexibility that these instruments offer is tremendous.

Forwards with Embedded Options

Options are also available when they are "embedded" into forwards. The forwards already discussed that involve an absolute obligation of the seller to deliver power to the buyer are known as *firm* forward agreements. To reduce the price of power purchased, buyers often embed an option that allows sellers to interrupt deliveries if prices rise by some amount. Such contracts are called *nonfirm* power purchases. If Z buys power in a forward from Y at $36/MWh, for example, Z may also choose to embed a short call struck at $40/MWh, which means that if prices rise above $40/MWh, Y can choose to "interrupt" delivery to Z and sell that power for the higher price in the real-time market. Because Z has sold the call option to Y, Z collects the option premium, which is applied to the forward purchase price and results in a lower all-in cost of power for Z than if Z had purchased firm power.

If Z wants to protect itself against catastrophic price increases above $50/MWh, for example, Z may also embed a *purchased* call struck at $50/MWh in the same contract. Called an *interruptible buy-through,* this position bundles a straight forward with a price of $36 with a short call struck at $40 and a long call struck at $50. As you can see, the possible combinations are practically limitless.

Financial Power Contracts

The vast majority of contracts in the wholesale power market involve the physical delivery of power. A handful of products, however, are purely financial—that is, they call for cash settlement based on a power price, but do *not* call for power deliveries. Forwards and options, for example, may be cash-settled, but rarely are in practice. Similarly, the New York Mercantile Exchange formerly listed exchange-traded forwards or *futures* that involved cash settlement, but those contracts were delisted in February 2002 because of inactivity.

A swap contract—also known as a *CfD* or *contract for differences*—is a financial contract in which two parties agree to exchange a series of cash flows over time based on differences between a fixed energy price and a floating energy price, where the latter is usually based on the spot price of electricity at a defined hub on the specified settlement dates. Swaps can be customized with many flexible features. Like forwards, parties that enter into swaps often do so to manage their exposure to future changes in electricity prices.

Multiasset swaps are increasingly popular in wholesale power markets. Such contracts facilitate cross-commodity risk diversification by defining cash flows based on the floating prices of different commodities. Consider, for example, a utility with a gas-turbine generator whose profit margin falls either when gas prices rise or when electricity prices fall. To protect against shrinking margins, the utility could enter into a swap on "the spark spread" in which the utility periodically receives (or, if negative, pays) a net cash flow equal to a floating gas price *less* a floating electricity price. When gas prices rise, higher swap income offsets higher turbine expenses. And when electricity prices fall, higher swap income offsets losses on electricity sales generated by the turbine.

BUMPY ROADS IN AN EMERGING MARKET

Electricity prices can be influenced by a wide range of factors such as geographical distinctions, weather unpredictability, transmission congestion, and the like, all of which make the determination of future electricity prices extremely difficult. These features also tend to make electricity prices highly volatile. Not surprisingly, the deregulated wholesale power market has had its share of bumps in the road.

Summer of 1998

In the beginning of 1998, the wholesale electricity market appeared to be running smoothly. There had been a large influx of new participants into the market that existed purely as trading entities with the purpose of making profits in electricity, and it appeared that the extra liquidity added by these independent power marketers was significant. Certain circumstances arose during the summer of 1998, however, that put the industry into a tailspin.

Starting in late June, the Midwestern and Northeastern parts of the United States experienced phenomenally high temperatures, resulting in high demands for electricity to power air conditioning. During this same period, several nuclear reactors in these regions were already off-line for regularly scheduled maintenance. And to complicate matters, several other unplanned plant and equipment faults created a sudden scarcity of generation capacity relative to loads. In addition, massive transmission congestion prohibited reliable movement of electricity from one region to another. Market participants without adequate generation capacity relied on purchasing electricity in the spot market to meet their contractual supply obligations. Bids for power in the real-time market in the Midwest soared from an average summer price of about $65/MWh to as high as $7500/MWh on June 26, 1998.

Many utilities had sought to balance their loads using forward purchase agreements. Unfortunately, not all the *sellers* of these agreements, it turned out, were relying on generation capacity of their own, or even on other forward contracts. They, too, were forced into the spot market, and a "daisy chain" of contract defaults soon began.

The first player to default on its contractual obligations was a small, independent power marketer named Federal Energy. Not unlike a large handful of new participants in this market, Federal Energy was basically an overnight trading operation with no generation assets. Another power marketer, Power Company of America (PCA), was buying a significant amount of its electricity supply from Federal Energy, so it was not long before PCA began defaulting on its contracts as well. Firms below PCA and Federal Energy in the delivery chain were forced to replace electricity from defaulted forward contracts at the extreme spot prices that in turn led to the failure of additional market participants such as Stand Energy and American Energy and led to huge losses at places such as the municipality of Springfield, Illinois. Louisville Gas & Electric—a large and significant market player—sustained a highly publicized $225 million in losses from purchases from PCA and decided to exit the trading industry entirely. Similarly, First Energy suffered defaults on contracts that led to $70 million worth of losses from covering what had previously been a balanced load until the counter party defaults occurred.

Before the summer of 1998, market participants had been well aware of *market* risk, or the risk of price volatility. Indeed, firms such as Enron were so successful as market makers in large part because they provided utilities with products designed to help other firms manage those market risks. But the summer of 1998 illustrated a new risk in the market—one well known to bankers but, unfortunately, largely ignored before then by power market participants—credit risk. Participants experienced significant losses of real income, and some regions even experienced reliability problems. The danger of having so many inexperienced, poorly capitalized independent power marketers with no generation assets came to light for the first time, as well as the awareness of the risks of highly concentrating transactions with single counter parties as opposed to diversifying.

The natural blame for these problems was placed on deregulation. Amid accusations of collusion and price fixing during the crisis by certain stronger players, FERC formed a special committee to evaluate the price reaction in the market. This committee concluded that there was no illegal market manipulation by any participants in the market. Rather, an unusual combination of unpredictable events precipitated market panic that resulted in the high price spikes. In addition, FERC blamed the inexperience and lack of caution used by market participants for the failures.[14]

California's Power Shortage

The second large crisis to hit the electricity industry began in California in 2000. This incident has perhaps had greater implications than the bankruptcies of 1998 because it visibly affected so many customers, going against the long-held industry standards of reliability.

California has long been faced with serious demand and supply shocks. The recent years have seen extreme weather patterns due to El Niño and strong economic growth in the area that led to increased demand. On the other side, a tremendous run-up of natural gas prices, combined with existing scarcity, led to dramatic increases in wholesale electricity prices in the region. In addition, California is constrained by tough antipollution controls that reduce generation opportunities. Starting in July 2000 and continuing through the end of the year, California faced real supply shortages, ultimately forcing the largest utilities into significant financial crises and causing disruptions in actual power delivery.

Once again, the most popular villain for California's electricity problems—before Enron, at least—was deregulation. The Energy Policy Act of 1992 encouraged each state to handle the retail aspect of deregulation on its own. The California Public Utility Commission (PUC), along with the state legislature, was responsible for designing a plan that had tremendous political support but turned out to create more problems than it solved.

The California plan had two key provisions. The first was the creation of a single *independent system operator*—Cal ISO—that was responsible for all transmission scheduling for the region, and the second was the creation of the California Power Exchange (Cal PX) on which all day-ahead and real-time spot power trading was to occur. In turn, the three major investor-owned utilities of California—Pacific Gas & Electric (PG&E), San Diego Gas & Electric, and Southern California Edison—were forced to cede all of their transmission control responsibilities to Cal ISO. To encourage transparency and price discovery, the utilities were also prohibited from using forward contracts and were required instead to make their power purchases in the spot market on Cal PX. Finally, retail prices were frozen so that utilities could not pass through any of their costs to customers.

Soon after the new plan was implemented in the late 1990s, Cal ISO imposed a power price purchase cap of $750/MWh that prohibited any purchases by the ISO at any prices above that amount. The price cap was first reached in May 2000 and marked the beginning of the California crisis. In July 2000, Cal ISO lowered the cap to $500/MWh and again to $250/MWh in August. As a result, fewer and fewer bids for power came into Cal ISO, and this severe bid insufficiency forced Cal ISO to meet current load requirements primarily in the spot real-time market. So, on the one hand, reliability was jeopardized by bid insufficiency, and, on the other hand, the utilities were hemorrhaging on forced purchases at the $250/MHh cap that could not be passed on to ratepayers.

FERC determined that the primary causes of the California crisis were twofold. The first was the extreme price volatility to which utilities were subject, mainly because of their inability to manage their risks with forward contracts. The second alleged cause of the crisis was market manipulation, in large part allegedly conducted by Enron. Trading abuses of which FERC has accused Enron include exaggerating load schedules, scheduling transmission on lines that were physically not functioning to get falsely based congestion payments, and selling power out of California at the price cap in the day-ahead market to a firm that preagreed to sell the power back to Cal ISO the next day in the real-time market at *uncapped* prices (because they were coming in from outside the Cal ISO control zone).

Many of the strategies with which Enron is alleged to have manipulated the market are actually ordinary transactions in wholesale power markets. Selling power in the day-ahead market to buy it back in the real-time market is more commonly known as *parking and lending* or *banking* power and, provided it is done within the FERC rules (e.g., still adheres to open access rules for transmission), is a legitimate "calendar spread" trade that is actually *liquidity enhancing*.

Other transactions in which Enron supposedly engaged in manipulative activities were, at least to some extent, a result of the specific rules of the California system. Several of Enron's activities alleged by both FERC and the recent grand jury to be manipulative in nature, for example, concern the firm's abuses of congestion charges assessed by Cal ISO. Specifically, when a transmission line is *scheduled* to be congested, users of the line must pay a congestion charge to Cal ISO. The proceeds from this congestion charge are then used to compensate holders of financial contracts called *fixed transmission rights* or to those firms that schedule transmission *against* a congested flow. The congestion charges typically were distributed by Cal ISO *pro rata* to all those that qualify. Enron attempted to abuse this system in several ways, including scheduling transmission on lines known to be nonworking. Enron thus could collect a congestion charge without ever having to engage in real transmission. Similarly, Enron was overscheduled in certain areas to create artificial congestion in an effort to make its fixed transmission rights more valuable.

Although the latter examples are clear indications of how Enron abused the system, equally true is that the system itself may well have been flawed at the design level. Cal ISO, after all, was a centralized government attempt to coordinate transmission, rather than allowing utilities to engage in that practice competitively among themselves. Enron may not be blameless for the way it "gamed" the Cal ISO rules, but the rules themselves should also not be held blameless.

ENRON'S FAILURE AND THE MARKET'S REACTION

Enron's involvement in electricity markets was not to blame for the company's demise. To put it simply, Enron failed because of a series of fundamentally bad investments in large capital-intensive projects, aided by fraudulent financing and misleading accounting that allowed the firm to conceal those losses for a long time. When, in late 2001, Enron finally began to disclose the full magnitude of these losses and the accounting shams on which it had relied to hide those losses and camouflage its true indebtedness, the result was a precipitous decline in the firm's stock price, a rating downgrade, a liquidity crisis, and, ultimately, the firm's bankruptcy filing in early December 2001.

There are many theories on who is to blame for Enron's collapse, and sorting these out will take an extremely long time to resolve. Meanwhile, it is worth looking instead at how the industry as a whole was affected by Enron's failure.

The impact of Enron's fallout has been extensive in the market, bringing again more heightened scrutiny to energy deregulation and credit issues within the market. A number of companies that had been trading counter parties to Enron were hit significantly on their share prices, such as Calpine, Dynegy, Mirant, and Williams. Other firms that did not lose money on Enron per se have, nevertheless, suffered indirectly. Despite initial claims to the contrary, few companies have emerged completely unscathed.

Apart from the pure market impact of Enron's demise, the credit exposures of firms to Enron through EnronOnline have also cast a pallor over the business-to-business and virtual exchange world. Unlike most traditional exchanges in which a large clearinghouse backs up all transactions, trades conducted on EnronOnline were all trades *with Enron*. Firms in a wide range of markets may now think twice before relying so heavily on an electronic trading platform in which a single, questionably capitalized sponsor is accountable for all the credit risk.[15]

Finally, the failure of Enron has brought to light a number of questions concerning the regulation of electricity markets in the United States. These issues are addressed in subsequent chapters of this volume.

NOTES

1. Attention by regulators to Enron's natural gas activities has also been significant, but these investigations have not received the same degree of *public* attention. Mainly for that reason, my attention in this chapter is confined to power markets. Enron's activities in natural gas and other markets are discussed in more detail in Chapter 1 of this volume.
2. Despite the conventional view of electricity as a "public good," numerous examples exist to demonstrate the success of private, competitive markets in providing fairly priced and reliable power to consumers.
3. See the *Houston Chronicle's* special Web site titled "Enron Timeline," available at http://www.chron.com/cs/CDA/story.hts/special/enron/1127125.
4. See http://www.enron.com/corp/pressroom/releases/1999/ene/EnronOnline.html for press release on Enron Online.
5. See http://www.enron.com under Press Releases, "Enron Milestone for March 2000."

6. Meanwhile, state legislatures and regulators could still determine the state of competition and pricing at the retail level.
7. See Federal Energy Regulatory Commission 18 CFR Parts 35 and 38, [Docket Nos. RM95-8-000 and RM94-7-001], "Promoting Wholesale Competition Through Open Access Nondiscriminatory Transmission Services by Public Utilities; Recovery of Stranded Costs by Public Utilities and Transmitting Utilities," ORDER NO. 888 FINAL RULE, Issued April 24, 1996 (FERC Order 888).
8. See http://www.americanhistory.si.edu/csr/powering/ titled "Powering the Past: A Look Back" by the Smithsonian Institute under the section "A New Era for Electricity" by Dr. Richard Hirsh, Virginia Polytechnic Institute and State University, December 2001.
9. See note 8.
10. See note 8.
11. See note 8.
12. Typically forward contracts in this industry are settled in arrears. In other words, invoicing for power delivered occurs after the actual delivery takes place.
13. Monthly strike options rarely call for power delivery 24 × 7 over the whole month. A typical monthly option would involve delivery of power during peak hours on weekdays, for example.
14. See Federal Energy Regulatory Commission's Staff Report titled "Causes of Wholesale Electricity Pricing Abnormalities in the Midwest during June 1998" released on September 22, 1998.
15. Herron discusses EnronOnline in more detail in Chapter 6 of this volume.

5

REGULATION OF WHOLESALE ELECTRICITY TRADING AFTER ENRON

ANDREA S. KRAMER, PAUL J. PANTANO JR., AND
DORON F. EZICKSON

A s explained in Chapters 1 and 4, Enron Corporation did not fail *because of* its participation in wholesale and retail electricity markets. But as Neves also noted in Chapter 4, electricity markets are typically viewed as *special* because of the reliability issues that surround the provision of wholesale power to public utilities and municipalities with an obligation to serve retail customers as well as to sell power directly to retail customer through a hodgepodge of state restructuring, direct access, and fixed retail price regulatory efforts. Not surprisingly, with the disclosure of questionable wholesale electricity trading practices by Enron, regulatory and legislative investigations and litigation have intensified, focusing on the propriety of wholesale electricity prices in California and the western United States in 2000 and 2001.

At this same time, the Federal Energy Regulatory Commission (FERC) and Congress are also considering reforms to the operation and oversight of wholesale electricity markets. While anticompetitive conduct must be investigated and penalized, we believe that the continued regulatory uncertainty caused by inconsistent legal standards governing wholesale trading practices poses a substantial risk to the viability of the developing wholesale and retail competitive electricity markets in the United States. Regulatory reform efforts must have as a primary goal the clarification of the legal standards by which wholesale electricity trading conduct will be judged. While the recent FERC staff investigation report into Enron's trading conduct suggests that the FERC is trying to establish clearer standards, more definitive steps must be taken to restore regulatory certainty to the competitive electricity markets.

We also fear that the recent Committee on Governmental Affairs majority staff memorandum criticizing FERC for its oversight of Enron may inappropriately pressure and immobilize FERC, slowing down commonplace and routine filings and further damaging the competitive electricity markets.[1]

Clear trading rules are a critical component of an efficient commodity market. Today, electricity market participants face a dizzying array of existing and proposed regulatory requirements. Aspects of electricity trading are subject to the overlapping jurisdiction of both the FERC and the Commodity Futures Trading Commission (CFTC), with both agencies currently investigating allegations of market manipulation in the western markets. Yet, the jurisdiction of each agency and the legal standards governing their reviews differ in material respects.

Moreover, a multitude of pending lawsuits, alleging manipulation of the electricity markets, seek to apply state competition laws to the same conduct being investigated by the FERC and the CFTC. In addition, FERC is conducting refund proceedings that may result in the recalculation or unwinding of hundreds of thousands of spot electricity transactions. While declaring its recognition of the sanctity of contracts, FERC has nevertheless allowed private parties to forward contracts to proceed to trial on their attempt to renege on those long-term contracts on which they are alleged to have lost money.[2] The FERC is also investigating wash trades, without the benefit of any market rules with respect to buy and sell transactions. Finally, FERC is considering a number of reporting and fundamental design and operational changes to the wholesale electricity markets that will take years to implement. This lack of regulatory authority and clarity makes it increasingly difficult for market participants to prudently manage the regulatory and legal risks associated with wholesale electricity trading.

We focus on the federal regulation of the wholesale electricity trading because the viability of wholesale trading drives the success of wholesale and retail competitive markets. We maintain that future regulatory reform must resist additional, burdensome regulatory requirements and must be focused instead on establishing clear and enforceable standards. The lack of clarity is, in and of itself, harmful to competition because it deters market entry and raises transaction costs. Future regulatory changes must, therefore, honor one of the fundamental principles of competition: transparency and predictability of market rules. Regulatory changes must not be driven by political pressure to find a scapegoat for Enron's failure.

To illustrate the complexity and inefficiency of the current regulatory regime, we first describe the physical and derivative products used by those market participants engaged in active commodity markets. Second, we briefly describe the current competitive wholesale power market in the United States. Third, we set out the different jurisdictional mandates of the FERC and the CFTC, with respect to trading electricity products. Fourth, we examine the jurisdictional interplay between the FERC and CFTC, reviewing their pending investigations in the West. Finally, we recommend steps to begin to restore some regulatory certainty to the wholesale electric markets.

THE POWER MARKET

Historically, the wholesale electricity market was not an active trading market.[3] Rather, electricity was generated for use by the customers of the regulated utility that had generated the power. If a utility had any excess generation capacity, it would typically sell its excess electricity to neighboring utilities. Trading was hampered by limitations in the electricity transmission system. Trading also was hampered and shaped by state regulation of retail markets, including limitations on the use of wholesale forward contracts by public utilities to supply retail load, state commission prudence reviews of generation planning and purchasing decisions, required purchasing from qualifying facilities (QFs) under Public Utility Regulatory Policies Act of 1978 (PURPA) at the public utility's marginal costs as fixed by the state commissions, and the public utility's traditional retail obligation to serve. With the start of federal deregulation efforts in the wholesale electricity markets, however, the power markets have been developing into active physical and derivative trading markets. In the past six or seven years, an entirely new business has developed for the purchase and sale of physical electricity and for entering into derivative contracts with values determined by reference to electricity prices.[4]

As Neves explains in more detail in Chapter 4, the physical power market primarily consists of spot and forward contract transactions. Parties to forward contracts generally contemplate that the delivery of the underlying commodity will occur at a future date. In practice, however, the majority of electricity-forward contracts are settled by book-outs, an agreement between forward contract parties to settle their respective obligations with a cash payment of the difference between the contract and reference (market) prices, as opposed to making and taking physical delivery. A book-out may occur when two parties have agreed to deliver the same commodity to each other or the participants form a *string* (many participants trading the same contract, allowing the first seller to deliver to the last buyer) or *circle* (a transaction beginning and ending with the same participant). Any party in a string or a circle can choose not to book-out the transaction and, instead, take delivery of the underlying commodity.

The derivatives power market is presently an OTC market with financially settled options, swaps, caps, and floors entered into between the parties to the transactions. Futures contracts on electricity (and options on those futures contracts) had traded on the New York Mercantile Exchange (NYMEX) from March 29, 1996, until February 15, 2002. On February 15, 2002, however, NYMEX delisted its electricity futures contracts and options because of insufficient contract liquidity. Low trading volume was attributed to limitations in the electricity transmission system. Low volumes also were attributed to variations in state deregulation efforts.[5] For example, states throughout the country were in various stages of (1) "unbundling" commodity costs from regulated transmission, distribution, and billing/metering services; (2) "stranded cost" recovery for generation and power purchase agreements rendered uneconomical through deregulation; (3) setting a viable "price to compare" for competitive retail market entry; and (4) establishing fair business and operations rules for retail power marketers. This hodgepodge between state deregulatory efforts and the varying success of deregulation and competitive access within the states and specific public utility distribution systems resulted in only a small percentage of residential and commercial customers switching to competitive retail providers. Retail power marketers were not able, and did not have the incentive, to serve retail customers. This reduced competitive opportunities and thus liquidity in both the wholesale and retail markets.

In an effort to compete with electronic trading platforms, NYMEX announced in May 2002 that it would offer clearing services for OTC energy contracts beginning on May 31, 2002.[6] In October 2002, NYMEX announced that it was planning to relaunch its PJM (Pennsylvania, New Jersey, and Maryland hub) electricity futures contract sometime in early 2003.[7] This relisted contract would have different terms and conditions than the previous PJM futures contracts that were delisted in 2002. Additionally, the new contract would be traded on the NYMEX ACCESS® electronic platform as well as through its open-outcry system.[8]

Current Regulatory Framework

Both the FERC and the CFTC have regulatory authority over certain aspects of the electricity market, with jurisdiction depending on the electricity product in question. FERC has exclusive jurisdiction over physical sales of wholesale electricity, including spot and forward sales. The CFTC, on the other hand, has exclusive jurisdiction over futures contracts and commodity options. Although the CFTC does not have regulatory jurisdiction over physical sales of electricity, it has jurisdiction to investigate and punish manipulation and attempted manipulation in the price of commodities, including physical transactions. Thus, in practice, two distinct federal agencies have jurisdiction that sometimes overlaps in regulating the wholesale electricity market.[9]

FERC Jurisdiction over Physical Transactions

The FERC, an agency under the Department of Energy,[10] receives its jurisdictional mandate under the Federal Power Act (FPA) over the interstate "sale of electric energy at wholesale."[11] Wholesale electricity sales include spot and forward sales. The FERC is charged with ensuring that rates charged for wholesale electricity are "just and reasonable."[12] The FPA also grants the FERC jurisdiction over the transmission of power, which includes both physical and financial transmission rights.[13] The FERC's jurisdictional grant does not apply to financially settled (physical or derivative) transactions of any kind.

In addition, the 50 states and the District of Columbia are vested with jurisdiction over retail power sales to end users, whether provided by the regulated public utility distribution company or by a licensed or registered competitive retail service provider. The state commissions also set public utility retail rates and returns on capital and equity, review the prudence of public utility generation and wholesale power purchasing decisions, and, in some cases, establish or approve integrated resource plans governing a public utility's addition of new generation and wholesale purchase-power resources and demand-side management and retail load response programs. In some states, public utilities bid out to wholesale power suppliers the wholesale supply component of their retail standard offer, default, or basic generation service obligations to customers that remain on the regulated supply and distribution utility service. State regulation often affects the type of wholesale power and demand/load response products required by public utilities serving retail load.

FERC's jurisdictional mandate is confused further by inconsistent definitions of covered transactions. Although the FERC has jurisdiction over wholesale spot transactions, it does not have a consistent definition of a spot transaction. For instance, the FERC has stated that a spot transaction is a sale for delivery in "24 hours or less and that [is] entered into the day of or day prior to delivery,"[14] and that the spot electricity market is "a market where goods are traded for immediate delivery."[15] Yet, in a FERC proceeding in 2001, an administrative law judge found that "spot power transactions" included sales for up to one month in length.[16] Although this definition is inconsistent with industry practice, the FERC has not indicated whether it will accept or modify this conclusion. This inconsistency creates substantial uncertainty as to those transactions subject to FERC jurisdiction.

Market-Based Rates   Wholesale sellers must obtain the FERC's approval to sell wholesale power at market-based rates (MBR). The FERC grants MBR authority if the wholesale seller (and its affiliates) lack market power with respect to the ownership or control of generation or transmission assets and the seller cannot otherwise erect barriers to market entry. Once the FERC authorizes an applicant to sell power at MBRs, the seller's rates are presumed to be "just and reasonable." FERC's regulation of MBRs seeks to ensure that wholesale sellers do not subsequently obtain "market power." This is because, absent a change in circumstances (that is, a seller subsequently obtains market power), the seller is presumed to be unable to manipulate prices.

As a general rule, a wholesale seller has market power if a portion of its capacity must be used to meet pool peak demand and its capacity exceeds the market's supply margin. The FERC has found that before such a seller can sell power at MBRs, it must mitigate its market power by offering to sell, in the relevant market, its uncommitted capacity in spot market sales at cost-based rates.[17]

MBR Reporting Requirements   Once the FERC approves a wholesale seller's MBR, the seller is subject to three reporting requirements. First, it must advise the FERC about any material changes in its status. Second, it must file quarterly and annual transaction reports. The FERC has recently adopted new quarterly transaction reporting requirements, under which sellers must electronically file and post on the FERC's Web site transaction information, including an index of customers, a summary of contractual terms, and short- and long-term transaction details. Third, the seller must file a triennial update to its initial market power analysis.

Although it is the CFTC that regulates derivative transactions, the FERC proposed in December 2001 that wholesale sellers report information with respect to their financially settled derivatives transactions to the FERC. This proposed rulemaking would require wholesale sellers to follow the Uniform System of Accounts, which currently applies to utilities that sell power at cost-based rates.[18]

On May 31, 2002, the FERC rejected the claim by the California attorney general that power marketers had failed to properly file their MBRs, as required by the FPA, because the FERC did not require the power marketers to provide the details of the rates of their transactions before the dates the rates were used.[19] The FERC rejected these claims, finding that the FPA does not dictate the rate-making methodology to be followed or the elements that must be included in a lawful tariff.[20] The FERC determined that its current filing procedures satisfy the "filed rate doctrine as required by the FPA."[21]

Courts have also affirmed that the FERC's reporting requirements for MBRs satisfy the provisions of the FPA. This affirmation is based on the fact that the FERC requires such sellers to lack, or mitigate, market power before allowing such sellers to sell electricity at MBRs, and the FERC requires quarterly informational filings to ensure that marketers are not exercising market power.[22]

FERC's Enforcement of MBRs   Under the FPA, MBRs must be "just and reasonable" to be lawful.[23] If FERC finds that a market is not functioning properly—or that a wholesale seller has market power (even if only in a niche market)—the FERC can take steps to ensure that rates are just and reasonable.[24]

If the FERC finds specific wholesale power transactions to be unjust and unreasonable, the FERC has various remedies available to it. First, FERC can initiate an action on its own, or a private party can file a complaint with FERC, requesting the FERC to determine that the rates, charges, or classifications are unjust and unreasonable and that a refund is appropriate.[25] Second, FERC can alter the market structure, implement additional reporting requirements (with respect to transaction-specific price data), impose price caps, institute mandatory sale requirements, or revoke a seller's right to sell power at MBRs. On a going-forward basis, FERC can also require a seller to change its MBR tariff (including numeric, formula, or capped rates).[26]

While FERC has exclusive jurisdiction over wholesale rates, the FPA does not provide guidelines as to how FERC should determine whether wholesale rates are just and reasonable. In addition, the courts have found that FERC is not "bound to the use of any single formula or combination of formulae in determining rates."[27] As a result, there is "no precise legal formulation for setting a just and reasonable rate and no precise bright-line for when a rate becomes unjust and unreasonable." With such a lack of statutorily mandated guidelines, FERC has taken the position that "if over time rates do not behave as expected in a competitive market, [FERC] must step in to correct the situation."[28] If FERC determines that rates are unjust and unreasonable, it will set rates that it considers to be "just and reasonable," issuing an order imposing those rates on the parties to any affected transactions. Recently, in the context of its broad investigation of Enron and the western power markets, the FERC staff stated it intends to apply the CFTC's market manipulation standard to questioned transactions.[29]

Allegations of unjust and unreasonable prices have included claims of market manipulation and electricity shortages and criticisms of power trading practices. In the past, the FERC has proposed a wide range of responses. The FERC proposed in August 2002 to condition a grant of MBR tariff authority on the requirement that the seller not exercise market power or act in an anticompetitive manner (including physical or economic withholding of capacity) and that the MBR transactions could be subject to refunds or "other" retroactive remedies.[30] The FERC staff also recommended in August 2002 conditioning market participation on an agreement not to misstate or omit information while trading.[31] In addition, the FERC issued a paper on March 1, 2002, discussing proposed rules to govern withholding power from the market, evaluation of market price, appropriate penalties, due process concerns, and potential tariff modifications.[32] In its investigation of western markets, the FERC is conducting refund proceedings concerning various spot and forward market transactions, and it is conducting a coordinated investigation of manipulation allegations with the CFTC, Department of Justice (DOJ), and SEC.[33] In July 2002, the FERC released a 600-page proposal on electricity market design that proposed a standard market design to apply across all wholesale electricity markets.[34]

Private Litigation of MBRs   In addition to the FERC's ongoing regulation of wholesale electricity rates, a number of private class action suits are pending in California. These lawsuits allege that certain wholesale electricity sellers engaged in unfair business practices, price fixing, and withholding of electricity.[35] These lawsuits clearly challenge the FERC's exclusive jurisdiction of wholesale electricity rates. Any court decisions would result in de facto regulation of wholesale market activities. In this regard, a long line of Supreme Court cases acknowledge the FERC's exclusive jurisdiction and support preemption of private plaintiffs' claims.[36] Despite the FERC's unquestionable jurisdictional mandate, however, the FERC has not currently asserted its jurisdiction before these courts or made efforts to have these cases dismissed.

CFTC Jurisdiction over Commodity Transactions

CFTC jurisdiction, established under the Commodity Exchange Act (CEA), is premised on a commodity's involvement in the transaction or activity at issue. The CEA defines a *commodity* to include 24 specified agricultural products, "all other goods and articles, except onions,"[37] and "all services, rights, and interests" in which futures contracts are "presently or in the future dealt in."[38] The CFTC has exclusive jurisdiction over futures contract transactions in a commodity.[39] The CFTC also has exclusive jurisdiction over option contracts on a commodity,[40] as well as options on futures contracts for a commodity.[41] Participants in these derivatives markets are regulated by the CFTC.

In what amounts to a jurisdictional power grab, the FERC recently amended its rules to require wholesale sellers to start reporting to the FERC their booked-out power transactions in addition to contracts that actually result in physical delivery of power.[42] Interestingly, in Order No. 2001-A, the FERC clarified that wash trades are a subset of book-out transactions that must be reported quarterly by power marketers because "collecting and disclosing these data . . . will promote confidence in the integrity of markets and will be helpful for market monitoring purposes to detect improper conduct."[43] The CEA, however, expressly prohibits wash sales.[44] The FERC is considering whether, and to what extent, it should also require wholesale sellers to report their power derivatives transactions on an annual basis. The FERC recently issued a notice of proposed rulemaking (NOPR) to require wholesale sellers to disclose power derivative transactions.[45]

Congress has generally exempted from CFTC regulation commercial merchandising transactions in physical commodities, whether delivery is in the spot market or in the forward market for deferred delivery.[46] As to spot and forward transactions, the CFTC's authority is generally limited to enforcement actions for the manipulation of commodity prices.[47]

The CFTC views *cash market* or *spot* transactions as "transactions for the immediate sale and delivery of a commodity."[48] Industry practice supports the view that the spot market is the immediate sale and delivery of a spot commodity.[49] In general, cash market or spot transactions are limited to transactions in which a commodity is delivered against payment on or within two days of the trade date.[50]

Transactions Subject to CFTC Jurisdiction

CFTC jurisdiction depends on the commodity transaction at issue being of a type subject to the CFTC's jurisdiction. For example, a futures contract for "sale of a commodity for future delivery" is subject to the CFTC's exclusive jurisdiction.[51] A forward contract for the deferred sale of a commodity ("for delayed shipment or delivery") is exempt from CFTC jurisdiction, except with respect to the CFTC's authority over price manipulation or attempted manipulation.

Under the CEA, the CFTC has exclusive jurisdiction over "accounts, agreements including any transaction that is of the character of or commonly known as an option, and transactions involving contracts of sale of a commodity for future delivery."[52] Although the CEA does not explicitly define *future delivery*, the CEA says that future delivery "does not include any sale of any cash commodity for deferred shipment or delivery."[53] As a result, spot power transactions (for immediate delivery) and forward power transactions (for deferred delivery) are not subject to the CFTC's jurisdiction except with respect to allegations of price manipulation.[54]

Because of the implications of the CFTC's precisely defined jurisdiction, with futures contracts subject to exclusive CFTC jurisdiction and forwards exempt except for allegations of manipulation, there has been considerable debate over how to draw the line between a futures contract and a forward contract. The CEA does not explicitly define what constitutes either a futures or a forward contract. As a result, the elements of these products have developed through judicial interpretations, CFTC interpretations, and CFTC policy statements.[55]

Before enactment of the Commodity Futures Modernization Act of 2000 (CFMA)[56] in December 2000, the distinction between *futures* and *forwards* was critical, not just because of the CFTC's exclusive jurisdiction over futures, but also because futures contracts were required to be traded on an exchange that was designated by the CFTC as a "contract market."[57]

With the CFMA, however, the distinction between futures contracts and forwards has become less important for energy products because the CFMA established several exclusions and exemptions from the CEA that are available to energy products.[58] Among other things, broad safe harbors now apply to transactions in so-called exempt commodities, which include electricity and natural gas, if certain requirements are met. For electricity and natural gas transactions to qualify as exempt commodities, the contracts must be entered into between eligible contract participants (ECPs).[59] In addition, for those entered into on a "trading facility,"[60] both parties must qualify as eligible commercial entities (ECEs).[61] Transactions in exempt commodities continue to remain subject to the CFTC's jurisdiction over manipulation and attempted manipulation.[62]

Book-Out Transactions   As in some commodity markets, many electricity-forward contracts are "booked-out," which means the contracts are financially settled between the parties without the actual delivery of power.[63] The CFTC has affirmed that the forward contract exclusion to CFTC jurisdiction is available to such forward contracts, provided that delivery "routinely" occurs.[64] Financial settlement does not change a forward contract into a futures contract if three requirements are met:

1. A forward contract is not viewed as a futures contract if the original forward contract is entered into between commercial participants in connection with their businesses.

2. A forward contract is not a futures contract if the original contract provides for delivery obligations that impose substantial commercial risks on the parties.
3. Financial settlement does not change a forward into a futures contract if the book-out transaction is separately agreed to in individually (or multilaterally, in the case of delivery strings or circles) negotiated, new agreements.[65]

Enforcement Powers over Manipulation   The CFTC jurisdiction over spot and forward contracts is limited to the power to investigate and prosecute manipulation or attempted manipulation of the market price of any commodity, in interstate commerce, or for future delivery.[66] Under its authority, the CFTC can compel persons to produce information about spot transactions in connection with a CFTC investigation or prosecution of an alleged manipulation of the price of a spot commodity or a futures contract.[67] CFTC jurisdiction over manipulation and attempted manipulation includes all physical and derivative transactions.[68]

CFTC's enforcement authority for manipulation goes beyond the FERC's power because, under Sections 6(c) and (d) of the CEA, the CFTC can impose civil penalties, issue injunctions, enter into cease and desist orders, and establish prohibitions from trading. The DOJ has brought a number of cases for criminal violations of the CEA.[69] Unlike the FERC, however, the CFTC does not have the authority to set, or retroactively adjust, market prices.

In 2001, the CFTC applied the CEA's anti-manipulation provisions to an energy trading company that engaged in a scheme to manipulate the settlement price of electricity futures contracts on NYMEX to increase the value of its trading company's spot and forward contract positions.[70] The CFTC concluded in August 2001 that the energy company had the financial ability to place, and did place, large orders that moved the market price. The CFTC found the evidence overwhelming that the company intended to, and did, influence the market prices for electricity. As a result, the company was ordered to cease and desist from further violations of the CEA, to pay a civil penalty, and to comply with certain undertakings specified in the settlement order.

JURISDICTIONAL INTERPLAY BETWEEN THE FERC AND THE CFTC

The interplay between the FERC and the CFTC jurisdiction over certain electricity transactions raises a number of issues as to the effective regulation of the physical and derivative markets for electricity. As a practical matter, both the CFTC and the FERC have overlapping jurisdiction with respect to manipulations of the spot and forward markets for power with potentially inconsistent regulatory requirements. As we discuss in the remainder of this section, the CFTC and the FERC have historically applied substantially different standards in monitoring the electricity market and analyzing whether spot electricity prices have been manipulated. Different standards result in regulatory and legal uncertainty for electricity market participants.

Market Manipulation

In analyzing market manipulation, the CFTC focuses on whether a price is "artificial."

In investigating a suspected violation of the CEA's antimanipulation provisions, the CFTC addresses four questions:

1. Did the party have the ability to influence market prices?
2. Did the party specifically intend to influence market prices?
3. Was there an artificial price?
4. Did the party's conduct cause the artificial price?

For a charge of attempted manipulation, the CFTC addresses only two questions:

1. Did the party intend to affect the market price?
2. Did the party engage in an overt act in furtherance of its intent?

If the answer to both of these questions is yes, a manipulation was attempted. Once manipulation or attempted manipulation is found, the CFTC can impose civil penalties, injunctions, cease and desist orders, and prohibitions against trading, and the DOJ could bring a criminal action for violation of the CEA.

The FERC, on the other hand, evaluates manipulation by reviewing whether wholesale spot transaction rates are "just and reasonable." Whether rates are "just and reasonable" is far less defined and much more subjective than the CFTC's test to determine whether a price is artificial. Once the FERC determines that wholesale spot prices for power are unjust and unreasonable, it can order refunds, alter the structure of the market, implement additional reporting requirements, impose price caps, institute mandatory sale requirements, require prospective MBR tariff changes, and revoke a wholesale seller's right to sell power at MBRs.

The standards used by, and the remedies available to, the CFTC and the FERC are very different. One key difference is that the CFTC, unlike the FERC, does not have the authority to set or retroactively adjust market prices.

Prohibited Transactions

The CEA prohibits certain transactions in futures contracts and options on futures contracts that are a "wash sale," "accommodation trade," "fictitious sale," or "transactions used to cause any price to be reported, registered, or recorded that is not a true and bona fide price."[71] The FPA, on the other hand, does not directly address wash sales or round-trip transactions. In connection with FERC's western power market investigation of potential manipulation, FERC issued an order seeking information related to wash or round-trip trades.[72] The FERC initially defined *wash* or *round-trip* trades as the "sale of an electricity product to another company together with a simultaneous purchase of the same product at the same price."[73] Subsequently, the FERC clarified that wash or round-trip trades were "between the same parties, at the same delivery point and for the same volume."[74] In July 2002, the FERC found that wash trades are a subset of book-outs for reporting purposes. Further confusion resulted when the FERC issued its initial report on its investigation in August 2002, stating that it has investigated as wash and round-trip those transactions that were buys and sells between the same counter parties for the same products at the same price "within a two-minute period."[75]

FERC's inconsistent statements on what it views as wash and round-trip trades are precisely the type of regulatory confusion that impairs the development of an active trading market. It is well recognized that certain types of transactions between parties involving a simultaneous purchase of the same product at the same price serve a legitimate business purpose, do not indicate a specific intent to avoid market risks, and thus should not be prohibited. The CFTC and federal courts have acknowledged that legitimate trading may produce an outcome identical to a wash sale.[76] The FERC should initially seek comments and then adopt a market regulation that clarifies its rules on wash and round-trip trades and takes into consideration the CFTC's existing standards.

FERC INVESTIGATION OF POTENTIAL MANIPULATION OF CALIFORNIA ELECTRIC PRICES

The separate CFTC and FERC investigations of potential manipulation in the western markets illustrate the inefficiency of the current regulatory scheme for electricity products and markets. The investigations do, however, provide the FERC and the CFTC with the opportunity to clarify regulatory standards and to develop a cohesive set of market rules that can be applied to the power market.

On February 13, 2002, the FERC issued an order directing its staff to investigate a potential manipulation of electric and natural gas prices by Enron Corporation or any of its affiliates (the February 2002 order).[77] The FERC sought information on whether any entity, including Enron (through any of its affiliates or subsidiaries, including EnronOnline), manipulated, or otherwise exercised undue influence over, short-term prices for electric energy or natural gas in the western United States, resulting in potential unjust and unreasonable rates in long-term power sales contracts. The February 2002 order initiated a broad investigation and allowed the FERC's staff to "obtain information on any and all matters relevant to potential market manipulation in the West."[78]

In an important step toward conducting a cohesive investigation, the FERC stated it intends to consult with the CFTC, the SEC, the DOJ, and the FTC. The FERC hopes this consultation will help it to better understand and analyze financial markets. In making this step toward regulatory coordination, the FERC acknowledged that its responsibility and jurisdiction lies primarily in the physical assets markets rather than in the financial assets markets, where so many of Enron's activities occurred."[79] In its August 13, 2002, staff report, the FERC confirmed its coordinated investigation and announced its intent to apply the CFTC manipulation standard to its ongoing investigation of the western markets. The staff is focused on the activities of three Enron affiliates (including Portland General Electric) and two investor-owned utilities with MBR authority. In response, the FERC issued three enforcement orders instituting formal investigations into whether the three parties engaged in market manipulation, including providing false information to the FERC.

The FERC also ordered wholesale sellers to the California Independent System Operator (Cal ISO) and the California Power Exchange (Cal PX) to respond to specific requests for admissions focused on certain alleged trading strategies, which were described in three Enron memoranda.[80] The request for admissions required wholesale power and ancillary services sellers to submit an affidavit, signed under oath by the company's "president, chief executive officer, general counsel, or a corporate officer of comparable authority and responsibility." The affidavit was to be submitted "after the company . . . has diligently conducted a thorough investigation into the trading activities of the company's employees and agents . . . in the U.S. portion of the Western Systems Coordinating Council (WSCC) during the years 2000 and 2001."[81]

On May 21, 2002, the FERC initiated an investigation into allegations of wash, round-trip, and buy/sell trades in the WSCC. The very next day, the FERC expanded its investigation to require all sellers of natural gas in the U.S. portion of the WSCC and/or Texas during 2000 and 2001 to respond to this request for admissions.[82] Responses were again required to be attested to by a member of the company's senior management in an affidavit signed under oath. These wash trade allegations are also subject to SEC investigations.[83]

The FERC has already proceeded against market participants pursuant to these investigations. On June 4, 2002, the FERC issued an *Order to Show Cause Why Market-Based Rate Authority Should Not Be Revoked to Avista Corporation, El Paso Electric Company, Portland General Electric Company, and Williams Energy Marketing & Trading Company.* The FERC issued this Order to Show Cause because it viewed the responses from these companies as "indicative of a failure by these companies to cooperate" with the FERC's investigation.[84] On August 13, 2002, the FERC instituted a formal proceeding against El Paso Electric Company to investigate whether the company had violated its MBR by ceding control of all or part of its electricity operations to Enron.[85] At the same time, the FERC also instituted formal proceedings against Portland General and Avista to investigate whether these companies had violated the FERC's affiliate trading rules in connection with transactions between Enron and Portland General and whether Portland General's trading practices violated its Code of Conduct and FERC's standards of conduct.[86]

In addition to the FERC's ongoing investigations, the CFTC has also initiated its own investigation into wholesale power trading in the West, recently subpoenaing documents from numerous marketers. We understand that the CFTC has sent requests for information or subpoenas to the same 150 companies that responded to the FERC's data requests. Although wash trades might be the CFTC's primary focus, the CFTC is nevertheless asking for full disclosure of all trading information with respect to relevant transactions.

LEGISLATIVE PROPOSALS TO AMEND FERC AND CFTC JURISDICTION

Given the confused state of energy market regulation, various legislative proposals were considered by Congress in 2002. In February 2002, Senate Bill 1951 (S.1951) was introduced to modify the CEA and the FPA.[87] This bill would have repealed CFMA provisions exempting energy derivatives from CFTC oversight, requiring the CFTC and the FERC to work together to ensure appropriate energy trading markets. It would have dramatically changed the application of the CEA to energy transactions, changing how the CFTC regulates energy derivatives. In addition, S.1951 would have allowed the FERC to regulate energy derivatives that fall outside the CFTC's grant of exclusive jurisdiction.

Although S.1951 was not enacted, a new version (incorporating many of the provisions of S.1951) was proposed in July 2002 as Senate Bill 2724 (S.2724).[88] We do not know if any of the proposals currently contained in S.2724 ultimately will be enacted by Congress. What we do know is that the issues will continue to be addressed and debated in Congress.

On November 12, 2002, the majority staff of the Senate Governmental Affairs Committee released a memorandum examining the FERC's oversight of Enron (majority staff memorandum),[89] which concluded that FERC failed to protect American consumers from Enron's alleged market abuses in California and the western United States in 2000 and 2001. According to the majority staff memorandum, FERC failed to understand the significance of the information it was provided about Enron's activities and lacked the thoroughness and determination to analyze Enron's activities. While FERC has been at the forefront of restructuring the wholesale electricity and natural gas markets, the memorandum nevertheless concludes that FERC "has yet to prove that it is up to the challenge of proactively overseeing the changing markets." In short, the memorandum asserts that FERC failed to protect consumers from market abuses that can occur in an MBR system and that FERC "was no match for a determined Enron." The memorandum does not advance any legislative proposals, instead focusing on criticisms of FERC.[90] This memorandum illustrates that the Enron blame game is far from over and that finger pointing continues between and among FERC commissioners, members of the U.S. Senate and Congress, the White House, and a host of state officials. The majority staff memorandum does not suggest a comprehensive or well-reasoned analysis of ways to amend FERC and CFTC jurisdiction. Rather, it merely criticizes the FERC in a highly political way.

RECOMMENDATIONS TO IMPROVE REGULATORY CERTAINTY

Although regulatory and legal risk are standard features of commodity markets, the high level of these risks in today's wholesale electricity markets impedes efficient trading. To improve regulatory certainty and reduce these risks, several short-term agency actions would assist in establishing the bare minimum level of regulatory predictability in the electricity markets. While we recognize the need for the continued transformation of the markets over time, these short-term steps should help to restore confidence in some of the basic market rules and processes for evaluating market conduct:

1. An important first step would be for the FERC to codify its application of the CFTC's manipulation standard to allegations of market manipulation. The CFTC and the FERC should also clarify how
   their overlapping jurisdictions will be resolved.
2. Both agencies should acknowledge the legitimate role that certain
   buy/sell transactions have in the electricity markets, clearly de-
   lineating those transactions that are not legitimate and that should
   be prohibited.
3. The FERC should clarify that it will not adopt its staff's recommendation for adoption of an *omission* standard to assess market conduct. An omission standard would severely complicate transaction
   planning and execution, while also providing another mechanism
   for parties to attempt to challenge transactions after they are closed.
4. The FERC should reaffirm application of the accepted industry
   definition of a spot transaction to the electricity markets.
5. The FERC should clearly reestablish the sanctity of bilateral contracts by rejecting the attempts of parties to rescind contracts due
   to unfavorable financial results.
6. The FERC should proactively assert its jurisdiction to preempt
   civil litigation alleging manipulation of the wholesale electricity
   markets.
7. The FERC should move quickly to implement its standard market
   design proposal.
8. The FERC should not bend to political pressure over criticisms of
   its Enron oversight in a way that slows down or stops its approval
   of commonplace and routine filings and further damages the competitive electricity markets.

CONCLUSION

Electricity markets historically have been regulated by two different regulators with two different regulatory mandates. The FERC has regulatory
oversight for power transactions by wholesale sellers of transactions that
result in physical delivery. The CFTC, on the other hand, has broad regulatory oversight over financially settled transactions, while its jurisdiction over other products is limited to investigating and prosecuting the
manipulation or attempted manipulation of prices.

    With the investigations and disclosures growing out of the western
power markets, it has become apparent that some trading activities currently are not subject to regulation, while many of the rules governing
trading conduct are unclear. Prompt delineation of transparent market

rules will bring needed regulatory certainty to wholesale electricity trading and will maximize the competitiveness of these important markets.

NOTES

1. Majority Staff Senate Committee on Governmental Affairs, Memorandum dated November 12, 2002, to the Committee on Governmental Affairs Members and Staff, Committee Staff Investigation of the Federal Energy Regulatory Commission, available at http://www.senate.gov/~gov_affairs /111202fercmemo.pdf (visited November 14, 2002).
2. See *Public Utility District No. 1 of Snohomish County v. Morgan Stanley Capital Group, Inc.,* FERC Docket No. EL02-56-000 (FERC filed February 11, 2002).
3. Electricity has been difficult to treat as a conventional commodity because storage and transmission restrictions make it a regional, rather than a fungible, product.
4. Salomon Smith Barney (2002), p. 7, Standard & Poor's (2002), and Moody's Investors Service (2002).
5. See "NYMEX Delists Electricity Futures Contracts" (2002).
6. NYMEX Notice #134 "Exchange Announces Introduction Of Over-the-Counter Energy Clearing On May 31, 2002" (May 13, 2002), available at http://www.nymex.com/jsp/shareholder/notice_to_member.jsp?id=ntm312 &archive=2002> (visited November 18, 2002).
7. "NYMEX Prepares to Wade Into Electricity Contracts Again, Relaunch PJM Futures" (2002), p. 22.
8. See note 7.
9. This overlap is reflected in the ongoing investigation by these agencies into Enron's trading practices in the West.
10. FPA § 201, 42 USC § 7171 (2001).
11. FPA § 205(a), 16 USC § 824d(a) (2001).
12. See note 11.
13. Transmission rights are used by wholesale sellers to hedge their exposure to congestion on interstate transmission lines, which results when electricity scheduled for delivery would exceed the capacity of the transmission path. The CFTC defines congested markets as squeezes or corners. See *In re Cox* [1986–1987 Transfer Binder] Comm. Fut. L. Rep. (CCH) ¶ 23,786 at 34,061 (July 15, 1987).
14. *FERC Order on Rehearing of Monitoring and Mitigation Plan for the California Wholesale Electric Markets, Establishing West-Wide Mitigation, and Establishing Settlement Conference,* Docket Nos. EI 00-95-031, EL00-98-030, EL00-98-033, RT01-85-000, RT01-85-001, EI01-68-000, EI01-68-001 at 2, n.3 (June 19, 2001).
15. Federal Energy Regulatory Commission (1998).
16. See *Puget Sound Energy, Inc. v. Sellers,* Docket Nos EL01-10-000, EL01-10-001, 96 FERC ¶ 63,044 (September 24, 2001).

17. See *AEP Power Marketing, Inc., et al.*, Docket Nos. ER96-2495-015, ER97-4143-003, ER97-1238-010, ER98-2075-009, ER98-542-005 (Not consolidated) ER91-569-009, ER97-4166-008, 97 FERC ¶ 61,219 (November 20, 2001).
18. See *Revised Public Utility Filing Requirements*, Order No. 2001, 67 Fed. Reg. 31,043 (April 25, 2002).
19. See *State of California, ex rel. Bill Lockyer, Attorney General of the State of California v. British Columbia Power Exchange Corp., et al.*, Docket No. EL02-71-000, 99 FERC ¶ 61,247 (May 31, 2002).
20. See note 19.
21. See note 19.
22. *Transwestern Pipeline Co. v. FERC,* 897 F.2d 570, 577 (D.C.Cir., 1990).
23. FPA § 205(a), 16 USC § 824d(a) (2001).
24. See note 23.
25. See *San Diego Gas & Electric v. Sellers,* Docket No. EL00-95-000, 93 FERC ¶ 61,294 (December 15, 2001).
26. FERC has established price and bid caps for certain power markets. For example, FERC has imposed a $1,000/MWh price cap for transactions in the real-time and day-ahead markets in New York, PJM, and ISO-NE. The FERC has also established a hard price cap in California of $91.87/MWh for the period July 12, 2002, through September 30, 2002.
27. See *San Diego Gas & Electric v. Sellers,* Docket No. EL00-95-000, 93 FERC ¶ 61,294 (December 15, 2001).
28. See note 27.
29. See "Enforcement Powers Over Manipulation," below, for a discussion of the CFTC's standard for market manipulation.
30. *FERC's Initial Report on Company-Specific Separate Proceedings and Generic Reevaluations; Published Natural Gas Price Data; and Enron Trading Strategies,* Docket No. PA02-2-000, p. 5 (August 2002).
31. See note 30.
32. *Order Removing Obstacles to Increased Electric Generation and Natural Gas Supply in the Western United States and Requesting Comments on Further Actions to Increase Energy Supply and Decrease Energy Consumption,* Docket No. EL01-47-000 (March 14, 2001).
33. *FERC's Initial Report on Company-Specific Separate Proceedings and Generic Reevaluations; Published Natural Gas Price Data; and Enron Trading Strategies,* Docket No. PA02-2-000, p. 2 (August 2002).
34. *Remedying Undue Discrimination Through Open Access Transmission Service and Standard Electricity Market Design,* 00 FERC ¶ 61,138 (proposed July 31, 2002).
35. *Wholesale Electricity Antitrust Cases I & II,* Case Nos CV02-0990-RHW; CV02-1000-RHW; CV02-1001-RHW (U.S.D.C. S.D.Cal. removed May 21, 2002).
36. *New York v. FERC,* 122 S. Ct. 1012, 1024 (2002) (stating that the FPA "unambiguously" authorizes the FERC to assert jurisdiction over the sale of power in wholesale markets); *Mississippi Power & Light Co. v. Mississippi ex rel. Moore,* 487 U.S. 354, 371 (1988) ("it is common ground that if FERC has

jurisdiction over a subject, the States cannot have jurisdiction over the same subject") (Scalia, J. concurring); *Nantahala Power & Light Co. v. Thornburg,* 476 U.S. 953, 966 (1986) (Congress meant to draw a "bright line" between state and federal jurisdiction under the FPA and the FERC has jurisdiction to regulate wholesale sales in interstate commerce); *New England Power Co. v. New Hampshire,* 455 U.S. 331, 340 (1982) (FPA delegates to the FERC "exclusive authority to regulate the transmission and sale at wholesale of electric energy in interstate commerce").

37. This exception conformed the CEA to a criminal statute enacted because speculative activity in the onion futures market was found to cause unwarranted fluctuations in the cash price of onions. Senate Comm. on Agriculture and Forestry, Trading in Onion Futures—Prohibition, S. Rep. No. 1631. 85th Cong., 2d Sess., reprinted in 1958 U.S. Code Cong. & Admin. News 4210.

38. CEA § 4(a), 7 USC § 6(a) (2001).

39. CEA § 4c(b), 7 USC § 6c(b) (2001). Although this section does not explicitly give the CFTC "exclusive" jurisdiction over options on commodities, it has been interpreted as doing so. See *Dunn v. CFTC,* 519 U.S. 465, 477 (1997).

40. Ibid. See also 17 CFR § 1.19 (prohibited trading in commodity options); 17 CFR § 30 (foreign futures and foreign options transactions); 17 CFR § 32 (regulation of commodity option transactions); 17 CFR § 33 (regulation of domestic exchange-traded commodity option transactions).

41. Before the NYMEX started trading electricity futures contracts, it requested an order from FERC that electricity futures were not "securities" as defined by the FPA. FERC found that a "plain reading" of the security definition under the FPA did not include electricity futures contracts. *New York Mercantile Exchange,* Docket No. EL95-81-000, 74 FERC ¶ 61,311 (1996). FERC noted that it would have jurisdiction "pursuant to sections 205 and 206 of the FPA if the electricity futures contract goes to delivery, the electric energy sold under the contract will be resold in interstate commerce, and the seller is a public utility." Ibid. In addition, FERC did not address whether it has jurisdiction over other derivative products.

42. See note 41.

43. "In a 'wash' [or round-trip] transaction, the parties agree in advance to offsetting transactions such that no power is delivered. Typically, the sales are made at the same price, so that no money changes hands." *Revised Public Utility Filing Requirements,* FERC Order No. 2001-A, 100 FERC ¶ 61,074 (July 18, 2002) ("Order No. 2001-A"), at P 23, n.25, and P 26.

44. Section 4c(a) of the CEA (7 USC § 6c(a)) makes "wash sales" and certain other transactions unlawful. To prove a violation, the CFTC must demonstrate that the trader did not intend to make a bona fide transaction. See 7 USC § 6c(a). By its terms, the section 4c(a) wash sale prohibition is limited to futures, options on futures, and options on commodity transactions.

45. Revised Public Utility Filing Requirements, 66 Fed. Reg. 67,134 (December 28, 2001) (issued December 20, 2001).

46. CEA § 2(a)(1)(A), 7 USC § 2 (2001). CEA § 4c(a) prohibits various manipulative transactions in commodities, as does CEA § 6(c). 7 USC §§ 4c(a) and 6(c) (2001).

47. CEA § 4c(a) and 6(c), 7 USC §§ 4c(a) and 6(c) (2001).

48. See, for example, *Salomon Forex, Inc. v. Tauber,* 8 F.3d 966, 970 (4th Cir. 1993), *cert. denied,* 511 U.S. 1031 (1994). See also *Dunn v. CFTC.* 519 U.S. 465 (1997) ("spot transactions [are] agreements for purchase and sale of commodities that anticipate near-term delivery"). The CFTC's Office of the General Counsel has defined a spot contract to include a contract between a producer and a merchant to make or take immediate delivery of a commodity at a price to be agreed to at a later time. CFTC Office of the General Counsel, Characteristics Distinguishing Cash and Forwarding Contracts and "Trade" Options, 50 Fed. Reg. 39,656, 39,660 (1985). The spot contract that was reviewed offered a minimum price guarantee to the seller in return for a premium that allowed the seller time to decide whether to take the guaranteed minimum price or to obtain a higher final price based on either the contract pricing formula or the cash market price for the commodity. Because both parties were obligated to perform under the contract and delivery was scheduled at the time the contract was made, the CFTC's Office of General Counsel viewed the contract as a spot contract. A spot contract is not an option because the seller's right to demand a price is not separated from the actual delivery of the commodity between the parties.

49. See, for example, *Bank Brussels Lambert, S.A. v. Intermetals Corp.,* 779 F. Supp. 741, 748 (SDNY, 1991) (referring to "the conventions of foreign currency trading" to determine what constitutes the "current market"); CFTC, Regulation of Noncompetitive Transactions Executed on or Subject to the Rules of a Contract Market, 63 Fed. Reg. 3708, 3712 (January 26, 1998) (noting importance of "prevailing cash market practice" in determining the delivery parameters of a cash market transaction); CFTC, Division of Trading and Markets, *Report on Exchanges of Futures for Physicals,* 51, 65, 124–47 (1987) (market practices in the cash markets for sugar, crude oil and foreign currency, call for delivery within 75, 30 and 2 days, respectively); see also *CFTC Interpretative Letter 98–73,* 1998 CFTC Ltr. LEXIS 85 (October 1998) ("In a spot transaction, immediate delivery of the product and immediate payment for the products are expected on or within a few days of the trade date").

50. 1 National Legal Research Group, *Regulation of the Commodities Futures and Options Markets,* § 9.01 (2nd ed. 1995).

51. CEA § 2(a)(1)(A), 7 USC § 2(a)(1)(A) (2001).

52. See note 51.

53. CEA § 1a (19), 7 USC § 1a (19) (2001). This is commonly referred to as the "forward contract exemption."

54. The term *future delivery* does not include "any sale of any cash commodity for deferred shipment or delivery." CEA § 2(a)(1)(A), 7 USC § 2 (2001).

55. See *Statutory Interpretation Concerning Forward Transactions,* [1990–1992 Transfer Binder] Comm. Fut. L. Rep. (CCH) ¶ 24,925 (September 25,

1990); *Exemption for Certain Contracts Involving Energy Products,* [1992–1994 Transfer Binder] Comm. Fut. L. Rep. (CCH) ¶ 25,633 (April 20, 1993).

56. See Commodity Futures Modernization Act of 2000, Pub. L. No. 106-554, 114 Stat. 2763 (December 21, 2000). The CFMA was prompted, in part, by the conclusions presented in President's Working Group on Financial Markets *Over the Counter Derivatives Markets and the Commodity Exchange Act: Report of the President's Working Group on Financial Markets* (November 1999), many of which were incorporated into the CFMA legislation. The President's Working Group consisted of the Secretary of the Treasury and the Chairmen of the Board of Governors of the Federal Reserve System, the Securities and Exchange Commission and the CFTC.

57. Prior to the CFMA, unless otherwise subject to an exemption under CEA § 4(c), the CEA required all futures contracts to be traded on a "contract market," approved by the CFTC. In addition, off-exchange trading of nonexempt futures contracts was illegal. CEA § 4(a), 7 USC § 6(a) (2001). CEA § 4(c) authorizes the CFTC to exempt, either retroactively or prospectively, any contract from the requirement that it be traded on a contract market if the CFTC determines that granting the exemption is consistent with the public interest and two conditions are met. First, the contract must be entered into solely between "appropriate persons." Second, the exemption will not have a "material adverse effect" on the ability of the CFTC or any contract market to discharge its regulatory responsibilities.

58. See "Legislative Proposals to Amend the FERC's and CFTC's Jurisdictions." Congress is considering repealing some of these exemptions.

59. An ECP includes certain specified financial institutions, regulated entities, corporations, and other entities with minimum total assets or net worth and individuals with minimum total assets. CEA § 1a(12), 7 USC 1a(12) (2001).

60. A trading facility is a physical or electronic facility or system in which multiple participants have the ability to execute or trade agreements, contracts, or transactions by accepting bids and offers made by other participants that are open to multiple participants in the facility or system. CEA § 1a(33), 7 USC § 1a(33) (2001).

61. CEA § 2(h)(3), 7 USC § 2(h) (2001). An ECE is an ECP (as defined in CEA § 1a(12)) that meets one of three requirements in connection with its business. First, it has a demonstrable ability to make or take delivery of the underlying commodity. Second, it incurs risks in addition to price risk, related to the commodity. Or, third, it is a dealer that regularly provides risk management or hedging services to, or engages in market-making activities with, ECEs involving physical or derivative transactions in the commodity. CEA § 1a(11), 7 USC § 1a(11) (2001).

62. CEA § 2(h)(2)(C), 7 USC § 2(h)(2)(c) (2001).

63. 58 Fed. Reg. 21286 (April 20, 1993).

64. See *Statutory Interpretation Concerning Forward Transactions,* [1990–1992 Transfer Binder] Comm. Fut. L. Rep. (CCH) ¶ 24,925 (September 25,

1990); *Exemption for Certain Contracts Involving Energy Products,* [1992–1994 Transfer Binder] Comm. Fut. L. Rep. (CCH) ¶ 25,633 (April 20, 1993).

65. 58 Fed. Reg. 21286 (April 20, 1993).

66. CEA § 6(c), 7 USC § 9 (2001) (proceedings before the CFTC); CEA § 6(d), 7 USC § 13b (2001) (cease and desist orders); CEA § 9(a)(2), 7 USC § 9(a)(2) (2001) (criminal penalties).

67. See CEA § 6(c), 7 USC §§ 9, 15 (2001).

68. The CFTC prosecuted price manipulation in the forward market for copper. See *In the Matter of Sumitomo Corporation,* order instituting proceedings pursuant to sections 6(c) and 6(d) of the Commodity Exchange Act and Findings and Order Imposing Remedial Sanctions, 1998 CFTC LEXIS 96; Comm. Fut. L. Rep. (CCH) P27, 327 (May 11, 1998).

69. *See,* for example, *U.S. v. Baggot,* 463 U.S. 476 (1983) (sham transactions to create paper losses for deductions on a tax return); *U.S. v. Kepreos,* 759 F.2d 961 (1st Cir. 1985) (prohibited market participation by a convicted felon and fraud by a CFTC registrant); *U.S. v. Bein et al.,* 728 F.2d 107 (2nd Cir. 1984) (sale of illegal commodity options); *U.S. v. Bailin,* 1993 U.S. Dist. Lexis 2003 (N.D. Ill. 1993) (aiding and abetting fraud).

70. *In the Matter of Avista Energy, Inc. and Michael T. Griswold, Order Instituting Proceedings Pursuant to Sections 6(c) and 6(d) of the Commodity Exchange Act, Making Findings and Imposing Sanctions,* CFTC Docket No. 01-21 (August 21, 2001). See also *In the Matter of Anthony J. DiPacido, Robert S. Kristufek, and William H. Taylor,* CFTC Complaint, CFTC Docket No. 01-23 (August 21, 2001).

71. CEA § 4(c), 7 USC § 4(c) (2001).

72. *FERC Office of Markets, Tariffs and Rates, Data Request to the Sellers of Wholesale Electricity and/or Ancillary Services in the United States Portion of the Western States Coordinating Council During the Years 2000–2001,* Docket No. PA02-2-000, p. 2 (May 21, 2002).

73. See note 72.

74. *Dynegy Power Marketing Inc.'s Response to the May 21, 2002 FERC Office of Markets, Tariffs and Rates, Data Request to the Sellers of Wholesale Electricity and/or Ancillary Services in the United States Portion of the Western States Coordinating Council During the Years 2000–2001,* Docket No. PA02-2-000, p. 2 (filed May 31, 2002).

75. *FERC's Initial Report on Company-Specific Separate Proceedings and Generic Reevaluations; Published Natural Gas Price Data; and Enron Trading Strategies,* Docket No. PA02-2-000, p. 54 (August 2002).

76. See, for example, *In re Glass* [1996–1998 Transfer Binder] Comm. Fut. L. Rep. (CCH) ¶ 27.337 (CFTC April 27, 1998); *In re Gilchrist* [1990–1992 Transfer Binder] Comm. Fut. L. Rep. (CCH) ¶ 24,993 (CFTC January 25, 1991).

77. See note 76.

78. *Order Directing Staff Investigation,* Docket No. PA02-2-000, 98 FERC ¶ 61,165 (February 13, 2002).

79. *FERC Office of Markets, Tariffs and Rates, Data Request to the Sellers of Wholesale Electricity and/or Ancillary Services to the California Independent System Operator*

and/or the California Power Exchange During the Years 2000–2001, Docket No. PA02-2-000, p. 2 (May 8, 2002).

80. Confidential Attorney-Client Memorandum from Christian Yoder and Stephen Hall, Stoel Rives LLP, to Richard Sanders, Traders, Strategies in the California Wholesale Power Markets/ISO Sanctions (December 8, 2000); Confidential Attorney-Client memorandum from Gary Fergus and Jean Frizzell, Brobeck, Phleger & Harrison LLP, Status Report on Further Investigation and Analysis of EPMI Trading Strategies, (undated). The "Enron Memoranda" are posted at http://www.ferc.gov/electric/bulkpower/pa02-2/pa02-2.htm.

81. See note 82.

82. *FERC Office of Markets, Tariffs and Rates, Data Request to All Sellers of Natural Gas in the U.S. Portion of the Western Systems Coordinating Council and/or Texas During the Years 2000–2001,* Docket No. PA02-2-000 (May 22, 2002).

83. See note 82.

84. *FERC Order to Show Cause Why Market-Based Rate Authority Should Not Be Revoked to Avista Corporation, El Paso Electric Company, Portland General Electric Company, and Williams Energy Marketing & Trading Company,* Docket No. PA02-2-000 (June 4, 2002). The FERC staff subsequently sent letters indicating satisfaction with the supplemental responses of Williams and El Paso. See *FERC's Initial Report on Company-Specific Separate Proceedings and Generic Reevaluations; Published Natural Gas Price Data; and Enron Trading Strategies,* Docket No. PA02-2-000, p. 14 (August 2002).

85. *FERC's Initial Report on Company-Specific Separate Proceedings and Generic Reevaluations; Published Natural Gas Price Data; and Enron Trading Strategies,* Docket No. PA02-2-000, p. 25 (August 2002).

86. See note 85, pp. 28–30.

87. S. 1951, 107th Cong., 2d Sess. (2002). Its sponsors were from the Western states: Senators Feinstein and Boxer represent California, Senator Cantwell represents Washington, and Senator Wyden represents Oregon.

88. S. 2724, 107th Cong. 2d. Sess. (2002).

89. Majority Staff Memorandum, supra note 1.

90. See note 89 at 2.

6

ONLINE TRADING AND CLEARING AFTER ENRON

JOHN HERRON

The world of financial markets often appears inscrutable to those on the outside. Enormous transactions that are executed in a peculiar yet convincing jargon are also scrutinized with a certain suspicion. Welcome to the world of derivatives. In many ways, the financial markets themselves looked on Enron in a similar manner. To those more experienced, there was certainly a feeling of déjà-vu. It was "masters of the universe" all over again, but this time in Houston, Texas.

Almost a year after Enron withdrew from the financial markets, the energy markets sound and smell disturbingly similar to dealing rooms across the globe immediately following the so-called "great derivatives disasters" of the mid-1990s—Barings, Metallgesellschaft, Procter & Gamble, Orange County, and others. Then, as now, there was a distinct move "back to basics" in which outright position taking has been replaced by vanilla hedging of risk. Many energy-trading operations carried out by the principals in the market—the energy-generating corporations themselves—have ceased operations and were, in many cases, willing to sustain significant losses often just to ensure their own long-run survival. This disturbingly familiar pattern that affected derivatives long before Enron has now arrived in the energy markets, as well. This will be the legacy of Enron.

This chapter deals specifically with the impact on global trading and clearing/settlement of the failure of EnronOnline, the automatic order execution system that acted as an extension of Enron's commercial trading arm. The first section offers a brief description of EnronOnline—what it was, how it evolved, and how it operated. The following section addresses the impacts of EnronOnline's failure on energy markets in general, with the next two sections considering specific implications for trading markets and clearing, settlement, and credit risk management, respectively. A final section offers some policy observations and conclusions.

ENRONONLINE

The *supply chain* for a financial transaction includes the processes of trading, clearing, and settlement. Trading involves the listing of financial products and the provision of a marketplace (i.e., platform, system, and rules) for transactions in those products. Clearing and settlement can be broadly separated into two categories. The first is the operational process by which securities and funds are transferred and may include the calculation of net obligations and entitlements across trading counter parties, collateral management, delivery- and/or payment-versus-payment services, back office reporting, and the like.

The second category of clearing and settlement involves the participation by the settlement agent as a central counter party (CCP) to all transactions conducted in the markets being cleared and settled by the CCP. Apart from becoming the post-trade contractual counter party to the original transaction, CCPs usually also provide performance and trade guarantees and a netting scheme. Most organized derivatives exchanges (e.g., New York Mercantile Exchange, London International Financial Futures and Options Exchange, Eurex) have a CCP to guarantee all trades, whereas most virtual exchanges, such as automatic trading systems (ATSs), electronic communication networks (ECNs), and business-to-business (B2B) verticals, do not.

Enron's financial market activities included at least some participation in all parts of the financial transaction supply chain across numerous financial products and physical commodities.[1] As a major player in exchange-traded derivatives, Enron engaged in trading on almost all of the world's major organized derivatives exchanges and not just in energy. In addition, Enron was perhaps the largest trader in energy wholesale and spot over-the-counter (OTC) derivatives, or bilateral privately negotiated contracts on assets such as natural gas and oil that are neither traded nor cleared on any organized exchange.

A trading culture permeated Enron under the stewardship of former trading head and CEO Jeffrey Skilling. His creation of the Enron Gas-Bank in 1991 (see Chapters 1 and 4) in which Enron acted as the intermediary between gas producers and consumers—principally via the creation of forward gas delivery contracts—was a huge success, selling more than $800 million worth of gas in the first week of operation (Bryce, 2002, p. 54). Following the departure of Enron president and COO Rich

Kinder in 1996 and his replacement by Skilling as the head of trading activities, the focus of Enron shifted almost entirely to energy deal making and trading. As such, Enron Capital & Trade Resources was formed in 1997 to oversee Enron's trading activities, which at that time included both market making in well-established organized markets and intensive forays into new OTC markets. It was hardly surprising when Enron launched its own trading platform on November 29, 1999.

EnronOnline was the brainchild of U.K.-based Enron employee Louise Kitchen. The EnronOnline system consisted of a Web browser-based platform that matched trades electronically based on the bids and offers for specific products submitted by different market participants. Instead of waiting for an exact match, Enron would execute transactions generally whenever they arrived, substituting Enron Corporation itself as the counter party to the original trade until a matching transaction with another customer could be identified. This meant that all firms trading on EnronOnline were trading with Enron, at least for some period of time. In highly liquid markets such as oil and natural gas, a match often could be identified with another customer in mere minutes, whereas EnronOnline users in less liquid markets such as pulp and paper or bandwidth might end up with Enron as the counter party for days or weeks until a matching order from another customer came in.

Many market commentators and Enronites referred to it as "the jewel in Enron's crown." The source of the value of EnronOnline to Enron, however, is not as obvious as it might appear. One possibility, of course, is that EnronOnline was a valuable new *trading system*. By December 2001, EnronOnline boasted around 5,400 average number of trades per day,[2] and the average number of users logged in at any one time was 4,800. Although seemingly successful, these numbers are nothing out of the ordinary in the world of automatic financial trading.

Enron could easily have replicated these statistics, moreover, by purchasing any of the numerous electronic trading platforms that are available for sale instead of designing its own system. An Enron technical advisor involved in the design and construction of the platform commented that the original cost of construction was around the $20 million mark. At the same time, the Cantor Exchange (now known as eSpeed) designed a similar electronic platform for a cost close to $100 million. In addition, EnronOnline was a "work-in-progress" system, continually being updated. The overall conclusion was that the EnronOnline electronic trading platform was one of several electronic markets that were being created at the time and, as such, held little value.

Alternatively, many contend that the market participants who used EnronOnline were the greatest source of value for Enron. In general terms, it is the liquidity that the market players literally brought to the table. Greater liquidity generally attracts a higher transaction volume to a marketplace. Normally, the market operator (in this case, Enron) would derive profit from taking a transaction fee from trades and thus increase revenue from increased trading. However, EnronOnline did not charge transaction fees, nor did it charge membership or entrance fees. If Enron benefited from higher transaction volume, it thus could not have been through direct volume-based revenues.

Because Enron was the counter party to all transactions, the prices and/or information that customers revealed to Enron through EnronOnline seem to have been the real value to Enron as a corporation. This is demonstrated in Figure 6.1, which shows the relationship between platform functionality and liquidity on EnronOnline.[3] In short, the more a customer traded through EnronOnline, the better Enron was able to serve the customer.

Many have regarded the visibility of position and price information to the market operator as a significant impediment to the proliferation to date of automatic trading platforms, especially for privately negotiated OTC derivatives in which dealers remain hypersensitive about the

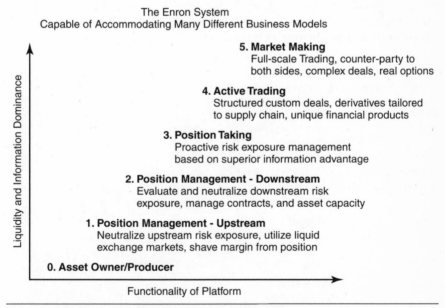

Source: Enron Discussion Papers, on file with the author.

FIGURE 6.1   EnronOnline System Capability

proprietary nature of their own trading activity. Nevertheless, such issues do not seem to have affected EnronOnline's customers. Market participants were perfectly aware that Enron was able to see their positions and/or trade at any given time but cited various benefits of the trading platform that allowed this potential cost. The principal reasons were the sheer number of products listed by EnronOnline (see Table 6.1) and, more importantly, the relatively narrow bid/offer spread that Enron-Online was able to produce on many of these products.

EnronOnline did not offer just a breadth of trading opportunities across commodities; it provided users with significant depth across different product types within commodity categories. EnronOnline users could engage in transactions involving physical commodities, financial products, basis and spread positions, index products, options, and the like. In short, a great variety of physical and derivatives products were uniquely available on EnronOnline.

Many products offered by EnronOnline were indeed truly innovative and, were it not for EnronOnline, may have taken many years to develop. This particularly applies to "exotic" derivatives such as those contracts whose values were based on weather and bandwidth. Enron's role as either a large or pioneering principal trader within these markets facilitated the process by which the markets evolved. Such participation also often left Enron holding unwanted and/or illiquid products that they were unable to offset through the order-matching process or offload through hedging.

Table 6.1   EnronOnline Products Listed for Trading

Power	NGLs, Petrochemicals, and Plastics	Natural Gas	Weather Derivatives
Australian	European LPG	Argentine	Asia Pacific
Austrian	European Petrochemicals	Belgian	European
Dutch	United States	Canadian	United States
German		Dutch	**Crude Oil**
Nordic	**Shipping**	German	Asian
Spanish	**Coal**	United Kingdom	United States
Swiss	International	United States	**Metals**
United Kingdom	United States	**Steel**	**Bandwidth**
U.S. East		**Credit Derivatives**	**Pulp and Paper**
U.S. West	**Emission Allowances**		

Source: "Enron Networks," Draft Presentation and Internal Discussion Document, November 2001 (on file with the author).

ENERGY MARKET IMPACT OF
ENRONONLINE'S FAILURE

Perhaps the greatest shock from Enron's demise was to the energy markets themselves. There was substantial "market noise" at the time of Enron's collapse, following in the wake of the market closures surrounding the September 11, 2001, terrorist attacks and the corresponding excessive volatility in energy and derivatives prices. Together with the sheer size and presence in the markets as a liquidity provider, the withdrawal of EnronOnline from the markets was bound to have an effect on overall energy market liquidity and price discovery.

Indeed, the failure of Enron also came at a time when other energy virtual exchanges and B2Bs were fast disappearing from the market. By the end of 2000, there were more than 900 B2Bs in the United States alone, but that number contracted to fewer than 70 by mid-2001 (Harrold, 2001). Many of the remaining B2Bs, moreover, have refocused on areas such as supply chain management and thus no longer emphasize the provision of financial products and trading markets.

Just how much liquidity EnronOnline provided to the market is not clear. By December 2001, EnronOnline had a total life-to-date transaction count of more than 1.7 million trades, a staggering $950 billion notional value of transactions, and more than 2,000 listed products.[4] However, statistics can be deceptive. Many of the listed products were traded only several times, and "notional value" is common in large energy derivatives trades despite never being exchanged by the trading parties and hence not representing a genuine amount of capital at risk. Nevertheless, that Enron was a huge market player is beyond dispute.

How does a market withstand the withdrawal of such an entity and still maintain market integrity? Art Gelber, principal at Gelber & Associates, commented that "of all the products the energy industry might utilize, integrity is the most demanded" (Gelber, 2002). One obvious answer—the one that seems to have occurred especially in U.S. energy markets following EnronOnline's failure—is that the market continues to operate but at a contracted pace and level.

Many of Enron's trading teams and resources, moreover, did not simply vanish, but rather split apart and changed employers. UBS Warburg, for example, acquired EnronOnline's trading platform and 800 traders in a successful application to the U.S. Bankruptcy Court in New York on January 18, 2002. According to one Enron insider, EnronOnline at one time had captured 25 percent of the entire U.S. gas trading market. UBS Warburg paid zero for the transaction and received free office space in the Enron head office for 10 years in return for paying Enron 33 percent of net profits for the first year, falling to 22 percent for the next year, and 11 percent for the remaining 10 years. The new entity—called UBS Warburg Energy—could even deduct up to $20 million from the royalty to cover information technology (IT) infrastructure development.

Yet, even the relocation of some of Enron's trading assets has not abrogated a significant contraction in the market. UBS Warburg Energy, for example, has already announced the layoffs of several hundred trading staff that it had acquired from EnronOnline.

A primary reason underlying the stagnation in current energy markets—especially in the United States—is the virtual disappearance of many of the market's most creditworthy potential trading counter parties—disappearance because of both downgrades and voluntary market exits. According to Fitch, the bulk of credit downgrades at energy companies occurred in the third quarter of 2002. This coincided with the mass exodus of some of the largest energy corporations from energy trading. Consider some of the most prominent examples:

- *Dynegy*, a major competitor to Enron, closed its trading platform in June 2002 and announced in mid-October that it was withdrawing from energy trading. It cited the need to renew $1.3 billion in credit as a major factor.
- *El Paso Corp.* announced the severe curtailment of its energy trading operations and several hundred layoffs.
- *Allegheny Energy, Inc.,* announced in mid-October 2002 that it was retreating from merchant electricity trading and limiting itself to activities involving assets it already owned.[5]
- *Aquila, Inc.,* announced in mid-September that it would abandon its trading business.
- *Reliant Resources* is completely scaling back its energy trading operations.
- *CMS Energy Corp.* has eliminated its energy trading business and reduced assets.
- *Williams Co.* is seeking a buyer for its energy trading business.

Despite the withdrawal of many principals from the energy and power markets, it is expected that the energy markets will continue to see a period of consolidation over the coming 12 months. Nevertheless, the market remains alive and kicking, perhaps demonstrating that a temporary contraction of volume and recentering of the market on only the most creditworthy participants is actually *good* for the market in the long run.

TRADING MARKETS IN A POST-ENRON WORLD

Was Enron *the* market, an innovator, or simply a product of the times? Extraordinarily, Enron was in part all of these. Certainly, there were fortuitous circumstances that foreshadowed the emergence, dominance, and eventual collapse of Enron. In particular, the global growth and deregulation of energy markets were a large factor. For example, in natural gas, the main commodity and original base of Enron, U.S. gas consumption rose 30 percent between 1983 and 2000, to 22.5 trillion cubic feet.[6] Corresponding trading in energy spot and forward contracts also rose sharply.

As noted earlier, the same was the case for emerging electronic markets and exchanges. By 2001, EnronOnline was one of several B2B electronic markets, and competitors such as Dynegy had embarked on the development of energy trading platforms. Moreover, derivatives trading in general experienced such explosive growth to total more than $100 trillion per day in transactions, much of which occurred on organized financial exchanges (Woods, 2002, p. 125).

Flight to Quality

The overall trading environment has experienced a profound reaction to the demise of EnronOnline. One apparent impact of the Enron failure has been an apparent "flight to quality" to traditional organized exchange markets. The years 2001 and 2002 brought record volume on traditional futures and options exchanges. Much of this growth occurred in financial derivatives, such as the interest rate and index futures that grew globally by 75 percent in 2001.[7] On the other hand, exchange-traded energy futures and options grew by only 7.8 percent over the same period. Since the demise of Enron, energy exchanges have grown more rapidly.

Further indication of a flight to exchange quality is the stellar performance in the natural gas futures and options contracts listed on the New York Mercantile Exchange (NYMEX), as shown in Table 6.2. Given the dominant position of EnronOnline in the natural gas market, there has been an obvious flow of volume to the NYMEX since Enron's failure. Interestingly, Enron was almost the largest trader on NYMEX, as well. As is common in the exchange-traded versus over-the-counter derivatives worlds, Enron frequently sought to offset/arbitrage/hedge OTC contracts from EnronOnline using the exchange-traded analogues on NYMEX.

Some financial market observers have suggested that in addition to a flight of volume from OTC to exchange trading platforms, the post-Enron environment has also created a substitution effect *within exchanges* back

**Table 6.2   Volume of Exchange-Listed Energy Derivatives Traded
Number of Contracts Traded, Year-on-Year as of June 2002**

Contract	Exchange	Average Daily Volume, May 2002	Year-to-Date Volume	Year-to-Date Change (%)
Light sweet crude oil	NYMEX[a]	196,244	19,054,550	+18
Natural gas	NYMEX	103,700	10,054,550	+78
Brent crude oil	IPE[b]	85,274	9,344,396	+22
Gasoline	T-Com[c]	91,901	7,468,377	+12
Gasoline	C-Com[d]	60,594	6,498,396	+10
Natural gas options	NYMEX	49,548	5,195,600	+188
NY unleaded gasoline	NYMEX	44,780	4,486,892	+3
Light sweet crude oil options	NYMEX	39,441	4,976,695	+72
Heating oil	NYMEX	35,898	4,328,682	+15
Gasoil	IPE	28,579	3,128,537	+11

Source: The data underlying this table was obtained from the June 3, 2002 and July 17, 2002, issues of *Futures and Options World*.

[a] New York Mercantile Exchange.
[b] International Petroleum Exchange (London).
[c] Tokyo Commodity Exchange.
[d] Central Japan Commodity Exchange.

to "floor trading." Although NYMEX has an electronic platform known as NYMEX ACCESS, only about 7 percent of all NYMEX transactions are traded online.[8] The remainder trade on the floor using the traditional open-outcry pit system, where floor locals trading for their own accounts transact about 40 percent of total volume. Simon Heale, the new CEO of the London Metals Exchange (LME), was recently asked in an interview about the impact on LME of the closure of EnronOnline. He responded, "The exchange's volume went straight to the [floor]."[9]

B2Bs and Virtual Exchanges

Much confusion actually surrounds the word *exchange*. In countries such as Australia, the United Kingdom, and Canada, any entity that purports itself to be an exchange must be registered, regulated, and approved by the relevant national (or regional) regulators as such. This is not so in the United States, where numerous B2B entities describe themselves as an exchange. The main distinction is the focus on financial products rather than institutions in U.S. derivatives regulation, as explained by

Neves (Chapter 4) and Kramer, Pantano, and Ezickson (Chapter 5). Whether an entity in the United States is a formal, regulated futures or securities exchange depends entirely on whether the exchange allows trading in nonexempt futures or securities, respectively.

As Kramer, Pantano, and Ezickson explain in more detail in Chapter 5, the Commodity Futures Modernization Act of 2000 (CFMA) affords the status of *exchange* to markets that list derivatives for trading and operate under guidelines set forth by the Commodity Futures Trading Commission (CFTC). Achieving this designation is trivial under the CFMA, although the ensuing regulations are not. And, ironically, fully operational and organized foreign futures and options exchanges must undergo a lengthy and expensive approval process to register their products and have them recognized by the U.S. financial markets.

Numerous electronic trading platforms, however, list only those products for trading that are specifically exempt from the regulatory domain of the CFTC, such as forwards and swaps (see Chapter 5). Provided the B2B does not list "futures," "futures options," or nonexempt "securities," CFTC and SEC regulation are not required. Accordingly, EnronOnline did not have to undertake any rigorous new product review before listing new products, provided the products listed were limited to those exempt from regulation under existing commodities and securities laws.

The general B2B model typically involves the provision of a marketplace for bilateral transactions without the market provider's playing any kind of CCP role. Because of its focus on providing a trading platform for mainly bilaterally negotiated OTC derivatives, EnronOnline was itself considered a B2B and thus was not subject to CFTC or SEC regulation. In typical OTC markets, intermediaries such as brokers may match trades in a discrete fashion, but the trade is still completed through a bilateral agreement between the original trading counter parties. In other words, intermediaries in the OTC derivatives world typically assume no credit risk. Therefore, the greater the credit standing and/or rating of the market participant, the greater their ability to either trade or influence the market as a whole.

The Enron model, with EnronOnline the counter party to every transaction, moved away from this bilateral B2B model. On the one hand, EnronOnline thus was an unregulated B2B listing products for trading that were exempt from U.S. regulation under commodities and securities laws. On the other hand, EnronOnline was providing central counter party-like services that made the entity look much more like a Clearing House Oranization (CHO) than just a B2B virtual market. As such, Enron had to maintain a very strong credit rating to be able to clear and execute trades on EnronOnline.

Distinguishing between the B2B agent as a provider of purely a trading environment and the B2B provider as a settlement agent is critical. Noting the previous issues, the financial markets could have been expected to totally abandon the B2B model following EnronOnline's failure. Interestingly, this was not the case. In short, the problem with EnronOnline does *not* appear to have been associated with how it operated as a B2B platform, but rather to the fact that EnronOnline was *also* providing CCP trade guarantees that are highly atypical for B2Bs and much more commonly associated with organized exchanges.

UBS Warburg certainly did not see the end of the B2B model, given its acquisition of the remnants of EnronOnline. And although the B2B model was in steep decline, there were notable exceptions. Of these, three in particular stand out: ChemConnect, ICE, and TradeSpark. The later two B2B entities have shown strong growth in the post-Enron environment. There are several reasons for this:

- Both ICE and TradeSpark operate on the bilateral model of matching and clearing transactions and do not provide central counter party settlement guarantees.
- Both are backed and funded by leading energy participants. ICE is backed by eight U.S. and European finance and energy companies (among others), and TradeSpark is the product of a partnership among eSpeed, Cantor Fitzgerald, and five other energy partners, including Dynegy and Williams.
- ICE diversified its revenues by the purchase of the London-based International Petroleum Exchange (IPE), making it a significant global energy market.
- TradeSpark has the experience of eSpeed and Cantor Fitzgerald, which were pioneers in electronic trading platforms and markets.
- Both ICE and TradeSpark drew OTC derivatives business from EnronOnline that could not be transacted on NYMEX.

The recent economic success of these two B2B energy markets is an example of how exchanges and markets in general have taken the demise of Enron in their stride. ICE witnessed a record 133 percent increase in natural gas trading between mid-November 2001 and mid-December 2001, the period over which Enron filed for Chapter 11 bankruptcy.[10] During the same period, new user applications increased by 400 percent. TradeSpark also reported significantly increased volumes, and its parent, eSpeed, posted impressive profits. However, eSpeed CEO Howard Lutnick correctly identified the fact that future liquidity may be debilitated by the withdrawal of several large energy players from energy trading. On this point, an Enron insider indicated that of natural gas volume on EnronOnline (estimated at 85 percent of total EnronOnline volume), up to 80 percent of the volume was once generated by only 10 of the largest market participants. Given the bilateral nature of B2B participants and the high credit quality required for OTC trading, the growth of these "exchanges" post-Enron thus may be limited. Nevertheless, the B2B model of exchanges will survive well into the future.

Market Transparency after Enron

EnronOnline and the army of marketers that operated the phones attracted over the years a significant number of energy companies that had never participated in energy and/or power trading, especially associated derivatives contracts. EnronOnline also prided itself on displaying numerous prices both constantly and at a fine bid/offer spread. As such, EnronOnline became a focal point for market information, a point that cannot be overemphasized.

NYMEX prices and data have been available freely for many years, but the same cannot be said for the other two major energy B2B entities discussed in the prior section. As such, transparency of market information in energy markets is bound to fall following EnronOnline's demise. And with the decline of transparent price information, liquidity and actual trading volumes may also suffer.

Numerous market rumors abound as to "market plays" that emerged during the final days of EnronOnline. There may be some validity to activities such as attempts of larger and more stable energy companies—and particularly investment banks with energy trading desks—to squeeze Enron and other smaller entities from certain products, especially as smaller traders attempted to exit from their Enron positions at any cost. Although these will most likely remain the secrets of traders' bar discussions, this activity is not unusual in less illiquid and/or distressed markets. As one trader commented, "For me, [Enron's failure is] virtually a nonevent, except for discussion of credit issues and Enron's NYMEX positions." He continued to say, "I don't hear people complaining about it being missing. It has, however, opened up opportunities for the NYMEX, which is pushing very hard to take advantage of the situation."[11]

CLEARING AND CREDIT RISK MANAGEMENT POST-ENRON

With EnronOnline acting as counter party to every transaction until an offset or match occurred, the credit risk that counter parties assumed when transacting on EnronOnline was Enron credit risk. EnronOnline thus operated as a CCP of sorts, but without the usual time-tested conservative safeguards traditionally associated with a CCP (e.g., capital requirements, a default fund, margin requirements, periodic mark-to-market resettlement). A normal B2B exchange, by contrast, is essentially *just* a trading platform that preserves bilateral credit agreements between trading participants, just as in OTC derivatives markets. However, as Woods (2002) explains, this "constrains the number of market participants that will be eligible counter-parties to any given transaction and thereby restricts the growth of the market" (Woods, 2002, p. 132).

In that connection, the failure of EnronOnline has focused attention of market participants on the potential benefits of centralized clearing and settlements for OTC derivatives products. Exchanges have for many years coveted the prospect of expanding the role of their clearinghouses and clearing products other than the traditional futures and options. Now with energy markets in disarray, several have been offering to clear energy OTC products. NYMEX has led the way successfully for several months. ICE has followed by announcing in July that it intends to offer new clearing services for OTC power products with the Board of Trade Clearing Corporation in Chicago.

However, the post-Enron environment is in many ways a double-edged sword. While the regulated exchanges have expanded into new areas of clearing, many moves to change clearing practices have also stagnated. In particular, the combined impact of September 11 and the fall of Enron have forced insurance companies and investment banks to abandon moves for the creation of insurance-type bonds to be incorporated into the guaranty funds of the exchanges' clearinghouses. Without adequate supplementary capital, OTC clearing by existing exchanges becomes less attractive, especially for the current users and owners of those exchanges.

Another worrisome consequence of Enron's collapse is the cancellation and litigation that surround forward and/or derivatives contracts. Many ex-counter parties of Enron are now seeking to renege on the performance of such provisions in their contracts. One interesting lawsuit involves Merrill Lynch's filing suits against Allegheny Energy, Inc., alleging the nonpayment for the sale of its energy trading business. For its part, Allegheny has cited alleged improprieties that occurred between Merrill and Enron, not to mention "other matters" relating to Merrill's past energy trading (whatever that may mean).

To date, it appears that corporations are merely trying to unwind their Enron exposure, and they are doing so via the U.S. courts. Kramer, Pantano, and Erickson have highlighted this problem and called for FERC to "reestablish the sanctity of bilateral contracts by rejecting the attempts of parties to rescind contracts due to unfavorable financial results." The greatest danger is that a precedent is being set for parties to renege on future payment and delivery obligations on their derivatives transactions, which could ultimately decimate the marketplace.

CONCLUSIONS

It appears that market forces have triumphed, and the fall of Enron is but a memory. Trading is often considered a zero-sum game, and, in this case, there are obvious winners and losers from Enron. And, as in all market disasters, the legal fraternity will triumph because litigation will surely continue over outstanding Enron exposures. We hope the outcome of such litigation does not adversely impact the nature of derivatives and forward contracts, which could have disastrous results for the global financial markets and economies.

Many markets do indeed benefit after absorbing a market shock. This is certainly the case with Enron. As to online trading, the net impact seems to have been beneficial, as the remaining markets have now become more efficient. Although some market participants have dropped out, the superior business models of the remaining trading exchanges can more easily accommodate energy trading over the long run than the Enron-credit-centric EnronOnline model. In this sense, the long-term viability of the energy markets may be well served by the migration of volume away from EnronOnline toward more established and time-tested trading systems.

The same can be said for clearing and settlement. EnronOnline represented an odd middle ground that did not represent the benefits of a full-blown central counter party settlement agent but, at the same time, did not constitute the pure bilateral credit risk model common to OTC derivatives. At least in the latter case, market participants *know* to manage their credit risks. By creating a false sense of security, EnronOnline may have actually been worse than either extreme. Not surprisingly, both bilateral credit risk management and centralized clearing and settlements of exchange-traded derivatives have gained ground following the death of EnronOnline. Again, energy markets will be more solid as these entities carry energy trading, which is expected to benefit them in the long run. Another familiar byproduct is always innovation, and, certainly, this will be the case with clearing.

There are also numerous regional considerations in energy markets. The home of Enron—the United States—has suffered unprecedented market shocks since the September 11, 2001, attacks and none more so than the various accounting disclosure crises. There is no doubt that this has affected domestic and international energy markets. More importantly, as the expected crisis in confidence in the United States builds apparent momentum (see Bassett and Storrie, Chapter 2), the importance of U.S. markets for venues of trading, risk-shifting, and liquidity formation will become even more essential.

In international markets, the withdrawal of Enron has reduced competition and so is a boon for domestic markets. This has particularly been the case in the European Union, where new energy markets have been appearing since Enron's demise. The pattern is also similar to the ones observed in the United States, where markets such as Eurex (the German/Swiss derivatives exchange), Euronext-LIFFE, and UKPX (the U.K. Power Exchange) have been steadily winning business and introducing new products. The same applies for more peripheral markets such as Australia, Canada, and Asia.

The return to *normality* (if there ever was such a time) in energy markets will ultimately be beneficial for all markets. Enron was certainly an aberration, and many lessons will have been learned in online trading and clearing. The facility to transact energy trades has not been damaged, and, although there may be some market distortions due to a small loss in price transparency, market efficiency has moved quickly to fill any void.

NOTES

1. For those seeking the lighter side of an Enron-related market analogy, I recommend Joe Bob Brigg's "How Enron Works: The Mule Market," *National Review* (January 22, 2002).
2. "Enron Networks," Draft Presentation and Internal Discussion Document, November 2001 (on file with the author).
3. A cautionary note is that superior platform technology does not always generate liquidity alone, as displayed on numerous global electronic exchanges that operate on substandard systems (e.g., The Korean Stock Exchange).
4. "Enron Networks," op. cit.
5. *Energy Info Source* (October 18, 2002).
6. Bryce (2002), p. 217.
7. Woods (2002), p. 125.
8. "A Conversation with the LME's Simon Heale." *Wall Street and Technology* (April 5, 2002).
9. See note 8.
10. See *Computerworld* (December 10, 2001).
11. *Power and Gas Marketing* (January/February 2002).

7

DO SWAPS NEED
MORE REGULATION?

DAVID MENGLE

T o be effective, government regulation must either (1) bring about a better result than the unregulated market or (2) improve the efficacy of the self-regulating mechanisms of swaps activity, namely, corporate governance, market discipline, and legal certainty. To demonstrate the need for further regulation of swaps activity, it is necessary to establish three things:

1. A market failure must exist that regulation might eliminate without introducing offsetting distortions.
2. It must be shown that current laws and regulations are not sufficient to control the problem.
3. There must be a realistic expectation that regulation would lead to a superior outcome.

MARKET FAILURE?

Examination of the failures and market crises of the past few years suggests that market mechanisms continue to function well. The self-equilibrating mechanism of the market has consistently absorbed shocks and then allowed business to return rapidly to normal levels. Enron is only the most recent—and possibly the most convincing—example of

Portions of this chapter are reprinted with permission from International Swaps and Derivatives Assocation, Inc., *Enron: Corporate Failure, Market Success*, 17th Annual General Meeting, Berlin (April 17, 2002).

how market mechanisms work to diffuse shocks. Further, each failure or market disruption has provided lessons useful in improving the self-regulatory mechanism. Procter & Gamble's problems, for example, led to increased management attention to understanding the risks a firm takes; the Barings failure led to increased attention to controls; and the market disruptions of 1998 helped focus attention on liquidity risk and counter party credit risk. Yet, throughout these difficulties, swaps have continued to grow in volume and are used by an increasing range of institutions.

Further, the market appears to have handled the Enron failure in an exemplary manner. For example, approximately 800 credit default swaps involving more than $8 billion in notional amounts were outstanding on Enron, all of which appear to have been settled without disputes, litigation, or mechanical settlement problems. In addition, closeouts occurred in an orderly manner: Obligations associated with the closeouts were apparently paid, where required, to Enron by the counter party, while counter parties that are owed money by Enron will have their claims considered by the bankruptcy trustee. Finally, the disappearance of Enron as a trader appears to have had little market impact as volume moved to other trading firms. It is difficult to see failure in the way the market functioned.

ADEQUACY OF THE CURRENT ENVIRONMENT

Even if you could demonstrate that market failure occurred, you must also show that current laws, regulations, and standards are not sufficient to cope with the problems encountered in the Enron failure. In fact, the Enron bankruptcy is replete with examples of failures to meet existing standards. In the Chewco transaction, for example, Enron's plan depended crucially on fulfilling two requirements for not consolidating the Chewco Special Purpose Entity (SPE) in Enron's books. (See Chapters 8 and 10 for a discussion of Chewco.) First, it would be necessary for non-consolidation that the ownership of a subsidiary consist of at least 3 percent outside equity; the requirement was not met. Although Chewco attempted to treat a bank loan of the required amount as equity, the bank's insistence on collateralization of the loan caused the outside investment to fall well short of the required 3 percent outside equity at risk. Second, it would be necessary to show that Enron did not control Chewco. Because Chewco's manager was also an employee of Enron, however, it is unlikely that this was the case. Despite failing to meet the requirements, Enron excluded Chewco from its consolidated financial statements, which led to errors in its reported income and debt. These were among the errors that finally were corrected in October and November 2001, after which the market lost confidence in Enron. Had Enron followed the rules that were in place, losses in the investments would have been recognized as they occurred and the restatement might not have been necessary and certainly would have been significantly smaller. But it is also true that, had Enron recognized the losses, the market would have seen through Enron's appearance of creditworthiness and consequently curbed, if not eliminated, its role as a dealer in derivatives.

Another example of a violation of standards already in place appears in the Raptor transactions (see Chapter 8). First, recognizing the value of the appreciation of a company's own stock, even if done by means of forward contracts, is inconsistent with accounting principles. Second, as the value of the investments hedged by the Raptors and the value of Enron shares fell, the Raptors' credit capacity deteriorated. Instead of recognizing the deterioration by setting up reserves, Enron undertook a series of questionable restructurings that delayed loss recognition but were ultimately unsuccessful. Given that the amounts involved were material, it is unlikely that these restructurings were consistent with current standards.

Third, as with Chewco, the Raptors did not meet the nonconsolidation requirements. But, unlike Chewco, the Raptors did not meet the requirements because the SPE that capitalized the Raptors was able to recoup its initial investment by means of a put option Enron purchased on its own stock but settled early. In each case, the premium was distributed to the SPE. Because the premium was sufficient to return not only the entity's invested principal but also a substantial (30 percent) return on the investment, the original investors had little, if any, risk left in the subsidiaries. This lack of capital at risk should have disqualified the Raptors from nonconsolidation.

Finally, Enron was obligated to disclose details of the SPE transactions, along with Chief Financial Officer Andrew Fastow's interest in them.[1] A great deal of information was disclosed in Enron's annual report, yet assertions were made without support and certain key items were missing or misleading. Enron, for example, asserted that the transactions such as those described in Chapter 8 were undertaken on terms that were "no less favorable than the terms of similar arrangements with unrelated third parties." But, as mentioned previously, an economically rational unrelated party would not have agreed to such transactions, so it was misleading to characterize such transactions as having been at arm's length. In addition, Enron did not disclose the significant initial premium income ($41 million) distributed by each of the Raptor entities to the LJM2 partnership (see Chapter 8).

CAN REGULATION IMPROVE THE CURRENT SITUATION?

Finally, it must be shown that additional regulation would work better than the swaps framework of strong corporate governance, market discipline, and legal certainty. Strong, effective corporate governance, for example, is essential to the functioning of swaps activity. As the Group of Thirty pointed out in its 1993 report *Derivatives: Practices and Principles*,[2] senior management attention and involvement is the starting point for risk management. Yet, regulators face a difficult task in attempting to influence corporate governance because each firm's internal controls must be consistent with its corporate organization, culture, and management style. Regulators might be in a position to evaluate governance through a supervisory approach, but more prescriptive regulatory approaches that involve detailed one-size-fits-all requirements incur the risk of reducing the effectiveness of corporate governance by ignoring the unique governance characteristics of a firm.

Second, government attempts to enforce market discipline, while well intentioned, should be approached with caution. A major concern among policymakers and industry participants is that regulation can create a moral hazard in a market even in the absence of an explicit government safety net. Individuals and firms might assume, for example, that government regulation creates a safer environment than is in fact the case.[3] The result is that they take more risk individually, leading to a higher level of risk in the system.

The same caution applies to attempts to augment market discipline by means of increased disclosure of relevant information to the market. Policymakers have taken steps in the past few years to shore up market discipline through increased information disclosure. An example is the Pillar Three of the New Basel Accord, which outlines disclosure standards and, significantly, carries the title *Market Discipline*. But there appears at times to be a tendency among policymakers to elevate transparency through disclosure to the status of an end in itself rather than a means to an end. Any policies geared toward increased disclosure and transparency should, therefore, keep three things in mind:

1. It is essential to be clear on the objectives of new disclosures and whether the required information will actually help accomplish the objectives.
2. Policies should take account of the explicit costs of new disclosure in the form of administrative costs.

3. Transparency policies should take account of the implicit costs of new disclosure in the form of information overload when new disclosures are added to ones already in place.

Early in 2002, there were repeated predictions in the media of new swaps regulation. The matter has not been laid to rest, but it is now apparent that, even in the wake of Enron, the case for new regulation remains weak. The proponents of new regulation still have not demonstrated a market failure; indeed, the main argument seems to be that regulation is needed because some parts of the industry appear not to be regulated the same as others. Further, there is no convincing evidence that sufficient regulatory authority is not already in place. Finally, the proponents of regulation have failed to demonstrate that additional regulation would improve the effectiveness of, let alone supplement, market mechanisms.

CONCLUSION

Enron's actions were the result of trying to reconcile two conflicting strategies: One was to invest in energy, telecommunications, and other technology businesses, which required substantial debt; the other was to grow into a major dealer in swaps, which required substantial creditworthiness. Enron executives knew that their firm's credit quality was essential to a counter party's willingness to do business with Enron. The market would not have it any other way. But rather than adapt the strategies to reality as the result of experience, the executives apparently sought to make it possible to pursue the strategies until they could no longer be reconciled. That they chose to exploit—or flout—accounting rules as well as the principles of corporate governance to maintain the appearance of creditworthiness is not an indictment of market discipline, but confirmation of it. It would be tragic if policy actions designed to correct a perceived market failure were to have the unintended consequence of undermining a self-regulatory structure that has proven to work and work well.

NOTES

1. Regulation S-K, Item 404 (U.S. Federal Securities Laws).
2. Global Derivatives Study Group. *Derivatives: Practices and Principles* (Washington, DC: The Group of Thirty, 1993).
3. For problems that persisted in a regulated environment, see, for example, "Daiwa Bank's rogue employee allegedly made 30,000 illicit trades. Why didn't anybody notice?" *Time* (October 9, 1995).

PART THREE

Structured Finance after Enron

8

AN INTRODUCTION TO THE BUSINESS OF STRUCTURED FINANCE

BARBARA T. KAVANAGH

Media coverage of the landmark Enron bankruptcy has been rife with reference to the large number of partnerships in which Enron was apparently hiding assets and debt from the general investing public. In consequence, many now believe that legitimate corporate finance should not involve *special purpose entities* or, alternatively, that current industry standards and practices surrounding use of such entities must be drastically altered. Some have suggested that additional and perhaps even *special* regulation needs to be directed at structured finance, and others even seem to believe that American businesses and investors would be better off if structured financing methods were abandoned or prohibited altogether.

In fact, structured finance—that part of corporate finance making use of special purpose entities (SPEs)[1]—is a sound business management tool when appropriately deployed. Further, the development and growth of this market has contributed substantially to both the American consumer and corporate prosperity characterizing the United States' most recent economic expansion.

As explained in this chapter, Enron's perverse use of structured financing vehicles hardly conformed to existing industry standards or convention. On the contrary, many of Enron's vehicles were contrived to hide or delay the impact of poor investment decisions,[2] hide debt, and manipulate revenue streams on certain derivatives transactions.[3] Through the simultaneous failure of a number of usual safeguards surrounding use of these structures, Enron was able to create structured financing partnerships that bear virtually no resemblance to those soundly constructed by most corporations today.

The concept of structured finance must be explained before the anomalous nature of Enron's activities and the inappropriateness of recent calls for tighter regulation can be fully appreciated. To that end, the next section begins by defining structured finance in broad terms and explaining the customary reasons for and use of SPEs. The following section then provides readers with background on the evolution of structured finance and its economic benefits to corporations, investors, consumers, and the economy. Having firmly set forth the sound economic function of this branch of finance, we turn back to discuss Enron's abuses of this financing technique, why those abuses occurred, and why caution should be used in extrapolating Enron's behavior to the need for greater regulation. Bockus, Northcut, and Zmijewski return to the issues of accounting, disclosure, and regulation of structured finance in Chapter 10.

THE EVOLUTION OF STRUCTURED FINANCE

Structured finance is a term widely used but rarely defined. For the purposes of this chapter, we stick to the simple and broadly accepted definition that a structured financial transaction is any transaction that makes use of an SPE. Unlike many other forms of financing, structured financing generally requires the participation *from inception* of more than one entity—for example, the ultimate buyer, selling party, and financial engineer, where the latter is often an investment or commercial bank. This definition and the roles of each party in structured transactions become clearer in the later examples.

Structured finance as we know it today has its origins in two different phenomena dating back to the 1970s: *securitization* and the use of special purpose subsidiaries. After discussing these two seminal early vehicles, several more recent and popular structured financing innovations are also presented.

Securitization

Securitization is the process by which the cash flows on one or more assets or claims are bundled and conveyed to end investors through the creation of debt or equity securities that represent claims on those underlying assets or their cash flows. In most cases, the original assets or claims are conveyed by the originator to a separate legal entity—the SPE—that then issues the securities to investors. Interest and/or principal paid on the new securities are financed by cash flows accruing to the underlying asset pool.

Asset Divestiture   The origins of securitization can be traced to the American residential housing markets. Government-sponsored enterprises (GSEs), such as the Government National Mortgage Association (GNMA), Federal National Mortgage Association (FNMA), and Federal Home Loan Mortgage Corporation (FHLMC or Freddie Mac), built the first structured transactions, aided by Wall Street engineers attempting to satisfy investors looking for certain specific attributes in their securities or investments.[4] Indeed, the heavy involvement of Wall Street early on attests to the often-neglected importance of *investor demand* in the design of securitization programs. Investors who wanted short-dated securities were sold claims on the *first* cash flows (both interest and principal) emanating from the pools of underlying mortgages the GSEs were seeking to "sell." And insurance companies, which preferred longer dated securities, ended up with claims on later cash payments in the mortgage pool, often payments that became available only after the short-term claims had been fully paid off.

Whereas the early securities were direct obligations of GNMA or FNMA, later deals were constructed using SPEs. In those cases, the securities issued against the underlying assets represented obligations of the SPE rather than of GNMA or FNMA itself. We return to this very important *separate entity* concept later.

In March 1987, Sperry Corporation undertook what is widely regarded as the first major securitization involving nonmortgage assets—an engineered security whose cash flows were backed by the receivables on Sperry's computer leasing program. Shortly thereafter, General Motors Acceptance Corporation (GMAC) indirectly issued securities supported by a pool of its car loans. GMAC created an SPE to which it sold (i.e., conveyed) a portfolio of its auto loans, and the SPE in turn issued securities representing claims on the interest and principal payments received on those loans. Since then, the population of assets underlying these structured transactions has diversified dramatically and now includes credit card receivables, corporate trade receivables, aircraft leases, stranded utility costs, plant projects, patents, and more. The underlying assets may be mortgages, auto loans, credit card receivables, or a myriad of others; the securitization process in general, regardless of underlying asset, is summarized in Figure 8.1.

Investment Demand   Who buys these securities and why? In particular, why would an investor buy, for example, GMAC's auto-backed security rather than stock in General Motors itself?

Institutional investors such as pension funds and insurance companies often buy securitized products for portfolio diversification. In the General Motors example, structured products allow investors to own a

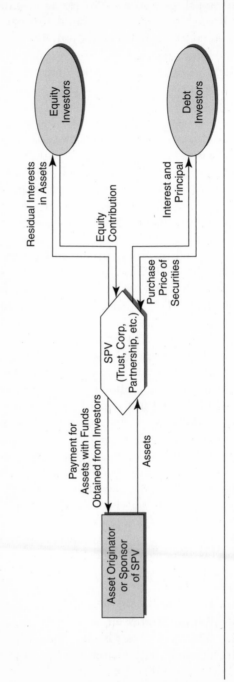

FIGURE 8.1 Securitization Process

156

particular *piece* of GMAC's risk profile rather than General Motors' *entire* risk profile, as reflected in GM's stock.

Importantly, the behavior of a structured security is generally different from the behavior of common or preferred stock of the originator. GM's stock performance will be affected not only by the behavior of consumers whose car purchases are financed by its subsidiary GMAC, but also by overall economic and stock market trends, steel prices, labor union costs, relative foreign exchange rates in overseas markets where GM might heavily sell its product, and many other variables. In contrast, the security representing an interest in a defined pool of consumer car payments owed to GMAC largely contains only the risk relating to credit quality and performance of the underlying car purchasers and the usual risk of relative interest rates (i.e., the yield on this security versus the yield on other securities available in the marketplace).

The Decision to "Structure"   Continuing the example of GMAC's consumer car loans, GMAC's treasurer has two general alternatives available to obtain the money for lending to car purchasers: *on-balance-sheet* and *off-balance-sheet* finance. The distinction is really only one of accounting. The former must go on GMAC's published financial statements, along with the assets themselves. Off-balance-sheet finance, however, enables firms to take the pool of car loans *and* the related securities financing them off GMAC's financial statements, provided the firm meets certain legal, accounting, and regulatory requirements.

GMAC's on-balance-sheet financing alternatives are several. It can issue a bond that is a direct obligation of GMAC itself and collateralize or secure the bond by the specifically identified pool of consumer auto receivables, borrow from a bank and pledge the specified pool of assets as collateral to the bank, or issue new stock. In the off-balance-sheet approach, GMAC creates a separate legal entity (e.g., a trust or partnership) and isolates the assets being financed in that SPE.[5] By taking this approach, the SPE insulates those holding the asset-backed securities from the potential bankruptcy of the originator—General Motors in this example. Remember also that the investor does not want the same risk exposure as GM stock, so the SPE helps ensure that the investor takes on only risks it desires—in this case, those of a diversified population of car loans.

The SPE's primary purpose in this case is to achieve what is often described as "corporate separateness." Simply incorporating a separate legal entity with legal title to the underlying assets in question does not alone constitute "separateness." Legal, accounting, and regulatory standards dictate that the SPE must also generally meet the following requirements to avoid consolidation with the originator or sponsor:

- The SPE's equity base is not subject to control by the originator. Historically, this meant that the equity base must be at least 3 percent of the value of all assets conveyed to the trust. In the wake of Enron, the governing bodies overseeing accounting convention are contemplating increasing this requirement to 10 percent.[6]
- The SPE cannot be controlled by the originator or its management.
- The risks and economic rewards associated with the underlying assets must be effectively conveyed and transferred to the SPE for the originator to remove the assets in question from its financial statements.

When we later analyze several of Enron's well-publicized vehicles, how those structures failed to meet the aforementioned criteria becomes apparent.

The originator obviously cannot build structured transactions in isolation. Coordination is required with firms attesting to its financial statements, specialized legal counsel, and, if the SPE intends to issue rated securities, the rating agencies. Each of these third parties usually acts as a check and balance on the structuring process and tends to ensure its integrity. The Enron transactions discussed later thus are aberrant, not only in terms of their structural characteristics but, more notably, that these three external checks simultaneously failed.

Special Purpose Subsidiaries

Parallel with the evolution of securitization, the concept of special purpose subsidiaries was born and refined. Unlike securitizations, in which SPEs are set up for the purpose of allowing firms to sell or divest themselves of particular assets and to raise funds, special purpose subsidiaries rarely involve asset disposition or fund raising as a primary goal. In consequence and in notable contrast to the SPEs that are set up to facilitate off-balance-sheet finance and asset divestiture, special purpose subsidiaries *usually* are owned and controlled by the firms that conceive of establishing them.

Dating back to the 1970s, certain corporations believed that their exposure to, and capacity to manage, particular types of risk was much better than the rising insurance and reinsurance premiums of the era dictated. As such, these firms set up separate special purpose subsidiaries, wholly owned by their parent firms, separately capitalized, *and* licensed to sell insurance. In their purest form, these "captives" then sold insurance back to the parent corporation at a much better rate than was available in the market. Self-insurance predated the use of special captive subsidiaries, but these captive structures had two advantages over straight self-insurance (e.g., through the use of earmarked reserves). As a separate entity, the company had "prefunded" its losses—there could be no temptation to spend the money on something else. At the same time, the premiums collected on writing insurance back to the parent firm gave captives an independent capacity to *service* claims arising against those policies, not to mention the investment income on the premium.

Having created a separate subsidiary specializing in managing a specific risk dimension, the logical next evolutionary step was for that same subsidiary to begin offering its services to third parties. This was particularly effective in industry sectors where individual insurers lacked sufficient size individually to justify the start-up cost of a captive. Thus was born the concept of *multiparent* captives.

By the late 1980s and 1990s, the specialty subsidiary concept had spread from the insurance sector to wider applications. Banks such as Goldman Sachs, Merrill Lynch, and NationsBank isolated certain financial trades in separately capitalized subsidiaries, in part to give trading counter parties greater comfort relative to credit quality. By creating these subsidiaries—often more highly rated than their parent companies because of protective mechanisms built into the structures—a piece of the capital base of the parent was segregated explicitly and exclusively to support specific trades with counter parties.

Finally, special purpose entities became more prolific in the 1990s as a mechanism for "ringfencing" specific business lines or risks for specialized management and capital allocation purposes. This has been particularly true in the energy sector, where Enron's competitors frequently isolate their trading operations and related financing needs in single-purpose subsidiaries.[7] In these cases, the operations of the subsidiaries are fully reflected in the consolidated financial statements of the parent—the SPE has not been established to hide transactions, assets, or debt from the public.

Liability Management

By the mid-1990s, structured finance was being applied to a much wider population of assets, limited only by investor appetite or Wall Street creativity. In addition, SPEs began to play an important role in helping firms manage their *liabilities,* as well.

The best examples of this are found in the "Cat bonds" now routinely used by reinsurance companies. Assume a reinsurer underwrites directly or reinsures catastrophic risks such as property damage arising from California or Japanese earthquakes or U.S. East Coast hurricanes. Suppose the company retains and reinsures the first $150 million layer of liabilities to claims it might receive, but, above that amount, classical reinsurance is not available and the firm's shareholders do not want to retain the risk. Despite its limited capacity to continue providing insurance, the firm may still have strong *demand* to keep underwriting. The firm can increase its underwriting capacity by buying reinsurance in excess of $150 million—for example, up to $250 million—*from the capital market at large.*

Specifically, the reinsurance company sponsors (but does not own) an SPE whose primary purpose is to write reinsurance back to the sponsor in return for a premium. The SPE takes the premium *and* proceeds from issuing Cat bonds and invests in low-risk securities that can be liquidated to fund future catastrophic insurance claims. In turn, investors in the Cat bond earn a very high interest rate but run the risk of losing all or part of their interest and/or principal in the event of significant catastrophic claims on the SPE. From the investor perspective, the unusual nature of the risk (typically uncorrelated with other major asset classes) helps them diversify their portfolio and achieve a relatively substantial expected return in exchange for a low-probability event—catastrophic losses in excess of $150 million.

Project Finance

The subsection of structured finance known as *project finance* is generally associated with large, fixed assets such as power plants.[8] Of the supposed 1,200 SPEs set up or controlled by Enron, many appear to have been for project financing purposes. A broad understanding of project finance thus is critical to understanding some of Enron's structured financing activities.

Project financing was historically undertaken by commercial banks in two phases: a relatively short-run construction/completion phase and a permanent financing phase with maturities ranging between 10 and 15 to 20 years. Because of their generally short-dated liabilities, banks generally prefer not to write long-dated loans. Accordingly, the second phase of project financing is typically supplied by banks with step-up interest rates designed to encourage the borrower to repay funds early. Notably, however, the expected lives of the underlying assets often extend well beyond the 15- or 20-year loan maturity date. The emerging trend for dealing with this dilemma has been found in structured finance—the creation of an SPE that issues debt to be serviced by cash flows stemming from the underlying project.

Project finance securitizations are generally undertaken by either the bank writing the long-term loan or the sponsor of the project itself as an alternative means of securing funds for the project. In a typical structure, the SPE issues senior and subordinated debt to be serviced by cash flows emanating from the underlying project(s). For example, a power generation plant generally has a contract purchasing its prospective energy production before construction of the plant even begins. Commonly, the bank would provide direct financing through the construction phase given the lack of cash flows in that period on which a structured transaction could be built.[9]

Once the plant is capable of generating cash flow, the contract representing purchase of the plant's future power production can be conveyed to the SPE and act as the source of return for debt and equity investors. From the plant sponsors' perspective, structured finance can provide much preferred fixed-rate financing rather than the floating, step-up interest rate associated with classic commercial bank finance. From the bank's perspective, the mismatch between its short-dated liabilities and the long-term nature of the loan has been eliminated by the SPE's prematurely retiring its debt.

As discussed in greater detail later in this chapter and in Chapter 9, the use of SPEs for project finance was important for Enron. A company regularly expanding in overseas markets, Enron sometimes bought a shared interest with other parties in fixed plant infrastructure in the host country, and other times chose to build. Being able to remove those fixed assets from its balance sheet as well as obtain financing for those projects from capital markets rather than banks became increasingly important for Enron over time.

MARKET SIZE AND ECONOMIC IMPLICATIONS

The structured transactions discussed previously cannot be considered a small, secular piece of global capital markets. Securities backed by mortgages and other pooled assets have assumed increasing importance over the past 15 years, aiding consumers, originating corporations, and investors in the process.

Consider the residential mortgage market. By virtue of being able to sell mortgages in a securitization, the originator is able to accommodate a much larger number of borrowers seeking home ownership than would otherwise be the case. At the same time, the originator maximally leverages its own internal expertise in mortgage originations, thereby benefiting its shareholders. And end investors—often insurance companies, pension plans, or other financial institutions—enjoy residential mortgage market exposure and returns without the start-up cost of internally building, developing, and maintaining the human capital and related support infrastructure. In no small part, the cost effectiveness of this process led to reduced financing costs for the mortgage borrower and greater ease in acquiring home ownership financing.

These same benefits also apply to nonmortgage assets, including credit card financing, auto loans, manufactured housing, and project financing. In our General Motors example, GMAC can provide a greater amount of financing to potential car purchasers than would be the case if it held all loans it originated on its balance sheet to final maturity. As a consequence, General Motors can produce and sell a larger number of automobiles.

ENRON'S PERVERSE APPLICATION OF THE SPE CONCEPT

In the preceding sections, we saw examples of legitimate uses of SPEs—corporations isolating specific pools of assets for securitization or self-insurance or creating separate specialized subsidiaries for risk management, capital allocation, or other strategic reasons. In this section, we consider some of Enron's most widely discussed vehicles, their raison d'etre, and how they differ from existing industry convention.

In general, we can say with some certainty that Enron built structured financing vehicles for the following reasons, in absolute contravention to usual industry objectives:

- To hide debt.
- To hide suspect investments and their deleterious financial statement implications.
- To manipulate revenue streams by marking trade contracts to market.

As is now coming to light, moreover, a number of Enron insiders also experienced extraordinary personal gain, largely by being equity shareholders and/or appointed executives of the SPEs in question. Whether a design objective, afterthought, or unintended consequence, this feature is categorically opposite to most others in the industry, where executives go to *great lengths* to avoid anything that might be construed as associating them or their corporations with the SPE in question.

Chewco

Chewco serves well as an example of an SPE whose sole reason for existence seemingly was to hide debt. In 1997, Enron and California's Public Employee Retirement System (CALPERS) were each 50 percent owners in the SPE called Joint Energy Development Investments (JEDI). Enron executives sought CALPERS as a partner in other ventures but did not believe CALPERS would invest in more than one Enron-related SPE at a time. Enron staff thus began looking for a third party to buy out CALPERS' stake in JEDI, then valued at $383 million.

Unable to find a third-party buyer, Enron's finance staff incorporated Chewco in November 1997 and named a mid-level Enron finance employee as its sole managing partner and investing member. Two banks then lent Chewco the necessary $383 million (unsecured) to fund the buyout of CALPERS' interest in JEDI. Although Enron staff supposedly intended to find an independent third party to step into Chewco and take an $11 million capital stake, they never succeeded. As a consequence, Chewco was formed with a nominal capital contribution from one Enron employee, and that same individual was the sole managing partner. By late 2001, that partner and his domestic partner had received personally more than $10 million from Chewco as a return on their $125,000 equity investment.

Enron could have simply borrowed funds directly and bought out its partner's interest in JEDI. But the consequences in terms of its financial statements would have been negative. By having to reflect greater bank debt by $383 million, Enron would have appeared to be more leveraged (negative from a rating agency perspective), and the limited amount of bank lines available to fund further expansion by the company would have been used disadvantageously. In addition, Enron would then have controlled 100 percent of JEDI's equity. Accounting convention would unquestionably have required line-by-line consolidation of JEDI's assets and liabilities onto Enron's financial statements. This ironically would have defeated the purpose in originally forming JEDI.

In 2001, Arthur Andersen required Enron to restate its financials and consolidate Chewco because of the company's inability to demonstrate that Chewco met the *corporate separateness* standards discussed earlier in this chapter. No independent party managed Chewco, and no equity owner could be identified, least of all an equity base in the requisite 3 percent amount. It is unclear why Chewco was originally treated as a separate entity and not consolidated in Enron's financial statements from inception.

The Chewco transaction demonstrates flaws on several fronts. First and most obviously, despite certain attempts at "restructuring" Chewco after inception, the *de minimus* 3 percent equity requirement was never met by this vehicle, either as initially incorporated or later in its life.

In addition, whereas most originating organizations go to great lengths to avoid controlling an SPE through managerial decision making (or even *appearing* to control the SPE), Enron made no such efforts. By appointing one of its own finance staff as the sole executive managing the SPE, Enron went to the opposite extreme. Even if an outside investor had contributed the necessary 3 percent of equity in this transaction, the issue of Enron's *controlling* Chewco would still broach the possibility of consolidation of the vehicle.

Note that no assets, claims, or financial instruments were housed in Chewco. Chewco existed simply for purposes of housing bank debt used to purchase CALPERS' interest in JEDI. This creates the appearance that Chewco was designed to help Enron avoid borrowing such debt directly and then reflecting both the debt and JEDI's underlying merchant investment on its own financial statements. The most that could be hoped for is that Chewco actually took legal title to CALPERS' 50 percent equity in JEDI, but that is unknown.

Chewco raised corporate governance questions, as well. Powers et al. (2002) note that Enron's board of directors approved formation of Chewco but only after representations from senior Enron officials to the Enron board that Chewco would (1) have $11 million in equity supplied from an undisclosed source, (2) obtain a $250 million bank loan Enron would have to guarantee, and (3) obtain an additional $132 million in debt from JEDI. The board was thus clearly mislead relative to Chewco's equity.

Finally, the convention in structured finance and accounting is to deem a "guarantee arrangement" of this type inappropriate. In effect, it means Enron is not truly transferring the risks to the SPE as required, but instead just assuming them indirectly. For this reason, corporations almost never use a guarantee arrangement of the type seen here because it typically results in consolidation of the SPE's assets and debt into that of the originator/guarantor and defeats the purpose of initially forming the SPE. In attempting to *reengineer* Chewco after its initial closure, Enron reportedly provided a guarantee supporting Chewco's bank borrowings, thus contributing substantially to the restatement of Enron's financial condition in 2001.

LJM1, LJM2, and the Raptors

The LJM1 and LJM2 partnerships entered into more than 20 transactions with Enron. Both partnerships were formed, at least in part, to minimize the deleterious effects of certain investments on Enron's published financial performance. Specifically, the accounting requirements concerning "marking investments to market" were causing Enron's income statement to change dramatically from period to period as the value of several underlying investments moved dramatically up or down from one quarter to the next.

Consider, for example, Enron's purchase of stock in 1998 of a company called Rhythms NetConnections (Rhythms). In 1998, Enron purchased $10 million of stock in Rhythms at $1.85 per share. Its ability to resell those shares was restricted until the year 2000.[10] Rhythms was subsequently taken public, and, by May of 1999, Enron's initial $10 million investment was worth approximately $300 million.

Accounting standards required that at each quarter's end Enron reflect in its income statement the increase or decrease in value of this investment from the preceding quarter. As we can see from the change in Rhythms' stock price, Enron would have to have reported a considerable increase in value of its investment, but this value was unrealized in the sense that Enron received no cash flow from this increase and likely would not until the stock was actually sold. Further, the value of Rhythm's stock could just as likely go down from one reporting period to the next, resulting in a decline of reported investment values for Enron from one quarter to the next. It was precisely this volatility in quarterly marks to market of Rhythms that led Enron executives to create the LJM structures.

As further background, Enron executives also chose to address another issue at the same time in these two structured transactions. Namely, Enron's stock had realized greater and greater increases in value during the time frame in question here, and, in that connection, a hedge contract[11] that Enron's treasury group had entered into with a major investment bank had appreciated considerably in value—similar to the increase in stock value of Rhythms. In a seeming moment of greed, Enron executives decided to use LJM1 and LJM2 as vehicles for realizing that increase in value.

LJM1   LJM1 was formed in June 1999 with Enron's Chief Financial Officer Andrew Fastow assuming the role of general partner in the SPE in exchange for a supposed $1 million capital contribution. Two unaffiliated corporations indirectly became limited partners in this SPE and jointly contributed $15 million at formation. According to representations made to Enron's board of directors in requesting its approval for this transaction, LJM1 was being formed for essentially three reasons:

1. To hedge the volatility of Enron's Rhythms NetConnections investment.
2. To purchase a piece of Enron's interest in a Brazilian power company subsidiary.
3. To buy the certificates of yet another Enron SPE known as The Osprey Trust.

What assets did LJM1 own, and what value did they have? LJM1 held shares of Enron stock whose resale was restricted for four years. These shares had been "gifted" to LJM1 at its inception, with LJM1 issuing a note to Enron in exchange representing a related debt obligation. And in September 1999, LJM purchased an interest in a Brazilian subsidiary from Enron for $11.3 million that is discussed later.

Rhythms   Enron's finance team made the strategic decision to create LJM1 in June 1999 and to have LJM1 enter into a derivatives contract with Enron that would supposedly act as an "earnings hedge" for Rhythms. By creating gains and losses based on the value of Rhythms stock from one period to the next, the hedge was intended to offset the impact of actual Rhythms stock price changes and reduce Enron's earnings volatility.

At the deal's inception, LJM1 created a subsidiary that issued a type of derivatives contract—a *put option*—to Enron on its shares of Rhythms stock. Under such a contract, Enron could require LJM1's subsidiary to purchase the Rhythms shares at $56 a share in June 2004. In other words, a put option acts as an insurance policy for the buyer, essentially guaranteeing for Enron a floor below which the value of Rhythm's stock would not fall. If, in public markets, shares of Rhythms stock traded below $56 a share, Enron could simply "put" the shares to the LJM1 for $56 a share. The seminal question, however, is how the SPE would have paid Enron $56 per share for the Rhythms stock if Enron's stock–the SPE's sole quasi-liquid asset—moved down in price at the same time as a decline in Rhythm's stock.

Subsequent to the initial implementation of LJM1 and the Rhythms hedge, Enron finance personnel realized its hedge was incomplete. Whereas Enron had purchased insurance against Rhythm's stock price falling below $56, *volatility* in Rhythm's stock price *above* that level continued to translate into earnings volatility for Enron because of the accounting mark-to-market convention. Enron thus quickly entered into four more derivatives with LJM1 and its subsidiary—all option-based products such as the one previously described. The terms of those contracts are not disclosed (Powers et al., 2002).

Despite its hedging efforts, Enron's finance team chose to terminate the Rhythms hedge toward the end of the first quarter of 2000. In November 2001, apparently as a result of Arthur Andersen's review of a number of these vehicles, Enron announced it would restate its financials to reflect, among other things, consolidation of LJM1's hedging subsidiary because it failed to meet the required 3 percent outside equity test.

Current discussion in the industry is to increase the *de minimus* equity standard to 10 percent for SPEs not subject to consolidation. Ironically, even if this subsidiary had 10 percent equity at inception, it still would have lacked a capacity to perform on its obligations because of the extraordinary price volatility in Rhythms' stock during this period.

Other Mark-to-Market Abuses   LJM1's Rhythms hedge illustrates an additional abuse endemic to Enron's use of SPEs—namely, its marking to market of trades with SPEs in a suspect fashion, apparently to manipulate its stated financial performance. Just as accounting convention required Enron to mark its merchant investments to current market prices, an analogous standard required that trading contracts such as the Rhythms put option also be marked to market as of the date of each published financial statement. Marking trading contracts to market, however, can be an art form, particularly when dealing with such unique, nonstandard, illiquid contracts as the Rhythms hedge.

Whereas many types of put options are publicly traded on exchanges with price quotes readily available, privately negotiated derivatives such as the Rhythms hedge require use of sometimes-complex valuation models that often call for subjective decision making in choosing inputs that affect mark-to-market values. For example, a standard input to virtually any common model for valuing a put option is the price of the underlying stock. However, the publicly quoted price of Rhythms would have to be subjectively adjusted to reflect the restricted nature of the underlying shares or the fact that resale of the stock shares was restricted for some period of time. And that price adjustment would change each quarter because we are moving closer and closer to expiry of the resale restriction.

If Enron had hedged with a major Wall Street counter party, as is market convention, Enron could have gone back to that dealer on each financial statement date to obtain an independent third-party valuation of the mark-to-market value of its hedge. Instead, Enron simply *decided* at each quarter what the Rhythms hedges were worth and adjusted its unrealized gains or losses accordingly. The extraordinarily unique nature of the hedges allowed for tremendous latitude in valuation and made this an obvious target for abuse by executives bent on manipulating financial statements and personal gain.

Cuiaba, Brazil   As increasing amounts of information become public about the extraordinarily large personal sums of money extracted by Enron executives from the company through SPEs, the source for at least some of these funds seems to be the transfer or "sale" of assets at less than market value, with subsequent resale (in some cases, back to Enron) at considerably higher prices. The price difference appears to have often been pocketed by Enron executives for personal gain. Enron's Cuiaba Brazilian investment falls into this category.

Enron owned a 65 percent interest in and controlled appointment of three of four directors of a Brazilian company that, among other things, was building a power plant in Cuiaba, Brazil. This level of equity ownership and control undoubtedly required line-by-line consolidation of this subsidiary into Enron's financial statements. Enron had been searching for a third-party buyer of at least part of its interest in this project but had been unsuccessful.

In September 1999, Enron sold LJM1 a 13 percent stake in the company and relinquished control of one director appointment for $11.3 million. Subsequent to this sale, Enron took the position that it no longer controlled the company and, as such, need not consolidate it in its financial statements.

Enron subsequently repurchased the 13 percent interest in August 2001 for $14.4 million, despite the fact that in the intervening period the Brazilian corporation likely lost value because of operating difficulties. Powers et al. (2002) make no note of any independent appraisals having been obtained relative to either the sale or repurchase of this interest, as would typically be the case in a transaction with a truly independent third party. Because Enron insiders were often shareholder beneficiaries of the SPE, their personal interests called for sale or transfer of assets to the SPE from Enron at a loss to Enron in exchange for high personal profits. The Brazilian transaction in LJM1 is a straightforward example of this.

We also note that Enron had a significant natural gas forward contract in place with the Brazilian company. When this company was a subsidiary and subject to accounting consolidation, this forward contract would have undergone intercompany elimination and would not been reflected in the consolidated Enron financials. However, the "sale" of the 13 percent interest and resulting nonconsolidation meant that Enron now had a privately negotiated forward gas contract with an unaffiliated third party subject to mark-to-market gains and losses. Enron realized a $65 million gain in the second half of 1999 on the forward gas contract with the Brazilian affiliate.

LJM1's Wind-Down and Some Lessons   In March 2000, Fastow apparently chose to terminate LJM1 for what appears to be two principal reasons: The restriction on Enron's ability to sell the shares of Rhythms stock expired, and the Rhythms "hedge" between Enron and LJM1 was not performing. The corporate record surrounding the transactional life of LJM1 is, according to Powers et al. (2002), incomplete. However, several conclusions can be unequivocally drawn in connection with that structured transaction.

First, as in the case of the Chewco structure, LJM1 resulted in tremendous financial windfall to Enron insiders. In March 2000, other Enron employees had become shareholders in LJM1 and its subsidiary, seemingly without taking risk, yet realizing phenomenal returns. Those financial returns seem to have been at the expense of Enron Corporation—corporate records are unable to validate what economic return Enron enjoyed in exchange for costs incurred. Second, Enron's use of a phantom SPE as a counter party for a hedge can only be described as the antithesis of market practice. We term LJM1 *phantom* in that it had no real assets to rely on should it ever have had to make payments to Enron as part of its "option-based insurance policy." LJM1's only assets were stock in Enron Corporation, whose sale was actually restricted, and an interest in the Brazilian project that was anything but liquid. This aspect of LJM contravenes existing standards in a number of respects.

Existing accounting standards and interpretations restrict dramatically the circumstances under which a corporation can make use of its own stock for anything other than direct issuance to the public or employees. OTC derivatives markets, moreover, are extraordinarily credit sensitive. Enron's corporate peers enter into derivatives to hedge earnings volatility only with the most highly rated, major global financial institutions and, after careful analysis, ensuring that the derivative contract provides considerable economic protection. The LJM1 structure was tantamount to a corporation's attempting to hedge its own exposure with a contract with itself, which is, of course, not a hedge at all. By the time LJM1 was terminated, Enron's own risk management staff had reportedly calculated the probability of LJM1's defaulting on its hedge with Enron as 68 percent!

Finally, just as in the case of Chewco, the "corporate separateness" of LJM1 is suspect. Although the limited partners in LJM1 reportedly had some management control despite Fastow's being sole general partner managing the structure, the amount of true equity in this SPE is subject to substantial question. Although Enron chose to unwind the vehicle in 2001, Arthur Andersen's restatements of the company's financials in November 2001 covering the 1999 and 2000 income statements did include downward adjustments to Enron's net income of $95 million and $8 million, respectively. These adjustments reportedly represent a "reconsolidation" of the subsidiary of LJM1 housing the "Rhythms hedge," in part because its ability to meet the 3 percent *de minimus* equity test was suspect. In the end, then, even Arthur Andersen employees questioned the use of Enron stock as a hedge.

LMJ2 and the Raptors   LJM2 was formed in October 1999. Based on Fastow's representations to Enron's board, it was intended to be a large equity fund that could invest in strategic assets that Enron might want to syndicate quickly. Supposedly, LJM2 thus should have been a source of quick funding for continued expansion. From what is known of LJM2, however, it was used as a mechanism for smoothing volatility in mark-to-market prices of investments made by Enron over a number of preceding years.

Fastow was again designated general partner in this structure, but this structure took on as many as 50 limited partners. Limited partners in LJM2 were, like those in LJM1 at inception, reportedly major corporate investors such as JP Morgan, Citicorp, Merrill Lynch, and a number of well-known pension/retirement plans. Contributions from all partners to LJM2 reportedly totaled $394 million.

LJM2 ultimately became a façade for *equity* contributions to a number of Enron's famous Raptor transactions. In each case, LJM2 would inject what appeared to be the necessary equity to capitalize a Raptor SPE, but in many or most cases, LJM2 would receive a phenomenal return of both principal and interest *before* the SPE in question would become truly activated. Once active, the Raptors were intended to engage in additional incestuous hedging transactions with Enron, designed to insulate Enron's earnings volatility. Hedging activities would generally commence only *after* the purported equity was returned to LJM2, making it anything but equity-like because true equity would remain at risk throughout the life of the SPE.

LJM2 itself had a complex, multilevel partnership structure, and often the SPEs in which it invested would in turn hold ownership interests in other SPEs. Two common themes underlie several of them, making them in substance similar to the Rhythms transaction described earlier. First, the SPEs were endowed with Enron stock (or its economic equivalent) in an effort to provide the SPE with some "economic value" and requisite capital to enter into hedges with Enron. Second, the SPE's hedges were often designed to mask the volatility associated with existing Enron investments. Contrary to apparent representations to equity investors in LJM2 and to Enron's own board, these SPEs and LJM2's funds were not used to fund new investment opportunities identified by Enron, but rather seem to have been used to prop up an increasingly fragile collection of existing investments. The Raptor vehicles in which LJM2 invested allowed Enron to avoid reflecting nearly $1 billion in losses on merchant investments from the third quarter of 2000 through the third quarter of 2001 (Powers et al., 2002, p. 99).

What exactly were the Raptors? For illustrative purposes, consider Raptor III. The New Power Company (TNPC) was a power delivery company in which Enron held a 75 percent interest. Enron intended to take TNPC public in the fall of 2000 and supposedly wanted to insulate itself from potential interim volatility in TNPC's value. To that end, Raptor III was designed with an SPE named *Porcupine*. Similar to the other Raptor transactions, LJM2 contributed $30 million to Porcupine, supposedly representing "equity." At the end of the same week it made its initial equity contribution, LJM2 received back $39.5 million in a single distribution from Porcupine for a calculated internal rate of return of 2,500 percent.

The other three Raptor vehicles were endowed with Enron stock, but the Porcupine SPE was endowed instead with warrants on TNPC—exactly what the structure was supposed to be hedging! Simultaneously, it had entered into a derivatives contract obligating it to compensate Enron when the price of TNPC fell. In effect, then, this "hedge" was really a *doubling* of Enron's exposure to price movement in TNPC stock. Porcupine's sole asset was warrants representing TNPC stock, and the warrants declined in value just when Porcupine would be most obligated to provide money to Enron—when TNPC stock was declining. As a consequence of this painfully flawed structure, Raptor III began disintegrating almost immediately after construction.

CONCLUSION

Unfortunately, media coverage surrounding Enron has led the public to believe structured finance is nothing more than an act of deception on the part of institutional management—a mechanism to defraud the investing public. In reality, it is a legitimate financial management tool with well-established roots in capital optimization and risk management dating back to the 1970s.

Structured finance generally has its own inherent checks and balances protecting the interest of all parties involved, from seller to investor. In the Enron case, however, a group of senior executives seems to have successfully bastardized the process in pursuit of personal wealth and power.

Current efforts to revamp materially fundamental aspects of structured finance, especially through new political restrictions on these activities, are, however, tantamount to "shooting the messenger." Fraud can, has, and will be perpetrated by insiders through any means at their disposal if insiders decide the criminal path is the one they want to take. Draconian constraints we might arbitrarily place on certain asset or income categories will not change that. If executives wish to lie and/or falsify corporate records for personal gain, they will do so with complete indifference as to the category of balance sheet or income statement affected.

No doubt, greater transparency would be beneficial in the form of more disclosure by executive management of the nature and extent to which structured finance is used as a means of financing a company or altering its balance sheet. However, disclosure itself is a *competitive tool* that firms can use to their advantage. Those with nothing to hide have a strong

172 STRUCTURED FINANCE AFTER ENRON

incentive to be even more transparent with their structured finance activities going forward. The early use of captive, special-purpose subsidiaries illustrates that firms are more than capable of disclosing all the details of SPEs when they desire. In some cases, firms considered publicizing a captive to be a "signal" of strength—why else would they self-insure with a captive unless they thought their loss record was better than insurance premiums reflected?

Regulatory changes designed to force more disclosure in a particular fashion thus may not be necessary and could even discourage firms from using their own disclosure techniques as a means of *attracting* investors and customers. Apart from disclosure, proposed changes such as the increase in required capital levels of SPEs from 3 percent to 10 percent will simply act to render uneconomic otherwise-sound business transactions. Capital levels should be commensurate with risk inherent in any structured transaction and thus determined on a case-by-case basis. Arbitrarily tripling required capital levels will simply render lower risk transactions economically unfeasible, to the detriment of both seller and investor.

Finally, the recent actions by the Securities and Exchange Commission requiring CEOs and CFOs personally to attest to corporate financial statements is noble. It may, perhaps, even be necessary to convince investors that the egregiousness of recent events has not gone unnoticed. For the majority of corporate treasurers who are honest, higher compensation will understandably be sought in exchange for this higher personal liability. But those executives willing to commit felony fraud will likely be indifferent to one more incremental crime (i.e., attesting personally to manipulated financial statements). It seems, then, to be just another misdirected penalty, albeit with an understandable point of origin.

NOTES

1. The terms *special purpose entity* (SPE) and *special purpose vehicle* (SPV) are essentially synonymous. Because of its use in connection with Enron, I adopt the convention throughout of using only the term SPE, although the term SPV probably has a wider following among practitioners.
2. Enron's demise was not a function of its structured transactions but rather of other fundamentally flawed aspects of its business decisions, as well as executive pursuits of personal wealth rather than that of shareholders.
3. Not all of Enron's SPEs appear to have been used for these illegitimate purposes. Even for those more obvious and egregious cases discussed here, all the facts are not in, so any conclusions in this article should be interpreted in the context of the author's admittedly limited information, all of which is public domain.

4. Some contend that securitization often requires the government to subsidize the initial creation of the market, as occurred with mortgages. The evidence for this claim is lacking, however. Indeed, numerous counter examples can be found of markets being created and assets securitized without any government assistance.

5. Often, the sole purpose of this legal entity is to house the transaction in question.

6. It is doubtful, however, that a 10 percent equity level would have fixed the problem with Enron's structures as those discussed in the Powers Report were fundamentally flawed in dimensions other than capital adequacy.

7. The Public Utility Holding Company Act (PUHCA) essentially *requires* investor-owned municipal and state utilities to ringfence their power marketing operations in this manner.

8. This section draws heavily on Kavanagh (2002).

9. The nebulous time frame for completion of construction also makes it hard to issue bonds and predict when a completed plant can begin servicing related debt.

10. As a cash-starved company always looking for funds to fuel its continued growth and expansion into new markets, investments such as Rhythms are hard to understand from the outset. The investment generated no cash—the resale restriction meant that Enron could not realize any gains in the stock if they did occur.

11. Enron had certain obligations to issue stock to employees as they exercised stock options that were part of its employee compensation plans. The cost to Enron of issuing that stock increased as the price of its stock increased. To minimize this cost, Enron had entered into a type of derivative known as a forward contract that "locked in" the cost to Enron of issuing these shares. As the price of its stock shares rose, the value of this "insurance policy" it had purchased from a major investment bank increased.

9

STRUCTURED COMMODITY FINANCE AFTER ENRON

Uses and Abuses of Prepaid Forwards and Swaps

CHRISTOPHER L. CULP AND BARBARA T. KAVANAGH

S ignificant criticisms have been leveled at Enron's use of energy derivatives contracts known as *prepaid forward* and *swap* contracts, or *prepaids* for short. The Senate Permanent Subcommittee on Investigations and at least one U.S. federal court, for example, have questioned whether the nearly $15 billion in cash prepaids that Enron received in the decade before its failure was actually "bank debt in disguise." Because of the consequent anathema concerning these products, even the most well-established uses of these contracts have waned in recent months. Energy market regulators, moreover, will surely be paying significant extra attention to these structures. Are the recent criticisms of Enron's use of prepaids justified? And are these criticisms unique to the Enron transactions, or do they generalize to all applications of these particular financial instruments?

Prepaid commodity derivatives are a form of *commodity finance* in which one firm uses derivatives contracts to achieve the economic equivalent of loaning a commodity to another firm by paying cash upfront and agreeing to delay taking delivery on the commodity. Commodity lending can help the borrower finance a development project or production facility in a way that the underlying project or facility being financed also serves as *economic collateral* for the repayment of the commodity loan. And because the borrower's repayment obligations are expressed in terms of the production of the underlying project rather than as a money interest rate, the commodity lender's credit risk is both greatly reduced and confined to the risk of the project being financed (as opposed to the other assets of the firm borrowing the commodity). So useful are prepaids for project finance, in fact, that the World Bank relied on them extensively in the 1980s for many of its development and project finance loans.

The dearth of publicly disclosed information about what Enron actually did prevents us from fully addressing the Enron transactions here, but we instead provide a number of more general conclusions that can be drawn even without a detailed Enron-specific analysis. We begin by explaining the distinctions between traditional and prepaid energy forwards and swaps, and we remind readers that even plain vanilla forward purchase contracts are economically equivalent to a money loan plus physical storage of the underlying commodity. We further explain why *traditional* forwards can be used to extend money credit, but *prepaid* forwards involve no money credit and, instead, are economically equivalent to borrowing and lending the underlying commodity. We then explain how prepaids and commodity loans play an important role in project finance, using an early program from Enron itself as an example. Next, we explain why Enron's more recent uses of prepaids have generated so much controversy. We outline the circumstances under which the more recent prepaid structures can be legitimately used for commodity finance, as well as when they can potentially be abused to disguise traditional debt. A brief conclusion ends with a cautionary note about the recent public and political scrutiny of prepaids.

THE ECONOMICS OF COMMODITY FORWARD AND SWAP CONTRACTS

Dating back to at least to the 12th century, forward contracts are among the oldest and most established forms of commodity derivatives—contracts whose values are based on underlying physical commodities such as natural gas or oil. A forward contract requires the *long* to purchase a fixed amount of the underlying commodity on some future date at a fixed price that is negotiated at the inception of the contract. The basic difference between traditional and prepaid forwards, as we explore in the following sections, simply concerns the timing of the payment by the long to the commodity seller.

Traditional Forward and Swap Contracts

In a traditional forward agreement, the payment of cash by the long *and* the transfer of the asset by the short both occur at the end of the life of the transaction (i.e., on its settlement date). Consider, for example, a three-month forward contract negotiated on September 15 that requires the long to purchase 1,000 barrels of West Texas Intermediate crude oil on December 15. The fixed price paid by the long (denoted $K/bbl) is fixed on September 15, although the payment by the long occurs on December 15. Figure 9.1 illustrates from the perspective of the short (i.e., the oil seller), where up arrows denote cash or asset inflows and down arrows denote outflows.

Instead of requiring the physical transfer of title for oil on the settlement date, some forwards are *cash-settled*. The long still makes a fixed cash payment to the short at maturity, but now the short also makes a cash payment to the long.[1] The cash payment by the short is equal to 1,000 bbls times the spot price of oil on the contract's settlement date. The *values* of the physical and cash-settled forwards are identical.[2]

One myth that has surfaced in the wake of the Enron failure is that cash-settled forwards do not serve legitimate *commercial purposes*. An example immediately illustrates why this is wrong. Consider a petrochemical firm that purchases oil every three months as an input to chemical production. As oil prices rise, its profit margin shrinks. The firm could, of course, lock in its oil purchase price using a traditional forward. Equally plausible, however, is that the firm prefers to buy oil competitively on the spot market to spread its business around and retain some degree of purchasing flexibility. In this case, the firm might use cash-settled forwards to lock in its fixed purchase price for oil indirectly—the forwards would generate cash income at the same time that oil price increases erode margins. This use of a cash-settled forward is clearly a legitimate part of the chemical firm's primary business activities, despite the absence of physical delivery.

Close cousins to forwards, *swaps* are essentially multiple forward contracts with different maturity dates bundled and sold as a single package.

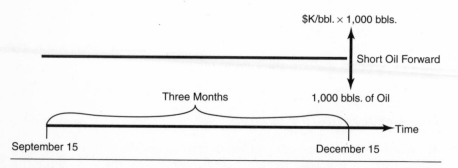

FIGURE 9.1   Inflows and Outflows from the Perspective of the Short

A swap involves not just a single exchange of cash for an asset but *several* such exchanges. Consider, for example, a nine-month oil swap with quarterly settlement dates. If the swap is negotiated on September 15 and specifies a fixed purchase price of $K/bbl, on December 15, March 15, and June 15, the long pays $K/bbl × 1,000 bbls to the short in exchange for 1,000 bbls of oil. Exactly the same result could have been achieved had the short entered into three forward contracts, each with fixed purchase price $K/bbl and based on 1,000 bbls of oil and with maturities of three, six, and nine months. Like forwards, swaps can be cash-settled.

Prepaid Forwards and Swaps

The sole difference between traditional commodity forwards/swaps and prepaid forwards and swaps is the timing of the cash and asset flows. Instead of making a cash payment to the short at the same time the short delivers the asset as in a traditional forward, the long in a prepaid makes a cash payment to the short *at the inception of the transaction.* Figure 9.2 illustrates, using an otherwise identical oil forward as in Figure 9.1.

Notice in Figure 9.2 that the fixed price received by the short when the prepaid deal is struck on September 15 is now denoted $M/bbl to indicate a different price than the $K/bbl received by the short in the traditional forward shown in Figure 9.1. We explore what this price difference is in the next section.

Like traditional forwards, prepaids may also be cash-settled. Similarly, prepaid *swaps* are just bundles of prepaid forwards, or contracts in which a single fixed payment is made at the beginning of the transaction in exchange for the subsequent delivery of a commodity on *several* future dates.

At face value, there is nothing particularly controversial about prepayment features in derivatives. Consider the most prevalent example

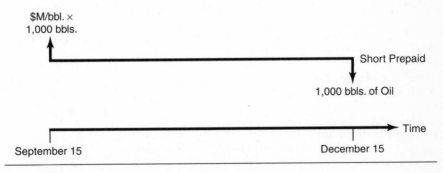

FIGURE 9.2   Prepaid Forwards and Swaps

of prepaid derivatives: options, or contracts in which the buyer pays an upfront premium to the seller for the subsequent right to buy or sell the underlying asset at a specified price. Even the most ardent critics of derivatives generally admit that options can serve a legitimate purpose. So, too, can prepaid forwards and swaps.

Forwards versus Physical Storage

Like all derivatives contracts, the usefulness of commodity derivatives comes from the tight linkage between derivatives and the underlying markets on which the derivatives are based. The ability to "replicate" and "arbitrage" the payoffs of derivatives with positions in the underlying asset market, for example, keeps the prices of derivatives in line and makes them reliable tools for hedging.

The economic distinctions between traditional and prepaid forwards can be better understood by examining the differences in the *replicating strategies* for these two derivative products—that is, strategies that involve no outlay at time t and produce the same payoff at time T for the traditional and prepaid forwards, respectively.

TRADITIONAL FORWARD CONTRACT REPLICATING STRATEGY

As Culp and Hanke explain in Chapter 1, going long a forward contract is economically equivalent to borrowing money and using the proceeds to finance the immediate (spot) purchase of oil and then storing that oil over time.[3] Table 9.1 shows the equivalence of a long forward with this borrow, buy, and store replicating strategy.

Table 9.1   A Traditional Long Forward and Its Replicating Strategy

	Time t	Time T
Borrow, Buy, and Store Oil from t to T		
Borrow $S(t)$	$S(t)$	$-S(t)\,e^{r(T-t)}$
Buy one bbl of oil at t	$-S(t)$	$S(T)$
Pay net storage costs from t to T	—	$-S(t)\,e^{z(T-t)}$
NET	0	$S(T) - S(t)\,e^{(r+z)(T-t)}$
Long Oil Forward Maturing at T		
Long forward on one bbl of oil at t	0	$S(T) - K$
NET	0	$S(T) - K$

where $S(t)$ $(S(T))$ denotes the spot price of oil at time $t(T)$, r denotes the money interest rate, K denotes the fixed purchase price for oil in the forward, and z denotes the cost of physically storing oil, net of any benefits to holders of actual oil inventories, and where both r and z are expressed as continuously compounded annualized rates.

Because both strategies involve no initial outlay and have identical risks, their values must be the same.[4] Table 9.1 thus tells us that the equilibrium fixed purchase price K in the forward must be the same as the cost of borrowing money plus storing oil, or

$$K = S\left(t\right)e^{(r+z)(T-t)}$$

The term $r + z$ is called the *net cost of carry*, where r represents the capital cost of carry (i.e., storage) and z represents the net physical cost of carry. The economical equivalence of the two strategies has led many to refer to a position in long forward contract as *synthetic storage* (Culp and Miller, 1995b).

Because the replicating strategy for a traditional forward requires the long to borrow, buy oil, and store oil, the long cannot escape the capital cost of storage (i.e., the interest due on the loan required to fund the physical oil purchase) by going long a forward contract.[5] True, in the traditional forward, the long no longer has to borrow to finance its oil purchase at time t, but the seller knows this and thus can raise the forward purchase price by exactly the capital cost of oil storage that the long avoided by using the forward contract.

In other words, there are no free lunches, and the long bears the capital cost of storage in *both* physical and synthetic storage strategies. In the physical strategy, those costs are paid explicitly to a lender to finance the initial purchase of oil. In the forward, the short is essentially extending money credit to the long by allowing the long to delay its cash payment, and the interest charges on that de facto loan are reflected in the price paid by the long to the short at the contract's maturity.

Prepaid Forward Replicating Strategy

If a traditional oil forward is economically equivalent to borrowing money plus buying and storing oil, then to what is a prepaid oil forward equivalent? Table 9.1 shows that borrowing, buying oil, and storing it is a zero-cost strategy. Now, the prepaid forward requires an initial outlay of M, where M is the fixed price paid by the long to the short at time t for delivery of oil at time T. The prepaid is *not* a zero-cost strategy. To invoke the traditional no-arbitrage valuation arguments of financial economics, we need to compare apples to apples and thus either need to convert the replicating strategy into a strategy with an initial cost of M or to convert the prepaid into a zero-cost strategy. We adopt the latter approach without any loss of generality.

As Table 9.2 shows, the original replicating strategy of borrowing, purchasing oil, and storing it is now economically equivalent to going long a prepaid forward *plus borrowing M* to fund the cash prepayment. In the absence of arbitrage, the fixed price M paid by the long in the prepaid thus is

$$M = S(t)\, e^{z(T-t)}$$

As in the case of the traditional forward, the long yet again bears the capital carrying costs of the commodity in both the physical replicating strategy and the prepaid. In the former case, the capital carrying cost is paid explicitly to a moneylender in the form of the money interest on the loan required to finance a spot market purchase of oil. In the latter case, the capital carrying cost is again paid to a lender, this time to finance the upfront payment in the forward. In both cases, *it need not be the case that the long has borrowed any funds from the short.*

Unlike the traditional forward, the long now bears the capital carrying cost explicitly when a prepaid is used in lieu of physical storage. The short is no longer extending credit to the long by allowing the long to delay its payment for the commodity. Accordingly, the short can no longer charge the long a higher price to reflect the foregone capital carrying cost. As a result, the fixed price paid by the long in the prepaid is exactly

Table 9.2   A Prepaid Long Forward and Its Replicating Strategy

	Time t	Time T
Borrow, Buy, and Store Oil from t to T		
Borrow $S(t)$	$S(t)$	$-S(t)\,e^{r(T-t)}$
Buy one bbl of oil at t	$-S(t)$	$S(T)$
Pay net storage costs from t to T	—	$-S(t)\,e^{z(T-t)}$
NET	0	$S(T) - S(t)\,e^{(r+z)(T-t)}$
Long Oil Prepaid Maturing at T and borrow		
Borrow M	M	$-M e^{r(T-t)}$
Long prepaid on one bbl of oil at t	$-M$	$S(T)$
NET	0	$S(T) - M e^{r(T-t)}$

equal to the *present value* of the fixed price paid by the long in the traditional forward—that is:

$$M = Ke^{-r(T-t)} = \left[S\left(t\right) e^{\left(r+z\right)\left(T-t\right)} \right] e^{-r\left(T-t\right)} = S\left(t\right) e^{z\left(T-t\right)}$$

IMPLICATIONS

A major implication of the foregoing discussion is one of the oldest and most basic tenets of commodity derivatives. As the great economist Sir John Hicks recognized in 1939, any forward transaction (prepaid or otherwise) can always be "naturally thought of as reducible to a money loan *plus* a spot transaction or forward transaction. In fact any loan transaction can be reduced in that way" (Hicks, 1939/1957, p. 141).

In that context, it should also now be clear that the oil purchaser *always bears the capital cost of storage.* In a physical storage program or a prepaid forward, the capital storage cost is paid in the form of the funding cost borne by the long to finance its initial cash outlay, whereas the long bears the capital carrying cost in a traditional forward contract through a higher forward purchase price for oil. This immediately implies that *absolutely all* commodity derivatives have a funding component and that the cost of this lending is always borne by the purchaser of the asset.

Another implication of the analysis in the previous sections is that the only extension of money credit from one counter party in a forward to the other occurs when the short agrees to let the long delay payment *in a traditional forward.* In that case, the simultaneous exchange of cash for the asset at maturity allows the long to avoid the cost of funding the purchase over time, but that savings is offset by a higher forward price. In the case of prepaids, the long must fund its initial outlay until it receives the underlying asset. Although the cash flow consequence of this is to put cash in the hands of the short earlier, this is *not* an extension of credit by the long to the short. On the contrary, this is an extension of credit by a third party to the long, and the long in turn uses this credit to finance *a commodity loan* to the short.

To see why the prepaid is equivalent to a commodity loan despite the obvious cash transfer from the long to the short, we need only recognize the fundamental difference between an asset purchased for immediate delivery and one purchased for future delivery. In a normal spot transaction, funds are exchanged for an asset that is delivered within a day or two of the funds transfer. In a forward transaction, the two parties mutually agree that funds will be exchanged *later* for an asset that will be delivered *later.* In this case, *both* counter parties bear some credit risk—the long has allowed the short to "borrow" the commodity by agreeing to delay delivery, *and* the short has allowed the long to "borrow" the funds by agreeing to take payment.

A prepaid represents the middle ground, where the short does *not* agree to extend credit to the long, but the long does agree to delay delivery. The long thus has bought and paid for a commodity on which it voluntarily delays taking delivery. The prepaid is thus equivalent to a purchase of the commodity for immediate delivery *plus* the simultaneous decision of the long to loan the commodity back to the short.

ECONOMICS OF COMMODITY LENDING

Why might a firm agree through a prepaid to lend a commodity back to the short that it has already paid for? There are two possibilities—either the short *needs* the commodity, or the short *does not yet have* the commodity. The latter, in particular, lies at the core of understanding prepaids as they are used in *commodity finance*.

The Economics of Commodity Lending

Commodity finance is essentially the lending of commodities to a producer that does not yet have the commodity in deliverable form. By paying for the commodity in advance, the producer can use the funds to acquire the commodity or transform it into a deliverable form. In markets such as gold, commodity lending occurs explicitly, whereas in markets such as oil and gas, commodity borrowing and lending are accomplished with prepaids.

In a money loan, the borrower either accepts cash on an unsecured basis and merely promises to repay it or posts collateral with the lender to guarantee performance on the loan. In a commodity loan, by contrast, the borrower commits to repaying the commodity itself over time. A *cash-settled* commodity loan involves the purchase of the cash equivalent of a commodity by the long on the trade date and the subsequent payment by the short to the long of cash amounts determined by the prevailing future spot price of the underlying commodity.

To see how a cash-settled commodity loan works, consider, for example, a U.S. bank that advances the Mexican government $1 million to fund the completion of a government-owned oil drilling operation. The loan is to be repaid over five years, with quarterly installment payments commencing one year after the initial advance of funds. The cash payment due on each installment date is explicitly linked to a fixed amount of oil and a floating reference oil price. The loan is thus equivalent to a prepaid, cash-settled oil swap.

From the perspective of the U.S. bank, a payment has been made for the cash equivalent of a fixed amount of oil, and the bank has then agreed to delay its collections of those oil price-based payments over time. From the bank's perspective, its credit exposure to the Mexican government is substantially reduced relative to an extension of money credit by the bank that would require fixed interest payments in return. If oil prices rise substantially, the Mexican government will have relatively little trouble servicing the commodity loan. Interest payments on the commodity loan are higher, but so are revenues from the oil rig. Similarly, the debt burden for Mexico falls at precisely the same time that its revenues fall—that is, when the spot price of oil declines.

Commodity-based loans of this kind date back to the fourteenth century where they were used by the Medici Bank to promote trade finance. (See Cochrane and Culp, 2003b; de Roover, 1963.) Similar commodity-index loans resurfaced in the early 1980s as a source of development finance. The World Bank, for example, frequently used commodity-based debt to provide funds to countries that relied heavily on commodity exports to service their borrowings.

Another common use of commodity loans is project finance. By pre-purchasing the production from an as-yet uncompleted oil field or production platform, the upfront cash can provide the commodity borrower with enough cash to complete the underlying project. This does not mean that the lender has made a *cash* loan to the borrower. Instead, the lender has made a loan *of the commodity* to the borrower, and the completion of the project acts as economic collateral to ensure that the commodity can be repaid as the underlying project begins producing and the commodity becomes available.

Does all of this mean that prepaids are "bank debt in disguise"? *Absolutely not.* On the contrary, prepaids are *commodity loans that are not disguised at all.* To use a forward contract to extend a money loan, the *short* would extend credit to the *long* by allowing the long to delay payment. A prepaid, by contrast, involves the *long* lending the commodity *to the short.* The commodity purchaser bears the interest costs of funding the commodity purchase regardless of the timing of the cash payment, as we have seen.

Enron's Volumetric Production Payments Program

To illustrate the actual mechanics and benefits of commodity lending through prepaids, we need look no further than Enron itself. As explained in Chapters 1 and 4, one of the great success stories of Enron was Jeffrey Skilling's GasBank, in which Enron provided long-term price protection and project financing to its natural gas customers. A pivotal component of the GasBank was Enron's Volumetric Production Payments (VPP) program, begun in 1990. These transactions were prepaid natural gas forwards in which Enron was the long—that is, Enron paid cash upfront to a customer in exchange for oil and gas production from the customer in the future.

As Kavanagh explains in Chapter 8, an important application of structured finance has always been the area of project finance, in which a lender agrees to help finance the completion of a project using the future revenues from that project as collateral for the loan. This was precisely the intent behind the VPP program. To keep the credit risk of the transactions limited to production fields, Enron's VPPs were set up in the form of SPEs that operated as legitimate affiliates of the oil and gas producers. The producers ringfenced their oil production fields in these SPEs, thereby enabling Enron to limit its credit exposure to the SPEs themselves. In other words, by prepurchasing the production from the fields set apart in the VPPs, Enron was essentially extending a loan to its customers whose interest payments in the form of gas and oil deliveries depended solely on the performance of the field underlying the VPP.

As we alluded earlier, commodity financing is an attractive alternative for would-be lenders to firms that may be questionable credit risks *but for* their involvement in or development of a commodity-related project that can serve as economic collateral for commodity financing. Not surprisingly, then, Enron set up VPPs primarily with producers that either were struggling and needed short-term liquidity to keep a gas or oil field producing or that were in need of project financing for a field. As an example of the former, Enron's first VPP was done in 1990 with Forest Oil, a cash-strained gas producer. Enron entered into a prepaid natural gas swap in which Enron paid $44.8 million upfront in exchange for 32 billion cubic feet of natural gas to be delivered over five years through the VPP. An example of the latter was the 1991 VPP Enron helped set up with Zilkha Energy. Under that agreement, Enron paid $24 million upfront to assist in covering the high upfront costs of Zilkha's planned Gulf of Mexico expansion in return for a portion of the subsequent production from those properties (Fox, 2002).

Enron's use of prepaids is a type of *structured* commodity finance for two reasons. The first is Enron's use of SPEs to house the VPPs. In addition, Enron looked to the structured finance market to *fund* the project finance credits extended through its VPP prepaids. Starting in 1991, Enron pooled its VPPs into a series of limited partnerships called the *Cactus Funds*. The terms of each individual VPP called for gas deliveries at varying frequencies and across differing maturities, but combining the VPPs into a single vehicle created a *net* position that looked like one giant prepaid gas swap with relatively uniform settlement dates. This, in turn, enabled Enron to hedge the risk that falling gas prices would erode the value of its future deliveries by entering into cash-settled natural gas swaps. (Hedging the *market risk* of project finance extended through prepaids is also a practice dating back to the World Bank in the 1980s.)

With a relatively stable stream of prepurchased future gas deliveries whose price risk was now essentially eliminated, the resulting exposure resembled a fixed-rate bond secured by a pool of commodities. Enron was thus easily able to securitize the future cash flows on its VPPs. In a typical Cactus securitization, Enron created two classes of securities: Class A sold to an SPE that financed the purchase of those securities with bank loans, and Class B securities sold to General Electric Credit. Interest and principal repayments on both classes of securities were based on the *hedged* income of the VPPs, which in turn was used by the Class A securities SPE to service its bank debt. In this manner, participating banks were able to avoid direct ownership interests in the Cactus partnerships (Fox, 2002). Figure 9.3 illustrates the process.

The first Cactus partnership was formed in 1991 and raised $340 million from 15 banks to fund Enron's VPPs. By mid-1993, Enron had raised nearly $1 billion to fund its VPP program (Fox, 2002).

ENRON'S LATER DEALS: LEGITIMATE COMMODITY FINANCE OR DISGUISED DEBT?

The contracts in which Enron was *long* prepaid forwards and swaps, as in the VPPs, have attracted virtually no political or public criticism. In other words, people seem to have accepted that Enron's VPPs were legitimate extensions of commodity loans for project finance purposes. But when Enron started to go *short*—that is, when Enron was *receiving* cash upfront in exchange for future delivery obligations or cash equivalents—claims quickly surfaced that Enron was abusing prepaid forwards and swaps to conceal what was really long-term money borrowing.

We have already seen that in isolation, comparing prepaids to bank debt is just plain wrong. The bulk of the Enron prepaid controversy, however, has surrounded structures that involved a bit more than just prepaids in isolation.

When Enron failed in December 2002, it had about $15 billion in cash prepayments from JP Morgan Chase and Citigroup booked against future oil and gas deliveries. Over time, Enron had entered into similar deals with other banks, including Crédit Suisse. The various deals into which these banks entered with Enron are numerous and diverse in terms (and perhaps in purpose). Instead of discussing these deals in any detail, we

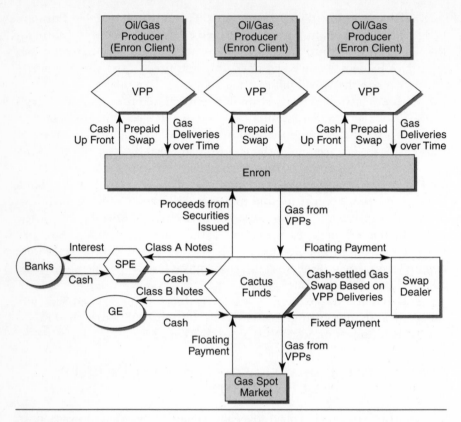

FIGURE 9.3   Enron's Volumetric Production Payments Program

explore a single *representative* structure. This is admittedly simplified for presentation and analysis purposes and is not intended to represent accurately a specific deal between Enron and any particular bank. Nevertheless, this stylized example is sufficient to facilitate an analysis of the controversy surrounding the actual transactions.

The Representative Deal Structure

Figure 9.4 illustrates our representative deal. The structure is easiest explained by examining the four numbers shown on the graph, each of which is associated with a major transaction or set of transactions. Assume for now that the SPE shown in Figure 9.4 is a company that is neither owned nor controlled by either Enron or the bank—we revisit the veracity of this assumption later.

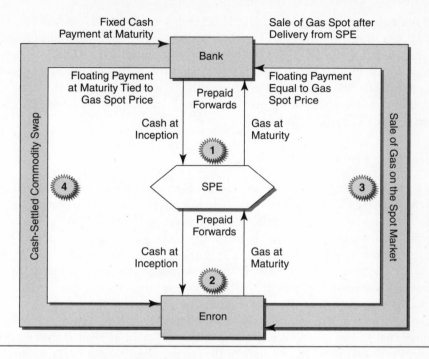

FIGURE 9.4   Representative Deal Structure

In transaction 1, a bank enters into prepaid gas forwards (or swaps) with an SPE in which the bank makes the initial cash payments and receives claims on future gas deliveries. Alternatively (and as in Chapter 10), a bank enters into a secured loan with the SPE, lending cash up-front secured by the subsequent delivery of gas. In transaction 2, the SPE executes prepaid forwards with Enron on essentially similar terms, paying cash in exchange for later transfers of title for gas from Enron to the SPE, which the SPE then uses to honor its own gas sale obligations to the bank. In transactions 1 and 2, the bank has done nothing out of the ordinary and has simply engaged in a typical prepaid forward with the SPE, which in turn has done the same with Enron.

Transactions 3 and 4, together with 1 and 2, complicate things. In transaction 3, the bank takes the gas that it receives from the SPE under the prepaid forwards and sells that gas for the then-prevailing spot price. In some cases, the bank sold gas on the spot market, but in other cases, as in Figure 9.4, the bank sold the gas *back to Enron*.

Recall from Figure 9.3 that Cactus entered into cash-settled commodity swaps to hedge its gas deliveries on the VPPs, as did the World

Bank before Enron in its project financing loans of the 1980s. As Enron did for Cactus, the bank in Figure 9.4 also enters into a cash-settled gas swap to hedge the price risk of its future gas deliveries on its various prepaid forwards. But in the VPP/Cactus structure, Enron entered into swap hedges with other swap dealers, *not* with the same customers into which Enron did the VPPs. In Figure 9.4, by contrast, the bank hedged its gas price risk in a swap *with Enron.*

Disguised Bank Debt?

The bank, acting like Enron in Cactus, has hedged away *all* of its market risk. Fluctuations in gas prices thus do not impact the bank's bottom line. But because the bank has also sold the same gas back to Enron that the SPE bought from Enron *and* because the bank has hedged the price risk of that spot gas sale in a swap with Enron, the structure starts to look rather incestuous. Specifically, the structure starts to look like a *wash trade,* or a trade in which only cash and no energy actually changes hands and in which there is essentially no net economic value.

Exacerbating suspicions about this structure is the accounting treatment that Enron could take on the prepaid forwards. As Bockus, Northcut, and Zmijewski explain in Chapter 10, Enron could, under certain conditions, account for the cash it received on prepaids as derivatives and not as term debt. This does not mean that the deals were undisclosed or even off-balance-sheet. On the contrary, the funds would show up as operating cash flows, and the subsequent delivery obligation would show up as a price risk management liability.

For the Enron customers engaged in VPPs, treating the upfront cash as operating cash flow may have made sense, given that the cash was invested in projects that were collateralizing the repayments of that initial cash receipt. But many contend that the structure depicted in Figure 9.4 was designed *specifically to get this accounting treatment* so that Enron could avoid direct disclosure of additional term bank debt.

Whether the structure shown in Figure 9.4 is a wash trade concealing a bank loan depends on the answer to several critical questions, discussed in more detail in Chapter 10. First, was the SPE a separate business with distinct ownership and control from both Enron and the bank? If not, the three legal entities shown in Figure 9.4 collapse into two entities—Enron and the bank—in which case the structure starts to look more like a wash trade.

A second and related consideration is whether the performance on the bank's cash-settled swap was materially tied to performance on its prepaids. If the SPE was not a separate entity, that would mean the bank bore Enron credit risk on both transactions. But that alone still does not mean the *performance* on the swap and prepaid were linked. As long as a default on the contract between Enron and the SPE or between the SPE and the bank does not automatically trigger an early termination of the swap—or conversely—the transactions are technically independent. But if the contracts are linked through "cross-default" provisions, a strong case can be made that the swap and prepaid together constituted a wash trade.

The third golden question is whether energy actually did flow through this structure. The answer to this question can be useful to legitimize the structures but proves unrevealing to indict them. Specifically, if the title to the gas actually was transferred from Enron to the SPE, from the SPE to the bank, and from the bank to other market participants, the structure was probably legitimate. Even if the gas flowed back to Enron in transaction 3, provided gas actually flowed through the pipelines, a case could be made that the transactions were all done for genuine commercial purposes.

What if gas did not flow through the structure? If the transactions were physically settled and no gas flowed, that gets suspicious. But if the prepaids between the bank and SPE and the SPE and Enron were *cash-settled*, we can conclude basically nothing. As we argued earlier, cash settlement in and of itself is neither unusual nor a priori cause for concern. Because energy *never flows* in a cash-settled transaction, however, it is essentially impossible to use this feature of the structure to differentiate between a wash trade and an actual, legitimate commodity derivatives transaction in a structure such as that shown in Figure 9.4. With cash-settled prepaids, the answers to the first two questions thus become significantly more important.

Evidence on the Actual Structures

Far too much evidence and too many facts remain outside public view for us to argue one way or the other whether the actual structures between Enron and JP Morgan Chase and Citibank were legitimate or not. At least one structure has been subject to enough public disclosure, however, to facilitate some further analysis.[6] Called *Mahonia Limited*, this structure was a Channel Islands SPE set up at the behest of Chase in December 1992 by Mourant du Feu & Jeune, acting on behalf of The Eastmoss Trust.

Mahonia was not established specifically to conduct transactions with Enron. At the time, Chase questioned (correctly, in our view) whether a national bank had statutory authority to accept physical delivery of commodities. Mahonia was established as a vehicle by which such deliveries from Chase customers could be made without posing regulatory problems for Chase. The transactions originally contemplated did not proceed, but the Mahonia entity had already been set up. Enron first approached Chase to do a prepaid in June 1993, and Mahonia was identified as a suitable vehicle for conducting that transaction (Harrison, 2002).

From 1994 to 2001, Enron engaged in another 10 prepaid transactions with Mahonia. All but the last of these transactions were physically settled and apparently involved the actual transfer of title of oil or gas. Over its life, moreover, Mahonia conducted business with customers apart from Enron. Mahonia also appears to have been neither owned nor controlled (in the sense described by Bockus, Northcut, and Zmijewski in Chapter 10) by Chase and later JP Morgan Chase (the latter as successor to Chase through merger with JP Morgan).

As a separate firm with separate ownership and control, Mahonia was free to reject any transaction that was off-market or unprofitable for the Mahonia shareholders. In at least one instance, Mahonia *did* reject a transaction proposed by Chase because it was too risky (Harrison, 2002).

Similarly, as a separate firm responsible for its own deals, the swap between Chase and Enron appears to have no link to the Mahonia prepaids. On the contrary, it seems that the usual cross-default provisions of the swap were actually waived to make sure that the transactions were independent.

After Chase ascertained that it could indeed accept physical commodity deliveries, it began to buy Enron's oil and gas from Mahonia and then sell that oil and gas to the open market. Not until late in the life of Mahonia did JP Morgan Chase sell the products back to Enron, as shown in Figure 9.4. Even then, JP Morgan Chase maintains that the sole reason transaction 3 was with Enron is simply that Enron was the largest spot market participant (JP Morgan Chase & Co., 2002, p. 3).

At face value, it thus looks as though the Mahonia structure was a legitimate commercial enterprise, formed with independent ownership at the suggestion of Chase—not unusual in the world of structured finance—to help Chase's customers engage in structured commodity finance using prepaids. Although Enron was the original customer, the firm also did business with other energy firms.

We should note, however, that this perspective is *not* shared universally. In fact, a U.S. district court judge commented in March 2002 that, to him, the prepaids among JP Morgan Chase, Mahonia, and Enron represented "a disguised loan."

CONCLUSIONS AND MARKET IMPACT

As in all commodity derivatives transactions, both traditional and prepaid forwards and swaps always contain an implicit money-lending component. Whether a forward contract is traditional or prepaid does not change the fact that the long always bears the costs associated with funding the asset purchase, nor does it change the value of those capital carrying costs. The prepayment provision merely alters when the capital carrying costs are paid.

The only time a forward contract represents an explicit extension of money credit is when the short in a *traditional* forward allows the long to delay its cash payment. This is admittedly counterintuitive. Because prepaids put cash in the hands of the short earlier than traditional forwards, it looks at first glance as though prepaids represent the extension of money credit and not the other way around. But when one realizes that the alternative is to buy the commodity *now* and store it, it becomes clear that the prepaid is actually equivalent to the purchase of oil or gas by the long for immediate (spot) delivery *plus* a loan of that commodity to the short for the life of the prepaid.

That prepaid forwards and swaps on their own are "bank loans in disguise" thus is quite the opposite of economic reality. A prepaid represents a *loan of the commodity* from the long to the short. The *risks* of a prepaid forward and swap are materially different from a bank loan, moreover, because the periodic repayments made by the short to the long are based on the underlying commodity price, not the money interest rate. Generally, this is precisely the attraction of these products for project finance—that is, extending commodity credit to firms for the development of a production facility whose production in turn collateralizes the original commodity loan.

Enron's early use of prepaids in its VPP program and Cactus securitization illustrates that these sorts of deals can be perfectly legitimate and legal. To classify structures such as VPP/Cactus as "bank loans in disguise" would be a basic failure of understanding about the economics of commodity markets. Similarly, to dismiss out of hand the later transactions of Enron with JP Morgan Chase and Citigroup as "bank loans in disguise" is premature and potentially equally wrong. If the SPEs used in these deals were independent entities, if the four transactions depicted in Figure 9.4 were not linked in a credit sense, and if gas and oil actually flowed through the structure, there is ample reason and historical precedent to believe that these recent deals were kosher. Even with cash settlement of the derivatives, the structure may well still have served an important commercial purpose other than "disguising debt." The bottom line is that the recent structures cannot be criticized without *significant* additional economic and financial analysis.

Unfortunately, the controversy over Enron's recent use of prepaids has cast pallor over this entire class of financial transactions. Calls for additional regulatory scrutiny have not been justified, and even if it turns out that Enron *did* abuse prepaids, that fact alone should not stop *other firms* from making appropriate use of these products, of which there are many. We urge regulators to move forward with caution, lest a wide range of beneficial activities be penalized for the sins of only one abuser. We also strongly encourage firms not to shy away from these valuable tools for fear of "guilt by Enron association." With proper attention to structuring, disclosure, and accounting, firms using prepaids have nothing for which to apologize.

NOTES

1. In cash-settled forwards, the cash payment obligations of the long and short are generally netted into a single payment.
2. To see this, simply imagine that the long in a physically settled forward immediately sells the 1,000 bbls of oil on the spot market at the prevailing spot price. The net proceeds from this are identical to a cash-settled contract in which the payment to the long is based directly on the spot price.
3. All of our discussions of "economic equivalence" are meant to apply to the marginal firm in equilibrium. As in many other situations in applied price theory, *inframarginal* firms may face a different opportunity set in the short run. See the discussion by Culp and Hanke in Chapter 1.
4. This does assume, of course, the usual asset pricing assumptions, including perfect capital markets and symmetric information.
5. As Culp and Miller (1995a) explain, the long cannot escape the cost of physical storage either by synthetically storing with a forward contract.
6. The reason for the significant public information on Mahonia pertains to a lawsuit filed by JP Morgan Chase against the insurance companies that provided Enron with surety bonds to be posted with Mahonia as guarantees of performance on their prepaid contracts. Culp discusses this lawsuit in more detail in Chapter 13.

10

ACCOUNTING AND DISCLOSURE ISSUES IN STRUCTURED FINANCE

KEITH A. BOCKUS, W. DANA NORTHCUT, AND
MARK E. ZMIJEWSKI

Not many people are interested in the debates about the rules that managers must use to prepare a company's financial statements (generally accepted accounting principles [GAAP]). Most people view those debates as esoteric and irrelevant. Thus, it is no surprise that these debates typically take place only within the confines of the private and governmental regulatory bodies that set the standards for financial reporting.[1] However, because of Enron's quick loss of billions of dollars of market capitalization and its bankruptcy, these debates gained widespread public interest, and accounting rules and their regulation fell into the center of the political arena.[2]

Is Enron's demise an example of the failure of accounting rules? Are the accounting rules inadequate? While we do not have the answers to these questions, in this chapter we contribute to this debate by describing and analyzing the accounting rules in the Enron controversy. Specifically, we discuss the accounting rules for consolidation of special purpose entities (SPEs) and how to account for a series of prepaid purchase transactions that are possibly linked or related, which, if treated as one transaction, are the equivalent to a loan (prepaids).

On November 8, 2001, less than a month before it declared bankruptcy, Enron announced that it was restating its financial statements because of accounting errors, reflecting its conclusion that three SPEs (Chewco, JEDI, and LJM1) did not meet certain accounting requirements and should have been consolidated (Enron, 2001). The retroactive consolidation resulted in a "massive" reduction in Enron's reported net income and a "massive" increase in its reported debt (Powers et al., 2002).

By that time, Enron had also received about $15 billion in cash prepayments from JP Morgan Chase and Citigroup that were booked against future oil and gas deliveries (see Chapter 9). In certain instances, the cash prepayments and future oil and gas deliveries were apparently booked as a series of transactions through SPE structures. These SPE structures and related transactions now have been alleged to be nothing more than *wash trades*, where only cash (and no energy) changes hands and thus potentially represented "bank debt in disguise."

In this chapter, we review and discuss how the accounting and disclosure of SPEs and related structured finance vehicles are highlighted by the controversy surrounding the failure of Enron.[3] The primary issue with respect to consolidation arises when a company's involvement with an SPE requires it to include the SPE's assets and liabilities in its consolidated financial statements.[4] Accordingly, the next section of this chapter summarizes the accounting and disclosure of issues pertaining to SPEs. A subsequent section then relates those broad issues to the two alleged abuses of accounting and disclosure policy by Enron. A final section offers a brief summary and concludes with some important public policy lessons.

CONSOLIDATION OF SPECIAL PURPOSE ENTITIES

In January 2003, the Financial Accounting Standards Board (FASB) issued FASB Interpretation No. 46, *Consolidation of Variable Interest Entities, an Interpretation of ARB No. 51* (FASB, 2003), which is the new guidance related to the consolidation of SPEs. The objective of the interpretation "is not to restrict the use of variable interest entities but to improve financial reporting by enterprises involved with variable interest entities."

Before turning to the current authoritative guidance specific to SPEs leading up to the new FASB interpretation, we first summarize accounting standards related to the broader topic of consolidation including full consolidation and "one-line" consolidation. These broader standards deal with only the general case of consolidation and do not deal with the specific case of SPE consolidation.

Full Consolidation

ARB 51 (American Institute of Certified Public Accountants [AICPA], 1959), as amended by FAS 94 (FASB, 1987), provides the primary guidance for full consolidation procedures. Fully consolidated financial statements represent the financial position and results of operations and cash flows for a single entity, although multiple legal entities may be included. All components of the parent's and subsidiary's assets, liabilities, revenues, expenses, and cash flows are combined. Consolidation must be used in substantially all cases where the parent controls, either directly or indirectly, 50 percent or more of the *voting interest* of a subsidiary. Consolidation should not be used when the parent's control is temporary or significant doubt exists concerning the ability of the parent to control the subsidiary (e.g., the subsidiary is in legal reorganization or bankruptcy). FAS 94 expanded the consolidation rules to include all majority-owned subsidiaries, for example, finance subsidiaries of manufacturing entities that were previously not consolidated.

One-Line Consolidation

For investments where the parent has *significant influence* with an entity but not control, APB Opinion No. 18 (AICPA, 1971) requires companies to use the equity method of accounting. Significant influence is generally defined as *voting interests* between 20 percent and 50 percent. The equity method can be thought of as a one-line consolidation because the investor's share of earnings from the investment is reported as a single amount in the investor's income statement. The original investment is recorded at cost as an asset on the balance sheet and is adjusted periodically to recognize the investor's share of earnings. Components of the investee's financial statements are not combined with the components of the investor's financial statements.

SPE Consolidation

The direct authoritative guidance leading up to FASB's new interpretation on the consolidation of SPEs has beginnings with accounting for the extinguishment of debt (FAS 76) (FASB, 1983a) and the transfer of receivables with recourse (FAS 77) (FASB, 1983b). FAS 76 provided that debt may be accounted for as extinguished if assets placed in trust outside the debtor's control were sufficient to satisfy the debt (i.e., in substance defeasance). FAS 77 permitted the transfer of receivables with recourse to be treated as a sale under certain conditions, including the seller's surrender of control of the receivables. The provisions of both FAS 76 and FAS 77 were superseded by the FASB in 1996 with the issuance of FAS 125.

Until 1996, all the direct authoritative guidance for SPE consolidation came from the Emerging Issues Task Force (EITF).[5] The first specific reference came from the EITF in 1984 with Issue No. 84-30, *Sales of Loans to*

Special Purpose Entities, which addressed the issue of whether the assets and liabilities of an SPE for the purpose of purchasing loans originated by the bank should be consolidated in the bank's financial statements even though the bank has no equity ownership interest in that SPE (FASB EITF, 1984). The EITF did not reach a consensus on the issue.

Consolidation of SPEs was mentioned next at an EITF meeting February 23, 1989, as described in EITF Topic D-14, *Transactions Involving Special-Purpose Entities* (FASB EITF, 1989). The SEC observer to the EITF raised the issue of whether SPEs should be consolidated and whether asset transfers should be recognized as sales. The SEC observer stated that nonconsolidation and sales recognition by the sponsor or transferor are appropriate only if the majority owner(s) of the SPE: (1) is an independent third party, (2) has a substantial investment in the SPE, (3) controls the SPE, and (4) has significant risks and rewards of ownership of the SPE's assets (FASB EITF, 1989).

In 1990, the EITF released Issue No. 90-15, *The Impact of Nonsubstantive Lessors, Residual Value Guarantees, and Other Provisions in Leasing Transactions* (FASB EITF, 1990). The EITF reached a consensus that a lessee should consolidate an SPE if all of the following three conditions exist in a lease transaction: (1) the SPE's activities are related to assets to be leased to one lessee; (2) the lessee is expected to have the substantive risks and rewards of the leased assets through such means as the lease agreement, a residual value guarantee, a guarantee of the SPE's debt, or the option to purchase at a fixed price other than fair value; and (3) the SPE owner(s) had not made a substantive residual equity investment that is at risk during the entire lease term (FASB EITF, 1990). Thus, to avoid consolidation, the transferor of assets to an SPE must avoid these three conditions. Although the EITF issue pertained specifically to leases, these three conditions became the general guidance by analogy for determining the consolidation of SPEs.

The SEC position with respect to Issue 90-15 was contained in a July 11, 1991, letter from the acting chief accountant of the SEC to the FASB staff (FASB EITF, 1989). The SEC staff indicated that although the three conditions of Issue 90-15 do not apply to nonleasing transactions, "they may be useful in evaluating other transactions that involve SPEs." Also, with respect to the meaning of a "substantive residual equity investment that is at risk" in condition 3, the SEC staff indicated that a working group that was formed with the SEC staff had indicated that an investment of at least 3 percent is substantive (i.e., a minimum acceptable investment). This response was the first quantitative guidance on what constitutes substantive residual equity investment. By analogy, this 3 percent guideline appears to have become an absolute standard for the nonconsolidation of SPEs in general, including the Enron-related SPEs.

The first FASB pronouncement to address the SPE issue but only in a limited context was FAS 125, *Accounting for Transfers and Servicing of Financial Assets and Extinguishments of Liabilities* (FASB, 1996). FAS 125 did not replace EITF 90-15 and did not address consolidation. It was intended to resolve narrow issues related to the securitization of receivables (see Chapter 8) especially related to control. FAS 125 established the conditions for determining when a transfer is accounted for as a sale. FAS 125 also introduced the term *qualifying SPE* (QSPE) to indicate a very limited scope SPE that meets a minimum standard for treating the asset transfer as a sale. FAS 125 did not mention the 3 percent guideline for the outside substantive residual equity investment and did not address consolidation of SPEs. FAS 125 was superseded in 2000 by FAS 140, *Accounting for Transfers and Servicing of Financial Assets and Extinguishments of Debt* (FASB, 2000a). Most of the provisions of FAS 125 were carried forward. However, FAS 140 stated that QSPEs "shall not be consolidated in the financial statements of a transferor or its affiliates" (FASB, 2000A, para. 46).

To summarize, the guidance in EITF Topic D-14 and EITF Issue 90-15 became the guidance for consolidation of SPEs. The guidance in FAS 140 is narrow in that it does not provide guidance on the consolidation of SPEs that are not considered QSPEs. Thus, the guidance in ARB 41, FAS 94, EITF Issue 90-15, Topic D-14, and the SEC staff letter should be applied to SPEs that are not considered QSPEs.

FASB Interpretation No. 46 (FIN 46)

In January 2003, FASB issued FASB Interpretation No. 46, its new guidance on SPEs. In doing so, the Board chose to refer to "variable interest entities" (VIE) rather than SPEs. The board changed the terminology because certain entities commonly referred to as SPEs might not fall under the guidance of FIN 46, while other entities not commonly thought of as SPEs might fall under its guidance. VIEs have one or both of two characteristics, the first of which is:

1. The equity investment at risk is not sufficient to permit the entity to finance its activities without additional subordinated financial support from other parties, which is provided through other interests that will absorb some or all of the expected losses of the entity.

In essence a VIE has an insubstantial equity ownership. The Interpretation notes that an equity investment of less than 10% of the entity's total assets would be insufficient to permit the entity to finance its activities under characteristic 1 above, though a greater percentage of equity ownership may be necessary.

The second characteristic of a VIE is:

2. The equity investors lack one or more of the following essential characteristics of a controlling financial interest:
   a. The direct or indirect ability to make decisions about the entity's activities through voting rights or similar rights
   b. The obligation to absorb the expected losses of the entity if they occur, which makes it possible for the entity to finance its activities.
   c. The right to receive the expected residual returns of the entity if they occur, which is the compensation for the risk of absorbing the expected losses. (FASB 2003)

The Interpretation also notes that the equity holders lack the "direct or indirect ability to make decisions about the entity's activities through voting rights or similar rights" when the voting rights of certain investors are not proportional to their obligations to accept losses or participate in gains, or when substantially all of the entity's activities are conducted on behalf of an investor that has relatively few voting rights. This prevents an enterprise from avoiding consolidation of a VIE by organizing it with nonsubstantive voting interests.

An enterprise will consolidate a VIE if that enterprise has claims that "will absorb a majority of the entity's expected losses, if they occur, receive a majority of the entity's expected residual returns if they occur, or both." This test involves a comparison with the enterprises' claims and obligations to the VIE with those of other parties. The ability to influence the VIE's results is important, as a "a direct or indirect ability to make decisions that significantly affect the results of the activities of a VIE" is taken as a strong indication that an enterprise should consolidate the VIE. Any entity that consolidates a VIE is referred to as the "primary beneficiary."

When determining whether it should consolidate a VIE, an enterprise is required to "treat variable interests in that same entity held by related parties as its own interests." For instance, variable interests held by an officer, an employee, or member of the board would be treated as owned by the enterprise for the purposes of the consolidation decision.

FASB believes that this Interpretation will "improve comparability between enterprises engaged in similar activities, even if some of those activities are conducted through VIEs." Further, FASB believes that consolidation of VIEs will provide more information about the "resources, obligations, risks and opportunities" of the primary beneficiary. It is too early to estimate the extent to which this Interpretation will improve the quality or comparability of financial reporting.

CONSOLIDATION AND CONTROL AT THE CORE OF ENRON ISSUES

As explained in Chapter 8, SPEs are not in and of themselves "guilty" or "innocent." But firms *can* use—and, unfortunately, sometimes abuse—accounting and disclosure policies related to SPEs to mislead the users of financial statements.

Concealing Debt and Assets

Figure 10.1 depicts the Chewco SPE discussed by Kavanagh in Chapter 8. This simple structure illustrates the manner in which Enron allegedly abused accounting and disclosure policies to conceal both asset values and leverage from the market.

Recall that the Joint Energy Development Investments (JEDI) SPE was set up by Enron as a joint venture with the California Public Employee Retirement System (CALPERS) in which each entity had a 50 percent equity interest. In 1997, the estimated value of the assets owned by JEDI stood at $766 million, or $383 million for each partner.

Enron felt that CALPERS could be a more effective partner for Enron if its capital were invested in Enron initiatives other than JEDI beginning in 1997. CALPERS, however, did not wish to invest in too many Enron initiatives at the same time. Enron and CALPERS thus sought to sell the CALPERS stake in the JEDI SPE.

Lacking a third-party buyer, Enron established Chewco in November 1997. Enron claims that it intended to find an independent third party to capitalize at least $11 million of Chewco—the required 3 percent to create a "substantive residual equity investment that is at risk" for a firm other than Enron or to satisfy condition 3 of EITF 90-15 for consolidation. Nevertheless, no such partner was ever obtained, and Chewco was thus capitalized solely by a nominal investment from one Enron employee, who also acted as the sole managing partner—thus failing to satisfy the nonconsolidation principles of EITF D-14 and 90-15 that required that an independent third party have a substantial investment in the SPE, control of the SPE, and derive significant risks and rewards of ownership of the SPE's assets.

As Figure 10.1 shows, two banks made an unsecured loan to Chewco that was used to buy out CALPERS' 50 percent interest in JEDI. Because Chewco does not appear to have satisfied the EITF D-14 and 90-15 nonconsolidation criteria, Chewco should have been subject to full consolidation. Because Enron did not account for Chewco as such, the $383 million in unsecured debt remained off Enron's books, as did the $383 million investment in JEDI until the restatements in 2001. Also, Enron owned almost

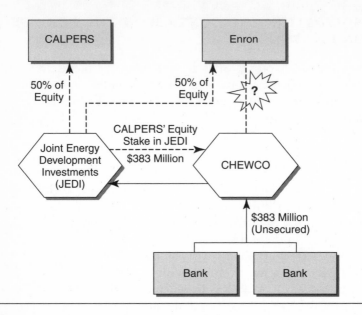

FIGURE 10.1   Chewco SPE

100 percent of the equity of JEDI (directly and indirectly through Chewco), but similarly failed to consolidate JEDI in its financial reports.

Debt by Any Other Name?

Figure 10.2 reproduces Figure 9.4, in which Culp and Kavanagh in Chapter 9 present an illustrative structure for how Enron and several of its prominent bankers engaged in prepaid forward and swap contracts. To summarize, the bank entered into a prepaid or made a secured loan to some SPE—for example, Mahonia Ltd. or Delta Energy Corp.—that the SPE used to fund the prepayment on a forward or swap, either physically or cash-settled. The subsequent delivery obligation to the SPE then served as collateral for the SPE to pledge to the bank on the original loan.[6] Subsequent physical deliveries by Enron to the SPE and the SPE to the bank created market risk exposure for the bank that was hedged using a cash-settled swap with Enron as counter party.

Enron accounted for the cash generated by its prepaid forward sales of energy products (or their cash equivalents in the cases of cash-settled prepaid forwards and swaps) as *operating cash flows* (as distinct from *financing cash flows* or *investing cash flows*). In turn, the forward delivery obligation was booked as a price risk management liability, which was the

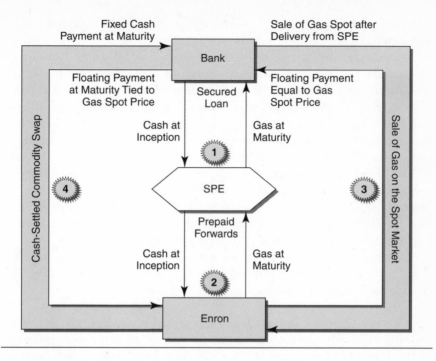

FIGURE 10.2   How Enron Engaged in Prepaid Forward and Swap Contracts

balance sheet line item in which Enron reported the unrealized gains or losses from its trading activities. This treatment is consistent with the manner in which Enron booked essentially all of its trading contracts, as Bassett and Storrie explain in Chapter 2.

Enron's accounting treatment of the prepaid forward cash receipts as operating activities did not increase the reported profitability of those activities. However, this accounting treatment did make it appear as if Enron's (operating) trading activities were generating more cash than it would have appeared if Enron had reported the cash receipts as financing cash flows. This could have led the users of financial statements to conclude that Enron was able to turn its trading gains into cash more quickly than they would have absent the prepaid swap transactions. Additionally, the unrealized trading gains that Enron reported were frequently based on financial valuation models rather than on market prices (i.e., they were *marking to model* instead of *marking to market*); using the prepaid swaps to monetize these unrealized gains could have given the readers of Enron's financial statements a level of comfort in the reliability of the reported trading gains that might not have been warranted.

A second consequence of treating the cash received as a price risk management liability (i.e., working capital) instead of debt was that it lowered the reported debt on Enron's balance sheet. This treatment could have affected financial statement users' views of Enron's long-term solvency risk. Ronald Barone, managing director of Standard & Poor's Ratings Service, testified before the Senate: "The effect on Enron's rating of approximately $4 billion in additional debt-like obligations would have, in all likelihood, significantly altered Standard & Poor's analysis of Enron's creditworthiness" (Barone, 2002). On the other hand, Enron did not use prepaids to generate off-balance-sheet debt; Enron's liabilities for the prepaid forwards appear to have been included on its balance sheet as price risk management liabilities (i.e., working capital).

Control of the SPE is an important consideration in accounting for the generic structure depicted in Figure 10.2. In this case, there are some other issues that affect accounting and disclosure.

Control   Control in the case of the prepaids pertains not to Enron, but rather to the banks that sponsored the SPEs. If an SPE satisfied the criteria under EITF 90-15 and D-14, it need not have been consolidated on the banks' balance sheets. But in the event the banks did have a significant and controlling stake in the SPEs, Figure 10.2 collapses into a wash trade as shown in Figure 10.3. Specifically, consider in Figure 10.3 how the collapsing of the SPE into the bank turns the series of transactions into a closed loop, noting the different numbering of the legs of the transactions than in Figure 10.2. Now, the bank makes an advance payment in transaction 1 in exchange for gas (or some other asset *or* the cash equivalent of that asset), which the bank receives from Enron in transaction 2. Transaction 3 then cancels out transaction 2 because the same amount of the commodity is returned to Enron. Transaction 4 represents the payment the bank receives for returning the commodity to Enron at the then-current market price, but this cancels out with transaction 5, or the floating payment made to Enron in the floating leg of the swap.

After transactions 2 and 3 cancel each other, as do transactions 4 and 5, the only two transactions left are 1 and 6—the fixed cash payment by the bank to Enron and the fixed cash payment by Enron to the bank, respectively. With all the commodity-related legs of the structure gone, the net result is essentially the economic equivalent of a bank loan. Or, more specifically, because the commodity trades wash out and serve no economic purpose, these wash trades could be regarded as concealing the net of transactions 1 and 6 as the real economic purpose of the structure.

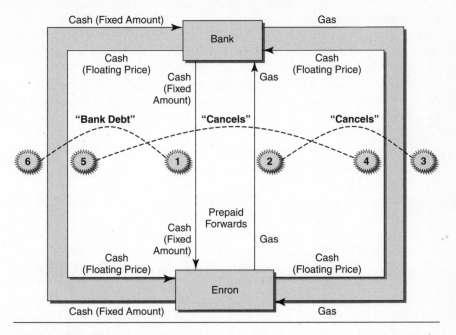

FIGURE 10.3   A "Wash Trade"

Other Issues   Independence of the SPE is essential to this structure's retaining its economic and accounting integrity as a series of commodity transactions. But even if the SPE is an independent firm, it is still possible that the transactions together constitute a wash trade. As Culp and Kavanagh explain in Chapter 9, the facts are not in about Enron's actual structures, so instead, we simply consider circumstances under which the structure in Figure 10.2 might collapse into the one shown in Figure 10.3 economically even with a nonconsolidated SPE.

Before 2000, there was a body of analogous accounting literature to which an accountant could appeal for guidance in recording a prepaid forward (Turner, 2002). In 2000, FASB issued guidance specific to prepaid swaps with *Statement 133 Implementation Issue, Definition of a Derivative: Prepaid Interest Rate Swaps* (FASB, 2000b).[7] At that time, the guidance was that prepaid swaps with a prepayment less than the notional value of the swap should be accounted by the seller as a derivative and that it could not be accounted for as debt. Without commenting on the specific characteristics of Enron's prepaid swaps, this FASB guidance was generally consistent with recording prepaid swaps the way Enron recorded them.[8] However, Lynn Turner, the former chief accountant of the Securities and Exchange Commission, asserted that "underlying [FASB's] conclusion is that the described transactions are not 'sham' transactions but rather swaps with a legitimate business purpose between independent parties who have assumed the risks and rewards of their respective transactions" (Turner, 2002).

Enron's auditor, Arthur Andersen, put forth a set of four conditions that appear to attempt to distinguish between sham transactions and legitimate trading activity. These conditions are as follows:

1. None of the individual agreements in the structured transaction is linked commercially or make reference to any of the other documents; in effect, each is a standalone, normally occurring derivative instrument, which continues to be in effect even if other pieces of the transaction are terminated for any reason.
2. The prepaid gas agreement and each swap are settled at current market values, and the prepaid includes provisions typical of trading instruments such as replacement cost provisions with monthly settlements.
3. Price risk related to the PGA is transferred from the gas supplier to the purchaser without the gas supplier further affecting the purchaser's management of this risk or the purchaser's or the purchaser's other PGA-related economics.
4. The purchaser of the gas must have an ordinary business reason for purchasing the gas and not in substance be an SPE established just to effect a secured investment in a debt instrument from a gas supplier (Turner, 2002).

These criteria do not appear directly in the authoritative accounting literature. Rather, these criteria are Arthur Andersen's attempt to distinguish between prepaid forward contracts that have economic substance from those that are, in substance, debt issuances. Other accounting professionals could have a different view of the criteria to apply in making decisions on the accounting for prepaid swaps. Lynn Turner, for instance, gave his criteria in testimony before the Senate, including:

- Does the transaction have a legitimate business purpose other than avoiding presenting the financing as bank debt on the balance sheet?
- Does the SPE engage in normal business operations? For example, does it undertake normal trading activities for the purpose of making normal trading profits?
- Does the SPE have more than nominal capitalization? From where does the SPE receive its funding?

- Does the SPE have officers and directors who function as they would in any normal trading company?
- Does the sponsor of the SPE or the entity it enters into transactions with have all the risks and rewards of the transactions, or does the SPE have them? Is there any economic substance to the SPE, or is it placed into the transaction merely as a third party to facilitate false and misleading financial reporting?
- Do the transactions among Enron, SPE, and the Wall Street bank actually transfer economic risk from or to Enron, the SPE, or bank? Are the transactions structured as a "round trip" whereby the cash flows and risks merely move in a circle and end up with the same party where they began?
- Are the transactions linked in such a manner that the risks or the ultimate obligations to repay financings are not really transferred?
- Are the forward sales contracts more like debt than a forward sale of a commodity or product?
- Are the contracts linked in such a fashion that Enron ultimately has the obligation to repay the funds used in the transaction? Does the Wall Street bank, via cross-default provisions or other contract terms, such as termination agreements, have the ability to obtain payments from Enron?
- Does the SPE have the ability to make the payments if Enron does not? (Turner, 2002)

As in the case of Andersen's criteria, these indicia are not listed in the authoritative accounting literature but are rather Mr. Turner's view of how to distinguish between prepaid forward contracts that have economic substance and those that are, in substance, debt issuances.

CONCLUSION

Did accounting rules cause Enron's demise? We see no evidence of that. Whether the accounting rules allowed Enron to portray itself as more creditworthy and having better financial performance is another question and one that is not answered easily. In November 2001, Enron restated its financial statements to correct for errors related to its consolidation of SPEs, but it has never restated for its accounting for prepaid forward transactions (Enron, 2001). Even according to Enron, it "broke the rules" on structures such as Chewco; on the other hand, Enron's accounting for and disclosure of its $15 billion in prepaid cash for subsequent actual or cash-settled commodity delivery obligations may not have involved rule breaking. Of course, Enron may yet restate for the prepaid transactions, and whether Enron did in fact break the rules as they stood at the time is up to the courts and the regulatory agencies to decide. From a public policy perspective, the more pertinent question is whether those rules are adequate.

As Bassett and Storrie noted in Chapter 2, accounting and disclosure regimes come in essentially two forms: principles-based and rules-based. A fundamental deficiency of a rules-based regime is the clarity with which the rules are available *to be broken*. As Roman Weil stated in his Senate testimony, "rules trump principles leading to, 'show me where it says I can't'" (Weil, 2002). A principles-based regime lacks the same degree of certainty but, in turn, also lacks the loopholes that excessive formalism can create.

Rules-based accounting standards, in the extreme, would provide detailed prescriptions for the accounting of each transaction. This has certain desirable properties. It can lead to greater comparability of financial statements across firms. It can also proscribe accounting treatments that are (almost) never appropriate.

On the other hand, rules-based accounting standards have limitations. They can be complicated and voluminous, as it is difficult (indeed, impossible) to create a rule for every possible transaction. As a consequence, rules-based accounting standards can be inflexible and inadequate when confronted with unexpected transactions. They invite financial engineering to construct complicated transactions that yield the same economic results as simpler transactions, but different, more favored accounting treatments. And as we have seen, a rules-based system does not prevent unethical management from releasing misleading financial statements. As we have described, Enron's accounting for certain of its SPEs simply did not conform to the accounting rules.

An alternative to rules-based accounting standards is principles-based accounting standards. According to FASB (2002):

> The main differences between accounting standards developed under a principles-based approach and existing accounting standards are (1) the principles would apply more broadly than under existing standards, thereby providing few, if any, exceptions to the principles and (2) there would be less interpretive and implementation guidance (from all sources, not just the FASB) for applying the standards. That, in turn, would increase the need to apply professional judgment consistent with the intent and spirit of the standards.

Principles-based standards would expand managers' ability to choose among potential accounting methods. This can allow well-intentioned management to choose accounting treatments that, in management's opinion, convey more information, or more reliable information, to the users of accounting reports. Applied properly, a principles-based approach is more likely to yield accounting treatments that conform to the substance of the underlying transactions.

In October 2002, FASB issued a proposal for principles-based accounting standards for the United States (FASB, 2002). FASB concluded its proposal with the following statement:

> On balance, the Board believes that if other participants in the U.S. financial accounting and reporting process make the changes required under a principles based approach, the benefits of adopting that approach would outweigh its costs. The result would be high-quality accounting standards that improve the transparency of financial information essential to the efficient functioning of the economy. Also, because the standards will be less detailed and specific, they will be more responsive to emerging issues in the changing financial and economic environment in which many companies operate. . . . Further, because a principles-based approach is similar to the approach used in developing IAS [International Accounting Standards] and accounting standards used in other developed countries, adopting such an approach could facilitate convergence as the FASB works with the IASB [International Accounting Standards Board] and other national standard setters in developing common high-quality accounting standards.

As of this writing, FASB has not held hearings on this proposal, and comment letters are not due until 2003. While the FASB board may advocate a switch to principles-based standard-setting, it is a quasi-regulatory agency, and accounting standards-setting is a political process with participants with conflicting desires, so the outcome of this initiative is difficult to predict.

NOTES

1. The private regulatory body that currently sets U.S. GAAP is the Financial Accounting Standards Board (FASB). The federal governmental regulatory body is the Securities and Exchange Commission (SEC). The SEC has the ultimate authority to set GAAP as well as disclosure rules for companies with publicly trade stock. The SEC, however, typically allows the private sector to set GAAP via a private regulatory body (currently the FASB).
2. An example of Congress's passing laws in reaction to such events is the Foreign Corrupt Practices Act. See Chapter 3 for a discussion of the political process that resulted in the passage of this Act.
3. We discuss these issues with respect to U.S. GAAP.

4. The use of an SPE is just one example of how companies can use structured financing to keep assets or liabilities "off the balance sheet." Other examples include operating leases, take-or-pay contracts, and throughput arrangements.
5. The EITF was formed by the FASB in 1984.
6. As Culp explains in Chapter 11, the lender banks managed their credit exposure to the SPEs—and, in turn, to Enron—either by demanding letters of credit or advance payment supply bonds or by engaging in credit derivatives transactions.
7. Note that many or most of Enron's prepaid transactions occurred before the issuance of this guidance.
8. In October 2001, FASB revised its initial guidance on the accounting for prepaid swaps and made it significantly more difficult to record them as derivatives (FASB, 2001).

PART FOUR

Credit Risk
Mitigation after Enron

11

CREDIT RISK MANAGEMENT LESSONS FROM ENRON

CHRISTOPHER L. CULP

As of June 1999, Enron had disclosed $34 billion in assets on its balance sheet, but another $51 billion in assets—many of which were troubled or impaired—lay hidden in Enron's unconsolidated special purpose entities (SPEs). As explained in Chapters 2, 8, and 10, these abuses of structured finance were not limited to concealing investment losses. Enron engaged in similar malfeasance to project an artificial image of financial resilience by camouflaging its total indebtedness. At the end of 1998, Enron had $7.37 billion in long-term balance sheet debt, but borrowing by unconsolidated Enron SPEs accounted for another $7.6 billion in leverage.[1]

Politicians and media commentators have been quick to argue that Enron represents a significant malfunction in the process by which firms self-police and monitor one other. As a result of this perceived "market failure" of credit risk management, greater regulations on accounting, disclosure, and financial transparency have been recommended, as well as heightened direct supervision of certain market participants by their regulators.

Credit risk management is the process by which firms attempt to monitor and control the potential for unexpected losses arising from an obligor's unwillingness or inability to honor all of its commitments. Despite an apparent unawareness in many cases of Enron's fraudulent activities, few firms dealing with Enron regarded the company as a "good" credit risk. Thanks to the proliferation in the past decade of financial products and techniques enabling firms to reduce or transfer away certain credit exposures, many firms doing business with Enron had taken considerable steps to reduce their Enron exposures well before news of Enron's troubles became public. This widespread use of credit risk transfer products also helped spread Enron credit risk fairly evenly around the global capital markets, thus preventing a significant buildup of Enron credit concentration in any single industry that might have made Enron's failure significantly more disruptive to global financial markets than it actually was. Indeed, that so many firms were able to manage their Enron credit exposures *despite* Enron's misleading financial statements suggests that the Enron debacle is a *success story* in credit risk management, not a failure.

This chapter begins with a brief review of the nature of credit risk. The techniques used by market participants to manage their credit risks are reviewed. The introduction of credit risk mitigation products is brief, but Kramer and Harris provide significantly more discussion of these solutions in Chapter 12. The next section then examines where Enron's failure appears to have precipitated credit losses, as well as examining where, thanks to successful credit risk management, losses did *not* occur. The final section provides some concluding policy observations.

THE NATURE OF CREDIT RISK

Credit risk exists only for assets. When a company *owes* money, services, or assets to another firm, the insolvency of the counter party does not affect the original obligation. But when a company *is owed,* the inability or unwillingness of an obligor to honor its commitments can translate into losses.[2] Credit risk has two components: the likelihood of default by the obligor and the amount that will be lost if a default does occur. The latter is often called the *loss given default* (LGD) or credit exposure of an asset or obligor.

An important determinant of a firm's credit exposure is what that firm can recover from a counter party in the event of a default. For simplicity, assume the default occurs because of insolvency. Insolvency laws in different countries then govern the recovery process, and claimants initiate that process by filing claims with the insolvency trustee.

Secured obligations are those for which collateral has been specifically pledged to cover any default-related losses—for example, a real estate loan that allows the lender to repossess an underlying piece of property if the borrower fails to make a promised payment. Assets that have been pledged as collateral must be applied to the obligations they secure and cannot be used to honor other outstanding obligations of the defaulting firm.

The amount a firm can recover on an *unsecured* claim depends on the value of the defaulting firm's remaining assets and the priority of claimants on those assets. Bank debt, for example, is often senior to other obligations. The proceeds from the liquidation of the defaulting firm's assets thus must be used to pay off banks and other senior creditors entirely before any lower priority claims can be honored. Junior unsecured creditors often recover only a pro rata portion of the remaining assets of the insolvent firm after all senior claimants have been made whole.

The credit exposure on traditional assets (e.g., coupon bonds) is typically known over the whole life of the transaction, at least to a first approximation. Contracts such as oil and gas forwards and swaps, however, can be either assets *or* liabilities depending on movements in oil and gas prices since the transaction was initiated.

When a counter party to a derivatives contract becomes insolvent or defaults on a required obligation, the contract is generally either "accelerated and terminated" or "assigned." In the former case, all remaining payments and/or deliveries on the contract are accelerated to the present and marked to their current market values. A single net termination obligation is calculated and either is due from the nondefaulting party or becomes a general unsecured claim of that party on the remaining assets of the insolvent firm.

If a derivatives counter party wishes instead to preserve its contract rather than accelerating and terminating it (e.g., to guarantee the subsequent physical delivery of an asset), the original counter parties and a solvent third party can all agree to an assignment of the old contract. The contract is first marked to its current replacement cost (i.e., the cost of negotiating a contract with the same terms at current market prices) and becomes either a payable or receivable of the insolvent firm. Unlike before, however, the contract is *not* accelerated or terminated; all remaining delivery and payment obligations of the insolvent firm are assigned to the new third party. Because the contract has been marked to its replacement cost, no payment is required to effectuate such a transfer, and the contract then runs on as before between the nondefaulting party and the new third party.

CREDIT RISK MANAGEMENT TECHNIQUES

As Palmer explains in Chapter 13, some firms have a "credit culture" and others do not. One aspect of a credit culture is the existence of a business unit within the firm whose objective is to monitor and perhaps manage credit risks assumed in the normal course of the firm's business. Historically, banks and insurance companies have had such divisions, whereas credit risk management is a newer arrival in the world of investment banking—and a *very new* arrival in industries such as power marketing, as the example in Neves' Chapter 4 of the U.S. electricity market credit crisis of 1998 illustrates.

Not surprisingly, the process by which firms actively manage their credit risk differs widely across types of firms. Nevertheless, this process invariably includes three common components discussed in the following sections.

Default Risk Monitoring

Predicting the failure of another firm is essentially impossible. Even with perfect financial disclosure, firms are subject to uncertain and random financial market movements whose impacts can never be perfectly anticipated. Nevertheless, monitoring the financial strength of obligors is an essential component of the credit risk management process at least to develop some idea of how likely it is that a firm can honor all of its obligations.

Direct Monitoring   Financial institutions—banks and insurance companies, in particular—typically rely on internal systems to estimate or rank the default risks of their counter parties. Internal rating systems encompass a wide range of methods, some of which rely almost exclusively on the subjective judgment of credit officers and others of which rely more on default risk models that infer default probabilities from a firm's published financial criteria, external ratings, industry characteristics, equity and asset volatility, and the like.[3]

Firms with significant credit-sensitive exposures to a given firm, moreover, often take internal monitoring beyond a review of public information. Due diligence, credit analysis, and ongoing credit surveillance of the obligor are all hallmarks of a well-developed credit risk monitoring process. These activities often include on-site inspections, interviews with key personnel at the obligor, a review of internal financial and risk management documents, and the like.

External Monitoring   For many firms, an independent credit analysis division is a luxury that the size and nature of their credit exposures cannot justify. Gas pipeline customers of Enron, for example, probably did not have internal credit departments. Such firms tend to rely instead on external monitoring to track their credit risks. External monitoring occurs when one firm relies on the credit analysis of a professional credit monitoring service for its information about the default risk of its obligors.

The most prominent external credit monitors are the rating agencies, although firms sometimes also look to external auditors (e.g., resignation decisions) and regulatory agencies (e.g., enforcement actions) for additional credit information. External monitors frequently use methods comparable to the internal credit risk analysis divisions of banks and insurance companies. Default modeling, due diligence, on-site investigations, and ongoing surveillance are all undertaken at some level by external monitors.

Delegated Monitoring   *Delegated monitoring* is based on the belief that banks have (or at least had when the theory was developed) a comparative advantage in assessing the credit risk of their customers. A senior bank lender's decision to roll over an unsecured revolving line of credit thus "sends a signal" of ongoing borrower creditworthiness and abrogates the need for relatively less-informed creditors such as bondholders to undertake an independent credit assessment of the borrower (Diamond, 1984; Fama, 1985; James, 1987; see also Diamond, 1991; Rajan, 1992).

Delegated monitoring, then, is the reliance on signals from senior unsecured creditors about the credit quality of their obligors as a substitute for engaging in independent credit risk analysis. This type of delegated monitoring is frequently combined with at least some reliance on external monitoring, as well.

Delegated monitoring is not only beneficial for those firms wishing to avoid the costs of performing their own credit risk monitoring, but also can be very sensible for the firms being monitored that want to avoid multiple repetitive credit checks by outsiders. The incentive to *be* a delegated monitor, however, is limited. Because delegated monitors cannot explicitly charge the firms that rely on their credit analysis, delegated monitoring of this type is essentially "free riding."[4]

Exposure Limits

Although the default probability of a potential obligor can and should be monitored, only the obligor can take actions to *change* its default prospects. The credit exposure of a transaction, by contrast, can be controlled by *either* party to the transaction.

One popular means by which a firm tries to keep its credit exposure below a maximum tolerable loss threshold is by maintaining a system of credit limits. For firms whose credit exposures are relatively static and homogeneous, limits are usually based on categories or types of counter parties rather than on specific obligors or "names" (i.e., individual companies). A power marketing firm, for example, may specify that all swap counter parties must be rated AA or above by Standard and Poor's (S&P).

Firms whose exposures are dynamic and involve multiple financial product types tend to rely instead on numerical obligor-specific limits that can be compared to actual estimates of credit exposure. Measures of credit exposure on which such limits are based range from crude approximations such as the size or notional principal of a transaction to more sophisticated forward-looking risk measures such as conditional expected loss or credit value-at-risk (Culp, 2001).

Exposure Reduction Techniques

Exposure reduction techniques allow firms to reduce their exposure or LGD to a given obligor or on a particular asset. Exposure reduction can enable firms to increase the volume of business they do with relatively riskier counter parties for a given exposure limit or risk tolerance. Exposure reduction methods also allow firms to bring risk exposures back in line with risk limits and tolerances in the event that a change in market prices or an unexpected decline in obligor credit quality increases the LGD of an existing asset. Exposure management methods come in at least five forms.

Exposure Management through Contracting Terms   Exposure management is often as simple as the judicious inclusion of certain provisions to the legal documentation underlying one or more transactions. Bond covenants, for example, have been used for many years to protect public creditors from expropriation and other unnecessary credit exposures (Smith and Warner, 1979).

The practice of documenting multiple transactions across product types with the same counter party under a single *master netting agreement* can also be an effective exposure management device by guaranteeing *close-out netting* in the event of insolvency. Close-out netting requires that all obligations between the firm and a defaulting obligor be marked to market and then netted down to a single net payment in the event of a default. If Firm A owes Enron $1 million on a swap and is due $2.5 million on a forward, for example, close-out netting requires Enron to net the two obligations into a single net payment of $1.5 million due from Enron to Firm A.

Close-out netting prevents "cherry picking," or an attempt by a defaulting firm to collect its receivables without honoring its payables to the same firm—for example, Enron demands its $1 million on the swap without paying its $2.5 million on the forward. Most master netting agreements (e.g., the ISDA Master Agreements) have been subjected to intensive legal scrutiny to minimize the risk that close-out cross-product netting provisions will be deemed unenforceable in the event of insolvency in a given legal jurisdiction (Culp and Kavanagh, 1994).

The credit exposure of a transaction can also be reduced through contractual requirements for periodic cash resettlement. By marking assets to their current replacement costs at regular intervals, a nondefaulting firm can never lose more than the *change* in the replacement cost of the contract since the last mark-to-market date.

Early termination and acceleration triggers are further examples of exposure management through contracting terms. Price triggers in derivatives, for example, allow the transaction to be terminated if the underlying asset price rises and/or falls by a specified amount. This guarantees that either party can get out of the transaction if it reaches a maximum tolerable credit exposure. Call and put provisions in bonds can serve a similar purpose.

Early termination and acceleration triggers can also be linked directly to indicators of credit quality. Some contracts terminate automatically, for example, in the event of a credit rating downgrade by one of the parties. Similarly, cross-default provisions in derivatives commonly allow for early termination by a firm if its counter party misses a single required payment on *any* of its obligations with the firm. In some cases, cross-default provisions even allow a firm to terminate a derivatives contract early if its counter party defaults on any obligation *to any firm*.

Credit Enhancements   Credit enhancements are assets or performance bonds that are attached to a credit-sensitive obligation to reduce the LGD. Secured loans are credit enhanced with the underlying collateral, so the credit risk of a secured loan is driven more by the credit risk of the collateral than the original borrower. Similarly, collateral requirements on derivatives typically mandate that one or both firms post a fixed amount of acceptable collateral at the inception of the transaction, in effect forcing firms to prepay some portion of their potential credit losses. Acceptable collateral usually includes Treasury securities, bank letters of credit (LOCs), and third-party performance guarantees from credit support providers as discussed in the next section.

In some cases, credit enhancements are combined with contractual exposure management tools, such as triggers that create *contingent* credit enhancements. Callable collateral, for example, is a supplemental amount of collateral that can be demanded on top of the initial collateral required in the event of a counter party rating downgrade.

Insurance   In the 1980s, insurance and capital markets began to converge rapidly in the alternative risk transfer (ART) market (Culp, 2002). Products that were once considered solely the domain of commercial insurance applications suddenly became popular for *financial* applications. One such product of the ART revolution was credit or asset insurance.

Credit or asset insurance reimburses its purchaser for actual losses incurred following an event of default by an obligor on one or more designated reference assets. As is standard in indemnity contracts that directly compensate a firm for actual economic damage sustained, the insurance purchaser must have an "insurable interest" (i.e., must in fact sustain damage to justify the reimbursement). To ensure that insurance purchasers remain vigilant in their own exposure management practices after the insurance is in place, credit insurance usually includes a deductible and policy limit.

Credit insurance is marketed in several different forms. The most general and unconditional is a *financial guaranty,* or an unconditional promise by an insurer to reimburse the protection purchaser if a loss is sustained following the occurrence of a specific "triggering event." Guarantees usually define the triggering event very narrowly—for example, the bankruptcy filing in a court by a specific obligor—but otherwise contain very few exclusions and are payable essentially on demand except in the case of fraud on the part of the insurance purchaser.

Credit insurance can also be provided through *surety bonds.* Shown in Figure 11.1, a typical surety bond involves the provision by an insurance company (the surety) of a performance bond to an obligee on behalf of a principal. In the event of nonperformance on some specific obligation by the principal, the obligee can make a claim on the surety.

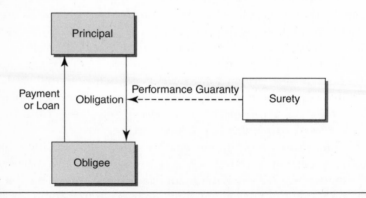

FIGURE 11.1   A Typical Surety Bond

The use of surety bonds to guarantee financial risks is a relatively recent by-product of the ART revolution. Historically, surety bonds were used more to facilitate aspects of commerce such as construction. Contractors, for example, are routinely asked by developers to post a surety bond so that funds are available for a developer to replace the original contractor and complete the work if the bonded original contractor cannot fulfill its obligations.

Using surety bonds to cover financial risks can be relatively tricky business. Lloyds' syndicates were not allowed to underwrite financial guarantees for many years, and only a handful have applied for the right to provide financial guarantees since the Lloyds' bylaws were amended to allow surety bonds and guarantees. Under New York law, moreover, financial guarantees may be provided only by *monoline* insurance companies. Monoline insurers provide insurance for only one type of risk—usually credit risk—and thus can more easily sustain a AAA credit rating than a multiline or composite insurer underwriting many different lines (e.g., property and casualty, life, health). Financial surety bonds offered by New York-chartered insurers thus are often called *monoline wraps,* or financial guarantees provided by monoline insurance companies to enhance the credit (and often the published rating) of securities such as bonds. The vast majority of asset insurance in the New York jurisdiction is provided by the four biggest monolines: Ambac, Financial Security Assurance (FSA), Financial Guarantee Insurance Corp. (FGIC), and MBIA Insurance Corporation (MBIA).

Financial guarantees and surety bonds can also be provided by multiline and composite insurers provided they are in a jurisdiction that recognizes the legality of such offerings. Indeed, the largest provider of financial guarantees globally is the multiline giant Munich Re. Multiline and composite insurers also sometimes provide surety bonds in the New York jurisdiction, as well, although they must be nonfinancial or hybrid in nature. An *advance payment supply bond* (APSB), for example, is a surety bond pledged to guarantee deliveries on long-dated commodity derivatives contracts. APSBs played an important role in the Enron affair, as a later section explains in more detail.

Credit Derivatives   Credit derivatives are bilateral derivatives contracts in which one party compensates another following an adverse triggering event on one or more reference names or assets. Virtually unused until 1992, credit derivatives have exploded in popularity in recent years. Nearly $1.6 trillion in notional principal was reported outstanding in credit derivatives in mid-2002.[5]

Credit derivatives include single-name and pooled contracts. Single-name credit derivatives are contracts in which the protection seller makes a payment to the protection buyer based on the credit risk of a single firm. In a single-name *credit default swap* (CDS), for example, the protection seller provides credit risk protection on a single name or reference asset in exchange for a fixed payment or series of fixed payments. This payment is usually a credit spread times a notional principal amount. A CDS functions much like credit insurance, except that the buyer of credit protection through a CDS often *need not* sustain damage in the event of a default and need not always own the reference asset. As a result, a CDS usually does not involve a deductible.

A CDS may be physically or cash settled. In a physically settled CDS (see Figure 11.2), a default on the reference asset triggers a swap in which the credit protection buyer receives the par value of the reference asset in exchange for giving the protection seller that reference asset (and thereby allowing the protection seller to pursue recoveries). In a cash-settled CDS, an event of default on the reference asset does not lead to an exchange of the bond for cash but rather to a single net cash payment from the protection seller to the buyer equal to the principal amount of the bond *less* the final market value of the bond (i.e., expected recoveries).

Another popular type of single-name credit derivatives transaction is called a *total return swap* (TRS), a contract in which the protection seller pays the London Interbank Offered Rate (LIBOR) plus a spread to the protection buyer in exchange for receiving LIBOR plus a cash amount equal to all realized interest payments on the reference asset(s) *plus* any change in the market value of the reference asset(s). Whereas a CDS compensates the credit protection buyer only for a loss resulting from an actual default, a TRS protects the buyer from the risk of defaults *or* declines in value associated with downgrades or other adverse credit events that do not necessarily result in any contractual nonperformance (Culp and Neves, 1998a,b).

Pooled credit transactions include CDSs and TRSs and function in a manner similar to single-name credit derivatives except that they are based on a relatively large portfolio of assets or names. A pooled credit CDS or TRS that pays off when *any* name or asset defaults, however, can be expensive, especially for a large population of names. Credit protection

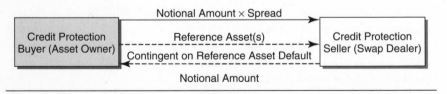

FIGURE 11.2   A Physically Settled CDS

buyers thus often prefer structures such as *first-to-default basket swaps,* in which the protection buyer identifies a basket of reference assets and pays a fee to the protection seller for the right to receive a payment when the *first* reference asset defaults. The protection seller's payment is equal to the par value of the defaulting asset less expected recoveries. If a *second* default occurs in the basket, however, the protection buyer in this contract structure receives nothing.

Another lower cost alternative to a pooled CDS is a *senior protection basket swap*—essentially the exact opposite of a first-to-default basket swap. In a senior protection basket swap, the protection buyer receives nothing following the first default on any asset in the reference portfolio. But on all subsequent defaults of assets in the reference portfolio, the protection buyer receives cash from the seller equal to the par values of the defaulting reference assets less expected recoveries.

Asset Divestiture, Securitization, and CDOs   If the default probability or exposure of an asset becomes excessive, selling the asset is generally a solution, albeit not usually as a first choice. If the rest of the market also senses trouble with the obligor, the price of the asset reflects those concerns. Selling the asset thus eliminates the *risk,* but the *expected loss* will be reflected in the discounted asset price and will be realized the moment the asset is sold (Culp, 2001).

Thanks to securitization techniques (as discussed in Kavanagh's Chapter 8), asset sales *prior* to credit crises have also become increasingly popular as ways of refining or diversifying the credit exposure of a given asset portfolio. Specifically, the credit risk of one obligor can be swapped for the credit risk of a *portfolio* of obligors by simultaneously selling an asset to and buying a security from what is known as a collateralized debt obligation (CDO).

In a typical CDO, depicted in Figure 11.3, a CDO manager (e.g., a bank or insurance company) buys a portfolio of bonds, loans, and other debt instruments. These bonds are held in custody by a trustee for the SPE, and the principal and interest earned is used to pay down the principal and interest of the securities issued by the CDO. These newly issued securities typically include fixed- and floating-rate notes that have different priorities on the assets held in trust by the CDO. Payments received on the underlying debt portfolio pay off senior securities first, and on down the line, so that the different tranches of securities represent varying degrees of credit risk exposure to the underlying pool of credit-sensitive debt instruments.

Essentially, CDOs enable firms to swap a single-name credit exposure for a portfolio of credit risks. A firm holding Enron bonds, for example, might sell those bonds to a CDO that holds bonds issued by all of

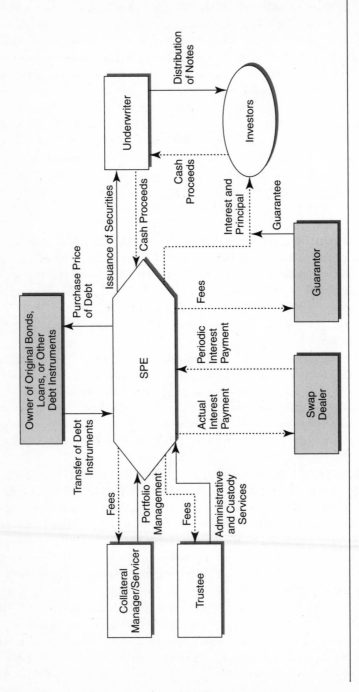

FIGURE 11.3 A Typical CDO

the top U.S. energy firms. The original Enron bondholder can then buy a senior or perhaps subordinated debt security issued by the CDO. The net effect is that the bondholder has exchanged Enron-only credit risk for a more diversified portfolio of credit exposures to the whole energy sector.

Even with the benefits of diversification typically achieved in a portfolio of assets underlying a CDO, the deeply subordinated and equity tranches of a CDO are often exposed to significant credit risk, as evidenced by some fairly substantial CDO losses over the past several years. Accordingly, CDOs are often big users of credit insurance and credit derivatives, as the box labeled *Guarantor* in Figure 11.3 suggests.

CREDIT EXPOSURES TO ENRON

Enron Europe's president John Sherriff stated: "Every part of our business involved granting and receiving credit. Really, we were in the credit business more than we were in gas or electricity or oil" (Fox, 2002, p. 188). Because of Enron's numerous and diverse activities—virtually all of which were credit-sensitive, as the quote suggests—the credit exposures to Enron when it filed for bankruptcy were significant. A closer examination reveals, however, that many of the credit exposures to Enron may *not* have been at firms with direct credit-sensitive relationships to Enron.

Debt

Azarchs (2001) estimates that approximately $13 billion of balance sheet debt was outstanding from Enron at the time of its failure, $4.5 billion of which was from banks. JPMorgan Chase and Citibank accounted for about $1 billion of that exposure, with other major bank lenders including Abbey National, ING, Deutsche Bank, and Commerzbank.

Around $1.5 billion in senior Enron bank debt was secured. This is a surprisingly high amount. Because senior creditors have priority in the recovery process, incurring the costs of securing senior claims is generally not done. The relatively high proportion of secured senior Enron debt thus indicates significant credit concerns among Enron's top lenders.

The other $8.5 billion in Enron's debt was unsecured and in the form of Enron bonds. The two largest concentrations of Enron bond holdings appear to be in the asset management ($3.8 billion) and life insurance ($2.6 billion) industries. Importantly, about a third of Enron's bonds ($3 billion) were held in CDOs as small parts of much larger credit pools (Azarchs, 2001).

To combat apparently significant credit concerns about the risk of its junior debt, Enron relied heavily on contractual credit exposure management devices. Especially popular with Enron were *acceleration triggers* in which a rating downgrade by Enron forced an acceleration of all remaining interest and principal payments on the debt. Although such triggers provided some comfort to Enron's unsecured creditors and allowed Enron to achieve a slightly lower cost of debt capital, these triggers also ultimately exacerbated the speed of Enron's demise.

When Enron was downgraded by S&P on November 9 from BBB to BBB– (negative watch) after some of Enron's previously hidden losses were disclosed, an acceleration trigger was hit on a $690 million loan to one of Enron's remaining *un*disclosed SPEs. Originally due in 2003, the entire balance on that loan was suddenly accelerated to a due date of November 27, 2001. Enron disclosed this in a restatement of its third-quarter earnings filed with the SEC on November 19, along with its disclosure at the same time of a massive decline in cash that signaled the beginning of a potential liquidity crisis. Enron also disclosed in that same release that a downgrade of Enron to below-investment-grade *or* a decline in Enron's common stock price below a certain threshold would trigger the acceleration of another $3.9 billion in debt—again, most of which was outstanding to undisclosed SPEs. The net impact of all this information was to exacerbate Enron's liquidity crunch. Indeed, the November 19 disclosure sowed the seeds of Enron's ultimate destruction two weeks later.[6]

Energy Derivatives and Commercial Counter Parties

Because Enron was such an active market maker in the gas, electricity, and power markets (see Neves, Chapter 4), the company's commercial customers and wholesale derivatives counter parties had significant credit-sensitive relations with Enron. In addition, all the trading counter parties with EnronOnline had at least some Enron credit exposure.[7]

Dodd (2002) estimates that Enron had about $773 billion in notional principal outstanding on derivatives contracts at year-end 2000: $152 billion in natural gas contracts, $267 billion in oil contracts, $338 billion in electricity contracts, $9 billion in interest rate derivatives, $7 billion in equity derivatives, and $550 million based on foreign exchange. S&P's estimate of the replacement cost of Enron's derivatives liabilities was about $19 billion on September 30, 2001 (Azarchs, 2001).

Replacement cost is a better measure of exposure than notional principal, but both measures potentially neglect credit enhancements and any credit exposure management tools used by Enron's counter parties. Whether Enron's customers used exposure management techniques on commercial contracts such as the Volumetric Production Payments program discussed in Chapter 9 is not known. But on its wholesale derivatives contracts negotiated with major swap dealers, Enron was viewed as a significant credit risk.

Even Enron's lifetime high credit rating of BBB+ was still well below standard for derivatives. Consequently, few dealers agreed to conduct derivatives business with Enron without appropriate exposure management. By 2001, many of Enron's derivatives dealers had exhausted their credit limits with Enron, and some had already put Enron on their *no trade* lists. In addition, most of Enron's derivatives counter parties required Enron to provide credit enhancements such as collateral. In many cases, callable collateral provisions were also included that required additional credit enhancement from Enron following a rating downgrade.

The extensive use of credit enhancements and other exposure reduction methods by Enron's derivatives counter parties has two interesting implications. First, it suggests that, like many of Enron's senior creditors, derivatives counter parties were not unaware of Enron's financial troubles. Second, the exposure estimates that have been released to date on Enron's open derivatives position may significantly overstate the actual losses. When collateral, other credit enhancements, and the possible use of credit derivatives by derivatives participants are taken into account, Enron's more savvy wholesale derivatives counter parties may have been much better prepared for the firm's failure than evidence now suggests.

Credit Derivatives

The risk of a default by Enron created two different types of exposures in the credit derivatives market. The first was the risk to credit protection sellers of assuming the default risk of the Enron name. Of the $8 billion notional in Enron-based credit derivatives rated by Mengle in Chapter 7, Khakee and Ryan (2001) estimate that around $2.7 billion notional principal was transferred to credit derivatives dealers in single-name or small-basket credit derivatives transactions. In addition, about 50 pooled credit derivatives transactions included an Enron asset in the reference portfolio. Those transactions had a total notional principal of around $79 billion and around $3.3 billion in replacement cost exposure.

Few credit derivatives dealers provide credit protection in that market on an unhedged basis. When possible, dealers hedge a CDS, for example, by selling the underlying bonds short. In the case of Enron, a protection seller could short Enron bonds against a CDS by borrowing those bonds in a reverse repurchase agreement. In the event of a default, the dealer makes a payment to the protection buyer equal to the par value of the Enron bonds but in turn receives the Enron bonds. These bonds are then returned to the reverse repo counter party in exchange for funds that should be close to sufficient to cover the payment made to the CDS counter party.[8] In this example—as is likely to have been the case in actual practice—the ultimate financial loss would be borne, not by the Enron credit protection buyer *or* the swap dealer, but rather by the party that loaned Enron bonds to the swap dealer in the reverse repo.

Apart from losses on credit derivatives referencing Enron as a name, a second exposure to Enron in the credit derivatives market was borne by firms that sought protection on *non-*Enron names through credit derivatives negotiated *with Enron as a counter party.* Khakee and Ryan (2001) estimate that Enron was the credit protection seller in at least three rated credit derivatives transactions with a notional principal of about $3 billion total.

Enron itself actually had a sophisticated internal credit risk management group. Indeed, Enron decided in February 2000 to make available its own transactional credit risk assessment models to other market participants—to become a delegated monitor of sorts. This effort gave rise to an adjunct of EnronOnline called EnronCredit.com on which market participants could negotiate structured credit derivatives online. In its last years, Enron also pioneered—ironically—the offering of "bankruptcy swaps" through EnronCredit.com (Fox, 2002, pp. 187–188).

Synthetic Enron Bond Holders

Enron's failure also precipitated losses to holders of credit-linked notes issued by Enron counter parties seeking to manage their own Enron credit risk. These losses are best illustrated by the most prominent example.

From December 1993 through 2001, Citibank made $4.8 billion in payments to Enron on cash-settled prepaid forward and swap transactions (prepaids).[9] As Culp and Kavanagh explain in Chapter 9, prepaids are economically equivalent (from the perspective of the bank) to a spot purchase of oil or gas plus a simultaneous loan of the commodity back to Enron for a period of time. In a typical Citibank prepaid, Citibank loaned the money to an SPE (e.g., Cayman Islands-based Delta Energy Corporation) that the SPE then advanced to Enron on cash-settled energy prepaids. The corresponding cash-equivalent delivery obligations to the SPE served as collateral for the SPE to secure the loan from Citibank. At the time of Enron's failure, $2.5 billion in cash-settled delivery commitments from Enron to Citibank (via the intermediary SPEs) remained outstanding on those prepaids (Roach, 2002).

The credit risk on a prepaid is significantly greater than on a traditional forward. In the event of a default by Enron on a prepaid, the prepaid would be accelerated, terminated, and marked to market to determine a final termination payment. Because the long had already advanced payment to Enron, however, the termination payment did not represent the usual replacement cost of the *net* purchase and delivery obligations, but rather the *gross* replacement cost of all remaining asset deliveries.

To address the significant credit risk of a default by Enron on its termination payments, Citibank used a credit-linked note, the history and mechanics of which are described in more detail in Culp (2002). Shown in its most basic form in Figure 11.4,[10] Citibank set up an unconsolidated credit SPE that issued notes and equity certificates to a broad range of investors. Proceeds from these securities funded the acquisition of investments by the SPE in securities rated at least AA-. Citibank entered into a credit swap with the credit SPE that reflected the terms of the loans the bank made to the prepaid SPE to finance the Enron prepays.

As long as Enron did not experience an adverse credit event, the credit SPE made regular payments to Citibank on the swap equal to the actual interest income on the credit SPE's investments. In return, the credit SPE received payments from Citibank in an amount sufficient to cover the interest payments due to investors in the debt notes. The gross interest payments from Citibank to the credit SPE for payment to note investors had two components: a pure interest component financed by the interest

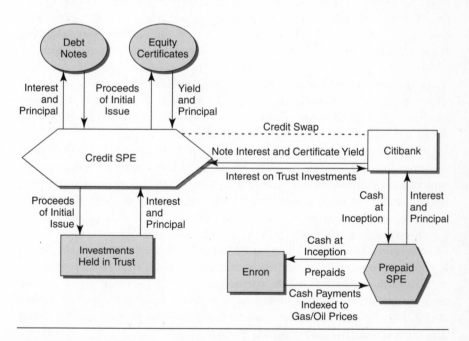

FIGURE 11.4   An Unconsolidated Credit SPE

Citibank received on its loans to the prepaid SPE and a credit insurance premium paid to credit SPE note holders to compensate them for bearing Enron credit risk.

In the event of an Enron default, the credit SPE would swap its low-risk investments with Citibank for senior unsecured Enron debt. The debt notes issued by the credit SPE thus functioned as synthetic Enron debt. As long as Enron remained a viable business, holders of notes issued by the credit SPE would earn a healthy premium over regular interest rates. But in the event of an Enron default, holders of notes issued by the credit SPE ended up holding senior unsecured claims on Enron.

Setting aside the significant political controversy over prepaids discussed in Chapters 9 and 10, these structures worked well enough for Citibank. Holders of the synthetic Enron bonds, rather than Citibank, ultimately had to absorb the $2.5 billion credit loss (before recoveries) from Enron's bankruptcy. Kramer and Harris, however, explore some legal questions that have arisen around structures similar to these in Chapter 12.

Credit Insurance

JPMorgan Chase (JPMC) was a lead creditor, derivatives counter party, project finance lender, securities underwriter, and a merger advisor to Enron. By 2001, Chase Manhattan Bank and later JPMC had arranged about $3.7 billion in commodity prepaids with Enron. The main vehicle through which JPMC conducted its Enron prepaids was Mahonia Ltd., a Channel Islands SPE whose history and mechanics were presented in Chapter 9. When Enron filed for bankruptcy protection, JPMC was owed $1.6 billion in loans made to Mahonia that had been used to finance now-defaulted oil and gas prepaids (Roach, 2002).

JPMC chose a different credit exposure management solution than Citibank for its prepaids. Initially, Mahonia was dealing with multiple customers and not just Enron, and JPMC required all of those customers to obtain bank LOCs that could be drawn in the event of default to make any required termination payment to Mahonia.

Beginning in 1998, Enron asked JPMC to let Mahonia accept APSBs (see previous discussion) in lieu of LOCs as collateral for the Mahonia loans that funded the Enron prepaids. In retrospect, that Enron preferred surety bonds to LOCs is hardly surprising. An LOC generally reduces the borrowing capacity of the principal, the surety bond does not. LOCs are also generally carried as contingent liabilities on borrowers' financial statements, whereas surety bonds are not.

Despite their obvious appeal to Enron, JPMC was initially hesitant to accept surety bonds in place of LOCs. To assuage its concerns, the bank requested that all the sureties backing the Enron APSBs provide several forms of assurance that the APSBs "would be the functional equivalent of letters of credit, and, like letters of credit, would constitute absolute and unconditional pay-on-demand financial guarantees."[11] These assurances were apparently provided, and with JPMC's consent, APSBs began to replace LOCs as collateral pledged to Mahonia. Providers of the APSBs were all multiline insurance companies, most of which were domiciled in New York, and included Liberty Mutual, Travelers Casualty & Surety, and St. Paul Fire and Marine. The essentials of the transaction structure are shown in Figure 11.5.[12]

On December 7, 2001—five days after Enron filed for bankruptcy protection—JPMC filed written notice with Enron's sureties of the nearly $1 billion due to Mahonia and JPMC under the APSBs. The sureties declined payment, arguing that the APSBs "were designed to camouflage loans by [JPMorgan] Chase to Enron, and that [JPMorgan] Chase defrauded the surety bond providers into guaranteeing what were purely

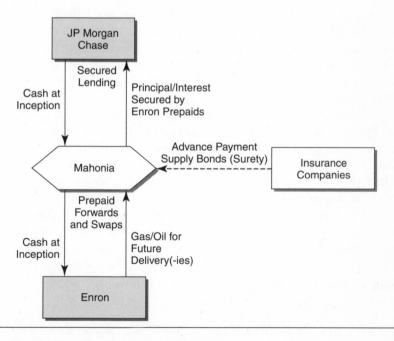

FIGURE 11.5   The Transaction Structure

financial obligations which they otherwise would not, and statutorily [under New York law] could not, have bonded."[13] In other words, the sureties claimed that because the prepaids were "bank debt in disguise," the APSBs represented *financial guarantees* that cannot be offered by multiline insurers under New York insurance law.

After the sureties failed to pay JPMorgan voluntarily, the bank filed a motion to compel the sureties to pay. The lower court denied motions for summary judgment and rescheduled a trial date in early 2003.

On January 2, 2003, JPMC announced that it was taking a $1.3 billion charge in the fourth quarter of 2002 largely to deal with Enron litigation matters. That charge-off reflected a settlement with insurers, reached on the same day the trial was to begin. As suggested by the 7.5 percent increase in JPMC's stock price the day word leaked out about the settlement, the settlement was a bigger victory for JPMC than expected. Under the settlement, the 11 insurers agreed to pay about 60 percent of their obligations to JPMC under the APSBs, or $655 million out of the $1 billion total owed.

CONCLUSION

By far, the greatest monitoring failure of Enron was a failure by virtually everyone—lenders, regulators, rating agencies, and counter parties—to recognize the depth of Enron's deceptions. Unfortunately, a firm that is absolutely intent on perpetrating a fraud often *can,* and neither new regulations nor changes in credit risk monitoring practices is likely to change that.

In virtually every other context, however, claims of a widespread market failure in the credit risk monitoring of Enron are overstated. Given Enron's duplicity in its financial statements, those firms with the prescience to have relied on credit risk mitigation and risk transfer to manage their Enron exposure should not be criticized but should be praised for their astuteness.

Although many of the conventional criticisms of credit risk management in the case of Enron are misplaced, the episode has served as a reminder of several important lessons and areas of ongoing concern.

Sound Credit Risk Management Does Not Imply Knowledge of Fraud

Royal Bank of Canada (RBC) made a $517 million loan to an Enron affiliate in November 2000 and hedged its credit risk by entering into a credit swap with the Dutch Cooperatieve Central Raiffeisen-Boerenleen-bank BA (better known as *Rabobank*). In June 2002, Rabobank announced a suit against RBC for $517 million on the grounds that RBC "knew Enron was a corrupt organization liable to implode at any time." Vehemently denying the allegations as "ridiculous," RBC indicated its intent "to defend this attack totally and with vigor" (Heinzl, 2002).

The Rabobank claim against RBC illustrates a fairly widespread misconception—namely, firms dealing with Enron that had suspicions about Enron *as a financial or credit risk* could not have been ignorant of Enron's broader efforts to mislead and defraud the market. How could firms have known that Enron was financially questionable without knowing about Enron's undisclosed investment losses and borrowings?

Counter party suspicions about Enron's credit risk, however, are hardly tantamount either to knowledge of or complicity with Enron's fraudulent activities. Swaps are arms-length transactions in which dealers frequently lack information about how the counter party is using the contract or how the transaction affects the counter party's total risk. If a counter party misrepresents the purpose of a transaction to a dealer, it is possible for the dealer to remain uninformed about any abuses in which their transactions are playing a part while still having concerns about the company's ability to pay its bills.

As Bassett and Storrie emphasized in Chapter 2, even Enron's *published* financials did not project the image of a strong firm. Enron had the reputation in the market for being aggressive and for taking risks, and Enron's top management fueled that image. Market participants had *plenty of reasons* to be concerned about Enron as a credit risk *without* being a coconspirator with the company.

Delegated Monitoring is No Substitute for Direct Monitoring

Enron provides a good case study of the dangers of *delegated monitoring,* or reliance on the credit decisions of other institutions as a substitute for independent credit risk analysis. Institutions that relied on delegated monitoring to ascertain Enron's creditworthiness probably found themselves in trouble.

As noted previously, firms that rely on delegated monitoring are essentially "free riders" on more senior creditors. An implication is that delegated monitors lack any real incentive to *inform* free riders of any change in their credit risk assessments or risk management practices. Consider, for example, a bank with an unsecured loan to Enron. Delegated monitors will view that bank's renewal decision as a signal about Enron's ongoing credit quality. But suppose the bank *hedges* its default risk and continues to roll over the loan to earn the servicing fees. In this case, creditors that look only at the rollover decision will draw the wrong conclusion.

Determining when and how much a financial institution hedges its credit risk to a particular obligor is no easy task. Harder still is for a junior creditor to determine how much credit is retained *by the credit protection provider*. Credit insurance providers, for example, routinely reinsure their primary policy lines instead of retaining 100 percent of their exposures. Similarly, credit protection sellers in the credit derivatives market regularly hedge through securities borrowing. If estimates of who bore the brunt of Enron's failures are *even now* unknown, the likelihood that a junior creditor could have figured that out in December 2001 is negligible indeed.

The problems of delegated monitoring that Enron highlights simultaneously raise a cautionary flag to purchasers of credit-backed securitized products such as CDO tranches. As the overall performance in the CDO market over the past few years has confirmed, purchasers of such products often confine their own credit analysis to the *actual issuer* of the securities—that is, the CDO manager or SPE. But as the Enron failure starkly illustrates, the credit risk of the *underlying population* of assets backing those structures is at least as important as the credit risks of the structures themselves. In the future, investors in securitized products backed by credit-sensitive assets would be well served to step up their direct credit monitoring a notch or two.

External Monitoring Is No Substitute for Direct Monitoring

Numerous commentators have been quick to criticize external monitors for having missed the Enron fiasco. Rating agencies, in particular, raised few of the traditional red flags that would normally be associated with a financial catastrophe of the magnitude of Enron. Worth remembering, however, is that although rating agencies are in the business of selling credit analysis and an assessment of an entity's ability to service its obligations, the rating agencies are no more capable of *predicting* financial failures than any other market participants.

To the extent that the rating agencies were late to classify Enron as teetering on the brink, they are even then not entirely at fault. To some extent, a false sense of trust and overconfidence in external delegated monitors have been encouraged over the years by regulatory and political biases that have overinstitutionalized the role of these organizations, as well as erected barriers to entry for their would-be competitors. And that problem is about to get worse. Under the planned revision of the Basel Capital Accord, bank capital requirements would be increasingly tied to the external ratings of their obligors. This will serve to entrench further the role of the rating agencies in the global financial system and discourage competition from "unrecognized" rating services.

With no real capital at risk (lawsuits aside), external delegated monitors are punished for being wrong only through a loss of reputation. But without free entry into the ratings provision arena, reputation risk is not a particularly compelling source of market discipline. Although blaming external monitors for missing the boat on Enron is tempting, more constructive is to blame the system that has drastically attenuated the incentives of external monitors to remain as vigilant as possible.

Regulation Is Not the Answer

Some have commented that the proliferation of credit risk management tools has destabilized the financial system by reducing front-line senior creditors' attention to direct credit risk monitoring. The theory is that the less risk a senior creditor has, the less monitoring a senior creditor will do. The popular solution proposed is to regulate more strictly and more broadly the use of credit derivatives and other credit risk management products by banks and other prominent financial intermediaries.

To blame the innovations in credit risk management for reduced attention to credit risk is backward logic for several reasons. First, many users of credit risk management tools still retain *some* exposure to their obligors and use those tools only to keep their exposures in line with credit risk limits and risk tolerances. Citibank, for example, succeeded in managing up to $2.5 billion in Enron exposure using credit-linked notes. But those were not the only exposures that Citibank had. Citibank *did lose* from Enron's failure. Credit risk management innovations simply reduced the amount of the loss, not the incentive of the bank to monitor and manage its exposure.

Second, to argue that the availability of better credit risk management tools abrogates credit monitoring ignores the fact that most firms would not know when to use exposure management tools without *even more careful and ongoing* attention to counter party credit risk. Credit enhancements and credit risk transfer is not free, after all. Knowing when to use credit risk management devices, which tool to choose, and how much exposure to manage *increases* the attention of firms to their credit exposures, not the other way around.

Finally, credit risk transfer mechanisms should be lauded for strengthening the ability of the global financial system to absorb the

Enron failure. Without these tools, the credit exposures to Enron would have remained very heavily concentrated in the financial and energy sectors. Instead, thanks to CDOs, credit derivatives, and insurance, Enron's default risk was, in fact, spread broadly and evenly throughout the whole financial system, including asset managers and insurance companies that had no direct dealings with Enron at all. S&P emphasized this as a major reason that the Enron failure did not precipitate "systemic" problems (Azarchs, 2001).

NOTES

1. See Fox (2002) for a good discussion of the investment losses that led Enron to slowly bleed to death financially. The numbers in this paragraph are also based on Fox (2002).
2. For simplicity, this chapter ignores *failed transactions,* or obligations that are not honored for purely operational reasons. Attention here is confined to unwillingness or inability to make payments or deliveries because of financial problems.
3. Surveys of techniques for modeling default risk can be found in Crouhy, Galai, and Mark (2000); Culp (2001); and Saunders (2002).
4. Delegated monitoring is what is known as a *positive externality.* Delegated monitors can charge the firms they are monitoring, but at least some part of the benefit to *delegated* monitoring cannot be priced because of *nonexcludability.* In other words, a delegated monitor cannot prevent firms from making decisions based on revealed credit decisions about bank borrowers.
5. International Swaps and Derivatives Association Mid-Year Survey of Derivatives Activity, 2002.
6. Probably the only reason the November 19 disclosure did not decimate Enron immediately was that the Dynegy merger was still on the table at this time.
7. EnronOnline was essentially a matching engine for financial transactions in which one party seeking to go long a contract was matched with a seller of a comparable contract. Until a match could be identified, however, Enron acted as counter party to the unmatched leg of the transaction. Matching in liquid markets sometimes occurred within minutes, but, in other markets, Enron remained a counter party for days or weeks. See Herron's Chapter 6 in this volume for a more detailed discussion.
8. CDS hedging and pricing is discussed in Fage and Liu (2002).
9. As described in Chapter 9, *cash-settled* means that no oil or gas was intended to be or was actually delivered. The cash payments made by Enron were nevertheless tied to oil and gas prices and thus financially equivalent to oil or gas deliveries.
10. Figure 11.4 is intended only to illustrate the basic form of a synthetic Enron bond, not any of Citibank's actual structures.

11. See *JPMorgan Chase Bank v. Liberty Mutual et al.*, USDC SDNY 01 Civ. 11523 (JSR) Amended.
12. This is not exactly the same as the figure shown in Chapter 9 because the issues being discussed are different. In particular, how Mahonia and/or JPMorgan Chase hedged its exposure to changing gas or oil prices is omitted here to keep the discussion focused.
13. See *Defendants' Memorandum of Law in Opposition to Plaintiff Motion for Summary Judgment* (February 11, 2002).

12

CREDIT DERIVATIVES POST-ENRON

ANDREA S. KRAMER AND ALTON B. HARRIS

Credit derivatives—bilateral contracts and debt securities, the value of which is linked to the credit status of a company, a debt obligation, or a pool of debt obligations—have been available since 1992.[1] The importance and frequency of use of these products, however, were transformed by the events of 2001. During that year, corporations defaulted on 211 bond issues valued at more than $115 billion, a record number and dollar value. More than 250 public companies filed for bankruptcy protection, a 46 percent increase over the previous year's 176, which itself had been a record (Li, 2002). And, the year ended with Enron's astonishing bankruptcy, the largest in American corporate history—until it was eclipsed just eight months later by WorldCom's even more extraordinary and unanticipated collapse.

As a consequence of what Alan Greenspan has referred to as this "sharp run-up in corporate bond defaults, business failures, and investor losses,"[2] the use of credit derivatives grew in 2002 at a rate that "exceeded all expectations."[3] For the first half of the year, the notional principal amount of reported outstanding credit derivatives was $1.6 trillion, 50 percent greater than the reported amount for all of 2001.[4] And the explosive growth in this market appears to have only begun. By 2004, the British Bankers Association (BBA) predicts that the global credit derivatives market will reach $4.8 trillion, a 500 percent increase over what it was in 2000.[5]

The increasing recognition of the value of credit derivatives in the post-Enron world has been accompanied by heightened attention to the different structures available for credit risk protection and a concerted effort to ensure that they perform as they are intended. In this chapter, we explain these different structures, contrast credit derivatives with insurance, discuss very briefly efforts currently underway to improve their documentation, and offer some predictions as to likely future developments with respect to credit derivatives. But before doing so, it may be useful first to address the deceptively simple question: Why credit derivatives?

MANAGEMENT OF CREDIT RISK

Credit risk "is the risk to earnings or capital arising from an obligor's or counter party's failure to meet the terms of any contract . . . or perform otherwise as agreed."[6] Although the credit derivatives market is of very recent origin, the recognition that the persons with whom you transact business may default on their obligations is as old as commerce itself, and the need, in appropriate circumstances, to manage or protect against credit risk is the reason for commonplace practices such as secured lending, letters of credit, financial covenants, guarantees, and margin requirements.

Yet, effectively protecting against credit risk while still continuing to conduct business can be difficult. Credit card debt cannot be secured, the full value of a loan may not be recovered on the sale of collateral, and margin may be insufficient in the event of an unexpectedly large market movement. Moreover, the established ways of transferring credit risk—for example, loan syndications and securitizations—require those assuming credit risk also to provide funding. Credit derivatives offer lenders and other credit risk counter parties an entirely new degree of flexibility in managing such risk. Many credit derivatives do not involve *ex ante* funding and require the party assuming the credit risk to make payment only *ex post* the occurrence of a credit event. Such credit derivatives, increasingly the majority, permit banks and other counter parties to manage their credit risk separately from their funding obligations. Other credit derivatives that do require *ex ante* funding permit that funding to be supplied through the capital markets from a far wider range of participants than was ever before possible.

Credit derivatives both separate credit risk from funding and commoditize such risk, transforming it into tradable market instruments. Both techniques provide the means for major financial institutions and corporations to manage their credit risk by distributing or laying off the type and amount of risk they do not wish to carry among a wide range of market participants. American banks, for example:

have effectively used credit derivatives to shift a significant part of the risk from their corporate loan portfolios to insurance firms here and abroad, to foreign banks, to pension funds, to hedge and vulture funds, and to other organizations with diffuse long-term liabilities or no liabilities at all. Most of these transfers were made early in the credit-granting process, and significant exposures to telecommunication firms were laid off through credit default swaps, collateralized debt obligations, and other financial instruments. Other risk transfers reflected later sales at discount prices as credits became riskier and banks rebalanced their portfolios. Some of these sales were at substantial concessions to entice buyers to accept substantial risk. Whether done as part of the original credit decision or in response to changing conditions, these transactions represent a new paradigm of active credit management and are a major part of the explanation of the banking system's strength during a period of stress.[7]

Precisely how credit derivatives perform "as a new paradigm of active credit risk management" is the subject to which we turn next.

What Are Credit Derivatives?

Credit derivatives refer to a variety of differently structured products that have as their common objective the protection of one party against credit risk associated with a specified third party (reference entity), the bonds or borrowings of a specified third party (reference obligation),[8] or a pool or portfolio of reference entities or reference obligations.[9] Neither party to a credit derivative needs to have any credit exposure to the reference entity or obligation. Nor does either party need to prove that it has incurred a financial loss to collect the payments specified in the derivatives contract. Like other securities and derivatives products, and unlike insurance contracts, payments are calculated and made pursuant to the terms of each particular credit derivative without regard to the obligations, liabilities, losses, or actual risks of the party to whom the payment is due.

Different user groups tend to use credit derivatives for different reasons. In a recent study by Greenwich Associates, market participants reported that they use credit derivatives to increase incremental returns (50 percent), for investment in a different asset class (48 percent), to hedge bond credit risk (34 percent), to exploit arbitrage opportunities (33 percent), to hedge loan credit risk (31 percent), to achieve greater leverage (20 percent), to reduce a portfolio's capital intensity (20 percent), to hedge counter party credit risk (18 percent), to speculate (16 percent), and for other reasons (16 percent) (D'Amario, 2002).

The various types of credit derivative used to achieve these objectives can be generally divided into those that are not funded before a credit event—for example, credit default swaps (CDSs) and total return swaps (TRSs)—and those that are funded *ex ante*—for example, credit-linked notes (CLNs) and collateralized debt obligations (CDOs). In the following sections, we describe these basic credit derivative structures, including the increasingly popular synthetic CDO (SCDO) structure.

Credit Default Swaps   In a CDS, one party buys credit protection (protection buyer) either with a single upfront payment or a series of fixed periodic payments for the term of the contract (the *premium* or the *default swap spread*). In return, the party selling credit protection (protection seller) agrees to pay the buyer if there is a "credit event" with respect to the reference entity or reference obligation. Neither the protection buyer nor the protection seller needs to have any actual credit exposure to the reference entity or obligation.[10] If a credit event occurs, the protection seller pays the buyer, and the buyer continues to make any required premium payments until the contract matures. If a credit event does not occur, the protection seller never makes a payment, and the buyer makes all required premium payments.

CDSs are almost always documented with an ISDA Master Agreement. The standard credit events that trigger payment by the protection seller are a specified price deterioration (the *materiality* standard) coupled with one of the following: bankruptcy, cross-acceleration, downgrade of reference entity or obligation, repudiation or moratorium, restructuring, payment default, or material default on a reference entity's debt obligations.[11] Depending on the terms of the CDS, on the occurrence of a credit event, either the protection buyer delivers to the protection seller the reference obligation and receives in return a payment equal to the notional amount of the contract (physical settlement), or the protection seller pays the buyer the notional amount minus the then-value of the reference obligation (cash settlement).[12]

CDSs can be entered into with respect to a single reference entity or obligation or with respect to a specified portfolio of reference entities or obligations. CDSs that reference a portfolio of some sort are often referred to as *basket default swaps*. In a *first-to-default basket swap*, the default on any of the reference obligations triggers payment to the protection buyer. Other types of default basket swaps are also available, such as CDSs that provide credit protection after credit events have occurred with respect to two or more reference entities or obligations.

Total Return Swaps   A TRS (or total rate-of-return swap) on a reference obligation typically provides for both *yield payments* and *value payments*. With respect to the yield payments, the total return payer (protection buyer) agrees to pay to the total return receiver (protection seller) the actual rate of return on the reference obligation, and the protection seller agrees to pay to the protection buyer a referenced interest rate (floating or fixed). With respect to the value payments, the total return payer pays the appreciation on the reference obligation, while the total return receiver periodically pays any depreciation on the reference obligation. The specified notional amount of a reference obligation is adjusted to reflect value payments.[13] Net value and yield payments can be made periodically or at the maturity or early termination of a TRS.

A total return payer that owns the reference obligation eliminates its credit exposure to the borrower without actually selling the reference obligation. While eliminating its credit exposure (to that borrower), the total return payer does not eliminate its market risk with respect to the payments from the total return receiver. A total return payer that does not own the reference obligation is synthetically transferring credit exposure on the reference obligation to the total return receiver, who is synthetically buying the reference obligation. Thus, TRSs allow counter parties to go long or short a particular credit-sensitive asset without necessarily funding the credit. A TRS—unlike a CDS—provides protection to the total return payer against loss of value irrespective of cause or the occurrence of a credit event.

Terminology   The payout of a CDS is similar to that of an option, with the protection seller receiving a premium in return for assuming the risk of having to make a payment in the event of a specified occurrence. But while CDSs share certain characteristics with options, they should not be confused with true *credit options;* that is, options on credit-risky instruments, such as bonds or loans, or on credit spreads. Just as receiving "fixed" in an interest rate swap is the duration equivalent of a long (financed) position in a bond, selling protection in a CDS (or, for that matter, being the total return receiver in a TRS) is the credit risk equivalent of a long (financed) position in a bond. The use of *swap* rather than *option* terminology in connection with CDSs and TRSs derives from this analogy. It is intended to convey the fact that a CDS or TRS effectively swaps the parties' positions in credit-risky assets, rather than their buying and granting options on positions in such assets. True *credit options,* just as other options in which the contingency is a market price development rather than a remote credit event, derive their value from the expected forward value and volatility of market prices. If an institution is capable of pricing a position in a loan or a bond, it is also capable of pricing a CDS. To price a credit option, however, additional information would be required about volatilities and implied forward credit spreads (J.P. Morgan, 1998).

Funded Credit Derivatives

Credit-Linked Notes   CLNs are debt securities, the value of which are linked to the creditworthiness of third-party reference entities or reference obligations. A CLN "represent[s] a synthetic corporate bond or loan, because a credit derivative (credit default or TRS) is embedded in the structure."[14] CLNs have "principal (par value) at risk depending on the credit performance of a reference credit."[15] CLNs are generally issued by operating companies and financial institutions but can be issued by SPEs. When CLNs are issued by an SPE, the SPE is typically "collateralized with high-quality assets to assure payment of contractual amounts due."[16]

CLNs are generally simple and flexible structures. The default contingency in a CLN can be based on a variety of underlying obligations, including a specific corporate loan or bond, a portfolio of loans or bonds, sovereign debt instruments, or an emerging markets index. It may also be based on a first-to-default CDS basket or a credit spread option. If a credit event occurs, the note typically matures, and the investor sustains a loss based on the reference obligation's loss. In effect, the investor is selling protection on the reference obligation, receiving a premium in the form of an attractive yield. The issuer of the note, on the other hand, is purchasing default protection on the reference obligation.

Investors find CLNs attractive for a variety of reasons. Because CLNs are on-balance-sheet assets, investors prohibited from entering into off-balance-sheet items, such as CDSs, can gain access to the credit derivatives market through CLNs. In addition, investors need not go through the ISDA documentation process. And banks can use CLNs to free up credit lines to particular borrowers, thereby providing access for nonbank investors to credit opportunities and customized maturity structures that are not otherwise available. A downside of CLNs, however, is counter party risk.

Collateralized Debt Obligations   Unlike CLNs, which are issued typically (but not exclusively) by operating companies, CDOs are always issued by an SPE. Similar in structure to collateralized mortgage obligations (CMOs), the CDO structure involves the transfer to the SPE of a portfolio of bonds, loans, or other assets; a sale by the SPE of debt securities (the CDOs) backed by the cash flows from the transferred portfolio; and a payment to the transferor of the proceeds of the CDO sale. While there are various types of CDOs (for example, arbitrage or balance sheet CDOs employing either cash flow or market value management), for purposes of this discussion, we view all such transactions simply as one more way to repackage and redistribute credit risk.

Key to the CDO structure is the securitization of the underlying collateral portfolio. In CDOs, just as CMOs, the SPE holding the collateral portfolio sells several different classes or tranches of securities, each of which carries a different risk/return configuration defined by the priority and timing of the payments due on it. In other words, in a CMO structure, the cash flow from the collateral portfolio is divided into a variety of principal and interest components that are allocated among the various security classes. This securitization process, known as *tranching*, turns the single risk/return profile of the underlying portfolio into multiple credit profiles. A CDO's tranches thus effects not only a redistribution of credit risk but a restructuring of it as well.

The risk/reward profile of the asset portfolio held by an SPE can be restructured in a variety of ways to appeal to a diverse array of investors. The tranches of a CMO typically have credit ratings ranging from triple A to single B or unrated. Thus, despite holding a collateral portfolio that has, for example, a double B credit quality, through the use of overcollateralization and subordination, an SPE may issue several tranches of significantly higher rated debt. Whatever the precise structure of a CMO's tranches, however, this credit derivative product allows one party (protection buyer) that is holding, for example, a portfolio of high-yield corporate bonds to eliminate its credit exposure to this portfolio by transferring that risk, in restructured form, to investors.

Synthetic Collateralized Debt Obligations While conceptually straightforward, CDOs are both complex to establish and expensive to administer. For example, it is costly to review loans or bonds for compliance with eligibility criteria, to transfer the legal title to loans, and to maintain the confidentiality of borrowers (critical in jurisdictions where this is required). To avoid the costs, legal, and administrative problems of transferring loans or high-yield bonds to an SPE, banks and other sponsors have combined the securitization structure of CDOs with unfunded derivative techniques to create so-called synthetic CDOs (SCDOs).[17] In such transactions, the sponsor retains the reference obligations but transfers the credit risk of the portfolio to an SPE through a CDS. The SPE then issues tranched notes, the proceeds of which are used to purchase high-quality assets, such as government securities.

The SPE pays the purchaser of the tranched notes with the interest income from the collateral, together with the swap premium paid by the sponsor. If default or loss occurs on the obligations in the reference portfolio, proceeds from the collateral are used to compensate the sponsor. Any collateral remaining at the maturity of the transaction is repaid to the note holders.

The SCDO market is dominated by three distinct products: (1) regulatory-driven balance sheet transactions, (2) tranched basket default swaps, and (3) managed arbitrage CDOs. "While balance sheet deals still represent the majority of synthetic [credit portfolio] outstandings," the largest growth has been in "tranched basket default swaps" and "managed arbitrage CDOs."[18] Even though the SCDO market is currently dominated by fixed portfolios of investment-grade corporate loans and bonds, "there has been a proliferation in the use of actively managed portfolios of new collateral types."[19]

MISUSE OF CREDIT DERIVATIVES

Credit derivatives have proved to be valuable and generally dependable products. When used properly, credit derivatives can diversify risk, improve earnings, and lower a bank or corporation's risk profile. But credit derivatives can be misused. A good example of the type of issues that can arise when credit derivatives are (allegedly) misused is the litigation growing out of a series of offerings of debt securities linked to Enron's creditworthiness (Enron CLNs).[20] In these transactions, introduced briefly in Chapter 11 by Culp, Citigroup and Credit Suisse First Boston Corp. (collectively, Enron lenders) transferred much of their Enron credit exposure arising from loans and structured finance transactions[21] to third-party investors through variously structured CLNs issued by SPEs. Under the terms of these notes, when Enron became insolvent, investors in the Enron CLNs were left holding the bag, and the Enron lenders walked away without loss.[22]

Six separate issuances of CLNs are the subject of the *Hudson Soft* litigation,[23] but the basic structure of various transactions appears to have been much the same.[24] An SPE issued one primary class of CLNs to investors and a second, much smaller, class of notes subordinate to the first to the Enron lenders. The SPE purchased highly rated debt securities with the proceeds of the note issuance and executed a CDS with the Enron lenders linked to Enron's credit performance. The CDS provided that the reference obligations would be exchanged for the SPE's collateral portfolio in the event of specified Enron credit events.

Before an Enron credit event, the SPE was to pay to the Enron lenders the interest earned on its highly rated investments, and the Enron lenders were to pay to the SPE the interest owed to the holders of the CLNs plus the yield on the subordinated notes. Upon an Enron bankruptcy, the

Enron lenders were to deliver to the SPE "senior obligations of Enron that rank[ed] at least equal to claims against Enron for senior unsecured indebtedness for borrowed money" having a principal balance equal to the notional amount of the CDS. The SPE was to deliver to the Enron lenders the SPE's investments with a principal amount equal to the amount of Enron debt delivered to the SPE, plus the base amount of the subordinated notes.[25]

When Enron failed, the Enron CLNs performed precisely as they were intended, relieving the Enron lenders of all loss with respect to the reference Enron obligations up to the notional amount of the CDS. But because of the generally unanticipated and highly suspicious nature of Enron's bankruptcy, considerable criticism has been leveled at the Enron lenders for shifting their credit exposure to the capital markets. Citigroup has responded that "[c]redit-linked notes are well-recognized financial instruments, widely issued and traded each year. . . . The instruments were sold to the largest, and most sophisticated, institutional investors in several Rule 144A offerings. Citi promised investors that the CLNs would perform similarly to straight Enron bonds—and they have."[26]

But the issues in the litigation over the Enron CLNs do not concern the legitimacy of the Enron CLN structure or the sophistication of the purchasers. Rather, the thrust of the litigation is that the Enron lenders were willing to lend great sums of money to Enron either without conducting appropriate due diligence or with knowledge that Enron's creditworthiness was not being accurately reported *because* they had no intention of ever being exposed to Enron's credit risk. In other words, the key allegations in the litigation involve an assertion that the Enron lenders "lent Enron more the $2.5 billion and invested at least $25 million in Enron's fraudulent partnerships in order to secure future investment banking business"[27] and that they were willing to do this because they intended "fraudulently [to] shift 100 percent of their risk of loss" to unknowing note holders.[28]

Obviously, the allegations in the *Hudson Soft* litigation are just that—allegations. Nevertheless, they raise a serious issue concerning the use of credit derivatives. A credit provider intending to reduce or eliminate its credit risk through the use of credit derivatives may well have significantly more information about the reference entity or portfolio than the potential counter party or note purchasers. The concern is that this information will not be shared either through the swap negotiation process or in the note sale disclosure documents. Certainly after Enron, counter parties to unfunded credit derivatives and investors in funded credit derivatives would do well to review carefully the representations by credit providers and all disclosures concerning the credit condition of the reference entity.

CREDIT DERIVATIVES OR INSURANCE

Credit derivatives and insurance have a number of similarities, and, indeed, credit derivatives are often characterized as functioning, in many circumstances, as the financial equivalent of indemnity contracts and financial guarantees. But functional equivalence is one thing and legal equivalence is another. If credit derivatives were deemed to be *insurance*, the consequences under state insurance law would be highly adverse for this vibrant and valuable market.

For example, a derivative that is found to be an insurance policy can be sold only by a licensed insurance broker. Thus, a protection seller found to have been selling an insurance contract would be acting unlawfully. In California, this would be a misdemeanor.[29] In Connecticut, fines, imprisonment, or both can be imposed for acting "as an insurance producer" without a license.[30] Under Delaware law, a Delaware corporation can lose its "charter" to do business[31] if it acts "as an insurer" without a "certificate of authority"[32] to conduct an insurance business.[33] In New York, insurance law violations are a misdemeanor,[34] with fines increasing for subsequent violations.[35] And in Illinois, no one can "sell, solicit, or negotiate insurance" unless licensed.[36]

Because the term *insurance contract* is separately defined by each of the 50 states and the District of Columbia,[37] it becomes important for the participants in the credit derivatives market to understand and abide by clear guidelines to ensure that credit derivatives—financial market transactions—are not treated as insurance, which are state-regulated service contracts.

Activities Associated with Insurance

The leading insurance treatise defines *insurance* as:

> A contract by which one party (the insurer), for a consideration that is usually paid in money, either in a lump sum or at different times during the continuance of the risk, promises to make a certain payment, usually of money, upon the destruction or injury of 'something' in which the other party (the insured) has an interest. [cite omitted] In other words, the purpose of insurance is to transfer risk from the insured to the insurer. Insurance companies act as financial intermediaries by providing a financial risk transfer service that is funded by the payment of insurance premiums that they receive from policyholders.[38]

In evaluating which "financial risk transfer services" are insurance, five characteristics are typically identified:

1. The insured must have an "insurable risk" (such as the risk of a financial loss on the occurrence of a disaster, theft, or credit event) with respect to a "fortuitous event" that is capable of financial estimate.[39]
2. The insured must "transfer" its "risk of loss" to an insurance company (referred to as *risk shifting* or *underwriting*), under a contract that provides the insured with an "indemnity" against the loss (with the indemnity limited to the insured's actual loss).
3. The insured must pay a "premium" to the insurance company for assuming the insured's "insurable risk."
4. The insurance company typically assumes the risk as part of a larger program for managing loss by holding a large pool of contracts covering similar risks. This pool is often large enough for actual losses to fall within expected statistical benchmarks (referred to as *risk distribution* or *risk spreading*).[40]
5. Before it can collect on an insurance contract, the insured must demonstrate that its injury was from an "insurable risk" as the result of an "insured event." In other words, the insured must demonstrate that it has actually suffered a loss that was covered in the contract.

In general, therefore, an insurance contract covers the risk that an insured will suffer an insured loss, and payment is due under the insurance contract only if there is "proof of an insured loss," and then only in an amount equal to the lesser of the insured's actual loss or the maximum loss covered by the contract.

Credit Derivatives Are Not Insurance

New York State is a key insurance regulator with jurisdiction over most of the largest insurance companies in the United States. As a consequence, New York's view of when a contract does and does not constitute *insurance* is highly influential. In New York, an insurance contract is defined as an agreement under which the insurance company is obligated "to confer a benefit of pecuniary value" on the insured or beneficiary on the "happening of a fortuitous event in which the insured . . . has . . . a material interest which will be adversely affected" by the happening of such event.[41] In determining whether a risk shifting contract falls within this definition or outside it, New York's basic approach is entirely consistent with the preceding discussion.

The New York Insurance Department (NYID) takes the position that derivative contracts are not insurance contracts as long as the payments due under the derivatives are not dependent on the establishment of an actual loss. For example, in considering catastrophe options (Cat options) providing for payment in the event of a specified natural disaster (such as a hurricane or major storm), the NYID stated that the Cat options were not insurance contracts because the purchaser did not need to be injured by the event or prove it had suffered a loss. In reaching this conclusion, the NYID distinguished between *derivatives products,* which transfer risk without regard to a loss, and *insurance,* which transfers only the risk of a purchaser's actual loss.[42]

Similarly, the NYID concluded that weather derivatives are not insurance contracts under New York law because neither the amount of the payment due nor the event triggering the payment necessarily relates to the purchaser's loss.[43] And most recently, the NYID concluded that because CDSs provide that the seller must pay the buyer on the occurrence of a "negative credit event" without regard for whether the buyer has "suffered a loss," they are not insurance contracts.[44] It appears clear, therefore, at least under New York law, that if the provisions of a credit derivative contract do not tie payment to the actual loss experience of the protection buyer, the derivative product will not be deemed an insurance contract.

Documentation Considerations

There are, nevertheless, certain conceptual overlaps between credit derivative contracts and insurance contracts. As a consequence, care should be taken in documenting such derivative contracts to avoid any implication that a party will receive a payment under the contract only for actual loss. To ensure that credit derivatives are treated as derivatives and not as insurance, the following drafting guidelines may be helpful:

- *Form of contract:* Unfunded credit derivatives should be documented with an ISDA Master Agreement with the specific terms of the agreement specified in the schedule, confirmations, and any credit support documents. The offering material for funded credit derivatives (notes) should specify the terms of the notes in language as similar to that of the ISDA definitions as possible.
- *Disclaimer:* The documentation for both funded and unfunded credit derivatives should include a disclaimer that the transaction is not intended to be insurance, the contract is not suitable as a substitute for insurance, and the contract is not guaranteed by any "Property and Casualty Guaranty Fund or Association" under applicable state law.

- *Marketing materials:* Marketing materials for a credit derivative transaction should avoid any references to similarities between the contract and insurance and should not use words such as *indemnity, guarantee,* and *protect.*

ONGOING EFFORTS TO IMPROVE DOCUMENTATION

The documentation of unfunded credit derivatives is generally done on ISDA-published forms.[45] Indeed, ISDA has taken the lead in standardizing the terms of credit derivatives. In 1998, it published a model "Confirmation of OTC Credit Swap Transaction." In 1999, it published the "1999 ISDA Credit Derivatives Definitions," which were followed in 2001 by three supplements that expanded and clarified the 1999 definitions.[46] As a result of Enron, Argentina, and numerous other credit defaults, ISDA worked throughout 2002 to draft and release a comprehensive set of revised credit definitions.

ISDA's 2003 Credit Derivatives Definitions, published on February 11, 2003, incorporate the three ISDA supplements issued in 2001 to the 1999 credit definitions, update many of the definitions, and generally bring documentation standards current with evolving market practices. As a result, we believe that the documentation practice for credit derivatives have been substantially improved.

CONCLUSION

As a result of the credit defaults during the early part of this century, the value of the credit derivatives market has become more apparent than ever. While representing a natural extension of the markets for products that "unbundled" risks, such as those for interest rate and foreign exchange derivatives, the credit derivatives market has provided a unique mechanism for assuming and shedding direct exposure to a reference entity's creditworthiness. As such, credit derivatives represent a unique and important development for the worldwide financial markets.

Despite concerns about the misuse of credit derivatives (as highlighted by the *Hudson Soft* litigation) and the desirability of further fine-tuning of ISDA documentation, the credit derivatives market has proven itself to be sound, effective, and vigorous through a very difficult credit period. Further, it is important to recognize that this market has developed and adapted without governmental regulation or supervision.

It is also interesting to note the development of the credit derivatives markets alongside the highly regulated insurance market. Primarily because of tax considerations, there remain enormous incentives for insurance companies to provide credit loss protection through *insurance contracts*. Nevertheless, we are seeing increasing intersections between the derivatives and insurance markets as the nature of the risks assumed by these markets converge. Thus, for example, more and more so-called *transformer transactions* are occurring whereby a financial instrument (e.g., a CDS) is transformed into an insurance contract or vice versa.[47] Insurance companies, prohibited under applicable state law from entering into credit derivatives, can often assume the same economic position as if they had "sold" protection to a derivatives counter party by issuing an insurance policy against a credit event specified in the derivative held by the insured. The insurance company thus assumes the economic results of holding the credit derivative while still complying with regulatory restrictions.

The expansion and strengthening of the credit derivatives market will unquestionably contribute to a more efficient allocation of credit risk in the economy. This market will allow banks efficiently to reduce undesirable concentrations of credit exposure by diversifying this risk beyond their customer base. This market should also lead to improved pricing information relating to both loans and credit exposures generally. In addition, this market will facilitate further specialization whereby financial institutions can fund participants in limited areas of commercial activity without having to bear the risk of excessive exposure to such limited sectors. Finally, by separating both risk from funding obligations and original risk from restructured risk, credit derivatives offer an extraordinarily important mechanism for financial market participants to play precisely the role at precisely the risk/reward level they deem prudent and appropriate.

NOTES

1. It has been reported that the International Swaps and Derivatives Association (ISDA) first used the term *credit derivatives* in 1992. "Evolution of Credit Derivatives," available at http://www.credit-deriv.com/evolution.htm (visited November 4, 2002).
2. Remarks by Alan Greenspan, chairman, Board of Governors of the U.S. Federal Reserve System, at the Institute of International Finance, New York (via videoconference) (April 22, 2002), available at http://www.federalreserve.gov/boarddocs/speeches/2002/20020422/default.htm (visited October 16, 2002) (hereinafter "Greenspan Remarks").
3. ISDA, News Release, "ISDA 2002 Mid-Year Market Survey Debuts Equity Derivatives Volumes at $2.3 Trillion; Identifies Significant Increase for Credit Derivatives," (September 25, 2002), available at http://www.isda.org/press/index.html (visited October 22, 2002).
4. See note 3.

5. BBA, Credit Derivatives Survey, 2001/2002, Executive Summary, available at http://www.bba.org.uk/pdf/58304.pdf (visited September 20, 2002).

6. Office of the Comptroller of the Currency, "OCC Bank Derivatives Report, Second Quarter 2002," available at http://www.occ.treas.gov/ftp/deriv /dq202.pdf (visited October 14, 2002), 1.

7. See note 2.

8. Reference obligations are also referred to in discussions of credit derivatives as *reference assets* or *reference credits*.

9. In fact, the 1999 ISDA Credit Derivatives Definitions simply define a *Credit Derivative Transaction* as "any transaction that is identified in the related Confirmation as a Credit Derivative Transaction or any transaction that incorporates these Definitions." 1999 Credit Definitions, at § 1.1.

10. Banking or insurance regulations may require a bank or insurance market participant to own a reference obligation, but that is not a requirement for entering into a CDS.

11. 1999 Credit Definitions 16–18.

12. For example, if after a credit event, a reference obligation is valued at $3 million and the notional amount specified in the contract is $10 million, the protection seller must pay the protection buyer $7 million. Alternatively, the protection seller may be required to pay a predetermined sum (a *binary* settlement) regardless of the then-value of the reference obligation.

13. Board of Governors of the Federal Reserve System, "Supervisory Guidance for Credit Derivatives," *SR Letter 96-17* (August 12, 1996), Appendix.

14. "Depending on the performance of a specified reference credit, and the type of derivative embedded in the note, the note may not be redeemable at par value. . . . For example, the purchaser of a credit-linked note with an embedded default swap may receive only 60 percent of the original par value if a reference credit defaults" (J.P. Morgan, 1998).

15. See note 14.

16. OCC, OCC Bulletin 96-43, "Credit Derivatives Description: Guidelines for National Banks," available at http://www.occ.treas.gov/fh/bulletin/96-43.txt (visited November 26, 2002).

17. Goodman (2002), pp. 60–61. SCDOs are referred to as *synthetic* because the credit exposure is created by the derivative contract and not with an actual obligation of, or relationship with, the reference portfolio.

18. Gibson, Lang, "Synthetic Credit Portfolio Transactions: The Evolution of Synthetics," available at www.gtnews.com/articles6/3918.pdf (visited October 1, 2002).

19. See note 18.

20. *Hudson Soft Co. Ltd. et al. v. Credit Suisse First Boston Corp. et al.*, Civil Action 02-CV-5768 (TPG) (October 8, 2002). (Amended Complaint).

21. We used the phrase *structured finance transactions* as it is used by Kavanagh in Chapter 8 as any transaction that makes use of an SPE or special purpose vehicle (SPV).

22. *Newby v. Enron Corp. (In re Enron Corp., Securities Litigation)*, Civil Action No. H-01-3624, 206 F.R.D. 427.

23. Hudson Soft Class Action Amended Complaint, supra note 25, at 44–58.
24. On November 4, 1999, Yosemite Securities Trust I 8.25 percent Series 1999-A Linked Enron Obligations in the aggregate amount of $750 million were issued. On August 25, 2000, Enron Credit Linked Notes Trust issues Enron CLNs in the aggregate amount of $500 million. On May 24, 2001, three separate Enron CLNs were issued: (1) Enron Euro Credit Linked Notes Trust 6.5 percent Notes in the aggregate amount of EUR200 million, (2) Enron Sterling Credit Linked Notes Trust 7.25 percent Notes in the aggregate amount of £125 million, and (3) Enron Credit Linked Notes Trust II 7.3875 percent Notes in the aggregate amount of $500 million. On October 18, 2001, Credit Suisse First Boston International JPY First-to-Default Credit Linked 0.85 percent Notes were issued in the aggregate amount of ¥1.7 trillion.
25. S&P Corporate Ratings, "New Issue: Enron Credit Linked Notes Trust, $500 million Enron Credit Linked "Notes (October 9, 2000), available at http://www.standardandpoors.com (visited November 26, 2002). Senate Permanent Subcommittee on Investigation, Appendix D, Citigroup Case History. See also, Opening Statement of Rick Caplan before the Senate Permanent Subcommittee on Investigations, July 23, 2002 (Caplan Opening Statement) available at http://www.senate.gov/~gov_affairs/072302caplan.pdf (visited October 22, 2002).
26. Statement of Rick Caplan supra note 30.
27. Hudson Soft Class Action Amended Complaint, supra note 25, at 153–156.
28. See note 27 at 157–162.
29. Cal. Ins. Code § 1633 (2001).
30. Conn. Gen. Stat. § 38a-704 (2001). The penalty for acting as an insurance producer without a license is a fine of not more than $500 or imprisonment of not more than three months or both. Ibid. An *insurance producer* is defined at Conn. Gen. Stat. § 38a-702(1) (2001).
31. 18 Del. C. § 505(c) (2001).
32. 18 Del. C. § 505(a) (2001).
33. 18 Del. C. § 505(b) (2001).
34. New York Ins. Law § 109(a) (2002).
35. New York Ins. Law § 1102(a) (2002).
36. 215 ILCS 5/500-15(a) (2002).
37. McCarron-Ferguson Act, 15 U.S.C. § 1011-1015.
38. 67 Fed. Reg. 64067 (October 17, 2002).
39. The *insured* must be able to demonstrate that it has both an economic and a legal connection to the asset or subject matter of the risk. Financial Services Authority, *Discussion Paper: Cross-Sector Risk Transfers* (May 2002) at Annex B1.
40. Because most business relationships involve risks and the assumption of risk, the key here is that an insurance company spreads or distributes the risks among a pool of contracts covering similar risks. See *Amerco v. Comm'r*, 96 T.C. 18 (1991), *aff'd* 979 F.2d 192 (9th Cir. 1992). See also, *Comm'r v. Treganowan*, 183 F.2d 288 (2nd Cir. 1950).

41. NY Ins. Law § 1101(a)(1) (LEXIS through Ch. 221, 8/29/2001). Key to this definition is the notion that the insured will be adversely affected by the specified fortuitous event. In other words, insurances require the establishment of actual loss.

42. NYID, "Catastrophe Options," *Office of General Counsel Informal Opinion* (June 25, 1998).

43. NYID, "Weather Financial Instruments (derivatives, hedges, etc.) *"Office of General Counsel Informal Opinion"* (February 15, 2000), available at http://www.ins.state.ny.us/rg000205.htm>.

44. NYID, Letter dated June 16, 2000, addressing a credit default option facility, available at http://www.ins.state.ny.us.

45. ISDA has developed standard agreements that have been widely adopted by parties to unfunded derivative contracts. The ISDA Web site is www.isda.org. Although CLNs, CDOs, and SCDOs are *credit derivatives,* we do not discuss their documentation in this chapter. CLNs, CDOs, and SCDOs are typically documented as privately placed notes.

46. Restructuring Supplement to the 1999 ISDA Credit Derivative Definitions (May 11, 2001); Supplement to the 1999 ISDA Credit Derivatives Definitions Relating to Convertible, Exchangeable or Accreting Obligations (November 9, 2001); Commentary on Supplement Relating to Convertible, Exchangeable or Accreting Obligations (November 9, 2001); Supplement Relating to Successor and Credit Events to the 1999 ISDA Credit Derivatives Definitions, (November 28, 2001).

47. Cross-Sector Risk Transfers (U.K. May 2002), supra note 44 Annex A: Transformers, available at www.fsa.gov.uk/pubs/discussion/index-2002.html. Press Release, "Risk Transfer: Benefits and Drawbacks Need Careful Balancing," May 3, 2002, available at http://www.fsa.gov.uk/pubs/press/2002/049.html cite visited September 16, 2002.

13

THE MARKET FOR COMPLEX CREDIT RISK

PAUL PALMER

T he failure of Enron and the widely publicized losses at WorldCom, Global Crossing, Tyco, and other firms have heightened market participants' attention to credit risk in general and to transactions that can be used to manage credit risk in particular. Recent events reinforce some fundamental structural inefficiencies that were already present in the market for structured credit assets. These inefficiencies center around the fact that banks and insurance companies that provide credit enhancement services rely extensively on rating agencies, which exercise significant power over these entities. To attract the capital required to make meaningful investments in the credit sector, banks and insurance companies need high debt and stock market ratings.

In the current environment, both the rating agencies and stock market analysts loathe the credit sector; and investors in credit assets are routinely penalized. Rating agencies, in particular, are anxious to be perceived as sages of credit, providing timely advice as opposed to the lagging indicators they are often accused of being. The ratings volatility we are currently experiencing is directly related to this push by rating agencies to be leading indicators of corporate creditworthiness. Consequently, credit spreads on noninvestment-grade (NIG) and story credits, especially, have widened tremendously because of the resultant lack of investor demand.

Thus, the paradox: Bank and insurance company investors that best understand complex credit risk are unable to fully capitalize on their specialized credit skills. As public, regulated entities, they are compelled to minimize credit risk to comply with regulatory and market requirements.

253

In particular, financial guaranty insurance companies, the natural investors in complex credit assets, are effectively prohibited from doing so by the rating agencies, which exercise virtual regulatory powers over these protection sellers by requiring punitive capital reserves, resulting in unattractive returns.

On the other hand, institutional investors, which are, environmentally, best suited to hold complex credit risks, often do not have the necessary skills, in-depth knowledge, and credit culture to confidently invest in the asset class and, consequently, opt not to allocate to the sector.

As a result, intermediaries, such as investment banks, are able to acquire and repackage assets for sale as securities and profit from what are often significant information asymmetries and skills mismatch among themselves, investors, and the original owners of the assets. This situation existed before Enron and the other recent disasters. A structural shortage of investors with the requisite sophistication, credit expertise, and risk appetite for NIG assets, subordinated tranches of structured credit, and other complex transactions has existed for some time. But post-Enron, deeper concerns about the very nature of credit risk (e.g., how accounting fraud impacts credit risk) will frighten more investors into *believing* that they lack the expertise to engage in serious credit evaluations, thus creating both additional gaps between the supply and demand for credit assets and additional opportunities for well-positioned intermediaries.

INEFFICIENCIES IN COMPLEX CREDIT INTERMEDIATION

Complex credit can be defined broadly as subordinated tranches of structured transactions as well as credit exposure related to derivatives transactions. Such transactions exhibit significant volatility and require analysis employing fundamental credit and quantitative disciplines as well as specific product knowledge concerning the underlying, or reference, assets.

A variety of regulatory and market factors contributed to the basic inefficiencies in this market. These problems predated Enron but, in virtually all cases, will surely be exacerbated rather than ameliorated by the events of the past year.

Financial institutions assume credit risk reluctantly. Credit exposure is the unwanted consequence of serving the funding, trading, and placement needs of preferred clients as well as of lucrative principal transactions. As a result, we are witnessing a massive and growing effort to transfer credit risk in existing portfolios to third parties. A recent proposal by the Bank for International Settlements (BIS) and the Federal Reserve to require banks to mark to market their loan portfolios will significantly increase banks' profit and loss (P&L) volatility and will serve to further hasten their retreat from credit risk. Banks are, now more than ever, clearly ill-suited to a "buy and hold" strategy as to credit risk.

Most notably, policies instituted by the Federal Reserve and the BIS have made banks unsuitable and unwilling holders of NIG credit assets. Concurrently, stock market analysts and the rating agencies have taken a negative view on the credit sector, further dampening the desire of banks and other publicly traded and ratings-sensitive institutions to be in this business. These factors, combined with the lack of a deep, stable market for complex and NIG credit risk, have created an arbitrage opportunity for sophisticated investors with the appropriate credit skills, corporate credit culture, and a business platform that is insensitive to regulatory and market pressures. It is this opportunity that the investment banks have seized on. Stepping into this market void, they have bought and repackaged credit assets for sale to institutional investors, in the process extracting the arbitrage profits—and little, if any, of the risk.

Industrial companies, too, are increasingly focusing on core activities and are seeking to outsource noncore functions such as credit risk management. In its August 2001 issue, *Euromoney* magazine reports that "Industrial companies have amassed many billions in credit exposure as a side product to their main businesses . . . The biggest 50 companies in Europe have a total of more than $500 billion of credit risk on their balance sheets . . . Now, under pressure from equity investors and rating agencies, some companies are starting to quantify and reduce their mountains of trade debt [customer credit risk]" (Michael Peterson, "The Accidental Credit Investor," August 2001).

Institutional investors tend to be better repositories of complex credit exposures because they are not subject to the regulatory capital requirements or earnings-consistency pressure of publicly held financial institutions. However, institutional investors often do not have the credit expertise and risk management competence to analyze and structure complex and NIG credit risks. Acquiring that competence is expensive, time-consuming, and requires a cultural change from a trading perspective to fundamental analysis and absolute value investing. Instead, we too often see investors being seduced by seemingly higher yielding assets with sexy-sounding appellations that mask fundamental structural flaws, hence, the myriad reports in the media of asset managers writing down the value of their high-yield portfolios, which are often the equity and mezzanine tranches of collateralized debt obligations (CDOs).

In the main, credit risk transfer activity is centered on relatively vanilla (standardized) risks. A ready market does not currently exist for complex and NIG credit risks, as is reflected in the current state of the high-yield market. Banks and other protection buyers that have sought to access institutional investors directly by issuing CDOs have had to retain the equity and, increasingly, the mezzanine tranches of these transactions. Insurers and hedge funds, investors that pride themselves as portfolio managers, have been voracious buyers of mezzanine and, to a lesser extent, equity tranches of structured products. They have now largely retreated because of heavy losses suffered on poorly structured deals pitched to them by investment bankers. The causes are twofold:

1. The significant information asymmetry and skills mismatch between the investment banks that broker these products and the investors that retain the risk.
2. The fact that the investment banks themselves are not necessarily best equipped to analyze and repackage these risks.

Again, trading-driven institutions tend to have neither the inclination nor the patience for the fundamental analysis and ongoing surveillance complex credit products require.

As indicated previously, public, rated financial institutions are increasingly penalized by the market, regulators, and rating agencies for holding credit risk, particularly unrated and NIG exposures. These penalties range from lower or volatile stock prices to higher capital charges and rating downgrades. Consequently, banks and similar financial institutions will continue to shift out of portfolio credit assets, abandoning their former role of credit risk repository and instead focus their efforts on becoming originators and traders of credit risk via credit transfer instruments such as credit derivatives and, increasingly, CDOs. However, banks and other issuers active in these markets have been increasingly unsuccessful in transferring all such exposures and have had to retain the more volatile subordinated tranches of these transactions as well as whole portfolios of complex credit exposures. This particular niche of the credit risk market is referred to in this chapter as the *complex credit risk market*.

The complex credit risk market is believed to be at the infancy stage of what will be a large and permanent market. Indeed, the sector should increase in size as market and regulatory pressures such as the promotion of increased usage of internal credit risk measurement systems by regulators and in Basel II, the new BIS proposal whose ultimate effect will be to cause banks to mark their loan portfolios to market. A number of major banks are already using these internal models, and some aspects of Basel II, such as the loan impairment rules, are already in place.

In summary, while success in this sector will be measured in above-normal returns, that success will in turn be premised on the investor's ability to be multidimensional—to function as an investor but also to simultaneously provide value-added solutions to address the following macro industry trends and phenomena affecting protection buyers:

- Financial institutions are increasingly reluctant to originate and hold credit exposures because of regulatory, rating agency, and market pressures and constraints, even under circumstances where they might otherwise find the risk-adjusted return attractive. To the extent these institutions retain any such exposure, it is usually due to (1) relationship pressures from the origination client, (2) market requirements to successfully facilitate syndication of the majority of the related transaction, or (3) a lack of sufficient buyers of NIG risk and, to a lesser degree, more complicated or "story" exposures.
- This reluctance to originate and hold risk is significantly exacerbated when dealing with highly structured, complex, and/or volatile exposures.
- These regulatory and rating agency pressures will increase over time and thus reinforce the need for financial institutions to remove these exposures from their balance sheets.
- However, these same market factors have contrived to constrain the development of investor interest and dealer liquidity for such exposures. Consequently, a sizeable or dependable market for this type of paper does not exist.

THE COMPLEX CREDIT RISK MARKET

Complex credit risks may also be thought of as those exposures that require customized, highly structured risk transfer solutions. The needs of the credit risk market are principally met by three product types: credit derivatives, insurance coverage (including financial guaranty), and complex credit risk solutions. If usage to date is the main indicator, credit derivatives are best suited to meet more straightforward, investment-grade (IG) risks. These instruments are mainly bought and sold by banks and represented, in 2000, $900 billion in global trading volume (according to the British Bankers Association), or 50 percent of the market.

Insurance covers are best suited to meet the needs of less sophisticated companies that have not yet invested in appropriate risk measurement tools and, therefore, seek blanket risk protection; insurers, including financial guarantors, represent 20 percent of the market.[1]

Complex credit risk transfer solutions are best suited to meet portfolio credit risk exposures, which represent 30 percent of the market or $600 billion in par value. However, if we focus on the subordinated tranches and

NIG segments, the target market is estimated to be 15 percent of the sector, or $90 billion. In general, the products and services available to this sector may be thought of as falling on a spectrum, with risk-specific solutions at one end and broad multirisk solutions at the other.

Credit Derivatives

At one end of the spectrum are the credit derivatives operations of banks and securities firms. These products permit the transfer of credit risks that are specific and well understood (i.e., plain vanilla risks), using contracts that are fairly standardized in form throughout the market. Thus, a protection buyer could readily call any credit derivatives dealer to buy, for example, $100 million worth of credit protection (via a credit default swap), over a five-year term, on Ford Motor Company. By contrast, banks are still not able to buy protection across their derivatives and/or commodity trading portfolios covering counter parties of varying credit quality for dynamic exposures in different countries and/or currencies.

Nonetheless, the credit derivatives market has grown tremendously in the past four years, with much of the recent growth fueled by general credit quality concerns and expectations of increased default rates in the corporate bond markets during the next 12 months. Indeed, the BBA believes that credit derivatives volume was $1.9 trillion in 2002 and will be $4.8 trillion by year-end 2004.

While credit derivatives continue to evolve and gain sophistication, significant segmentation has occurred and is being reinforced across the credit risk market. Recall that the complex credit risk needs of financial institutions is an area that is generally not well understood and, in any case, requires sophisticated, customized solutions. Banks and securities firms that sell credit derivatives, motivated by their need for scale and liquidity, are focused on standardization and creating a mass market for their products. This is why credit derivatives are used primarily for plain vanilla risks. The credit derivative instrument could be tailored to any kind of credit risk, but banks and securities firms have significant economic incentives (high costs) to continue their focus on the high-volume end of the market. This is a problem of inappropriate infrastructure, a legacy of how banks and securities firms were organized and developed, that will not be solved in the near term, if at all. For this reason, and the environmental reasons discussed elsewhere in this chapter, the complex credit risk sector is unlikely to be targeted by credit derivatives sellers or other providers of other standardized products in the near future.

Banks and securities firms remain the leading participants in the credit derivatives market. Significantly, however, bank activity is increasingly focused on the demand side: Whereas banks still account for 81 percent of credit derivative purchases (i.e., as buyers of protection), their share in credit derivative sales has fallen to 47 percent, with insurance companies and other entities picking up the slack (again, according to the BBA). This disparity suggests that banks' relative interests increasingly lie in using the instruments to offload credit risk, as opposed to retaining or making a market in credit.

Monoline Financial Guaranty Insurance

Financial guaranty insurance is the traditional method for improving credit quality of corporate and municipal bonds. Leading companies in this market are Ambac Assurance Corporation (Ambac), MBIA Insurance Corporation (MBIA), Financial Security Assurance, Inc. (FSA), and Financial Guaranty Insurance Company (FGIC). Like credit derivatives, financial guaranty is a fairly standardized method for dealing with the sorts of credit risks that it addresses.

To varying degrees, monoline insurers have used their core credit analysis skills to diversify into related business areas, such as wrapping asset-backed transactions that are structured and originated by investment banks. Financial guarantors, however, face constraints that will limit their ability to compete directly in the complex credit risk segment. Chief among these constraints is that financial guarantors rely on their own credit ratings to attract business and are, therefore, subject to considerable ratings agency pressure. The primary result of this pressure is that financial guarantors are unable to assume NIG risks. Additionally, financial guarantors are required by the ratings agencies to buy and hold a portion of the credit risks that they insure to encourage proper credit analysis and ongoing risk management.

The result, from the perspective of the investors that hold bonds covered by the financial guarantor, is an exacerbation of concentration risk. In effect, bondholders simply substitute the insurer's credit rating for that of the original issuer, thereby taking on credit exposure to the insurer itself. In the case of banking organizations mitigating their own risks, this results in a failure by the banks to achieve the maximum level of regulatory capital relief.

Investment Banking Products

Investment banks provide various products that could potentially be used to provide complex credit risk transfer solutions. First, they are major writers of credit derivatives, as described previously. Second, through their fixed income and asset-backed securities operations, they originate and structure asset-backed transactions that transfer credit risk from issuing institutions. While such transactions are primarily in plain-vanilla asset categories, they have equity tranches that the banks will seek to place. The placement process is naturally much smoother if there are sophisticated, credit-savvy investors to which banks can reliably turn.

Additionally, banks have significant credit risk transfer needs that arise from principal transactions undertaken on their own accounts or on behalf of their clients. Rather than being perceived as competitors, credit investors may well find themselves welcomed to a beneficial and symbiotic relationship with select investment banks based on the investors' independence and noncompetitor status. Consequently, such investors should have ready access to business opportunities that will not be targeted by investment banks, given the combination of perceived small market size (by Wall Street standards) and transaction complexity, or that will not be accessible to major Wall Street firms for competitive reasons (exposures on the books of other investment banks).

Property and Casualty Insurance and Reinsurance

While not traditionally active in the financial guaranty markets, property and casualty (P&C) reinsurers have developed products that may, in a broad sense, indirectly provide some of the benefits of credit protection. Additionally, some reinsurers have, in recent years, become active sellers of IG credit protection in the credit derivatives market. Certain insurers have also established structured finance departments.

Global, large capitalization companies may purchase enterprisewide catastrophe coverages that insure them against loss of income from a wide range of causes including credit risk. Such coverages have a stabilizing effect on the insured, and may, therefore, enhance the credit quality of securities issued by the insured. However, these insurance coverages are expensive and do not efficiently isolate and transfer the specific types of credit risks. Moreover, any credit that is enhanced by this method is subject to the same credit risk substitution dilemma that was described in the earlier discussion of monoline insurers.

Finally, certain offshore multiline P&C insurers and reinsurers have entered the monoline financial guaranty market, either through acquisition (Ace's acquisition of Capital Re) or start-up (Swiss Re, XL Capital, CDC) and will now be subject to the aforementioned rating agency pressures.

CONCLUSION

The appropriate platform for this type of business is one that captures both the environmental advantages of being privately held and unrated as well as the operational configuration necessary to originate, analyze, and structure credit transactions in-house. From such a platform, customized credit risk solutions may be provided to global financial institutions and industrial companies and thereby originate assets directly from these institutions instead of from investment banks. With this configuration, such a firm may use its structuring skills and proprietary analytics to purchase certain classes of credit risk from its clientele and transform these risks into a format palatable to its institutional investors, creating, thereby, a new asset class for them to invest in.

Worldwide demographic trends, new political realities, and globalization have conspired to make investment management more complex and risky. Across the globe, retirement schemes are being outsourced or privatized, resulting in a greater supply of funds chasing finite quality opportunities. While regulators, boards, and the market are placing an increased emphasis on risk management, the clients of professional investment managers are demanding better performance (stable and higher yields). Increasingly, asset managers will be more focused and will have to acquire deep expertise in the sectors they focus on.

The credit risk sector offers significant growth and superior returns but requires substantial credit expertise, focus, and a deep credit culture. These qualities are not found in typical institutional investors or traditional asset managers. In the main, the popularity of the credit risk market with these entities is due to higher yields that are available in this market, not a sudden inheritance of credit risk management skills by institutional investors.

The recent misfortunes of American Express and other institutions evidence what happens, eventually, to market participants that assume credit risk without the requisite skills, discipline, and culture. Nonetheless, institutional investors have not demonstrated sufficient understanding of the fundamental nature of credit risk by making the necessary and substantial investments in people, risk measurement, and management technology. Doing so would require a level of specialization and focus that would be inconsistent with the trading-driven, relative value strategies employed by many fixed income investment managers currently.

Investment banks are not the reason for this situation; they did nothing to bring it about. They were simply the first to figure out that there was an opportunity to be exploited. To be fair, they have come a long way up the credit learning curve in the past five or so years. But their focus remains relative value and a near obsession with credit spreads—to be expected, because this, after all, is the classic investment banking function of ruthlessly pursuing arbitrage opportunities until the window of opportunity closes. That opportunity exists for the reasons documented earlier and will continue to do so as long as there are naïve institutional investors that are either unwilling or unable to originate, analyze, and structure their own transactions. The banks are, strictly speaking, doing their jobs. Institutional investors should do the same.

Where does this leave us? The rating agencies remain the de facto regulators of the credit sector. They are also the quintessential tax collectors, exhibiting impressive creativity in extending the scope of their revenue base. In an environment beset with economic malaise and accounting scandals and an increasing willingness on the part of investors to outsource decision making to intermediaries "with no skin in the game," rating agencies and investment banks are able to reap risk-free arbitrage profits based on asymmetric information. For the intermediaries, rating agencies in particular, this is a wonderful business: They live in a protected world; their arbitrage profits protected from competition by virtue of their nationally recognized statistical rating organization (NRSRO) status. Their protector, the Securities and Exchange Commission, has elected to limit ratings competition by restricting NRSRO status to just three rating agencies. Naturally, the rating agencies have done nothing to jeopardize their protected status and operate in virtual lockstep with each other.

Investors, thus constrained, end up seeing the world with the same lens, responding to the same stimuli, earning market rates, individual members all of a massive investment herd. The solution is clear. Market participants must decide whether to acquire the skills and learn the discipline of credit investing and thus be able to confidently make investment decisions based on their own analyses and judgment. Or, they may follow the herd and abdicate investment decision making to intermediaries with nothing to lose.

NOTES

1. These estimates are based on the author's knowledge of the industry, the views of other market participants, and credit derivative dealers and insurance brokers with whom the author has had discussions.

PART FIVE

Regulating Corporate Innovation after Enron

14

COWBOYS VERSUS CATTLE THIEVES

The Role of Innovative Institutions in Managing Risks along the Frontier

FRED L. SMITH JR.

From the Fall from Grace to the fall of Enron, it has always been with us. It has been the primary reason that man is so often trapped into fatalistic acceptance of poverty and ignorance. And once mankind accepted the Promethean challenge to improve his condition, the issue of how best to deal with it has been a central element of controversy. Should the elites control it centrally, or should individuals deal with it directly? And when the unpleasant aspects of it occur, should we retreat or evolve institutions to make future mishaps less likely? In any event, it involves degrees of uncertainty and, invariably, an element of danger; therefore, it must be addressed in a balanced and careful fashion. Progress—civilization itself—may be seen as the gradual evolution of institutions and strategies to manage it.

It is risk—the possibility that a desired event will not occur or that a feared outcome will.[1] Risk was—and remains—the major factor limiting mankind's existence. And, even though mankind evolved in a risky world and is continually forced to choose between risky alternatives, risk is the major factor limiting our future. This is tragic; yet, as the late Aaron Wildavsky noted, the greatest risk of all is the effort to avoid all risk! (Douglas and Wildavsky, 1983). Civilization began when mankind came to realize that there were risks as well as lost opportunities in a world of stasis, a world where innovations were restricted or banned. Moreover, our existence on this earth creates changes—we use the more readily available resources and must continually engage in a risky search for replacements; we employ vaccines and antibiotics to save lives and find that diseases become resistant. As we change the earth and our institutions, we find again and again that our older risk management arrangements are inadequate. To retain stability, to gain access to the wealth-enhancing opportunities of change, it is essential that we continually evolve new risk management institutions and technologies to address these newer risks and older risks in their new guises. In effect, mankind is doomed to live in an *Alice in Wonderland* world: To stay in place, we must run; to progress, we must run more swiftly. We must take prudent risks to reduce these emerging risks!

But how should we discipline and regulate such innovative risk-taking activities? Certainly, we must manage such risks; behavior must be regulated. The dispute is about the best way of doing so (Hayek, 1978b). The question, in other words, is not whether risks should be regulated, but rather how should they be regulated and by whom?

The primary regulatory alternatives to managing risks are hierarchic (or political) and decentralized or competitive. Both types of regulation seek to ensure that only prudent risks are assumed, but they do so in very different ways. Political risk management relies heavily on central hierarchical bodies—tribal councils in traditional societies, regulatory agencies in the modern world. Political risk management is generally precautionary—nothing should be allowed until the experts decide the risks are appropriate.[2] This centralized gatekeeper role tends to reduce the risks of innovation (by reducing the rate of change) but may well increase the risks of stagnation (by reducing the rate of risk reducing change).

Competitive risk regulation, by contrast, encourages prudence by targeting the impacts of the innovation on the innovator, by allowing the parties to better attain that level of risk they prefer, and by remaining open to further refinements over time. Competitive risk management institutions evolve to enforce a set of general principles rather than to explicitly prescribe permissible behavior on a case-by-case basis.

Civilization can be seen as the gradual evolution of ever more creative risk management—from the family and private property to derivatives and structured financing arrangements. The goal is to permit an ever greater scope for the prudent assumption of risk. Because knowledge is dispersed, only that expanded scope offers any hope of fully using the varied skills of all the peoples of this planet. Civilization is the story of the advances and retreats of such prudent risk management expansions.

Civilization makes it possible to better manage risks in the financial, technological, and social fields. Indeed, a reasonable metric for assessing the level of civilization is mankind's success in evolving institutions that permit an ever-larger scope of prudent risk taking. Prudence is best defined as a careful calculation of the risks of change versus the risks of stagnation—and the development of institutions that encourage that careful balancing.

Risk management is most important and least developed at the frontier of civilization. There, not only do new risks emerge, but also old risks are encountered in new guises. Moreover, innovation on the frontier is undertaken by individuals who are self-selected risk takers. Finally, the institutional arrangements for managing risks in these areas are often embryonic. Note that the cowboys of the Old West were often portrayed as renegades and misfits, yet they played a critical role in policing borderless boundaries—reducing the risks to the cattle herds from wandering and rustling. Indeed, until the advent of barbed wire, the cowboy was *the* central feature of the risk management landscape, as well as perhaps the most often misunderstood.

Most individuals attracted to the frontier share similar goals—love of adventure, the spirit of competition, the thrill of innovation and discovery, and the willingness to take chances. It is not always easy to distinguish legitimate entrepreneurs and risk managers from frauds and miscreants. A thin line separates the cowboy from the rustler—in some cases, cowboys succumb to the weak monitoring of their activities and themselves *become* the cattle thieves.

Of course, all organizations face this traditional principal/agency risk—the risk that an employee will take advantage of his localized knowledge and power to advance his personal agenda at the expense of the organization. The confusion that characterizes activity on the frontier makes this all the more likely. And the focus on the novel risks present along the frontier too often leads to weakened scrutiny of traditional risks. Often old errors occur in these new settings, largely because they are not recognized as such and the older risk management strategies are less effective in the new setting.

And, when the inevitable errors do occur and potential risks become real losses, the instinctive response is often to retreat, to restrict the innovation. Rarely do policy makers consider whether existing policies might have made such losses more likely or whether modifying or strengthening some element of the competitive process might have reduced them. Too often, the inevitable losses associated with the trial and error process lead to quixotic attempts to seek a trial without error approach.

The Enron story follows this scenario. That Enron was staffed with cowboy entrepreneurs is not disputed. The real question is: When, where, how, and why did some of these legitimate risk-managing cowboys stray and become rustlers? And, more important, why did the traditional safeguards that had prevented such straying in earlier years fail? Why did the institutions—both private and political—designed to detect and prevent such a migration from legitimate entrepreneurship to abusive corporate malfeasance cease to discipline Enron management?

Many critics seem to believe that it was the company's involvement with novel financial products such as *derivatives* and *structured finance* that led to its financial losses. Had Enron avoided such complex and poorly understood innovations, it would have escaped its subsequent fraud and deception problems. Wrong, wrong, wrong! As discussed in the preceding chapters of this volume, Enron's problems arose from more traditional business mistakes—paying too much for acquisitions, acquiring companies that required management skills that Enron did not possess, and failing to put in place internal checks and monitoring requirements to ensure that employees were adhering to corporate policy. Enron's failures largely reflected the mismanagement of the traditional risks faced in any corporation—the "old cloudy wine in new but equally cloudy bottles" problem.

Enron did operate at the frontier. Its corporate financial policy, specifically its innovative ways of raising funds for its often-creative energy market activities, were pathbreaking. *Some* of Enron's corporate financing innovations, as discussed in Chapters 8 and 9, have been adopted by most global energy market participants as legitimate financing methods. Enron's derivative operations were actually largely profitable; they reduced rather than increased the overall riskiness of its operations. Enron's financial *market maker* role allowed other firms to reduce their commodity price and inventory risks. In brief, Enron's frontier-area activities in financial markets appear to have *reduced* overall societal risk. It is true that Enron's operations at the corporate finance frontier did leave it somewhat exposed. Still, Enron's problems arose less from the innovative nature of its financing strategies than from its failure to adequately *monitor* the use of these innovative financial instruments.

Doing so, of course, was not easy. Traditional accounting and tax reporting rules proved inadequate to clarify the riskiness of the special purpose entities (SPEs), stock options, and other innovations implicated in the Enron fall. The procedures developed to ensure prudent business practices in the tangible asset-based sectors of the economy failed to keep pace with Enron's increasingly complex—sometimes *overly* complex—financial activities.

Enron's problems, it should be noted, emerged only after the firm had shifted from a traditional energy firm focused on the distribution of oil and natural gas to a new economy firm dealing with the *financial* aspects of these physical energy transactions. After the partial deregulation of the 1990s, Enron's management began to see its comparative advantage as managing the virtual rather than the physical aspects of energy production and distribution. Enron pioneered the now famous *asset lite* strategy explained in Chapter 1. In this brave new world, Enron would allow others to manage the physical flows; it would focus on managing the financial risks associated with these flows. Enron's background as an energy services firm gave it the knowledge needed to address these risk issues, to design new financial instruments and strategies to help manage these energy-related financial risks. Enron also provided liquidity to make these emerging markets possible. Despite later monitoring failures, Enron's innovations in these areas were beneficial.

Enron's losses reflected the misuse of its creative innovations. It was its failure to prevent dishonesty and misrepresentation in this new setting that triggered the disaster.

The outrage over the Enron experience reflects in part the egalitarian concern that such innovative financial practices—even when honest—generate excessive profits. Yet, as Joseph Schumpeter noted long ago, extraordinary profits are "the baits that lure capital on untried trails" (Schumpeter, 1942, pp. 89–90). This confusion at the frontier, coupled with year after year of continued high profits, led many in corporate management to fall asleep at the switch. The errors and crimes now uncovered would have been less likely had Enron been operating in the "interior" of the economy. Still, Enron's innovations remain valuable; its failures demonstrate the nature of man, the fallen angel, rather than man the manipulative genius. Enron demonstrates that trial and error can be extremely costly. Yet, it remains the only viable path to the future. Trial without error is a utopian fantasy.

RISKS AND CULTURE: VALUES AND ATTITUDES TOWARD RISK

Human nature has changed little over recorded history. Humans value the immediate more highly than the more distant—both in time and space. We emphasize those things that affect us rather than others, and we continually face conflicts of interest between competing goals—for example, more food today versus the potential tightening of our belts tomorrow. And all this occurs in an environment where mistakes have consequences, often very painful consequences. Effective risk management institutions, therefore, create incentives relevant to man as he is—not man as we would have him be.

Douglas and Wildavsky suggested that cultural factors determine the way in which various societies respond and adapt to risk (or, more exactly, those risks that are not directly relevant to that individual). Attitudes toward such risks, they argued, are best viewed as "selected" to reinforce the legitimacy of the values they hold. Risks, in effect, aren't "out there" but rather are "internal constructs" useful for structuring a complex world. Douglas and Wildavsky (1982) defined four cultural values that they believed captured much of the varied views various peoples and societies hold toward risk and how best to manage it: fatalism, hierarchy, individualism, and egalitarianism.

Fatalism

The fatalist believes that risk is random. The appropriate response is to resign oneself to whatever fate the capricious gods might dole out.[3] Progress is an illusion; whatever one person gains, another has certainly lost. Wealth creation and the prudent risk-taking activities necessary for its advance have little traction in such cultures. In fatalist cultures, prudence is irrelevant since risk is random. Fatalists aren't political—there's no use fighting city hall!

Such extremely risk-averse societies were characteristic of man's early history—when our powers were weak compared to nature and our understanding of the world was rudimentary. Even today, many nondeveloping nations and some minorities within developing nations adhere to this dead-end cultural value. There are few risk takers in societies where the potential of action is viewed as nil and where the successful individual is seen as harming others. The fatalist culture gives way to more change-oriented cultures only when forced to do so by external circumstances or by internal collapse.

Hierarchy

Hierarchists believe that society should be ordered—that those most expert, most capable of leading society should be granted power and authority. Risk taking is necessary, even valuable, but the risks must be carefully monitored and supervised by the wise. Prudence is best ensured by leaving the decision as to which risks can be taken in the hands of those most qualified to decide for all.

Traditional societies and much of modern society have long been organized along hierarchic lines. The tribe or hunting band looks to the headman or chief to decide which risky actions should be banned and which encouraged. Today, similar faith and power are given to bureaucrats manning the various centralized political risk management institutions—the Securities and Exchange Commission (SEC), Environmental Protection Agency (EPA), Commodity Futures Trading Commission (CFTC), Food and Drug Administration (FDA)—and a host of other risk management agencies.

Hierarchic regulators realize that risk taking is essential; however, they are the sole arbiter of what constitutes "prudent" risk.[4] Note that hierarchic regulators do not capture the full gains of prudent risk taking (regulators are rarely residual claimants); however, they will face heavy criticism if their approval leads to some mishap. As a result, hierarchic agencies tend to adopt some variant of the *Precautionary Principle*—the policy that the risks of innovation should generally be weighed more heavily than the risks of stasis.

In practice, hierarchical risk managers seek *trial without error* and thus, in practice, tend to slow or even ban institutional and technological change. Hierarchic risk managers operate at some distance from the actual risk-taking activity, which makes it very difficult for them to incorporate the specialized knowledge that is dispersed widely. Further, the costs incurred in gaining approval to take some specific risk discourage some innovations.

Hierarchic societies can be very stable—there are few internal tensions to encourage reform. Regulators typically liberalize their anti-change rules only when faced by external competitive pressures from less restrictive risk management regimes (other political jurisdictions, for example). National hierarchic cultures are even more stable. For example, Japan, after its civil war, moved to create a stable world and largely succeeded. Change did not occur until the Europeans entered Asia in force in the nineteenth century.

Individualism

Individualist societies view risk as largely a personal matter—especially in areas where institutions are believed adequate to contain and target the impacts of risk taking. Society's role is to develop generalized rules to assign responsibility and to ensure that the consequences of individual actions are isolated. (Individualists tend to believe that this separation has largely been achieved.)[5] Individualist societies arise both as risk-targeting institutions allow the risks associated with an individual decision to be localized and as external pressures on hierarchic societies force liberalization. Individualist cultures enlist a greater fraction of the citizenry in the critical task of exploring the economic frontier. Because risk taking is individualized, each person is able to use the information that he or she alone possesses—thus society benefits from dispersed information unavailable in hierarchic risk management systems.

Individual risk taking requires, of course, a wide array of institutional arrangements to ensure that the well-being of the society isn't endangered by the careless acts of a few aberrant members. Modern society, as discussed in the next section, has evolved a wide array of institutions—private property, contracts, and the rule of law—to advance that objective. These generalized rules make decentralized risk taking more palatable to the society's more risk-averse members. Moreover, as risks are incurred and sometimes disasters result—that is, when the potential risks of the trial and error approach become reality—individualist societies respond by seeking out new institutional arrangements to reduce the likelihood of a reoccurrence of such disasters. By opening the frontier to entrepreneurial risk takers, individualist cultures have greatly accelerated economic and technological growth.

Egalitarianism

In modern societies, the major struggle is between hierarchic and individual risk management. Yet, the policy debate often focuses on another cultural value—the egalitarian concern over whether risk taking is compatible with fairness. In a society already characterized by vastly different rewards and status, egalitarians worry that entrepreneurial risk taking, if successful, will worsen existing inequities. Initially, new technologies will be available only to the powerful; thus, any wealth or life quality improvements that might result will accrue only to the few.[6] Besides, egalitarians argue, while the innovator will gain the benefits, the risks are too likely to fall largely on the downtrodden. For such reasons, modern egalitarians increasingly view change negatively.[7] The world is too fragile and change too likely to prove destructive to allow hierarchic—much less individual—risk taking. We should not expend time or energy in the impossible search for ever-greater economic and technological growth; rather, we should seek fairness by finding ways to equate wealth and power in the current world.

In many ways, the modern egalitarian has returned to the negativism of the fatalist.[8] Unlike the fatalists, however, egalitarians do have a political agenda. Believing that change makes the world a less fair place, they view our planet and our societies as extremely fragile—one misstep and disaster is ensured.[9] Thus, they oppose all novel risks: biotechnology, global warming, and derivatives. In a world that has become freer (satisfying those seeking greater individual freedom) and wealthier (reassuring those seeking a well-ordered society), the egalitarian perspective has become more significant. And, because total opposition to all change would render them politically irrelevant, egalitarians seek instead ever-stricter hierarchic regulation, seeing in that approach their best hope of blocking, or at least delaying, change.[10]

The Evolution of Risk and Culture

The hierarchic *enterprise-wide* approach to risk management has many virtues *for individual firms*. Indeed, the firm itself is best seen as an institutional arrangement for managing and coordinating the various risks associated with the production and marketing of goods and services. The managers of the firm can more readily consolidate positions and exposures for integrated risk measurement, can more easily monitor the evolving risks, can more readily address those risks as they are revealed, and can adjust the overall risk profile of the firm to that desired by its shareholders.

In contrast, *socially* centralized and hierarchical risk management (e.g., SEC regulation) is far less adaptable to tailored risk management. Neither the SEC nor any other centralized political risk manager is able to make full use of the knowledge dispersed across the numerous market participants. Those localized individuals who will benefit or lose based on the wisdom of specific investment decisions are far more knowledgeable about the prudence of a specific financial risk, yet their knowledge is inaccessible to the bureaucrats. The complexity and tempo of modern financial markets, moreover, makes them extremely difficult to monitor. How can any central authority understand in a timely fashion the ever-changing local situation? How can they ensure that their policies are being implemented? Individuals with the wisdom and foresight to accomplish that task may exist but they are unlikely to be found in governmental agencies.

As noted earlier, the fact that the gains from innovation accrue to the innovator and not the regulator creates a residual claimant problem—the regulator bears the risks of approval but does not gain the economic rewards that might accompany that approval. These difficulties encourage political regulators to move slowly, to shy away from approving any novel technology. It also makes them susceptible to any information suggesting reasons for delay or denial. Because successful innovations threaten existing economic interests, the centralized regulator will be lobbied fiercely by competitors providing many reasons why the innovation is too risky for approval. An interesting example of this special interest effort to block technology was Edison's efforts to frighten America away from alternating current; that ban would have made direct current—his entry into the electricity sweepstakes—a winner.

Political agencies also are influenced by *realpolitik*. They will consider more carefully the impact of their decisions on the powerful—and those relying on current technology and arrangements will generally be more powerful *today* than the innovators representing *tomorrow*. Powerful groups may be allowed risk-taking privileges denied to those perhaps better prepared to incur such risks. Again, the evidence on the riskiness of the innovation will be weighed more heavily. And if such preferred firms or individuals incur losses, they may find themselves reimbursed from taxpayer funds.

That passive fatalistic societies would gradually be replaced by limited risk-accepting hierarchic cultures is understandable, as is the fact that competitive pressures would gradually liberalize centralized hierarchic regulatory systems. In time, individualistic risk taking schemes would gain greater sway. However, we should not be surprised that egalitarians, distrustful of both individualism and hierarchy, would urge retreat from innovative risk taking whenever errors—inevitable in a system of trial and *error*—occur. The history of mankind's gradual effort to manage risk (summarized in more detail in the next major section) is a tale of slow advances and many retreats, sometimes for centuries. Even today, most financial risks are heavily regulated by a host of political risk managers. And, as the response of the Administration and Congress to the Enron crisis demonstrates, this progress is fragile, all too easily reversed when disasters occur.

History suggests that civilization is never secure. The innovative entrepreneurial society has no deep roots, and few passionate defenders. Yet, hierarchic regulatory bureaucracies are poorly designed to balance the risks of innovation against the risks of stagnation. In contrast, the competitive marketplace encourages that balancing very well. A business would always prefer to play it safe; yet, in competitive markets, the firm that spends nothing on R&D will soon be outflanked by firms that do make such productivity and quality-enhancing investments. Market prices guide firms toward prudent risk taking (rising prices suggest the value of investments in that area). If their intuition is correct and their innovation proves viable, they may well profit handsomely, attracting other resources to this new field. Prices signal the risks for which prudent investment is warranted; profits determine which investments are appropriate. Together, these competitive market forces guide risk taking at the economic frontier.

However, both fatalist and egalitarian values are biased against such competitive risk management. Fatalists lack any confidence that risks can be managed. Egalitarians fear the inequities that reliance on prices and profits might create. Moreover, the hierarchic view that centralized risk management offers greater security does have deep roots. Current society is influenced by the fact that for many millennia we obeyed the autocratic leadership of tribal priests and chiefs. Taboos blocked risk taking on all sides to protect the tribe against the risks of the wayward individualist. Given the fact that early societies operated close to the edge—even minor setbacks might well lead to the destruction of the tribe—these anti-innovation rules had some validity. Moreover, for much of mankind's prehistory, the risk-management institutions that today help to isolate risks, targeting their impact on those directly involved, were weak or nonexistent. In that era, competitive regulation of risks was often unfeasible. This prehistory has left society with a profound bias toward "priestly" control over risk taking. Even today, many believe that "objective" experts freed from any economic motive are far more likely to choose wisely for society than would economically motivated individuals disciplined by competitive markets.

That instinctive preference for hierarchic control over change often leads—in times of crisis—to the imposition, or reimposition, of centralized regulation. This weakens the evolving competitive forces that promise to make such disasters less likely in the future. Indeed, political intervention in response to economic mishaps often increases risk from *moral hazard*—the tendency of individuals to act in a riskier fashion if they believe any costs of such risks will be borne by others. In America, for example, the bank collapses of the 1930s led to federal deposit insurance, the "hostile" takeover battles of the past half century led to state and federal rules strengthening traditional management against outsiders (and weakening the incentive of outsiders to monitor errant performance by corporate managers), and failing corporations (airlines most recently) were granted access to federal loan guarantees. These interventions undermine competitive pressures for prudent risk taking.

Institutions that alleviate the pain when risks become reality and socialize the losses associated with those adverse events misdirect resources and energies toward imprudent risks. We spend too little in areas where prudent risk taking would be beneficial; we spend too much on imprudent risks in areas that have been socialized. Also, we weaken the incentives of the parties most knowledgeable about risks to innovate, to explore improved ways of focusing the gains and losses associated with such risks.

INSTITUTIONAL RISK MANAGEMENT— A BRIEF HISTORY

Having developed in the previous sections the broad framework for the evolution of risk management from the Fall from Grace to the fall of Enron, I now review very briefly some of the major events in this process. Civilization, as noted earlier, can be viewed as the gradual development of improved risk management capabilities, but that process is erratic. Mishaps, as noted, often lead to sharp reversals that slow or even block creative risk opportunities for long periods.

Important Historical Events and Changes

The move from tribal fatalism to hierarchy to modern individualism was made possible only by the development of institutions that limited the fallout of risks. These institutions make it possible to better reconcile the risk-averse attitudes of the majority and the risk-taking propensities of the entrepreneur.

The earliest risk-management stratagems (e.g., joining together to hunt larger animals) tended to place great weight on acting as a team. The individual who failed to hold the ring could permit the escape of the stag, leaving everyone hungry that night. But that value also led to a general suspicion of individual experimentation. Because most innovations fail, and, in the tribal collective, a loss by one was a loss to all, tribal cultures place a high premium on conformity and disparage the innovator. Tribal man first invented the Precautionary Principle—the rule that the risks of innovation should be weighed far more heavily than the risks of the status quo. In a world where the Gambler's Ruin outcome (the prospect of exhausting all resources) was always a very real possibility, such risk-averse policies made some sense.

Yet, the greatest risk is the refusal to take risk. Optimizing for an unchanging world is rational only if the world is indeed stable; but it is not stable. Societies that overly specialize, that eschew all forms of risk taking, become vulnerable. There are risks in innovation but there are also risks in the status quo. Folk wisdom has long noted this tension in well-known aphorisms: "He who hesitates is lost!" and "Fools rush in where angels fear to tread!"

Americans, now among the wealthiest people in history, seem increasingly willing to shut their eyes to this risk/risk reality. As the flurry of recent securities fraud shareholder suits and SEC fines suggests, the current demand is for risk-free investment opportunities. The current whine is: "They didn't tell me I could lose money!"[11]

Having attained much, we seem to want it all. Americans seem no longer content to take the bitter of uncertainty with the sweet of progress; instead, we insist on having the sweet only and rely on government to protect us from the bitter.[12] But, as Wildavsky (1988) has shown, the effort to "have it all" is both paradoxical and futile. It is paradoxical because we become safer only by allowing dangerous innovations that are less dangerous than the older products they replace. It is futile because the risk management strategies of today will increasingly prove inadequate to address the risks of tomorrow. We *must* change because the risks that we face are also changing. For example, resource depletion requires that we undertake risky explorations and developments around the world, that we finance risky new processing technologies, or that we explore substitute materials or technologies that may not prove out. Disease risks are also constantly changing—the flu vaccine of last year has little value today.

This decline in the value of existing risk management stratagems—this growing *resistance* to any given risk management strategy over time—means that almost every risk managed today will require different risk management techniques tomorrow. As noted earlier, ours is an *Alice in Wonderland* world: To stay in place, you must run; to get ahead, you must run even faster. The remainder of this section discusses key milestones in that race to get ahead.

Domestication of Wildlife   Mankind arose in a highly risky environment. Animal attacks were a fact of life; acquiring food involved risky hunting and foraging efforts. Domestication of flora and fauna drastically reduced these risks. Wolves became dogs; pigs, cows, and horses were brought under man's dominion, greatly reducing the risk that such resources would not be available when required.[13]

The Family as a Risk Management Institution   The basic family unit is an excellent example of a risk reduction strategy. Father, mother, and children have strong mutual reasons to work together to create a better life. The family workforce could specialize, allowing greater productivity without increasing risk. The family unit also permitted risks to be taken at the subtribe level, thus allowing experimentation at lower risk. Entrepreneurial families could move out to the frontier, where the freedom to innovate was greater. If their efforts were successful, the tribe benefited; if they failed, only the one family unit was lost.

The risk-taking propensities of individuals in tribal society was constrained by cultural norms. Although the family permitted some degree of innovation, the tribe still might be held liable for transgressions by one of its members. Richard Posner has discussed one of these cultural risk management rules—the *blood guilt* concept in which all members of the tribe were held liable for any act of violence committed by any individual member of that tribe. This custom, Posner argued, reflected the high cost of policing violence committed by outsiders. Because a tribe would have greater knowledge about the violence potential of its members, this collective assignment of risk responsibility was an efficient risk management rule. The classic clan feuds such as those between the Hatfields and the McCoys are survivors of early risk-management strategy.

Private Property   One of the most significant risk management innovations was the evolution of private property. Prior ownership arrangements were collective—land and goods were owned in common. Such collective ownership regimes allow little scope for innovation. Private ownership— and the associated institutions of fencing, monitoring, and protection— made possible a much wider variety of management experiments. And as fencing technologies improved, the consequences of successful and failed experiments could be more readily constrained to a person's own property. The entrepreneur gained the freedom to manage resources in a novel way. The greater scope of action made possible by privatization made it far easier to explore the technological and institutional frontiers. That advance in prudent risk taking greatly accelerated change.

Institutional mechanisms for policing private property rights are an essential component of frontier risk management. In the early days of western settlement, cowboys were virtually the only institutional device for policing borderless parcels of land, of protecting the crops and animals on that land. But as the cowboys and cattle thieves became harder to distinguish, the need for a more efficient fencing technology became evident. That technological innovation took the form of barbed wire, an invention that not only helped protect property rights but also made it easier to distinguish between the cowboys patrolling those now-fenced boundaries and the trespassing cattle thieves.[14] Note, also, that the institution of private property enlists non-owners in the risk management process. Those inventing and manufacturing barbed wire, for example, weren't concerned about reducing the risks associated with land management, but rather with their selling a new product. Yet, innovation did reduce such risks!

Contracts   Once resources were under collective or private ownership, owners sought to make arrangements about their transfer or use. These agreements evolved into modern contracts. The first contracts were highly ritualistic promises between chiefs, specifying the agreements of each toward the other. Contracts were solemn affairs, sometimes sworn in blood. Contracts greatly extended the risk-taking abilities of society by allowing parties to bind themselves to take certain actions if a risk did materialize. This ability to protect against the worst aspects of a risky venture greatly expanded the risk-taking options available. Because contracts are most valuable when widely used and honored, contracts strengthened the power of the individual. This point is made explicit in Richard Wagner's musical drama work *Der Ring des Nibelungen,* where the giants successfully resist the threats of the god Wotan, because his power rests on the sanctity of contract (Wagner, 1997).

Trade   Decentralized control over resources led to a vast increase in voluntary exchanges, at first within the tribe but then gradually to outsiders. Trade is a major risk management strategy because it allows the trader to acquire resources that are locally scarce (though often only temporarily). The first trades occurred in hierarchic societies where traders would sometimes be adopted into the village before being allowed to exchange goods.

Arbitrage   In *The Wealth of Nations,* Adam Smith reviewed eighteenth-century public attitudes toward specialized types of trade that were among the first important and then-innovative risk management strategies. In his discussion of the evolving trading arrangements, he discussed two: *forestalling* and *engrossing.* Forestalling was an activity in which corn was purchased during times of plenty in hopes it could be resold when prices rose. Engrossing was a similar activity in which corn was purchased in one region and transported to another in hopes of being sold at a profit greater than the transportation cost. Both innovations were fiercely opposed by merchants in areas enjoying favorable prices—the arbitrage role of these innovators tended to drive prices up in areas where corn was abundant and to lower prices in areas where corn was scarce. The traditional merchants in both areas saw these newcomers as interlopers who were profiting at their expense. After all, they noted these *middlemen* produced no corn—they simply benefited by taking advantage of the local conditions.

The antitrade Corn Laws were intended in part to restrict forestalling and engrossing. Smith, nonetheless, noted the obvious (but neglected) risk reducing benefits of those activities:

> By making [people] feel the inconveniences of a dearth somewhat earlier than they might otherwise do [forestallers and engrossers] prevent their feeling them afterwards as severely as they certainly would do, if the cheapness of price encouraged them to consume faster than suited the real scarcity of the season. (Smith, 2001)

Smith went on to call forestalling and engrossing a "most important operation of commerce." He noted:

> The popular fear of engrossing and forestalling may be compared to the popular terrors and suspicions of witchcraft. The unfortunate wretches accused of this latter crime were not more innocent of the misfortunes imputed to them, than those who have been accused of the former. (Smith, 2001)

Smith's view ultimately prevailed; the Corn Laws were repealed, and England's economy grew to be one of the largest in the world. Still, popular reaction to almost all economic innovations is hostile. The value of such innovations is often not well understood; existing businesses are often discomfited by the introduction of the new arrangement, and the profits earned in such frontier areas are often large. Egalitarians and hierarchs alike view such situations with suspicion. Civilization advances slowly in the face of such reactionary pressures.

Insurance   Insurance is the development and marketing of risk contracts, specifying the payments to be made if a risk materializes. Insurance contracts allow the shifting of risks associated with an investment to specialized risk pooling groups, while retaining the management of the enterprise itself with the specialist in that area.

Insurance originated in the maritime industry. Early insurers would lend money to shippers, collecting a healthy premium from the shipper if that ship came home safely, forgiving the loan if it did not. Such non-recourse conditional loans evolved into the modern insurance contracts of today. Underwriters evolved to correctly "price" insurance contracts; then these contracts would be syndicated among wealthy individuals (the Lloyd's model).

Insurance was the first business based solely on risk management. Insurance requires assessing the level of the risk, determining what contractual terms would best limit those risks (e.g., requirements that sea captains be highly trained, that fire suppression systems be installed, that loss limits and deductibles be included to discourage frivolous claims), and then investing the premium income anticipated to produce a cash flow suited to the risks being covered. Were insurance not available, a vast array of risky activities would not take place—or would occur at much reduced levels. That point was made evident in the aftermath of the 2001 terrorist attacks in New York City and Washington. The lack of coverage weakened the recovery, as firms proved unwilling to invest in new construction without some assurance that they would have access to risk coverage.

Insurance has also played a largely unrecognized role in allowing homeowners to accept risks that have improved the aesthetic quality of our communities. An example is homeowner acceptance of the risks of large trees adjacent to their homes. Absent homeowners' insurance, the modern city would be largely absent of such inherently risky flora.

The Corporation   To Nobel laureate Ronald Coase, the firm is a creative arrangement to assemble a set of tasks that are better performed within the hierarchic command-and-control structure of the firm rather than the exchange arrangements of the market (Coase, 1990). The decision as to "correct" bundling of activities (what to do under "one roof" and what to do separately) is always provisional and depends on many factors.

These include the culture of that society, the sophistication of the market including legal liability and contract rules, the nature of unionization, and technology. Generally, tasks involving exchanges of tangible goods or services are more likely to be handled via market exchanges. Tasks involving goods and services that are intangible and not readily valued are often best handled by being bundled into the corporation.

The firm must address a range of internal risk management problems. One key example is the management of the inherent conflicts of interest that occur whenever one individual is assigned a specialized subtask within a larger organization. In fulfilling this task, will that individual create excessive problems for others within the firm? This is the widely discussed "agency problem."

The development of the modern corporation allowed great gains in risk management. The limited liability aspect of the modern corporation reduces the risks to the investor and permits specialized management skills to be deployed without requiring ownership in return. A firm could acquire the specialized skills to perform some valued service, organize those skills to efficiently produce that good, and profit accordingly. Investors need only consider the broad capacity and prospects for that adventure; they are not held liable for any misadventure of the firm itself.

To further reduce risks to investors, the firm specifies the nature of its charter, the terms and selection criteria for its governing board, and the financial reports it will file for public (or, at least, shareholder) review. The evolution of accounting as a means of reporting its condition has become an important part of the firm's reporting obligation. Investors are more likely to invest in firms that clarify their status and the riskiness of their operations.

Note that the evolution of the modern corporation was preceded by the joint stock company. The events were not dissimilar to those around today's Enron affair. Investors had become intrigued by the potential of foreign investment and had poured money into various schemes. A crash occurred—the South Sea bubble—and politicians rushed to punish the miscreants and ensure against any future risks of this type. Laws were enacted that virtually prohibited joint stock companies—in England, one such law was the Bubble Act of 1720. That act was not repealed until 1825, which forced England to rely on alternative capital acquisition arrangements such as limited liability partnerships. The Bubble Act is thought to have curtailed the ability to acquire capital to develop the frontier.[15]

Accounting   To ensure accurate reporting of the firm's financial condition, accounting has evolved. This is a heroic attempt to assign static value to a dynamic concern. Accounting data assist management in determining internally the wisdom of alternative policies. External use of such data is to determine the viability of the firm, the wisdom of investing in it. The firm's accounting data provides one glimpse of the firm; external analysts and takeover experts provide other perspectives.

Double-entry bookkeeping was perhaps one of the most important elements in the evolution of accounting, making it harder to make mistakes and more difficult to defraud. The problem, of course, is that valuation techniques are highly subjective. Audits essentially inform both parties of gross discrepancies but are limited by the honesty of the data provided. Few firms conduct the expensive forensic audits that seek to determine the validity of the data itself. Most audits, therefore, are of the "if what you told us is true, then here's your condition" nature. Therefore, the ability of an auditor to ensure accuracy is minimal.

Accounting has worked reasonably well for firms whose assets are tangible (brick and mortar, machinery) but has proven far less adaptable to newer forms of asset value. However, the modern firm has much of its value in complex assets such as intellectual property (whose value depends on innovations elsewhere in society), goodwill, and "going concern" value. The accounting profession is well aware of the growing discrepancy between such critical valuation efforts and the assigned value of the firm but has made little headway in recent years in developing precise valuation techniques.

The Enron situation has been viewed as a failure of accounting—and, in one sense, that assessment is correct. However, there is little evidence that accounting is up to the task assigned it. The highly specialized and thinly traded financial instruments employed by Enron are clearly useful but inherently difficult to value. The inherent risk of such difficult-to-value instruments was clearly not well understood by either management or the external investment community. The best sources of value information may well be those external to the firm—analysts, customers, and rivals. Yet, as discussed elsewhere in this volume, these guardians relied on the same type of information as did management.

Accounting changes designed to better value the modern firm may have made matters worse. One example was the attempt to mark intangible assets to market. This effort was again an even more heroic attempt to quantify the nonquantifiable.

External Monitoring   Another institutional response to risk management concerns is the monitoring of a company's decisions by outsiders. Sometimes these outsiders have a direct relation with the firm they are monitoring, while in other cases external monitors have evolved as monitoring businesses in their own right.

Direct monitoring is performed by financial institutions with significant credit exposure to the monitored enterprise. In some cases, junior creditors rely on the credit analysis of those more senior "delegated monitors" for financial information and credit quality assessments.

In Europe, banks became the specialized financiers and external watchdogs of many corporations. In the United States, this evolution was blocked by populist fears of excessive corporate power. American banks were, however, more free to develop the modern credit industry—developing elaborate statistical methods to determine the riskiness of extending credit to individuals. Credit databases and credit scoring schemes evolved, which made it possible to predict reasonably well the risk associated with providing varying amounts of credit to specific groups of consumers. The resulting loans were then bundled, securitized, and syndicated. This process dramatically lowered the cost and increased the availability of consumer credit in America. In Europe, political restrictions on the ability of financial institutions slowed a similar evolution.

Some firms also function as *indirect* monitors of the credit risk of other institutions. These monitors—chiefly, the major rating agencies—are indirect monitors inasmuch as they have no direct exposure to the firms whose financial integrity they are policing, but rather provide such watchdog services for a fee. Corporate credit benefited from this parallel effort to rate corporate financial instruments (bonds and equities) and again lowered the costs of acquiring capital. These rating services, like accounting, worked best on established firms with well-traded instruments dealing with tangible assets. For the reasons mentioned previously, they were less accurate when dealing with the modern firm based on intangible, thinly traded assets.

Derivatives   Another important institutional response to the need for better corporate risk management naturally occurred with the growth of *derivatives activity,* or transactions that derive their value from some underlying asset, reference rate, or index. Derivatives may be either *exchange-traded* or *privately negotiated* (i.e., over the counter [OTC]). Derivatives are themselves primarily a risk management instrument—another example of how private contracts can facilitate the transfer of certain risks to firms best able to retain those risks. In that sense, the use of derivatives by institutions is often an important signal of prudent internal risk management.

In addition to their role in helping companies best achieve the level of risk their shareholders seek, derivatives have also created an important additional layer of monitoring and discipline on firms' other risk-taking and risk-management activities. Exchange-traded derivatives are relatively standardized and are negotiated in a transparent organized marketplace. Further, performance on exchange-traded derivatives is generally guaranteed by a *central counter party* (CCP), or a clearinghouse, that becomes counter party to all transactions after the trade is done. Because of the risks this creates for the CCP, risk management by CCPs is among the most conservative in the world and includes credit risk management features such as regular cash resettlement of open positions, margin or performance bond requirements on trading participants, capital requirements on participants, and regular financial surveillance and monitoring.

By contrast, OTC derivatives traditionally are privately negotiated and thus do not trade in a transparent organized marketplace. This makes such transactions hard for outsiders to observe, and this often makes people nervous. At the same time, the fact that OTC derivatives do *not* have a clearinghouse guaranteeing performance makes derivatives participants almost hypersensitive to counter party credit risk concerns. Risk mitigation mechanisms adopted by OTC derivatives "dealers" include bilateral and close-out netting provisions, credit enhancements such as collateral, and periodic cash resettlement.

The primary use of derivatives is by firms seeking to *reduce* their own risk exposures. Despite this fact, as well as the heightened degree of risk monitoring to which users of exchange-traded and OTC derivatives alike are subject, derivatives have long been subject to the types of witch hunts we have come to expect on the frontiers of financial innovation. U.S. politicians in the 1930s initially sought to blame financial activities and "speculative excesses" for the Great Depression. Legislation was enacted, for example, to eliminate financial contracts called *privileges,* which were viewed as tools by which people could gamble recklessly on company stock prices. The hysteria prevailed and succeeded in a ban on those contracts, which were not finally deemed "economically beneficial" enough to legalize until 1981. When they did reappear, they were called *options.* Options on company stock, foreign exchange, commodities, interest rates, and other physical assets and financial products now dominate the global financial landscape, and even the most populist politician would hesitate today before attacking their merits.

The futures industry has also been a frequent victim of political attacks. Senator Arthur Capper (R-KS), a sponsor of the 1921 Grain Futures Act regulating futures markets, referred to the Chicago Board of Trade as a "gambling hell" and "the world's greatest gambling house" (Markham, 1987). In 1947, President Harry S. Truman claimed that futures trading accounted for the high prices of food and that "the government may find it necessary to limit the amount of trading." He continued, "I say this because the cost of living in this country must not be a football to be kicked about by gamblers in grain" (Markham, 1987). Indeed, since futures began trading in the United States in the 1800s, more than 200 bills have been proposed by Congress to prohibit, limit, tax, or regulate futures markets.

Derivatives traded on organized exchanges, of course, did become accepted as not only beneficial, but in fact a necessary component of commerce. Without futures and options markets, corporations would be left at the mercy of the volatility of global financial markets. That futures and options have significantly enhanced the resilience of the financial architecture can no longer be questioned.

In the 1990s, however, concerns arose about OTC derivatives. Close on the heels of major public derivatives-related losses at entities such as Procter & Gamble, Orange County, Barings, and Metallgesellschaft, politicians were quick to condemn OTC derivatives. Former House Banking Committee Chairman Representative Henry Gonzalez (D-TX) said of derivatives: "Is it money . . . for the procurement of goods, for firing the engines of manufacturing and production? No. It is paper chasing paper, reduced to highly speculative and instantaneous transactions of billions of dollars . . ." (Congressional Record, 1993). Despite such claims, derivatives have numerous benefits for their users, global capital markets, and the economy. Corporations, governments, and financial institutions have benefited from derivatives through lower funding costs, diversified funding sources, enhanced asset yields, efficient management of exposures to price and interest rate risk, and low-cost asset and liability portfolio management.

Like other financial activities, derivatives also have risks. These risks are no different from the risks inherent in making a mortgage loan or holding equity, but they are risks that must be managed. Naturally, firms sometimes fail in the risk management process, and when established firms such as Procter & Gamble encounter losses, the long knives come out. Politicians are quick to decry these innovative practices as involving "too much rocket science and not enough sweat." Novel innovations rarely get respect; the criticisms here of derivatives and related financial instruments are all too similar to the earlier criticisms of the innovative middlemen functions of forestalling and engrossing.

Ironically, the failure of Enron has simultaneously vindicated concerns about most OTC derivatives. Now the great villain is *structured finance,* or the use of SPEs to couple asset divestiture decisions with risk management and corporate financing decisions. And many of those who have been quick to criticize Enron's abuses of structured finance have been equally quick to argue that had Enron used plain vanilla derivatives instead, where market controls are more mature and better established, Enron might not have been allowed to get away with the same degree of abuses.

Lessons from History

Several observations can be drawn from this brief survey. First, the development of institutions that localize and target risk—and thereby provide the confidence needed to permit a wider range of risks to be taken by a higher percentage of the population—is evolutionary, not revolutionary. Second, this process seeks to allow the citizenry the flexibility to attain *their* risk preferences—the result may be less *or more* risk. The goal is to allow widespread prudent risk taking—risk aversion per se is not a societal goal. Third, as novel mishaps arise in the innovative frontier region—that is, when the inevitable "errors" of the *trial and error* process materialize— some will argue that these losses could or should have been prevented, that we must tighten political control over risk taking in this area. Yet, losses are inevitable in any learning experience, and the risks reduced by that innovation are almost certainly more than those incurred. The loss event, moreover, will likely already have triggered changes, making future errors of this type less likely. But these are all points too rarely raised in the heated political debate. Most important, the call for a retreat from the risk frontier and the championing of more restrictive political control over risk taking are all too likely to weaken the competitive pressures to continuously improve risk management practices. The result? Civilization's slow progress slows still further.

Still, as noted previously, all societies are risk averse and naturally biased against innovation and entrepreneurial activity more generally. In most societies at most periods, novel practices and innovators are viewed with suspicion, and blame for disasters is placed on the novel aspects of the situation rather than on their misuse. Note the attacks on Enron's use of SPEs and derivatives, rather than on its failure to consolidate the financial impacts of these essentially internal arrangements. As noted earlier, this response is not new: From Prometheus onward, societies have feared both the innovation and the innovator. Cowboys were initially viewed with a mixture of skepticism and fear, as was the advent of barbed wire (surely one of the most important risk containment innovations in the area of property rights). Opponents were quick to point out that this technology would surely increase the risks to children and animals that might haplessly wander into the sharp metal fencing.

Experience suggests that the all-too-likely response to unanticipated risk is a retreat to more restrictive hierarchical risk management approach. Today, that retreat generally takes the form of hasty federal legislation or administrative action to impose greater restrictions on that sector of the frontier economy. The result is to slow the innovative process, to weaken the incentives to devise arrangements to address risk directly—why concern yourself with risk when government promises to assume the burden? An excellent example is the overreaction to the South Sea Bubble disaster cited previously. The retreat response led to a century-long suppression of joint stock companies in England that, almost certainly, slowed the Industrial Revolution in that nation. That the private losses stemming from this event might well have been adequate to "civilize" this frontier sector, to reduce the likelihood of this type of failure, seems not to have been considered.

To better understand the risks that a retreat response entails, consider the Promethean legend again. Note that Prometheus democratized fire, by taking it from the gods and making it accessible to mankind. His critics argued that this would increase the overall fire risks—at worst, only the elite priesthood should be authorized to take on such risks. And, of course, they were right—as to fire risk alone. However, restrictions on fire use would also limit its risk-reducing value. The risks reduced by fire—animal attacks, harsh weather, and starvation—were much greater than the novel risks fire introduced. Also, decentralized fire management accelerated the development of fire-risk management practices. Individuals found innovative ways of banking fires at night, of keeping flammables far enough away, and of providing adequate ventilation. Moreover, these risk reduction innovations were quickly shared among the community. Decentralized risk management encourages more rapid development of enhanced risk management practices. A wide scope for trial and error more quickly reduces the magnitude of error.

This chapter is not concerned with *whether regulation is warranted* but rather with the question of whether private competitive or political hierarchic risk management is the better path. In the aftermath of the Enron crisis, competitive risk management was dismissed as impractical, as totally inadequate to address the risks of modern financial instruments and methods. Too often, such dismissals are accepted as soon as they are voiced. For the moment, America seems to have fallen in love with political risk management. One consequence is a transformation of public expectations concerning risk. In other areas, we are more rational. We expect insurers to mitigate the effects of unfortunate events, not to prevent their occurrence. We expect doctors to cure diseases (most, anyway), not to make us immortal. But, today, many seem to feel that the SEC and other political risk regulators will somehow eliminate financial risk.

This expectation is as much the result of modern political risk management as it is its source. Once society demands the elimination of risk, government gains a vast advantage over private risk management. Only government would even purport to pursue the utopian goal of eliminating risk; only government has the power and the resources to compensate losers—with no regard for their own coresponsibility—by raising revenues from less visible and less powerful sources.[16] Only politicians promise "free" health care, "zero" pollution, and "risk-free" investment.

The desire for zero risk—and the belief that government regulators can somehow bring it about—dovetails with today's general distrust of markets and corporations. The underlying notion is that the profit motive encourages businesses to cut corners, to sacrifice safety and the environment for profits. This notion presupposes that consumers and intermediaries (such as insurers, rating agencies, or purchasers somewhere along a product's distribution chain) have little interest in the riskiness of a product or service and fail to discipline producers when problems become evident. Sometimes, it is argued, political risk management is necessary in those areas where the purchases are large and infrequent—auto and home sales, moving services, some investment services. In these areas, it is said, firms are indifferent to the risks of losing repeat business and thus face weak competitive disciplines. But that presumption ignores the role of reputation as the screening device for risky services. And reputation can easily be destroyed by even a few horror stories that gain attention all too easily in the modern low-cost information world. Markets are very effective risk management institutions.

By promising the impossible, regulation becomes subject to a variant of Gresham's law: Deeply flawed, political regulatory schemes drive out more realistic efforts to enhance risk management institutions. Regulations become ever more restrictive; fewer entrepreneurs are willing to explore that sector of the economic frontier. In effect, we address frontier risk by closing the frontier, reducing the incentives to devise improved competitive risk management alternatives. The tendency to retreat to hierarchic regulation when frontier disasters occur is atavistic and reactionary. Our hope is that, as inflated public expectations are chastened by reality, this love affair with political regulatory schemes will also end and we will reexamine the case for competitive risk regulation.

Indeed, financial risks were once primarily considered a private matter. After all, most economically valued resources at risk were privately owned, and their owners protected them, relying on the courts when necessary, against trespass, theft, fraud, and misrepresentation. Individuals negotiated on risk matters, typically through private contractual agreements. Risks were shifted to private insurers as desired, while private rating services provided information about the nature and level of risk in countless fields.

Of course, private parties make mistakes. Managers fudge financial reports, and some commit actual fraud. Rating agencies do not always spot imminent financial failures. Private systems are not immune from sabotage or error, either. Indeed, for those who are predisposed to distrust markets, Enron-style failures come to signify the inevitability and catastrophic consequences of allowing free and nonpolitically controlled markets. Markets, it is argued, cannot adequately discipline risk.[17]

Appealing as this *market failure* argument may seem, though, it is too facile. The fact that markets are imperfect does not, in itself, demonstrate the superiority of political strategies; rather, it calls for a balanced comparison of the respective ability of private and political institutions to regulate the risks of financial transactions. Competition is indeed a process of creative destruction; many firms based on outmoded institutions or technologies disappear continually. Still, history mandates skepticism toward attempts to remedy such ills by replacing market-based competitive discipline with grandiose hierarchic political regulatory schemes.

Unless we want to march mindlessly down the road mapped out by the market failure paradigm and pave the road to serfdom with investor-protection bricks, we must begin to take the task of financial reform seriously. Enron's bad management was perhaps less to blame than were earlier "reforms" that weakened the ability of the market to discipline corporations and halt such bad management before getting to Enron-like levels of trouble. Would, for example, Enron's problems have been as severe if the caveat emptor instincts of investors had not been anaesthetized by SEC assurances? Had prior reforms not limited hostile takeovers, would not outside analysts have devoted more effort to understanding Enron's supposed profitability—to raid the corporation or sell it short?

Past regulatory policies have often weakened the incentives that might have addressed the deep-rooted institutional and political incentives that sometimes incline some in business toward imprudent risks. Expanded investor protection laws, improved financial risk assessment procedures, increased public participation in corporate decision-making processes, larger compliance and surveillance budgets for the agencies, new governance and oversight regulations, enhanced accounting and disclosure standards—all do little to counteract these biases and do little to strengthen the incentives for other market participants to monitor and challenge aberrant corporate behavior.

Consider the idea of expanding *public participation* in the corporate governance and risk management process. For the public at large, the costs of obtaining sufficient information and setting aside sufficient time to participate in a meaningful way are prohibitive, so participation is never really *public*. Instead, the likely participants are either business interests or the leaders and attorneys of ideological "public interest" groups. Thus, public participation in effect shifts power from *shareholders*—the owners of the firm—to well-organized *stakeholders*—nonowners who seek to force the firm to act in their interests. This increases the risk that the firm may take actions not justified on economic grounds. Enron, for example, was very active in the politically correct "green energy" field, spending hefty sums for solar and wind power companies. All these proved non-profitable and added to the underperforming assets that ultimately killed Enron (see Chapter 1). In practice, granting self-appointed "publics" power over corporate decision making is likely to exacerbate an already-existing bias favoring the politically powerful interests of the present, against the emerging promise of the as yet unidentified producers and consumers of improved risk management products.

Civic education is also unlikely to resolve these problems. It is unquestionably true that the public is often inadequately informed or positively misinformed about the operations and functions of financial institutions and markets. Civic education has value; indeed, this volume calls for a radical revision of the way in which we as a society think about risk—a civic education project of monumental proportions. However, civic education is an undertaking fraught with perils, especially when it is done by government.

In a very real sense, ignorance may be not only bliss, but also rational. Rational ignorance serves to filter out remote and exotic risks, thus leading individuals to focus on those risks which are more substantial and more immediate. It may seem desirable that shareholders be made aware of all financial dangers, including those posed by complex business practices. Realistically, though, most people have little incentive to spend much effort becoming well educated on such remote and insignificant (to them) risks. Thus, the SEC could play a positive role in countering hysterical and misleading calls for bans on innovative risk management practices. The SEC might well educate the public on the causes of investor fraud and suggest steps to strengthen the competitive regulatory process (e.g., by clarifying the positive role of hostile takeovers and by reviewing the way in which bans on insider trading weaken incentives to develop more accurate information on the financial status of a firm). However, experience gives little hope that the SEC—or indeed any government agency—will actually play that role. The line between education and propaganda is not always very clear, and it is crossed with particular ease when the issues are highly uncertain, as they typically are in the world of derivatives, structured finance, energy markets, and other frontier financial activities.

Political agencies such as the SEC and CFTC, moreover, have a strong incentive to emphasize the ill effects of risks that fall within their jurisdictions. Agencies are plainly motivated by a desire to build political support for an expansion of their mandate and budget. Thus, the basic agency bias is to alarm, not to inform.

Reforms must simulate and institutionalize the internal and external forces that should discipline and inform risk taking by corporate management. But political controls are designed and monitored far from the modern world of intangible assets, rapidly changing institutional and technological realities, and complex financial accounts. Political regulators experience only indirectly—if at all—the costs of their actions; thus, the costs of restrictive regulation—most important, the slowing of the risk management evolutionary process—are weighed too lightly. Moreover, the bias of the political agency—its reluctance to approve changes that harm powerful interests—naturally inclines it against innovation.

THE CASE FOR COMPETITIVE RISK REGULATION

The Enron crisis has blinded us to the value of competitive regulation— to the idea that the best way to discipline the financial investment sector is to encourage the evolution of institutions that would profit by discovering and profiting from uncovering inept corporate management. To achieve this goal, we should mobilize forces both internal and external to the firm.

The corporation itself is an evolving arrangement for ensuring that employees keep management informed of what is really going on. Given the strong incentives that exist in any bureaucracy for employees to present only positive information to their superiors, this principal/agency problem is always a serious one (see Chapter 3). Employees have little reason to blow the whistle on aberrant behavior—and many reasons to remain silent. The obvious counterincentive—their ability to profit by capitalizing on their knowledge that profits are misstated—is highly limited because of current rules against insider trading. The result is that current policy ensures that the most informed information about the future state of the corporation never reaches the market.

External monitors are less well advantaged to obtain this information; moreover, the incentives to gain control over a company that is more or less valuable than generally perceived have been weakened by anticorporate takeover regulations. The result is that the very idea of competitive regulation as a substitute for political regulation now seems strange to most people.

This policy blindness, we may hope, is temporary. Societies that suppress innovation cannot thrive long. In most economic areas, we do not seek to control private risk taking, even though competition does entail serious risks: business failures, job losses, and, sometimes, the ruin of entire cities or regions.[18] We accept competition because we understand that competition is a process of creative destruction and that we cannot prevent these costs of change without losing the risk reduction benefits of creativity and innovation. Perhaps more important, we understand that the alternative to centralized political management is not anarchy—it is decentralized private risk management arrangements by competition itself.

To see this, let us reexamine the very concept of regulation itself. All human activities must be disciplined and regulated in some way. Everyone desires that problems be handled as rationally as possible. In so doing, we should use as much foresight as we can command. In this sense, everybody who is not a complete fatalist accepts the need for regulation. The debate over regulation is, therefore, not a dispute on whether we ought to choose intelligently among the various possible organizations of society; it is not a dispute on whether we ought to employ foresight and systematic thinking in planning our common affairs. It is a dispute about what is the best way of doing so (Hayek, 1978b, p. 234). The question, in other words, is not whether risks should be managed, but who should manage them for whom?

Private and political risk managers face many of the same tasks: They must seek out data, assess the level and nature of any emerging risks, and determine whether any action is appropriate. The case for private competitive risk management rests on the proposition that the knowledge base for risk management is far too dispersed and fragmentary to permit central planning.[19] Competition regulates risks by placing a premium on creative risk management within the firm and by creating a rich array of external institutions eager to discipline the firm for any aberrant behavior. The challenge to the firm is to encourage creative entrepreneurship while still retaining adequate oversight authority. Firms approximate this ideal by formal reporting requirements, internal reviews and audits, rotating job responsibilities, salary and bonus arrangements, and a host of other formal and informal mechanisms designed to align the interests of the employee and the firm. Firms also seek to match the risk skills of their employees to their assigned roles within the firm. The result is a wide array of firms—some operating very cautiously within the economic frontier; others blazing boldly out in the most innovative regions of the economy.

Competitive regulation recognizes that all checks and balances can fail and thus relies on external actors to reinforce internal firm-specific regulatory controls. External groups routinely monitor the firm, assess its performance, and stand ready to discipline aberrant behavior in various ways. Such external checks and balances include outside directors, insurers, auditors, rating agents, creditors, suppliers, and customers—and, perhaps most important, current and potential investors (both long and short) and corporate raiders. Outsiders are sometimes motivated to play this role because of their close relationship to the firm—as supplier or customer—or their financial stake in the enterprise.

Most important, outsiders are prompted by the fact that information about the viability of an enterprise is valuable. Firms may be under- or overvalued, and it is very profitable to gain that information before others do. There is much profit in buying or shorting the shares of a poorly valued firm and, thus, in acquiring the information to determine that status. Outsiders may also believe that a firm has lost its core—that its assets are being used unwisely—and seek to take it over.

Political regulators must also solve somehow the knowledge problem—what risks of what type exist where? Unfortunately, central bureaucracies are too far from the action to have access to the localized knowledge essential to wise risk management. Moreover, even if they could somehow achieve this incredible feat, political risk managers would still face the even more daunting task of motivating millions of people to act in accordance with their decrees. Competitive risk management allows us to approximate that standard: Markets entail myriads of voluntary transactions allowing the risk averse and the risk takers to coordinate their risk preferences. As such, markets register private risk preferences and tolerances far more accurately than even the most informed and open political process.

The private sphere facilitates the development of this risk management function. Many private investors seek to shift their residual risks to others. In a world where risk can be managed privately, insurance and other institutions evolve to meet that demand. For example, users of price-volatile commodities such as chocolate historically sought to escape that price risk, and cocoa and other commodity futures markets developed accordingly. Notice that the goal of private risk management is not to *reduce* risk but rather to allow more parties to more closely achieve the level of risk they seek. Private risk arrangements would take full account of the parties' concerns—but *only* the parties' concerns. Third parties might comment on private arrangements, but they have no power to determine them.

Although error is inevitable in both the private and political worlds, you can expect better performance from private risk managers. The incentives to *get it right* are superior! However, the proper comparison is not between the political risk manager and the *average* private actor but between the politician and that one marginal private actor who, among millions of others, *does get it right:* His or her actions will soon dominate the market.

Private risk managers are far more likely than political institutions to consider risks in a more balanced fashion. Risks are ubiquitous—any decision increases some risks and reduces others; therefore, the question of balance is critical. Consider the issue of whether a new technological process or institutional arrangement should be approved: Both private and political groups will weigh heavily the risks of change. On the other hand, stagnation and doing nothing are also dangerous. If only for competitive reasons (e.g., fear of losing market share), a private firm will take the risk of stagnation seriously. In contrast, few political risk managers experience any pain by delaying or even blocking change. The victims of inaction are statistical artifacts of the wealthier, safer world that might have been; their voices are scarcely heard in the political process.

RECONSIDERING THE ENRON SITUATION

The market failure case for political regulation is not persuasive. Indeed, the market failure argument actually works in favor of competitive, not political, regulation. Private risk management can, after all, create costs for which private managers and market participants escape liability. Sometimes—as in the case of force and fraud—those activities are criminal, requiring state action. Other times, however, potentially mutually advantageous agreements are blocked by the lack of key underlying market institutions. Such market failures might best be addressed by removing all barriers to competitive market regulation of financial risk. As the economist Ludwig von Mises stated concerning the case for political regulation of environmental risk:

> It is true that where a considerable part of the costs incurred are external costs from the point of view of the acting individuals or firms; the economic calculation established by them is manifestly defective and their results deceptive. But this is not the outcome of alleged deficiencies inherent in the system of private ownership of the means of production. It is on the contrary a consequence of loopholes left in the system. It could be removed by a reform of the laws concerning liability for damages inflicted and by rescinding the institutional barriers preventing the full operation of private ownership. (von Mises, 1966, pp. 657–658)

Rather than viewing Enron as a market failure, we should consider whether political controls might have blocked competitive forces, which would have identified and addressed the problem earlier.

We do not (yet) have a Federal Bureau of Secure Investment charged with defining the socially correct level of financial risk that an individual investor may assume, although several recent SEC chairmen seem to have interpreted securities laws in this fashion. And we certainly do not have any agency charged with eliminating investment losses. In America, private investors are considered adults and thus able to determine for themselves the level of acceptable investment risk. And investors in turn discipline the firm by deciding to buy or sell the stock.

Real problems do occur in the marketplace, as some of the shenanigans of Enron, WorldCom, and others have plainly illustrated. But the task of distinguishing deception from puffery, complexity from fraud, mistakes from willful nondisclosure—cowboys from cattle thieves—is never easy. It is doubtful that it could ever be performed better in the political arena. The interests involved, the bias against innovation, and the incentive to build agency power rather than to protect investors all suggest the superiority of private, competitive risk regulation.

Because the optimal level of investment losses is not zero, moreover, the inherently risk-averse nature of the political process may unnecessarily raise barriers to innovation and thus make capitalization of financially innovative firms much more difficult than it is today. To hold the future of our economy hostage to the investment acumen of government bureaucrats would exacerbate, not reduce, risk.

Under a private regime, firms fail, investors suffer losses, and monitoring processes do not always work as expected. Monitoring boards are not foolproof, nor are accounting firms and other external monitors. Yet, too often, the response to major losses and monitoring failures is to blame any business practice that cannot readily be explained. This "blame-the-innovation" bias threatens the evolutionary process that offers the best hope of improved risk management over time. The public, goaded on by the press and crusading politicians, can all too easily agree that innovation itself is the culprit. That risk is evidenced by the demonization of joint stock companies, forestalling and engrossing, derivatives, structured finance, and the like.

In contrast, as noted earlier, in a competitively regulated world, the market does respond quickly to unexpected problems by developing new risk management institutions or technologies. The private market's response to business failure is not paralysis; it is innovation and capital reallocation. After the Enron debacle, hundreds of billions of dollars moved from firms that had failed to clarify to the investor community adequately their internal risk management strategies. The level of that discipline dwarfed any fines that even the most aggressive SEC regulator might have levied. Note also that the inventions of outside boards of directors, frequent audits, quarterly reports, and disclosure policies were the market response to earlier business failures. A world that looked only to government to manage risk might never—or only belatedly—have developed such investor-protection arrangements. Moreover, the great variety in people's sensitivities to risk suggests that the decentralized competitive approach would explore a much broader range of innovative solutions, far earlier than the typical crisis-driven political approach.

Some of the monitoring institutions that evolved in response to earlier failures did not function as intended in the case of Enron. That simply means another wave of innovation in the monitoring process is at hand. Those institutions whose monitoring failed will be disciplined by the market, and those gaps that we now realize were left open will create opportunities for new innovative institutions to close them.

Markets are not rigid, frozen arrangements unable to address emerging concerns. They are exquisitely sensitive to changed expectations and flawed reporting. For this reason, we need to place greater reliance on private risk management to strengthen the demand for more accurate monitoring of corporations' financial status. Monitoring intelligence firms specializing in determining the actual profitability of a firm—and the wisdom of its investment, employment, production and internal management policies—will flourish. Such external monitoring will give a comparative advantage to investors active in either shorting or purchasing the stock. Moreover, such external information will encourage takeovers of mismanaged firms. Political regulators, in contrast, have little incentive or capability to conduct such detailed monitoring of the modern firm. They have even less incentive to encourage private firms to acquire such monitoring capacity. Indeed, they may view it as a threat to their authority. Established firms have political clout and, too often, the political authorities will view their mission as preserving the status quo, not encouraging the creative destruction necessary for a more efficient economy.

The major impediment to competitive regulation of future Enrons is political regulations that restrict the *market for corporate control* (see also Chapter 3). A vigorous market for corporate control is a powerful disciplining agent on companies that deviate from acceptable business conduct. Indeed, even firms that cannot explain their practices clearly, might well attract takeover bids. Sadly, the Enron debate has largely ignored the role of such competitive regulatory devices.

Pending such strengthening of competitive regulation via the removal of the protective policies introduced to shield errant firms and political regulators from market disciplines, we might consider reforming the political regulatory process. One idea that might counter the institutional and political bias against innovation would be to assign financial regulatory authority only to agencies having both a promotional and a risk management role.[20] Because private investors do face this conflict of interest (the desire for security and high returns), so also should the SEC. This capital formation role should conflict with the SEC's mission to reduce the risks to investors. If the SEC is unable or unwilling to play that role (a

most likely outcome), an Office of Economic Advocacy—a "devil's advocate" agency charged with making the most compelling case possible
against regulatory impositions in the economic risk area—should be established elsewhere (perhaps in Treasury where that tax collection agency
has already established a National Taxpayer Advocate which heads the
Taxpayer Advocacy Service). The Advocate's Office should receive a budget comparable to those financial risk regulatory agencies it monitors. It
should have access to all agency data and help mobilize constituencies
that bear the costs of regulation.

Other legal and institutional problems also make private risk management difficult, and those should be seriously reconsidered in light of
the Enron affair. For example, the predisposition of U.S. securities laws
allows class action lawsuits against the officers and directors of companies.
Of course, a firm's shareholders should be able to hold their manager and
directors accountable. But current laws allow suits to be filed on behalf of
a class of investors before that class has even been certified by the courts.
Attorneys may directly threaten officers and directors with the prospect
of huge personal liability. Suing officers and directors discourages qualified individuals from serving those roles.[21]

CONCLUSION

Enron has taught us a valuable lesson. Sometimes the innovators and entrepreneurs on the frontier cross the line from cowboys to cattle thieves.
Institutions must be in place—or should be allowed to evolve quickly—to
detect such problems when they occur, and cattle thieves, when caught,
should be severely punished. But in our effort to address such risks, we
should remain vigilant to several cautionary axioms.

First, the need to penalize cattle thieves does not create an open license to attack all cowboys.

Second, while the private institutions to detect and deter inappropriate activities sometimes fail (especially on the frontier), that does not
justify a hierarchical, political approach. We should first consider whether
some existing political policy might not have weakened superior private
risk management institutions. The greatest risk is not always the cattle
thief, but rather the political risk that a regulatory agency will go after
cowboys and cattle thieves with equal vengeance—or even worse, that our
efforts to prevent the risks of theft endanger the values created by the
honest cowboys.

Despite the numerous causes for frustration, the reform case is not
hopeless. The political response to the Enron problem has assigned financial regulators extraordinarily ambitious tasks that they cannot

fulfill without great harm to technological and economic growth. As the Enron crisis fades and its consequences are viewed more dispassionately, the risk of political overreach will become more evident. And Americans are already aware that excessive political control can be very risky indeed.

Like disease, political risk regulation is not an inevitable element of life—it can be addressed, treated, and cured. As the utopian excesses triggered by the Enron situation fade, risk reform will again become viable. Life is inherently risky, but it need not be inherently political. A world without risk is impossible, but one with reduced political risk is not. Thinking about the evolution of risk management institutions is a useful starting point. The Enron disaster may yet prove a valuable step in civilization's long term efforts to improve its risk management capabilities.

NOTES

1. Parts of this introduction draw heavily from Smith (1992).
2. A caution is needed here. There are risks of moving ahead too fast (of ignoring the risks of innovation), and there are risks of moving ahead too slowly (of ignoring the risk reduction benefits of innovation, the risks inherent in the status quo). That is, the real world presents us with a risk/risk trade-off. Political agencies prefer the simplicity of dealing with one or another of these risks. Thus, political agencies tend to be either *precautionary or promotional*. Either bias can make the world a more risky place. This chapter focuses on the risks of precautionary agencies; however, the recent disintegration of the space shuttle *Columbia* illustrates that promotional agencies can also increase risks. The strong institutional desire of the National Aeronautics and Space Administration to increase its visibility by launching more shuttles more frequently, led to suppression of information about risks. The results were tragic.
3. In a fatalist culture, risks can be portrayed as a marble on a flat plane. The marble may move or not—there is no direction, no rising or falling.
4. The appropriate view of prudent risk taking in hierarchical cultures is that of a marble in a narrow shallow bowl. Within limits, the marble can move around; but once the marble has exceeded those bounds, it will fall. To hierarchs, risk taking must be carefully controlled to prevent disaster.
5. The individualist view of risk is akin to a marble resting in a deep high-lipped cup. Society is inherently stable. The individualist may or may not be cognizant of the rich array of institutions that act to focus the consequences of risk taking on the innovator and that, therefore, account for this stability.
6. Note, however, that first-generation innovations (the first central heating systems, automobiles, computers, and cameras) are often costly. The rich, by providing a test market for such novelties, pay dearly for what (in historic terms) are low quality products. I've argued that we might see the rich as the "white mice" of society—the subpopulation used to test out

innovations—that, if successful, will eventually become available at much higher quality and much lower price to the larger population. Egalitarians have largely ignored this aspect of change.

7. See the discussion of this trend in Wildavsky (1991).

8. I use the term *returned* here because egalitarians once were far more optimistic about change and more skeptical of the virtues of centralized risk management. Thomas Paine and Andrew Jackson, two early populist egalitarians, saw no virtue in granting power to political institutions. Nor were they opposed to change. Egalitarians today—or perhaps more precisely, modern liberals—have displayed an increasingly negative attitude toward change. But that shift, in my view, reflects their belief that time is no longer on their side—that the cultural tides have shifted and their values are losing ground to resurgent individualism.

9. Risk is viewed by egalitarians as akin to a marble balanced delicately on an upturned globe. The slightest perturbation in any direction and the marble will fall. Nature and society are fragile and we must tread very carefully, lest they be damaged irrevocably.

10. It should be noted, however, that this creates a major tension within this cultural group. Thus, one sees calls for increased government regulatory power coupled with severe criticisms of the existing use of such powers. For instance, Naderites seem convinced that all existing government agencies have been captured by special (generally economic) interests but still demand that the powers of these agencies be increased!

11. As this article is being completed, the SEC has informed Credit Suisse First Boston, for example, that it will have to pay $250 million to settle probes into whether its analysts misled investors so as to benefit the firm's investment banking practice. Citibank has been told the price tag to end a similar probe there is around $500 million. Other firms under investigation include Bear Stearns, Goldman Sachs, JP Morgan Chase, and UBS Warburg. All this follows an agreement by Merrill Lynch to settle a similar claim for a fine of $100 million.

12. Douglas and Wildavsky (1982) have noted that values determine what people choose to fear. Individuals focus on risks that validate and reinforce their values. Modern intellectuals, who distrust free enterprise, focus on the risks of economic and technological change and weigh natural risks much less heavily. For example, environmentalists give little attention to the massive quantities of chlorine, particulates, and acidic material spewed forth by volcanoes, while attaching great significance to the CFC residues from aerosol containers.

13. The story of plant and animal domestication is told with great skill in Diamond (1996).

14. For an interesting account of the evolution of property rights in the West, see Anderson and Hill (1975).

15. This paragraph relies on personal correspondence between the author and Colin Robertson and Forrest Capie (e-mail July 3, 2002). See also Harris (1999/2000).

16. Of course, the courts also play a similar risk compensation role. The *predation through litigation* problem has grown dramatically in recent decades. Today, the guilt or innocence of a party may have little relevance to its liability.

17. The rhetoric of the policy debate often prejudges the outcome. Competitive regulation, for example, is often referred to as *self-regulation* as though the firm would have sole control over the type and nature of these disciplining forces.

18. The exceptions, of course, are force and fraud, which are *criminal* activities.

19. This observation is key to the analysis of Hayek and other economists of the *Austrian school* (see Chapter 1). See, for example, Hayek (1945).

20. The Federal Aviation Administration (FAA) for many years was responsible both for promoting air travel and for ensuring that air travel was safe. These conflicting roles—the first arguing for lower cost air travel, the second demanding ever more expensive safeguards—encouraged the FAA to trade off the safety advantages of additional expenses (three engines instead of two, three pilots instead of two, and mandatory child safety seats rather than lower cost family airfares). Sadly, that "conflict" was removed recently when the promotional role of the FAA was eliminated by Congress. The all too likely result is that the FAA will now become another risk-averse precautionary agency—concerned only with ensuring air safety to the detriment of overall travel safety (forcing travelers from the three-dimensional safety of air travel to the two-dimensional world of land travel will generally increase risks).

21. Private risk management means little unless such ownership encompassed the rights to manage your property. Regrettably, the rights of property and contract have been seriously eroded by legislatures and by the courts. Contractual arrangements have been replaced with tort law, which, in turn, has been almost completely socialized. Today, courts often award compensation to parties who have suffered no demonstrable damages while imposing liability on parties who have caused no harm. In fact, modern tort law has become an even more ambitious and misguided effort to redress risk harms than regulation; government regulators, at least, are subject to budgetary and political constraints that establish some minimal threshold of regulatory concern. Civil liability is constrained by little other than the ingenuity of lawyers.

REFERENCES

"Accounting Failures Aren't New—Just More Frequent." 2002. *BusinessWeek* (January 28). Available at www.businessweek.com/magazine/content/02_04/b3767713.htm.

Alchian, A. A., and H. Demsetz. 1972. "Production Information Costs and Economic Organizations." *American Economic Review* 62.

Allen, W. T. 1992. *Redefining the Role of Outside Directors in and Age of Global Competition.* Ray Garrett, Jr. Corporate and Securities Law Institute, Northwest University, Chicago.

American Bar Association, Section of Business Law. 1978. "Corporate Directors' Guidebook." *The Business Lawyer* 33 (April).

American Bar Association, Section of Business Law. 1994. *Corporate Directors' Guidebook.* 2nd ed. Chicago: Author.

American Bar Association, Section of Business Law, Committee on Corporate Laws. 2001. *Corporate Directors' Guidebook.* 3rd ed. Chicago: Author.

American Bar Association, Task Force on Corporate Responsibility. 2002. *Preliminary Report* (July 16).

American Institute of Certified Public Accountants (AICPA). 1959. *ARB 51: Consolidated Financial Statements.* Retrieved from FARS/Original Pronouncements/Committee on Accounting Procedure Accounting Research Bulletins (ARB), CD-ROM, Release September 1, 2002. Norwalk, CN: Financial Accounting Standards Board.

American Institute of Certified Public Accountants (AICPA). 1971. *APB 18: The Equity Method of Accounting for Investments in Common Stock.* Retrieved from FARS/Original Pronouncements/Accounting Principles Board Opinions (APB), CD-ROM, Release September 1, 2002. Norwalk, CN: Financial Accounting Standards Board.

American Law Institute. 1994. *Principles of Corporate Governance: Analysis and Recommendations.* St. Paul, MN: American Law Institute Publishers.

Anderson, T. L., and P. J. Hill. 1975. "The Evolution of Property Rights: A Study of the American West." *Journal of Law and Economics* 18(1).

Arrow, K. J. 1974. *The Limits of Organization.* New York: Norton.

Azarchs, T. 2001. "Enron Credit Exposures Widely Dispersed Through Global Financial System." *Standard and Poor's RatingsDirect* (December 6).

Bainbridge, S. M. 1995. "The Politics of Corporate Governance: Roe's Strong Managers, Weak Owners." *Harvard Journal of Law and Public Policy* 18.

Barone, R. M. 2002. *Testimony of Ronald M. Barone, Managing Director, Standard & Poor's Ratings Services Before the Permanent Subcommittee on Investigations Committee on Government Affairs, United States Senate.* Washington, DC: Governmental Affairs Permanent Subcommittee on Investigations, United States Senate.

Barroveld, D. J. 2002. "The Enron Collapse: Creative Economics or Criminal Acts." *Writers Club Press* 10.

Bazerman, M., and D. Messick. 1996. "Ethical Leadership and the Psychology of Decision Making." *Sloan Management Review* (January).

Belstran, L., and J. Rogers. 2002. "Andersen Skeletons Come Out in Trial." *CNNMoney* (May 7). Available at money.cnn.com/2002/05/07/news/companies/Andersen.

Berenson, A. 2002. "Ex-Tyco Chief, a Big Risk Taker, Now Confronts the Legal System." *New York Times* (June 10).

Berle, A. A., and G. C. Means. 1991. *The Modern Corporation and Private Property.* Reprint ed. New Brunswick, NJ: Transaction.

Berman, D. K. 2002. "Before Telecom Bubble Burst, Some Insiders Sold Out Stakes." *Wall Street Journal* (August 12).

Bhagat, S., and B. Black. 1999. "The Uncertain Relationship Between Board Composition and Firm Performance." *Business Law* 54.

Blumenstein, R., and J. Sandburg. 2002. "WorldCom's CEO Ebbers Resign Amid Board Pressure Over Probe." *Wall Street Journal* (April 30).

Bratton, W. W. 2002. "Enron and the Dark Side of Shareholder Value." *Tulane Law Review* 76 (May).

Brennan, M. J. 1958. "The Supply of Storage." *American Economic Review* 48.

Bronson, D. M. 1983. "Countertrends in Corporation Law: Model Business Corporation Act Revision, British Company Law Reform, and Principles of Corporate Governance and Structure." *Minnesota Law Review* 68 (October).

Broehl, W. G., Jr. 1992. *Cargill: Trading the World's Grains.* London: University Press of New England.

Bryce, R. 2002. *Pipe Dreams.* New York: BBS Public Affairs.

Buffett, W. E. 2002. "Notes from Omaha." Speech presented before the Berkshire Hathaway, Annual General Meeting, as reported in *The Motley Fool*, a Special Report by Selena Maranjian (2002).

Business Roundtable. 1978. *The Role and Composition of the Board of Directors of the Large Publicly Owned Corporation* (January). Reprinted in *Corporate Governance.* New York: Practicing Law Institute.

Business Roundtable. 1997. *Statement on Corporate Governance* (September 10). Washington, DC.

Business Roundtable. 2002. *Principles of Corporate Governance* (May 14). Available: http://www.brtable.org/pdf/704.pdf.

Cassidy, J. 2002. "The Greed Cycle." *New Yorker* (September 23).

Clark, R. C. 1986. *Corporate Law.* New York: Aspen.

Clayton, R. J., W. Scroggins, and C. Westley. 2002. "Enron: Market Exploitation and Correction." *Financial Decisions* (spring).

Coase, R. 1990. *The Firm, the Market, and the Law.* repr. ed. Chicago: University of Chicago Press.

Cochrane, J. H., and C. L. Culp. 2003a. "Equilibrium Asset Pricing: Implications for Risk Management." In *The History of Risk Management*. London: Risk Books. Forthcoming.

Cochrane, J. H., and C. L. Culp. 2003b. "Prepaids from the Medici Bank to Enron." Manuscript. (February).

Congressional Record. 1993. "My Advice to the Priviledged Orders." House of Representatives (June 10) H3443, Time: 20:20.

Crouhy, M., D. Galai, and R. Mark. 2000. "A Comparative Analysis of Current Credit Risk Models." *Journal of Banking and Finance* 24.

Culp, C. L. 2001. *The Risk Management Process: Business Strategy and Tactics*. New York: Wiley.

Culp, C. L. 2002. *The Art of Risk Management: Alternative Risk Transfer, Capital Structure, and the Convergence of Insurance and Capital Markets*. New York: Wiley.

Culp, C. L. 2003. *Risk Transfer: Derivatives in Theory and Practice*. New York: Wiley. Forthcoming.

Culp, C. L., and B. T. Kavanagh. 1994. "Methods of Resolving Over-the-Counter Derivatives Contracts in Failed Depository Institutions: Restrictions on Regulators from Federal Banking Law." *Futures International Law Letter* 14(3/4) (May/June).

Culp, C. L., and M. H. Miller. 1995a. "Hedging in the Theory of Corporate Finance." *Journal of Applied Corporate Finance* 8(1) (spring).

Culp, C. L., and M. H. Miller. 1995b. "Metallgesellschaft and the Economics of Synthetic Storage." *Journal of Applied Corporate Finance* 7(4) (winter).

Culp, C. L., and M. H. Miller. 1999. "Introduction: Why a Firm Hedges Affects How a Firm Should Hedge." In *Corporate Hedging in Theory and Practice: Lessons from Metallgesellschaft*. C. L. Culp and M. H. Miller (Eds.). London: Risk Books.

Culp, C. L., and A. M. P. Neves. 1998a. "Credit and Interest Rate Risk in the Business of Banking." *Derivatives Quarterly* 4(4) (summer).

Culp, C. L., and A. M. P. Neves. 1998b. "Financial Innovations in Leveraged Commercial Loan Markets." *Journal of Applied Corporate Finance* 11(2) (summer).

D'Amario, P. B. 2002. "North American Credit Derivatives Market Develops Rapidly." Greenwich Associates (January 9). Available at www.gtnews.com /articles6/4133.shtml (visited September 15, 2002).

de Roover, R. 1963. *The Rise and Decline of the Medici Bank: 1397–1494*. Washington, DC: Beard Books.

Diamond, D. 1984. "Financial Intermediation and Delegated Monitoring." *Review of Economic Studies* 51.

Diamond, D. 1991. "Monitoring and Reputation: The Choice Between Bank Loans and Directly Placed Debt." *Journal of Political Economy* 99.

Diamond, J. 1996. *Guns, Germs, and Steel*. London: Norton.

Dodd, R. 2002. *The Bigger They Come, the Harder They Fail: Enron's Lesson for Deregulation*. Special Policy Brief, Derivatives Study Center, Washington, DC (February 7).

Dooley, M. P. 1992. "Two Models of Corporate Governance." *Business Lawyer* 47.

Douglas, M., and A. B. Wildavsky. 1982. *Risk and Culture: An Essay on the Selection of Technical and Environmental Dangers.* Berkeley, CA: University of California Press.

Douglas, M,. and A. B. Wildavsky. 1983. *Risk and Culture: An Essay on the Selection of Technical and Environmental Dangers.* Reprint ed. Berkeley, CA: University of California Press.

Drucker, P. F. 1981. *Toward the Next Economics.* New York: Harper & Rowe.

"Dunlap to Leave Sunbeam Board." 1998. *Financial Times* (August 7).

Eichenwald, K. 2002. "Waste Management Executives Are Named in SEC Accusation." *New York Times* (March 27). Available at query.nytimes.com/search /restricted/article?res=F40E17D3B5F0C748EDDAA089.

Eisenberg, M. A. 1976. *The Structure of the Corporation: A Legal Analysis.* Boston, MA: Little, Brown and Company.

Enron Corporation. 2001. *Enron 2000 Annual Report.*

Fage, P., and X. Liu. 2002. *The Credit Default Swap-Bond Basis.* Credit Suisse First Boston Emerging Markets Sovereign Strategy Paper (August 15).

Fama, E. F. 1985. "What's Different About Banks?" *Journal of Monetary Economics* 15.

Federal Energy Regulatory Commission. 1998. *Staff Report to the Federal Energy Regulatory Commission on the Causes of Wholesale Electric Pricing Abnormalities in the Midwest During June 1998.* Offices of the Chief Accountant, Economic Policy, Electric Power Regulation, and General Counsel G-3 (September).

Federal Energy Regulatory Commission. 2002. *Staff Report to the Federal Energy Regulatory Commission on Potential Manipulation of Electric and Natural Gas Prices.* Docket No. PA02-2-000 (August).

Fields, G. 1998. "Dunlap Ousted as Sunbeam Head." *Knight-Ridder Tribune Business News* (June 16). Available online at nrtgls.djnr.

Financial Accounting Standards Board. 1983a. *FAS 76: Extinguishment of Debt.* Retrieved from FARS/Original Pronouncements/Statements of Financial Accounting Standards, CD-ROM, Release September 1, 2002. Norwalk, CN: Financial Accounting Standards Board.

Financial Accounting Standards Board. 1983b. *FAS 77: Reporting by Transferors for Transfers of Receivables with Recourse.* Retrieved from FARS/Original Pronouncements/Statements of Financial Accounting Standards, CD-ROM, Release September 1, 2002. Norwalk, CN: Financial Accounting Standards Board.

Financial Accounting Standards Board. 1987. *FAS 94: Consolidation of All Majority-Owned Subsidiaries.* Retrieved from FARS/Original Pronouncements/Statements of Financial Accounting Standards, CD-ROM, Release September 1, 2002. Norwalk, CN: Financial Accounting Standards Board.

Financial Accounting Standards Board. 1996. *FAS 125: Accounting for Transfers and Servicing of Financial Assets and Extinguishments of Liabilities.* Retrieved from FARS/Original Pronouncements/Statements of Financial Accounting Standards, CD-ROM, Release September 1, 2002. Norwalk, CN: Financial Accounting Standards Board.

Financial Accounting Standards Board. 2000a. *FAS 140: Accounting for Transfers and Servicing of Financial Assets and Extinguishments of Liabilities (a replacement of FASB Statement 125)*. Retrieved from FARS/Original Pronouncements/Statements of Financial Accounting Standards, CD-ROM, Release September 1, 2002. Norwalk, CN: Financial Accounting Standards Board.

Financial Accounting Standards Board. 2000b. *Statement 133 Implementation Issue, Definition of a Derivative: Prepaid Interest Rate Swaps*. Norwalk, CN: Financial Accounting Standards Board.

Financial Accounting Standards Board. 2001. *Statement 133 Implementation Issue, Definition of a Derivative: Application of Paragraph 6(b) Regarding Initial Net Investment*. Norwalk, CN: Financial Accounting Standards Board.

Financial Accounting Standards Board. 2002. *Proposal: Principles-Based Approach to U.S. Standard-Setting*. Norwalk, CN: Financial Accounting Standards Board.

Financial Accounting Standards Board. 2003. *Interpretation No. 46, Consolidation of Variable Interest Entities: An Interpretation of ARB No. 51*. Norwalk, CN: Financial Accounting Standards Board.

Financial Accounting Standards Board, Emerging Issues Task Force. 1984. *EITF 84-30: Sales of Loans to Special-Purpose Entities*. Retrieved from FARS/EITF AbstraConn.s/Full Text of EITF AbstraConn.s, CD-ROM, Release September 1, 2002. Norwalk, CN: Financial Accounting Standards Board.

Financial Accounting Standards Board, Emerging Issues Task Force. 1989. *EITF D-14: TransaConn.ions involving Special-Purpose Entities*. Retrieved from FARS/EITF AbstraConn.s/ Appendix D—Other Technical Matters, CD-ROM, Release September 1, 2002. Norwalk, CN: Financial Accounting Standards Board.

Financial Accounting Standards Board, Emerging Issues Task Force. 1990. *EITF 90-15: ImpaConn. of Nonsubstantive Lessors, Residual Value Guarantees, and Other Provisions in Leasing TransaConn.ions*. Retrieved from FARS/EITF AbstraConn.s/ Full Text of EITF AbstraConn.s, CD-ROM, Release September 1, 2002. Norwalk, CN: Financial Accounting Standards Board.

Fox, L. 2002. *Enron: The Rise and Fall*. New York: Wiley.

Fusaro, P. C., and R. M. Miller. 2002. *What Went Wrong at Enron?* New York: Wiley.

Gelber, A. 2002. "Industry Changes After Enron." *Power and Energy Marketing* (March/April).

Goodman, L. S. 2002. "Synthetic CDOs: An Introduction." *Journal of Derivatives* (spring).

Gordon, J. N. 2002. "What Enron Means for the Management and Control of the Modern Business Corporation: Some Initial Reflections." *University of Chicago Law Review* 69.

Greenspan, A. 2002. *Federal Reserve Board's Semi Annual Monetary Policy Report to the Congress* (July). Available at www.federalreserve.gov/boarddocs/hh/2002/july/testimony.htm.

Harris, R. 1999/2000. *Industrialization without Free Incorporation: Legal Organization in England, 1720–1844*. Cambridge: Cambridge University Press.

Harrison, W. B. 2002. *Letter from William B. Harrison, Chairman and Chief Executive Officer of JPMorgan Chase, to The Honorable Carl Levi and The Honorable Susan M. Collins, United States Senate Permanent Subcommittee on Investigations* (July 29).

Harrold, H. 2001. "Exchanges Serve and Survive." *Infoworld.com* (June 8).

Hayek, F. A. 1937. "Economics and Knowledge." *Economica* 4.

Hayek, F. A. 1945. "The Use of Knowledge in Society." *American Economic Review* 35(4) (September).

Hayek, F. A. 1949. "The Meaning of Competition." In his *Individualism and Economic Order.* London: Routledge and Kegan Paul.

Hayek, F. A. 1978a. "Competition as a Discovery Procedure." In his *New Studies Philosophy, Politics, Economics, and the History of Ideas.* Chicago, IL: University of Chicago Press.

Hayek, F. A. 1978b. "The New Confusion About Planning." In his *New Studies Philosophy, Politics, Economics, and the History of Ideas.* Chicago, IL: University of Chicago Press.

Hays, Kristen. 2002. "Enron's Ex-CFO Seeks Civil Immunity." *Washington Post* (June 22).

"Heard on the Street." 2002. *Wall Street Journal* (January 23).

Heinzl, M. 2002. "Royal Bank of Canada Is Sued Over a Loan Related to Enron." *Wall Street Journal* (June 25).

Hicks, J. R. 1939/1957. *Value and Capital.* 2nd ed. London: Oxford University Press.

Hicks, J. R. 1973/2001. *Capital and Time: A Neo-Austrian Theory.* Oxford: Oxford University Press.

International Swaps and Derivatives Association. 2002. *Enron: Corporate Failure, Market Success.* White Paper presented at the 17th Annual General Meeting, Berlin (April 17).

James, C. 1987. "Some Evidence on the Uniqueness of Bank Loans." *Journal of Financial Economics* 19.

Jensen, M. C., and W. H. Meckling. 1976. "Theory of the Firm: Managerial Behavior, Agency Costs and Ownership Structure." *Journal of Financial Economics* 3.

Johnson, L. L. 1960. "The Theory of Hedging and Speculation in Commodity Futures." *Review of Economic Studies* 26.

J.P. Morgan. 1998. *Credit Derivatives: A Primer.* New York: J.P. Morgan & Co.

J.P. Morgan Chase & Co. 2002. *Statement Submitted to the Permanent Subcommittee on Investigations, Committee on Government Affairs, United States Senate* (July 23).

Kaldor, N. 1939. "Speculation and Economic Stability." *Review of Economic Studies* 7.

Kavanagh, B. T. 2002. "Securitization and Structured Finance: Legitimate Business Management Tools." *FMA Online* (summer).

Keynes, J. M. 1930. *The Theory of Money: Volume II, The Applied Theory of Money.* London: Macmillan.

Khakee, N., and M. Ryan. 2001. "Enron Exposure Evident in the Credit Derivatives Market." *Standard & Poor's RatingsDirect* (November 30).

Klinger, S., C. Hartman, S. Anderson, J. Cavanagh, and H. Sklar. 2002. *Executive Excess 2002*. Ninth Annual CEO Compensation Survey, Institute for Policy Studies and United for a Fair Economy (August 26, 2002).

Knight, F. H. 1921. *Risk, Uncertainty, and Profit*. Boston, MA: Houghton Mifflin.

Kramer, A. 2002. "Weather Derivatives or Insurance? Considerations for Energy Companies." In *The ART of Risk Management: Alternative Risk Transfer, Capital Structure, and the Convergence of Insurance and Capital Markets*. C. L. Culp (Ed.) New York: Wiley.

Kurtzman, J., and G. Rifkin. 2001. *Radical E: From General Electric to Enron— Lessons on How to Rule the Web*. New York: Wiley.

Labaton, S., Jr., and R. A. Oppel. 2002. "Enthusiasm Ebbs for Tough Reform in Wake of Enron." *New York Times* (June 10).

Lachmann, L. M. 1978. *Capital and Its Structure*. Kansas City, MO: Sheed Andrews and McMeel.

Langevoort, D. C. 2001. "The Human Nature of Corporate Boards: Law, Norms, and the Unintended Consequences of Independence and Accountability." *Georgetown Law Journal* 89 (April).

LaPorta, R. F., F. Lopez-de-Silanes, A. Schliefer, and R. Vishny. 2000. "Investor Protection and Corporate Governance." *Journal of Financial Economics* 5.

Lauria, P. 2002. "Adelphia Bottoms Out." *Daily Deal* (June 27).

Leuz, C., D. Nanda, and P. D. Wysocki. 2001. "Investor Protection and Earnings Management: An International Comparison." Working Paper. The Wharton School of the University of Pennsylvania, the University of Michigan Business School, and MIT Sloan School of Management (August).

Levitt, A. 1998. *The Numbers Game* (September 28). Available at www.accounting .rutgers.edu/ raw/aaa/newsarc/pr101898.htm.

Li, M. Y. 2002. "Transfer That Risk." *U.S. Banker* (March). Available at http:// www.us-banker.com/usb/articles/usbmar02-4.shtml (visited September 16, 2002).

Lipton, M., and J. W. Lorsch. 1992. "A Modest Proposal for Improved Corporate Governance." *Business Lawyer* 48.

Lipton, M., and E. H. Steinberger. 2001. "Takeovers and Freezeouts." *Law Journal Press* 1.

Lorsch, J. W. 1995. "Empowering the Board." *Harvard Business Review* 107.

Lublin, J. S., and J. Sandberg. 2002. "Deadbeat CEOs Plague Firms As Economy and Markets Roil." *Wall Street Journal* (August 1).

Mace, M. 1970. *Directors: Myth and Reality*. Boston, MA: Harvard Business School Press.

Markham, J. W. 1987. *The History of Commodity Futures Trading and Its Regulation*. New York: Praeger.

Manne, H. G. 1965. "Mergers and the Market for Corporate Control." *Journal of Political Economy* 73.

Manne, H. G. 2002. "Bring Back the Hostile Takeover." *Wall Street Journal* (June 26).

Maremont, M., and J. Barnathan. 1995. "Blind Ambition: Part 1: How the Pursuit of Results Got Out of Hand at Bausch & Lomb." *BusinessWeek* (October 23). Available at http://www.businessweek.com/1995/43/b34471.htm.

Mautz, R. K., and F. L. Neumann. 1977. *Corporate Audit Committees: Policies and Practice.* New York: Ernst & Ernst.

McGeehan, P. 2002. "Goldman Chief Urges Reforms in Corporations." *New York Times* (June 6).

Menger, C. 1871/1974. *Principles of Economics.* Grove City, PA: Libertarian Press.

Millstein, I. M. 1993. "The Evolution of the Certifying Board." *Business Lawyer* 48 (August).

Min, M. 2001. *Quantitative Measures of the Quality of Financial Reporting.* FEI Research Foundation. PowerPoint presenation published by Financial Executives Research Foundation Inc. Available at http://www.fei.org/download /QualFinRep-6-13-2k1.ppt.

Monks, R. A. G., and N. Minow. 2001. *Corporate Governance.* 2nd ed. Oxford, England: Blackwell.

Moody's Investors Service. 2002. *Special Comment, Moody's View on Energy Merchants: Long on Debt—Short on Cash Flow: Restructuring Expected.* Global Credit Research (May).

Morgenson, G. 2002. "What If Investors Won't Join the Party?" *New York Times* (June 2).

Norris, F. 2000. "Rite Aid to Pay $200 Million to Settle Shareholder Lawsuits." *New York Times* (November 10). Available at query.nytimes.com/search /restricted/article?res=F60D13FF3F5C0C738DDDA80994.

Norris, F. 2001. "SEC Accuses Former Sunbeam Official of Fraud." *New York Times* (May 16). Available at query.nytimes.com/search/restricted/article ?res=F40611FF395E 0C758DDDAC0894.

Norris, F., and D. B. Henriques. 2000. "3 Admit Guilt in Falsifying CUC's Books." *New York Times* (June 15). Available at query.nytimes.com/search /restricted/article?res=F70717FF3A5A0C768DDDAF089.

"NYMEX Delists Electricity Futures Contracts." 2002. *Megawatt Daily* (February 19).

"NYMEX Prepares to Wade Into Electricity Contracts Again, Relaunch PJM Futures," *Platts Power Markets Week* (October 7, 2002).

NYSE and NASD. 1999. *Report and Recommendations of the Blue Ribbon Committee on Improving the Effectiveness of Corporate Audit Committees.* (February 8). Available at http://www.nyse.com/pdfs/blueribb.pdf.

Parris, M. 2002. "Another Bold Initiative, No Change There Then." *Sunday Times* (August 10).

Powers, W. C., Jr., R. S. Troubh, and H. S. Winokur, Jr. 2002. *Report of Investigation by the Special Investigation Committee of the Board of Directors of Enron Corp.* (February 1).

President's Working Group on Financial Markets. 1999. *Over-the-Counter Derivatives Markets and the Commodity Exchange Act: Report of the President's Working Group on Financial Markets* (November).

Rajan, R. G. 1992. "Insiders and Outsiders: The Choice Between Informed and Arm's-Length Debt." *Journal of Finance* 47 (September).

Rappaport, A. 1998. *Creating Shareholder Value: A Guide for Managers and Investors.* New York: The Free Press.

Roach, R. 2002. *Testimony Before the Permanent Subcommittee on Investigations on the Role of Financial Institutions in Enron's Collapse* (July 23).

Rozhon, T., and Treaster, J. B. 2002. "Insurance Plans of Top Executives Are in Jeopardy." *New York Times* (August 29).

Salomon Smith Barney. 2002. *Merchant Energy Primer* (January 22).

Sandberg, J., R. Blumenstein, and S. Young. 2002. "WorldCom Internal Probe Uncovers Massive Fraud." *Wall Street Journal* (June 26).

Sapsford, J., and A. Raghaven. 2002. "Trading Charges: Lawsuit Spotlights J.P. Morgan's Ties to the Enron Debacle—Insurers Balk at Paying Up to $1 Billion Claims on Complex Transactions—Update in a Glass Room." *Wall Street Journal* (January 25).

Saunders, A. 2002. *Credit Risk Management.* 2nd ed. New York: Wiley.

Schumpeter, J. A. 1942. *Capitalism, Socialism, and Democracy.* New York: Harper & Row.

Sirower, M. L. 1997. *The Synergy Trap: How Companies Lose the Acquisitions Game.* New York: Free Press.

Smith, A. 1776/1992. *An Inquiry into the Nature and Causes of the Wealth of Nations.* General Editors R. H. Campbell and A. S. Skinner, Textural Editor W. B. Webb Todd. Oxford: Clarendon Press.

Smith, A. 2001. "Digression Concerning the Corn Trade and Corn Laws." In *An Inquiry into the Nature and Causes of the Wealth of Nations,* Vol. 4, On Systems of Political Economy. Online ed. London: Adam Smith Institute. Available at http://www.adamsmith.org/smith/won-b4-c5-digression.htm.

Smith, C. W., and R. M. Stulz. 1999. "The Determinants of Firms' Hedging Policies." Reprinted in *Corporate Hedging in Theory and Practice: Lessons from Metallgesellschaft.* C. L. Culp and M. H. Miller, (Eds.) London: Risk Books.

Smith, C. W., Jr., and J. Warner. 1979. "On Financial Contracting: An Analysis of Bond Covenants." *Journal of Financial Economics* 7.

Smith, F. L., Jr. 1992. "Environment Policy at the Crossroads." In *Environmental Politics: Public Costs, Private Rewards.* M. Greve and F. Smith, (Eds.) New York: Praeger.

Standard & Poor's. 2002. *Energy Trading and Marketing: How It's Done.* Research Department (March 29).

Stewart, J. 2002. "Master of Disaster: How L.A.'s Super-Rich Gary Winnick Is Trying to Wash Blood from the Global Crossing Implosion Off His Hands—And Make More Money in the Bargain." *New Times Los Angeles* (April 25).

Telser, L. G. 1958. "Futures Trading and the Storage of Cotton and Wheat." *Journal of Political Economy* 66.

Treaster, J. B. 1999. "The Markets: Market Place; Investors Settle for $2.8 Billion in a Fraud Suit." *New York Times* (December 8). Available at query.nytimes.com/search/restricted/articles?res=F20712F6355A0C7138CDDAB0994.

Treaster, J. B. 2002. "Adelphia Files for Bankruptcy." *New York Times* (June 26).

Treaster, J. B., and T. Rozhon. 2002. "Doubts Grow on 'Covering' of Options." *New York Times* (August 30).

Turner, L. 2002. *The Role of the Financial Institutions in Enron's Collapse.* Washington, DC: Governmental Affairs Permanent Subcommittee on Investigations, United States Senate.

von Mises, L. 1966. *Human Action: A Treatise on Economics.* 3rd rev. ed. Chicago, IL: Henry Regnery.

Wagner, R. 1997. *Der Ring des Nibelungen* [Ring Cycle] G. Solti, (Ed.) Polygram Records.

Weil, R. 2002. *Fundamental Causes of the Accounting Debacle at Enron: Show Me Where It Says I Can't.* Washington, DC: The Committee on Energy and Commerce, United States House of Representatives.

Weinberg, N., and B. Capple. 2002. "Going Against the Grain." *Forbes* 170(11) (November 25).

Wildavsky, A. B. 1988. *Searching for Safety.* New Brunswick, NJ: Transaction.

Wildavsky, A. B. 1991. *The Rise of Radical Egalitarianism.* New York: National Book Network.

Williams, J. 1986. *The Economic Function of Futures Markets.* Cambridge, MA: Cambridge University Press.

Williams, H. M. 1978. *The Role of the Corporate Secretary in Promoting Corporate Accountability.* Reprinted in Practicing Law Institute, *Corporate Governance* (1979).

Wing, J. A. 2002. "Executive Compensation Is Skewed." *Journal of Global Financial Markets* (summer).

Woods, W. A. 2002. *B2B Exchanges 2.0.* Bermuda: ISI Publications.

Working, H. 1948. "Theory of the Inverse Carrying Charge in Futures Markets." *Journal of Farm Economics* 30.

Working, H. 1949. "The Theory of Price of Storage." *American Economic Review* 39.

Working, H. 1962. "New Concepts Concerning Futures Markets and Prices." *American Economic Review* 52.

Young, S. 2002. "WorldCom Slashes Revenue Outlook; Quest Is Pressured to Reduce Debt." *Wall Street Journal* (April 22).

Young, S., C. Mollenkamp, J. Sandberg, and H. Sender. 2002. "WorldCom Seeks Court Protection From Creditors Under Chapter 11." *Wall Street Journal* (July 22).

INDEX